Editor: Joe Funk
Creative Director: Jason Hinman
Art Director: Daniel Tideman

VG Sports
President: Bert Ingley
Staff Writer: Paul Gleason
Staff Writer: Jon Faulkner

Prima Games
An Imprint of Random House, Inc.
3000 Lava Ridge Court, Suite 100
Roseville, CA 95661
www.primagames.com

The Prima Games logo is a registered trademark of Random House, Inc., registered in the United States and other countries. Primagames.com is a registered trademark of Random House, Inc., registered in the United States. Prima Games is an imprint of Random House, Inc.

Senior Product Manager: Donato Tica
Editor: John Browning
Manufacturing: Stephanie Sanchez

ISBN: 978-0-7615-5925-2
Library of Congress Catalog Card Number: 2008921537
Printed in the United States of America

08 09 10 11 GG 10 9 8 7 6 5 4 3 2 1

NCAA® FOOTBALL 09

PRIMA Official Game Guide

Contents
Primary Sections

Getting Started

This section of the guide will give you an overview of what comprises *NCAA Football 09*. Each mode will be discussed so that you can get the absolute most replay value out of the game.

NCAA Football 09 is packed with new features. The What's New pages will show you all the changes, tweaks and additions that EA SPORTS has packed into this year's edition of the game. We cover all the gameplay enhancements, new game modes, Home Field Advantage and Wide Open game play features.

Wii and PS2 owners will find special sections devoted specifically to improvements and enhancements to those platforms. In addition, all the Xbox 360 Achievements are explained so you can blow up your Gamerscore.

We had a ton of fun putting together the guide this year, and we are confident that you've been given the tips and strategies you need to fully enjoy *NCAA Football 09*.

Introduction

WELCOME

College football is all about traditions, mascots, passion and pageantry. Fans take pride in their teams, and live and die with their performance on the field. There is no greater joy than when your team stomps your bitter rival in front of 80,000 screaming fans.

College football has the greatest mascots in all of sports. Sparty the Spartan, Albert the Alligator, Smokey the dog, the Alabama Elephant, the Penn State Nittany Lion and more roam the sidelines and pump up the crowd with their crazy antics.

College Football has the rivalries: Tennessee vs. Florida, Auburn vs. Alabama, Florida State vs. Miami, Pittsburgh vs. West Virginia, Ohio State vs. Michigan, Michigan vs. Notre Dame, USC vs. Notre Dame, Texas vs. Oklahoma, Nebraska vs. Oklahoma, USC vs. UCLA, Georgia vs. Florida, and many more!

College football has the traditions: the Gator Chomp, the FSU Chop, the checkered endzone at Tennessee, the Old Oaken Bucket, and the Jeweled Shillelagh.

EA SPORTS delivers all of what makes college football the greatest American sport around. We hope you enjoy this comprehensive strategy guide of the most complete, realistic, and enjoyable college football game ever made: *NCAA Football 09*.

▲ The Checkered Endzone

▲ The Gator Chomp

▲ More Elusive Ball Carriers

▲ Thunderous Hits

WIDE OPEN GAME PLAY

When EA SPORTS set out to make *NCAA Football 09*, they had one major gameplay goal in mind: wide open game play!

You'll notice right from the start that *NCAA Fooball 09* plays fast and plays fun. Big hits, amazing catches, and ankle-breaking jukes abound. Ball carrier combo moves add a whole new level of responsiveness to the running game as you can string together jukes, spins, and stiff arms to break through tackles and explode into the secondary.

Against weaker opposition, you'll notice bigger holes in the line and open receivers making the game feel more wide open than ever before. New features like directional pump fakes will let your QB get out of the pocket and fake defenders right out of their shoes.

Don't worry, the defense gets plenty of love as well. A new tackling engine will give you outstanding variety with big hits, shoestring tackles, and bone crushing gang tackles. Everything about *NCAA Football 09* is smoother, more realistic, and (did we forget to mention?) wide open!

Home Field Advantage

NCAA Football 09 is all about Home Field Advantage. Screaming crowds, rattled quarterbacks, and players going into the zone are all covered in the game this season.

PRE-PLAY CONFUSION

If you are the visiting team and get rattled while on the road, squiggly lines will replace your play art and your passing icons will become question marks. It'll take a good solid drive to silence the crowd and reveal your normal play art.

TURN UP THE NOISE

▲ HFA Play Art Confusion

If the home crowd gets heated up, it will be very difficult for your players to hear your

audibles and hot routes. Your controller will begin to vibrate in your hands to further affect your concentration. If you are the home team, be sure to Pump Up the Crowd and put your opponent in trouble.

QUARTERBACK QUIZ

Throw an interception and the Quarterback Quiz will pop up. You'll be able to see the play again and try to determine the coverage the defense called. Get it right and your Quarterback will recover some of his com-

▲ QB Quiz

posure. Get it wrong and he could become rattled.

ICE THE KICKER

The game is on the line. Your kicker steps up to hit the game winner. But wait, your opponent calls a time out to Ice the Kicker. Your kick meter will be covered in ice and the camera view will change to make the kick more difficult.

INTERACTIVE TIMEOUTS

Now a timeout doesn't just stop the clock. You'll be able to give your team coaching points that will affect their attributes during the current drive. Watch out: your opponent can counteract this boost by targeting the same facet of the game with his coaching points.

Football Should Be Fun!

COKE ZERO MASCOT MASH UP

This is your chance to have a little bit of fun as you go mascot vs. mascot. Special mascot moves are included to provide over-the-top gameplay and excitement.

▲ Acrobatic Mascot Moves

INTERACTIVE TD CELEBRATIONS

You'll keep control of your player after the score and can run to celebrate with your mascot or teammates. Some teams have school-specific animations like the Gator Chomp or FSU Chop.

AP Images

College Atmosphere

▲ *Packed Sidelines*

▲ *Cheerleaders*

▲ *New Clear Visors*

DYNAMIC ATTENDANCE

Just like in real life, crowd attendance responds to what is happening on the field. Lay an egg on your home field and the fans will exit the stadium en masse. Put it to a rival in your stadium and the crowd will go into a frenzy. In Dynasty mode, the better your season is going, the bigger the crowds and the longer they will hang around a blowout game.

PACKED SIDELINES

The sidelines are alive in *NCAA Football 09*. Teammates, mascots, and cheerleaders react to the events of the game and create a living, breathing atmosphere on the benches.

PLAYER AND FIELD MODELS

Player models have been improved yet again. In addition you'll find 50 alternate uniforms and even clear visors! Field textures have been greatly improved this season as well. You will notice the turf degrading and tearing up under the stress of the game.

CUSTOM STADIUM SOUNDS

Now you can add your own stadium sounds to the game. Score a touchdown and the speakers will blare with your favorite tune. There are over 20 different situations to which you can add your own custom sounds.

BREAKAWAY REACTIONS

The crowd will ooh and ahh as you make outstanding plays and break off long touchdown runs. Experience the roar of the crowd as you take that interception back to the house for six points.

END OF GAME HIGHLIGHT MONTAGE

At the end of the game, the team in the booth will show clips of the best plays of the game. Relive that kick off return for a touchdown or bone-crushing quarterback sack. You can even save your best highlights to share with your friends.

Game Enhancements

EA SPORTS did not rest on its laurels when it came to updating the gameplay for *NCAA Football 09*. The game is packed with new features that make strategic adjustments more important than ever before.

CO-OP PLAY

Offline co-op play is back in the game this year. You can play 1-4 players in any combination. Play 3 vs. 1 or match up in a 2 vs. 2 showdown.

RETURN MISSED FIELD GOALS

If it's in the game, it's in the game. Now you can pull a guy back on a long field goal and look to return it for a huge momentum changer.

▲ *Missed Field Goal Return*

However, if you don't make it back to at least the original line of scrimmage, you can lose valuable field position.

BLUFF PLAY ART

You've come to the line of scrimmage, and don't remember your routes in a head to head game. Now you can view your play and show two false play art screens to your opponent so you can learn what you need without giving away your play.

FORMATION AUDIBLES

This feature lets you audible to a run play, quick pass, deep pass, or play action pass from within any formation. Broaden your playcalling possibilities and never get caught in a bad play choice again.

▲ *Formation Audibles*

SMART ROUTES

In *NCAA Football 09* you can tell your receiver to extend his route to the first down marker or endzone. No more throwing a 5-yard curl when you need 7 yards to move the chains.

SLIDE PROTECTION

Coach up your offensive line to help pick up the blitz. You can have them shift left, right, pinch, or take an aggressive spread technique when creating your passing pocket.

BOBBLE CATCHES

▲ *Bobbled Catch*

Not every catch is a clean one. At times players will bobble and bat the ball around before bringing it down. When on defense, try to put a big hit on a receiver that is bobbling the ball.

EASY PACKAGE CYCLING

When in the play call screen, you can use the Right Thumbstick to switch forward and backward through packages. This is much quicker than the old method of pressing a single button. You'll be able to have more diversity in your game as you move players around within each formation.

RANDOM PLAY CALL IN PRACTICE MODE

Want to work on your I-Form Normal plays against the 4-3 defense? You can set up practice mode to make random play calls from within each formation. Test your schemes against a variety of plays and see if they hold up to the pressure.

AP Images

Game Mode Updates

ONLINE DYNASTY

Ever since the NCAA Football franchise went online, players have clamored for Online Dynasty mode. This year EA SPORTS delivers the complete Dynasty experience and then some. With 60 years of continuous play and up to 12 players competing at a time, Online Dynasty is sure to be one of the most played game modes this season.

Online Dynasty gives you everything that its offline counterpart does: full recruiting, redshirts, stats, NCAA News, custom schedules, and more.

Dynasty mode begins as you invite your friends to compete in your league. The Commissioner has full control to make sure that things go smoothly. Using Dynasty Headquarters you can track everyone's progress and see easily when it is time to advance to the next week.

Online Live Chat will even allow league members to talk online while they are managing their depth charts and doing their recruiting.

FLEXIBILITY

Online Dynasty mode is incredibly flexible. You can convert it to an offline dynasty if you want, or take your existing dynasty and move it online.

Automatic file uploading and merging makes everything effortless. You don't even need a hard drive to participate.

Invite new players at any time, kick out those that are problems and put control on autopilot when players are going to be out of pocket for a while.

You can even start Online Dynasty mode with customized or edited rosters!

New Dynasty Features

RECRUITING STRATEGY

▲ Recruiting Strategy

College coaches don't have time to manage every aspect of recruiting. That is one of the jobs of their assistants. With the recruiting strategy setting you can set recruiting priorities and tactics for your assistants and hand off the dirty work. If you prefer, you can roll up your sleeves and handle everything yourself. The choice is yours!

QUICKCALL

▲ QuickCall

The QuickCall system allows you to set the amount of time for a call and whether to offer a scholarship. The call is "simmed" and you'll find out loads of prospect information in just a couple of seconds.

QUICK SEARCH

Quick Search will automatically add players to your recruiting board based on a set of preferences that you establish. Save time digging through all of the potential recruits and get your board loaded with quality prospects in seconds.

New Mini-Games

HORSE

▲ Horse

Take on the CPU or a friend in a Field Goal kicking game of H.O.R.S.E. or P.I.G. This mode is great for working on those game winners.

SPECIAL TEAMS

▲ Perfect your special teams play

Imagine Tug-o-War mode, but with Special Teams. Field Goals, Punt Returns, and Punt Coverage can be improved quickly by spending time in this mode.

See our special section on Mini Games for a full breakdown of all the different modes.

▲ *You have full control of your experience*

▲ *Jump right into a game*

▲ *Play even teams*

If you are looking to jump straight into a game against the computer or a human opponent then Play Now is the perfect mode.

Once on the team select screen you have 120 FBS Division 1 Teams to choose from. If you selected your favorite team in My Settings, your team will be pitted against one of its rivals by default. Each team's overall, offense, and defense ratings can be viewed. This allows you to quickly determine how the teams match up against each other.

▲ *Setting up a Big Ten battle*

If you just want an even game, but want to sport your team colors, press the RB button (Xbox 360) or R1 button (PS3). The teams will now be evenly matched.

Before moving to the next menu screen, there is an option to choose your team's uniform, offensive playbook, and defensive playbook. You can choose your team's default playbook, or any of the other 119 teams. There are also a couple of style specific offensive playbooks to choose from.

▲ *Pick your favorite playbook*

The final menu screen you get to before getting into the game lets you set the following options:

Quarter Length: This setting allows you to choose how long the quarters are for each game. You have a choice between 1 and 15 minutes. The default setting is 5 minutes.

Skill: This setting allows you to choose between one of four skill level settings: Freshman, Varsity, All-American, and Heisman. If you are new to the game, start on Freshman or Varsity. If you are a seasoned veteran, play on All-American or Heisman.

Stadium: If you don't want to play in the home team's stadium, then choose one of the other 119 team stadiums in the game. You can also choose NCAA bowl stadiums such as the Sugar, Rose, and Orange Bowl.

Time: If you want to play at a different time than your console's system clock, you can play at one of four different times.

Weather: This option allows you choose between the current weather in your area (as provided by a Weather Channel feed), or you can change the weather to your liking manually.

Temperature: Manually change the temperature from between -20 to 105 degrees Fahrenheit.

Clouds: Cloud cover can manually be changed between one of three settings. They are as follows: Partly cloudy (default), Overcast (rain or snow), or Clear.

Precipitation: If you are looking to bring some weather elements to the game, use this setting to add rain or snow. The colder the temperature, the more likely it is that it will snow. Choose between none, light, medium, and high.

Wind: Choose between calm, light breeze, moderate, or very windy. The windier the game, the harder it is to make a successful field goal.

Dynasty & Campus Legend

▲ *High School Playoff Game*

Dynasty Mode

In Dynasty Mode, you have the chance to turn your favorite school into a collegiate powerhouse. Start out with a perennial Top 25 team, or build a program from the basement to the BSC National Championship game.

You can begin with an edited roster or let the CPU auto-generate names for your players. You control all aspects of your team.

PRE-SEASON RECRUITING

▲ *Recruiting Board*

Dynasty Mode begins with Pre-Season Recruiting. The game gives you the option to create a prospect before diving into your recruiting. Populate your recruiting board and then start making calls to prospects. Be sure to keep an eye on your recruiting time, as you'll only have so many resources to apply to recruiting.

REDSHIRTING PLAYERS

After you wrap up your pre-season recruiting, you'll have the opportunity to go through your team and redshirt players. You'll want to reshirt as many guys who won't see playing time as possible. If you have a stud QB that won't see any time on the field during his first season, you will definitely want to slap a redshirt on him. Getting that extra year is critical to developing your prospects.

DEPTH CHARTS

Go through your depth chart and sort players in the order you want them to play. You can also have the CPU Auto-Reorder your depth chart for you. Here's a word of caution for you. Don't put your star players in as kick/punt returners. There is a high chance of injury and you don't want your stud receiver knocked out for the season.

CUSTOM SCHEDULES

If you play in a conference, your conference schedule will be locked in. You'll still have a lot of leeway with your schedule. Do you want to warm up and pad your stats with a patsy, or go for national recognition and schedule a Top 10 team early in the season?

Note: *For more information about Dynasty Mode, see the section on Advanced Dynasty Tips.*

Campus Legend

▲ *Our Campus Legend*

Campus Legend is your opportunity to take over a current player, or create your own High School prospect as you battle for legendary status at your school. You'll have the chance to be recruited, try to crack the starting lineup, and eventually go for the Heisman Trophy.

Campus Legend mode plays similar to last season's edition, but there are a couple of new features that you will want to be aware of as you get started.

▲ *New Practice System*

A new achievement system has been added to determine your legend score. In addition, EA SPORTS has dramatically streamlined practices so that you can get a full weeks worth of reps in a single session. Practice makes perfect and now practice isn't painful.

Note: *For more information on Campus Legend Mode, see the section on Advanced Campus Legend tips.*

Mini Games

Don't have time for a full game with a friend? Looking to improve your fundamental skills? This is the place that Mini Games shine. You can take on your friends or the CPU in 5 different challenges. You'll work on every aspect of your game here: special teams, red zone, field goal kicking, option, and of course, running and passing.

NEW H.O.R.S.E.

▲ Play a quick game of H.O.R.S.E.

EA SPORTS converts this long time basketball favorite for the gridiron. You can play against a friend or duel the CPU. Choose different spots on the field, adjust the wind to increase the difficulty of the kick, and fire away. If you make it and your opponent misses, he'll get a letter and you retain control of where the next kick will be. If you miss, your opponent gets to pick the spot and put you in jeopardy of getting a letter. You can also play P.I.G. if you are short on time.

NEW SPECIAL-TEAMS CHALLENGE

▲ Work on your kick returns

Work on your kickoff and punt return skills with this new mini game. The game starts with a kickoff and then both teams take turns running only special teams plays until someone returns a kick for a score or makes a field goal. Kicks out of bounds are penalized, unless you can nail it inside the 10 yard line.

TUG-OF-WAR

▲ Battling for yardage

Starting from midfield, each team takes a turn running a single play until someone scores. There are no punts or field goals here; only touchdowns and safeties count. You will only be able to choose plays from the Ask Corso set. Interceptions can be returned, but if you don't make it back to the original line of scrimmage, you'll get the ball there instead.

BOWLING

▲ Can you bowl a perfect game?

Play "ten frames" in the redzone by yourself or against another player. A touchdown on the first play counts as a strike. A second play touchdown is a spare. Anything less and you get credit for the number of yards you gain. An incomplete pass is a gutter ball.

OPTION DASH

▲ Perfect your option game

The option is one of the most dangerous plays in football when it is executed properly. The Spread Option schemes of West Virginia and Florida are bringing this tactic back to the mainstream, so this is the perfect way to practice your skills. You'll be given two minutes to try to score as many times as possible using only option plays. If you play against another player, you'll each get two minutes to rack up points. Option Dash players can rack up points using all the different special play moves during the play. Each one adds a multiplier, so showing off your moves if you break into the open field can really boost your score.

Practice Mode

Every good player has one thing in common. They spend a lot of time in Practice mode. Practice mode is like your mad scientist laboratory. It's where you concoct new schemes to tear up the opposition.

NCAA Football 09 has a robust practice mode where you can work on both your offensive and defensive skills.

You begin practice mode by choosing a team for offense and defense (you can also practice kickoff or just run offense against no defenders). Bear in mind the team that your most common rival uses and put them opposite you in practice mode.

Next you choose your playbook for the practice session. Practice mode is the perfect place to learn the timing of new plays and try out different package options.

One of the nice features in Practice mode is the ability to call a Random Play for any formation. This really comes in handy when you want to practice your plays against different formations and sets.

▲ Work on your favorite plays

Call your play, then match up against the formation on defense that you want to practice against. Press the Y button (triangle on PS3) to have the defense call random plays from that defensive set.

Now you can run your play over and over and see how it works against the defense.

You can do the same, of course, on the other side of the ball. Call your defensive play and then run random plays from an offensive set that you want to match up against.

When working on your defensive schemes and blitz setups, we recommend setting up

▲ Get your reps in

two controllers: one on offense and one on defense. This way you will have time to set up your play and try out different shifts and defensive hot routes.

Snap the ball and then switch back to the defensive controller quickly to test out your scheme.

Note: *If you have a practice partner, you can get even more out of your practice session. Have your partner throw different types of deep routes while you practice your user catching skills to intercept the ball.*

Coke Zero Mascot Mash Up

The Coke Zero Mascot Mash Up is your chance to explore the lighter side of *NCAA Football 09*. Play a friendly game of mascot vs. mascot where everybody is rated a 99 overall. Juke moves are replaced by special mascot power flips, but otherwise the gameplay is similar to normal game modes.

We've included a list of all the mascots in the game.

Air Force The Bird

Alabama Big Al

Arizona Wilbur The Wildcat

Arizona State Sparky

Arkansas Big Red

Auburn Aubie the Tiger

Boston College Baldwin the Eagle

BYU Cosmo

Clemson The Tiger

Colorado Chip

Florida Albert E. Gator

Fresno State Timeout

Georgia Hairy Dawg

Georgia Tech Buzz

Iowa Herky the Hawk

Iowa State Cy

Kansas State Willie the Wildcat

Kentucky The Wildcat

LSU Mike the Tiger

Maryland Testudo

Miami Sebastian the Ibis

Michigan State Sparty

Minnesota Goldy the Gopher

Mississippi State Bully

Missouri Truman the Tiger

NC State Mr. Wuf

Nebraska Herbie Husker

North Carolina Rameses

Northwestern Willie the Wildcat

Notre Dame The Leprechaun

Ohio State Brutus Buckeye

Oklahoma State Pistol Pete

Penn State The Nittany Lion

Pittsburgh ROC the Panther

Purdue Purdue Pete

South Carolina Cocky

Tennessee Smokey

Texas Hook'em

UCF The Golden Knight

UCLA Joe Bruin

Vanderbilt Mr. C

Virginia CavMan aka Chester

Virginia Tech Hokie Bird

Washington Harry

West Virginia The Mountaineer

Wisconsin Bucky Badger

▲ *Bulldogs vs. Spartans*

▲ *Hairy Dawg shows off his moves*

▲ *Sparty gets outside for yards*

▲ *Buzz runs the QB option*

▲ *Cy drops back to pass*

▲ *Bucky Badger brings the wood*

▲ *The Bird makes a Big Swat*

▲ *Albert runs the option*

▲ *Timeout makes the catch*

Xbox Live

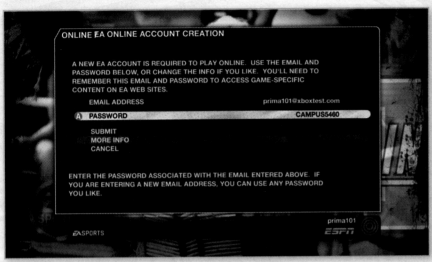

▲ EA Online Account Creation

Playing against the CPU can be challenging, but playing against a human online is a completely different animal. Being able to test your skills against other online players is the ultimate rush. Many of the hardcore players who go out and buy *NCAA Football 09* on the game's release date will hit online play the moment they get home.

EA Online Account Creation

Besides needing an Xbox Live Gold membership and a high-speed internet connection, you will also need to create an EA Online Account. Once you have created your account you are ready to hop online.

MAIN ONLINE MENU

Once you get to the main menu, there are several options to choose from. They are as follows:

Quick Match: This jumps you right into an

▲ XBox Live Menu

online game. There is no waiting in the lobby to challenge someone to play. There are four quick match options to choose from: ranked, unranked, custom match, and create session. Custom match and create session allows you to refine your search for games a bit more.

Dynasty: Online Dynasty mode is new to the NCAA Football franchise this year. You can have up to 11 friends join you to play. We cover Online Dynasty in more detail in the Advanced Strategy section of the guide.

▲ Take your Dynasty Skills online

Lobby: Hang out in the lobby to chat or challenge other players online. There are a few different rooms to choose from. The East and West rooms are where most players hangout. If you are new to NCAA Football, Beginners is a good choice to get your feet wet in the online environment. If you are an advanced player, then you will want to choose Advanced. Be warned, the players that play there are the hardest of the hardcore online players. They know all the tricks and have good stick control. Be prepared to bring your A game when

▲ The East Lobby

entering this room. Your level must be at least twenty to get in. There is an Xbox 360 Headsets room for players that want to chat while they play their games. Find players with your same level in the My Level room.

Leaderboards: Look at stats to see how the top players are doing. Choose between overall, weekly, and monthly leaderboards.

▲ Xbox Live Leaderboards

EA SPORTS World: Check out your stats.

Online Settings: Check out news and recent offers from EA SPORTS. There is an FAQ page to help walk you through different

▲ Online Settings

topics such as how to achieve levels.
ESPN: Use ESPN on Demand to find out the latest college football scores in real time or read about other sports related news.

EA Locker: Use this to upload, download, and delete rosters.

New Playstation 2 Features

While the future of NCAA Football is certainly Next Gen technologies, EA SPORTS did not leave the tried and true PS2 players hanging. They have continued to advance the Legacy Gen gameplay features to make *NCAA Football 09* a must-have title.

BALL CARRIER COMBO MOVES

The PS2 game has long been lauded for the responsiveness of the controls and the importance that stick control has in the game. EA SPORTS adds more to your arsenal this year with Ball Carrier Combo Moves.

Simply put, these combo moves allow you to string movements together almost like you would in a fighting game. You can juke left, then break off into a spin and break out with another juke.

▲ *New Combo Moves*

You'll be breaking ankles and leaving defenders in the dust more than ever before. Double spins and multiple jukes are your most effective options for this new feature.

FAMILY PLAY

One of the goals for all of the EA SPORTS franchises this year is accessibility. Family Play allows you to modify the game to your level of play by streamlining controls and play calling. You can of course still opt for the full advanced play call screens and myriad of control options.

Note: *Family Play is available for cross mode play now. The more advanced player can use the full options, while the game can be set up for Family Play for the more novice user.*

The controls have been modified so that four buttons are all you need on offense and defense. Play art is streamlined where just the routes and important assignments are highlighted, making it easy for beginners to get the gist of a play.

▲ *Streamlined Play Art*

The Passing system has been adjusted as well. Simply point the stick in the direction you want to pass and hit the X button. The ball will be thrown to the green highlighted receiver.

▲ *Easy to use Passing System*

Further gameplay hints will walk you through the game and help you get over the learning curve.

MASCOT CHALLENGE

NCAA Football 09 on the PS2 rolls out a unique game mode with Mascot Challenge. In this game mode, you will compete against Mascots from all around the country in four different drills, with three difficulty levels to each one.

PASSING CHALLENGE

▲ *Mascot Passing Challenge*

Similar to the pocket presence drills of the past, this drill is all about keeping your composure and finding the open target. Watch out for the mascots, as they will step in front of your passes if you mistime them.

RUSHING CHALLENGE

If you are looking to work on your running moves, then this challenge will be right up your alley. You will face a gauntlet of mascots. Perform the action listed above their heads and you'll avoid being tackled. Be careful, as one of the mascots will overtake you from behind if you take too long.

DEFENSE CHALLENGE

Step up to the plate and stuff those mascots. You'll get to work on your pursuit and tackling in this drill. Tackle each mascot by performing the move listed above their head. Each tackle will back the mascot up further. Back them all the way their endzone and you win.

RECEIVING CHALLENGE

The ball will be thrown out to one of several highlighted areas. Get your player in position to make the catch before the mascot does. You'll have to be on your toes as you move back and forth all over the field to receive the ball. This drill is great for working on your strafe and catching skills. Catch 6 out of 10 passes to win.

FAST FACT: Win at all three difficulty levels and you can play as your favorite mascot!

Wii Tips & Strategies

▲ Arcade style visual effects

The NCAA Football franchise makes its debut on the Wii this season with tons of family friendly features sure to have everybody picking up a remote to play. EA SPORTS didn't scrimp on the details as the Wii version of the game is packed with enough teams and game modes to keep even the most diehard NCAA fan busy for quite a while.

Both FBS and FCS teams are included, 198 teams in all. *NCAA Football 09* supports a full Dynasty Mode, Practice Mode, and you can even play Rivalry games for bragging rights.

The game provides fast arcade action and visual effects with ball trails, big hits and sprint trails.

ALL-PLAY CONTROLS

EA SPORTS All-Play Controls allow you to manage all of the commands and actions during the game with just a shake of the Wii remote. You will be able to control all of your main actions including snapping the ball, tackling, evading, kicking and passing.

You can also disconnect the Nunchuk, and the CPU will handle your player movement for you. This will allow family members of all ages to join into this virtual gridiron competition.

ALL-PLAY SETTINGS

▲ Accessible to the whole family

All-Play Settings allow you to get into the game without having to deal with penalties or the play clock. Novice gamers can take their time before the snap and won't feel rushed in their playcalling. You might want to play longer games if you are playing with the clock off so you'll be able to get enough snaps in. Once you get the hang of the playcalling, you can go back to a 3 or 5 minute game and have plenty of time to run up the score.

Choosing Even Teams allows both teams to compete at the same skill level. You can now play with your favorite team colors without feeling like you are at a disadvantage against a higher rated team.

Penalties: You can disable these to prevent penalties from being called.

Play Clock: Turn this off and you'll have all the time you want to select a play and snap the ball.

Gameplay Assists: Provides assistance to players and enables them to have more success at running, passing, catching and kicking.

PLAYCALLING SCREEN

▲ Did we call the right play?

EA SPORTS provides three different playcalling options to make sure that the needs of every style of player are covered.

Ask Coach: Chooses the appropriate play for you based on down and distance. This is the best choice for absolute beginners.

Basic Playbook: Contains a condensed playbook. This is much easier for beginner to intermediate players as it has a simpler set of plays.

All-Plays: Contains complete team-specific playbooks with multiple formations, sets and play calling options. This is for advanced players who know their way around the game and understand basic football.

CROWD HYPE

▲ Hype up the Crowd

After big plays, you'll have the opportunity to pump up the crowd and whip them into a frenzy. The faster you swing your controller, the wilder the crowd gets. More Crowd Hype earns you additional Mii fans, which gives increased stats to your team. You'll also receive a momentum boost.

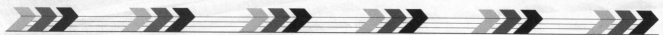

▲ *The Coin Toss, Wii Style*

BLUFF PLAYS

If you are playing against an opponent in a head-to-head game, you don't want them to know what plays you are going to run. Find the play that you want to call and hold down the A button. You will feel your controller rumble after a second or two. This locks in your play. Now you can scroll to another play and press the A button again to bluff. If you change formations, this will reset the bluff play.

Don't neglect this feature. If your opponent knows what you are going to call, he'll be able to easily shut you down.

MASCOT GAME

▲ *Sparty vs. Buzz*

Perfect for the younger members of your family, this mode lets you battle it out as your favorite mascot. All of the best mascots are in the game, including Albert, Buzz, Mike the Tiger, Sebastian the Ibis, Sparty the Spartan and dozens more.

TUTORIALS

▲ *Big Hit!*

NCAA Football 09 for the Nintendo Wii gives you tons of context sensitive tips to walk you through the game. Action icons above the heads of players will instruct you on what to do. You can also press the 1 button at various times to pull up a tutorial for that particular area. For example, when you line up for a kick off, pressing 1 will take you to the kicking tutorial.

You can go to the pause menu and view all of the tutorials in the game. NCAA Football 09 for the Wii can be played with family accessible controls, or you can get as advanced with X's and O's as you want to. Don't neglect the tutorials, as they will help you reach the full depth of game play.

Here's a list of what you will find in the Tutorial Menu:

OFFENSE PASSING GAME

☐ Snap the ball
☐ Fake the snap
☐ Passing
☐ Pre-Snap Camera Look
☐ Select Receiver
☐ Catching

OFFENSE RUNNING GAME

☐ Running with the Ball
☐ Juking
☐ Stiff Arm
☐ Power Move
☐ Break Tackle
☐ The Option
☐ Fake the Option

DEFENSE

☐ Jump the Snap
☐ Defensive Controls
☐ Swat
☐ Rip/Swim/Spin
☐ Big Hit
☐ Choose Receiver

DEFENSIVE AUDIBLES

☐ Defensive Shifts

OFFENSIVE AUDIBLES

☐ Audibles
☐ Hot Routes
☐ Slide Offensive Lint

KICKING GAME

☐ Kicking
☐ Fair Catch
☐ Block the Kick
☐ Bail Out of the Kick

Team Management

VIEW & EDIT ROSTERS

▲ Choose a player to View/Edit

A coaching staff's ability to determine what their players can and can't do is one of the most important aspects of developing their system. Having this understanding is beneficial to both player and coach. For the player, he'll be more confident that he can perform the task that's asked of him. For the coach, he'll be more confident in a play's success rate knowing that each player can successfully carry out his responsibility within the play.

One of the first things you should do before playing a game is to get familiar with your team personnel. Study each individual attribute for your players. For example, who's your

▲ Making changes to #1

fastest receiver? Who's the best offensive lineman for run blocking? Does your quarterback have a strong arm? Do your cornerbacks have enough speed to play man coverage?

Once you feel comfortable in knowing your players strengths and weaknesses you can then determine how best to use them.

You can use the View & Edit Rosters option to take a look at your team and determine your top performers. In addition, you can adjust the attributes and appearance of your players.

DEPTH CHART

Your team will be set up in a default depth chart to start the game, but this doesn't always

▲ Sorting the Depth Chart

mean that the players are in the best possible position or order. You should feel free to adjust the depth chart to match up with the way you want to play.

For example, with the Florida Gators, Sprint Option plays out of the Shotgun are very effective. We like to move HB #8 up the depth chart to take advantage of his high speed rating.

This gives the power of QB #15 matched up with a speedy halfback that can get to the corner and take it to the house.

If you don't want to go through the depth chart yourself, you can pick the auto-reorder depth chart and the CPU will order the chart by the best overall rating at each position.

Create A Player

Create A Player lets you design your own player from scratch. There are four parts to the Create A Player process.

BIO

▲ Creating a player

This screen lets you set all of the basic attributes for your player. You'll fill in your player's name, jersey number, school, home state, etc.

The most important choice, of course, is the player's position.

APPEARANCE

The appearance menu is where you set the physical attributes of your player. You can determine the height and weight of your player, skin tone, and set up his build.

EQUIPMENT

▲ Making equipment adjustments

The equipment screen lets you modify the uniform equipment of your player. You can edit his facemask, determine whether he wears a visor, and control everything from wristbands to ankle tape.

SKILLS

You can set any value for all of the different skill attributes in the game. All the basics are covered like speed, agility, and acceleration. In addition, you can adjust position specific attributes like throwing power, throwing accuracy, route running, etc.

The ratings you choose for your player will change his tendency. For example, load up on your QB's throwing power and accuracy, but give him limited speed and he will show the Pocket Passer tendency.

Once you finish creating your player, he will show up on the roster for the team that you selected.

Note: Auto-Name Rosters *If you want to play with names for your players instead of just numbers, you can let the CPU Auto-Name your players. It will randomly assign names to all the players in the game. They will now be announced by name during games.*

My Settings

The My Setting menu allows you to change multiple gameplay options and penalty sliders, customize the AI and game controls, set preferences, audibles, and auto subs, and adjust volume control and your video calibration. In this section of the guide, we are going to take a look at each one of these settings in more detail.

House Rules

There are three House Rules menus that can be used to change various gameplay settings.

▲ Adjust your settings

GAME PLAY OPTIONS

There are 8 gameplay options adjustments that can be made. They are as follows:
- **Skill:** Determines the skill level of the CPU AI.
- **Injuries:** Set this to On if you want them in the game.
- **Fatigue:** If you want players to get tired as the game progresses, have fatigue on.
- **Quarter Length:** Set quarter lengths between 1 and 15 minutes.
- **Play Clock:** This setting turns the gameplay clock on or off. Turning it off can be used to practice plays in game without worrying about getting delay of game penalties.
- **Home Field Advantage Effects:** By default, these are turned on. This causes the visiting team to have a harder time calling audibles at the line of scrimmage and viewing their play art.
- **Ice the Kicker:** With this setting on, the kicker has a harder time making clutch field goals.
- **Quiz the Quarterback:** Each time an interception is thrown while this setting is on, you will be asked to identify the

▲ Gameplay Options

pass coverage. Answer right, and you will increase your quarterback's composure. Read it wrong and your quarterback will lose composure.

PENALTIES

▲ Adjust Penalties

Penalties settings can be set from 0 to 100. The higher the percentage, the more likely the penalty will be called. The default slider setting for each penalty is set as 50 percent. A few of the different types you can adjust are offsides, facemask, clipping, and roughing the passer.

CUSTOM AI

▲ Customize AI Settings

This menu allows you to customize the AI's QB Accuracy, Pass Blocking, WR Catching, RB Ability, and Run Blocking. By default, each slider is set at 50 percent, but each can be adjusted from 0 to 100.

User Menus

There are four user settings menus:

GAME CONTROLS

▲ Game Control Settings

Use this menu to get a visual of all the game controls in *NCAA Football 09*.

PREFERENCES

▲ Preference Settings

This menu allows you to set various user settings such as favorite team, offensive and defensive playbooks, and random team filter.

AUDIBLES

Use this menu to set your offensive and defensive audibles. There are five audibles that need to be set for offense and defense. You can also use this menu to view information about the playbook you have chosen such as how many quick pass plays are in the book.

SYSTEM

Use this menu to change the game's volume settings for music, commentary, and noise on the field. Video calibration can be used to adjust video settings on your TV screen.

Xbox 360 Achievements

Achievements are awarded after completing a specific in-game task as listed below—an "Achievement Unlocked" icon will appear when this occurs.

5 POINTS EACH

- ☐ **Old Spice Red Zone Shutout:** Complete a Play Now or Dynasty Mode game without allowing a touchdown from the Red Zone
- ☐ **What Were You Thinking?:** Throw the ball away on 4th down

10 POINTS EACH

- ☐ **Break The Ice:** Make a Field Goal when "iced"
- ☐ **QB Quiz Success:** Successfully complete a Quiz the QB challenge
- ☐ **Sick 'Em Smokey:** While playing as the Tennessee Volunteers, celebrate a touchdown by running to your mascot
- ☐ **Don't Mess With Texas:** While playing as the Texas Longhorns, celebrate a touchdown by running to your mascot
- ☐ **Got Gator Bait?:** While playing as the Florida Gators, celebrate a touchdown by running to your mascot
- ☐ **Cue the Fat Lady:** Win a Play Now or Dynasty Mode game by 21 points or more
- ☐ **HIT STUCK:** Jar the ball loose with a User-Controlled Hit Stick tackle
- ☐ **Take Control In The Clutch:** Sack the QB with a user-controlled defender on 3rd down to force a punt situation
- ☐ **Up and Over:** Take it "up and over" the linemen, diving into the endzone for a touchdown
- ☐ **Join The Ranks:** Play a Ranked Game
- ☐ **Conference Champs!:** Play and win a conference championship game in single team Dynasty Mode or Campus Legend Mode
- ☐ **Out on a High Note:** Play and win a bowl game in single team Dynasty Mode or Campus Legend Mode
- ☐ **Place at the Table!:** Become the Starter in Campus Legend Mode

15 POINTS EACH

- ☐ **Play a Mascot Game:** Play a Mascot Game with any mascot teams
- ☐ **Let the Air Out:** As the away team, score within the first 30 seconds of the opening whistle
- ☐ **Pick-Free:** Do not throw any interceptions in a Play Now or Dynasty Mode game
- ☐ **Pick Two:** Intercept 2 passes in a Play Now or Dynasty Mode game
- ☐ **Old Spice Red Zone Perfection:** Complete a Play Now or Dynasty Mode game with a Red Zone Efficiency rating of 100%

20 POINTS EACH

- ☐ **On the 1's and 2's:** Create a custom Stadium Sound event
- ☐ **Triple Threat:** Score a receiving, rushing, and passing touchdown with one player
- ☐ **Go Deep for 50+:** Complete a pass for 50 or more yards in a Play Now or Dynasty Mode game
- ☐ **Breaker Breaker 4-9:** Break a run for 49 or more yards in a Play Now or Dynasty Mode game
- ☐ **Ice In Your Veins:** Be the hero and win a game by taking the lead as time expires
- ☐ **Pick 6!:** Take an interception back to the house in a Play Now or Dynasty Mode game
- ☐ **Scoop and Score!:** Scoop a fumble on defense and take it to the house in a Play Now or Dynasty Mode game
- ☐ **On Lockdown:** Hold the opposition to under 100 total yards in a Play Now or Dynasty Mode game
- ☐ **Is That Even Legal?:** Return a missed field goal for a touchdown. Only valid in Play Now or Dynasty Mode
- ☐ **I'm Special!:** Take a punt or kickoff back to the house for a touchdown. Valid only in Play Now or Dynasty Mode
- ☐ **A/V Club President:** Upload a Video or Photo Highlight
- ☐ **Win at H____:** Win the H.O.R.S.E. mini game
- ☐ **Special Teams Challenge Winner:** Win the Special Teams Challenge mini game
- ☐ **High School Hero:** Become a 5-star legend prospect

25 POINTS EACH

- ☐ **That Just Happened!:** Score a touchdown with your punter in a Play Now or Dynasty Mode game
- ☐ **Record Breaker—Interceptions:** Break the game record for interceptions with one player (5) in a Play Now or Dynasty Mode game
- ☐ **BCS Conference Invite:** Get an invite to a BCS conference in single team Dynasty Mode
- ☐ **Heisman Memorial Trophy:** Win the Heisman Memorial Trophy in single team Dynasty Mode or Campus Legend Mode
- ☐ **Oil Tycoon:** Develop a new pipeline state in single team Dyansty Mode

30 POINTS EACH

- ☐ **Tippy Toe! Lemon Tree!:** Score a touchdown with your receiver by performing a toe-drag animation
- ☐ **Get Creative:** On a non-option play, score a TD with at least one lateral
- ☐ **Safety And Sound:** Force a safety in Play Now or Dynasty Mode
- ☐ **Mmmm…..Donut:** Pitch a shutout by holding your opponent to zero points. Valid only in Play Now or Dynasty Mode
- ☐ **Reach out and Crush Someone:** Join or Host an Online Dynasty
- ☐ **National Champions!:** Play and win a BCS championship in single team Dynasty Mode or Campus Legend Mode
- ☐ **Mr. February:** Have the #1 ranked recruiting class in a season in single team Dynasty Mode
- ☐ **Pontiac G8 4th Quarter Comeback:** Win a Play Now or Dynasty Mode game when down by 14 to start the 4th quarter (min. difficulty: Varsity)

40 POINTS EACH

- ☐ **Russell High School Champ:** Win the Russell High School Championship Game in any state

100 POINTS EACH

- ☐ **The Legend of Campus Legend:** Earn more than 1,000 points in Campus Legend Mode

RIVALRY TROPHIES

Rivalry Trophies are obtained by winning rivalry games. Dynasty and Legend trophies are added to the trophy case by reaching certain goals and achievements in Dynasty and Campus Legend modes.

Getty Images/David Stluka

TROPHY NAME	TEAM 1	TEAM 2
Apple Cup	Washington	Washington State
Battle of I-25 Trophy	New Mexico	New Mexico State
Bayou Bucket	Houston	Rice
Beehive Boot	BYU/Utah/Utah State	BYU/Utah/Utah State
Black Diamond Trophy	West Virginia	Virginia Tech
Bronze Boot	Colorado State	Wyoming
Commander-in-Chief's Trophy	Air Force/Army/Navy	Air Force/Army/Navy
Commonwealth Cup	Virginia	Virginia Tech
Cy-Hawk Trophy	Iowa State	Iowa
Floyd of Rosedale	Iowa	Minnesota
Fremont Cannon	Nevada	UNLV
Golden Boot	Arkansas	LSU
Golden Egg Trophy	Ole Miss	Mississippi State
Golden Hat	Texas	Oklahoma
Governor's Cup	Kansas	Kansas State
Governor's Cup	Kentucky	Louisville
Governor's Victory Bell	Minnesota	Penn State
Illibuck	Illinois	Ohio State
Ireland Trophy	Notre Dame	Boston College
Iron Skillet	SMU	TCU
Jeweled Shillelagh	Notre Dame	USC
Keg of Nails	Cincinnati	Louisville
Land Grant Trophy	Penn State	Michigan State
Little Brown Jug	Michigan	Minnesota
Marching Drum	Kansas	Missouri
Megaphone	Notre Dame	Michigan State
Missouri-Nebraska Bell	Missouri	Nebraska
ODK–Foy Sportsmanship Trophy	Alabama	Auburn
Old Brass Spittoon	Michigan	Indiana
Old Oaken Bucket	Indiana	Purdue
Paul Bunyan Trophy	Michigan	Michigan State
Paul Bunyan's Axe	Minnesota	Wisconsin
Peace Pipe	Bowling Green	Toledo
Purdue Cannon	Purdue	Illinois
Seminole War Canoe	Florida	Miami
Shillelagh Trophy	Notre Dame	Purdue
Silver Spade	New Mexico State	UTEP
Stanford Axe	Cal	Stanford
Sweet Sioux Tomahawk	Illinois	Northwestern
Telephone Trophy	Iowa State	Missouri
Territorial Cup	Arizona	Arizona State
Textile Bowl Trophy	Clemson	NC State
Tiger Rag	LSU	Tulane
Victory Bell	Cincinnati	Miami (OH)
Victory Bell	Duke	North Carolina
Victory Bell	USC	UCLA
Wagon Wheel	Akron	Kent State
Williams Trophy	Rice	Tulsa

Football 101

Each game in *NCAA Football 09* is broken down into four quarters that last up to 15 minutes per game. The game defaults to 5 minute quarters which allows you to get in a quick game, but with enough time to have plenty of action.

Many Dynasty mode players prefer 7 minute quarter games when it comes to getting accurate stats.

We won't get into a full explanation of the basic rules of football here, but instead we are going to focus on the guys that make things happen...the players.

There are 11 players on the field for each team at a time. Each player has a very specific role and unique skill set. Players in *NCAA Football 09* are rated in 45 different categories, and thus no player plays the same.

In this section of the guide we will explain the most important skills for each position and show you the top 5 performers for each one.

Player Ratings

Each player in *NCAA Football 09* is rated in 45 different categories. The higher the rating in a specific area, the better the player is at performing that skill. Not all ratings apply to every position on the field. For instance, kicking accuracy does not apply to the quarterback. We have included the definitions and abbreviations for each rating below:

PLAYER RATINGS	DEFINITION
Acceleration (ACC)	How fast a player can reach his top speed
Agility (AGI)	Ability of a player to move laterally and avoid tacklers
Awareness (AWR)	Football intelligence. Higher AWR players react quicker to plays and are less likely to be fooled by misdirection
Ball Carrier Vision (BCV)	Ability of the ball carrier to spot the open hole
Block Shedding (BSH)	Ability of a defender to shed a blocker against the run or pass
Break Tackle (BTK)	Ability of a player to break a tackle
Carrying (CAR)	Ability of a player to carry the ball without fumbling
Catch (CTH)	Ability of a player to catch the football and hold on
Catch In Traffic (CIT)	Ability a receiver to make tough catches over the middle in traffic
Elusiveness (ELU)	Ability of a ball carrier to avoid being tackled
Finesse Move (FMV)	Ability of a defender to go around a run or pass blocker using a swim or spin move
Hit Power (POW)	Ability of a defender to use the Hit Stick to make a tackle or cause a fumble
Impact Blocking (IBL)	How well an OL, FB, or TE can block while controlled by the lead blocking system
Injury (INJ)	How injury prone a player is. Higher INJ players are less likely to get hurt
Juke Move (JKM)	How well a ball carrier can perform a juke move
Jumping (JMP)	Jumping/Vertical leaping ability of a player
Kicking Accuracy (KAC)	Ability of a player to aim and kick or punt a football
Kicking Power (KPW)	How far a player is able to kick or punt a football
Release (RLS)	Ability of a receiver to beat press (bump-n-run) coverage. The higher the rating, the quicker the receiver will beat the jam
Man Coverage (MCV)	Ability of a defender to play man coverage on a receiver
Overall (OVR)	Player's overall ability. The exact formula used to reach this rating is an industry secret
Pass Block Foot Work (PBF)	Ability of a blocker to use his feet to run block
Pass Blocking (PBK)	Ability to pass block
Pass Block Strength (PBS)	Ability of a blocker to use his strength to pass block
Power Move (PMV)	Ability of a defender to use a power move to disengage from a run or pass blocker
Play Recognition (PRC)	Ability of a defender to read the play once the ball is snapped
Press (PRS)	Ability of a defender to jam the receiver at the line of scrimmage. The higher the rating is, the longer the jam
Pursuit (PRS)	Ability of a defender to pursue the ball carrier
Return (RET)	Ability of a punt or kick returner to return the ball
Route Running (RTE)	Ability of a receiver to run precise pass routes
Run Block Foot Work (RBF)	Ability of a blocker to use his feet to run block
Run Blocking (RBK)	Ability to run block
Run Block Strength (RBS)	Ability of a blocker to use his strength to run block
Spectacular Catch (SPC)	Ability of a receiver to make spectacular catches. Only receivers with a high SPC can make these types of catches
Speed (SPD)	Measure of a player's top end and overall speed
Spin Move (SPM)	Ability of a ball carrier to use the spin move
Stamina (STA)	Ability of a player to regain their energy after each play. Low stamina players will have to be subbed more often to perform at peak levels
Stiff Arm (SFA)	Ability of a ball carrier to shove a would-be tackler away just before being tackled
Strength (STR)	Measure of a player's upper body strength
Tackle (TAC)	Ability of a player to make tackles
Trucking (TRK)	Ability of a ball carrier to run over a defender
Throwing Accuracy (THA)	Ability of a QB to hit his receiver and complete passes in tight spaces. A QB with a high THA rating can also throw better on the run
Throwing Power (THP)	Ability of a QB to throw the ball for distance and velocity
Toughness (TGH)	Ability of a player to recover from injuries
Zone Coverage (ZCV)	Ability of a defender to play zone coverage

Player Positions

▲ *A highly ranked quarterback: #15 (Junior) from Florida*

Quarterback (QB)

The quarterback is the team's field general on offense. In *NCAA Football 09*, there are three types of quarterbacks: balanced, pocket passer, and scrambler. The type of offense you plan on running should determine the type of quarterback you choose to lead your offense. For example, if you plan on running the option offense, then a scrambling quarterback should be your choice.

TEAM	NUMBER	OVR	AGI	SPD	AWR	THP	THA	BTK	INJ	STA
Florida	15	99	82	84	88	97	93	84	95	93
Missouri	10	97	76	76	84	90	97	72	92	90
West Virginia	5	97	95	92	84	94	88	65	70	94
Texas Tech	6	96	66	65	92	90	97	48	88	88
Oklahoma	14	94	68	72	82	93	95	56	92	86

▲ *A highly ranked halfback: #28 (Junior) from Ohio State*

Halfback (HB)

Outside of the quarterback, the team's top halfback normally gets his hands on the ball more often than any other player. There are three types of halfbacks. There are balanced, power, and scat backs. A balanced back is able to do everything well. A power back moves the chains through tough running inside. A scat back has the speed to get outside, and often is a good receiver out of the backfield.

TEAM	NUMBER	OVR	AGI	SPD	ACC	AWR	CAR	BTK	INJ	STA
Ohio State	28	97	90	92	94	86	87	99	92	86
Georgia	24	96	97	94	96	85	86	91	92	90
Clemson	1	95	94	93	94	88	82	92	89	90
Clemson	28	95	97	96	98	85	82	84	90	96
Boise State	41	93	94	91	93	81	90	90	92	94

▲ *A highly ranked fullback: #3 (Senior) from Texas*

Fullback (FB)

Fullbacks don't get the same recognition as their fellow backfield teammates. However, they are often one of the keys to having a successful run game. They usually are the lead blocker that opens the holes for the halfback to follow. Some fullbacks are also good ball carriers and receivers out of the backfield.

TEAM	NUMBER	OVR	SPD	AWR	CTH	CAR	BTK	RBK	INJ	STA
Texas	3	93	85	84	68	84	87	62	89	85
Navy	36	93	86	78	65	82	82	68	90	86
Wisconsin	44	89	65	80	59	76	82	76	87	87
Pittsburgh	30	87	85	68	68	80	80	62	85	83
Washington	32	87	76	74	62	68	82	68	86	88

Player Positions

▲ A highly ranked wide receiver: #1 (Junior) from Florida

Wide Receiver (WR)

Wide receivers tend to get the spotlight more than any other player on the field, except perhaps the QB. There are two types of receivers in the game: possession and speed. Possession receivers make all the tough catches over the middle of the field. Speed receivers stretch the field vertically and can turn a simple catch into a big play at any given time.

TEAM	NUMBER	OVR	AGI	SPD	ACC	AWR	CTH	JMP	INJ	STA
Florida	1	96	99	98	99	90	93	91	65	92
Texas Tech	5	96	94	94	95	88	96	97	88	88
Rice	81	95	94	96	97	90	96	88	89	91
Missouri	9	94	97	97	98	86	93	82	87	88
Illinois	9	93	96	94	96	82	90	94	87	82

▲ A highly ranked tight end: #45 (Senior) from Missouri

Tight End (TE)

One position that has lost some of its importance over the last decade or so is the tight end position. With so many teams now running some form of the spread offense, teams tend not to use the tight end as much. College teams that still run a more traditional pro style offense almost always have a tight end that can stretch the defense down the middle of the field. If you plan on running a pro style offense, having a tight end with speed and blocking ability is a huge asset.

TEAM	NUMBER	OVR	AGI	SPD	ACC	AWR	CTH	RBK	INJ	STA
Missouri	45	95	84	85	87	92	94	58	92	85
Wisconsin	9	94	88	88	90	90	92	58	90	88
Oklahoma State	87	93	82	81	82	75	88	68	88	87
Oklahoma	18	92	84	87	90	88	92	56	90	86
Ohio State	88	90	86	83	78	84	84	62	86	88

▲ A highly ranked center: #51 (Senior) from Cal

Center (C)

The center is generally known as a jack-of-all-trades. He must be able to both run and pass block. He also is the offensive line's leader. He calls out all the run and pass blocking assignments based on what he sees the defense doing. They may also have the duty of being the team's long snapper for field goals and punts.

TEAM	NUMBER	OVR	STR	AGI	ACC	AWR	PBK	RBK	INJ	STA
Cal	51	95	90	62	68	88	95	94	86	76
Oregon	60	95	90	65	62	88	94	94	87	80
Oklahoma	50	93	88	65	65	83	94	96	90	76
Arkansas	63	92	91	59	65	86	91	94	82	74
Louisville	77	92	90	59	68	84	91	93	88	78

Tackle (T)

Each team has a left and right tackle. Their primary job is to protect the quarterback. On most teams, the left tackle tends to be a better pass blocker than the right tackle. The left tackle is usually responsible for protecting the quarterback's blind side. In *NCAA Football 09*, you will find more highly rated left tackles than right tackles.

▲ *A highly rated tackle (LT): #71 (Junior) from Alabama*

TEAM	NUMBER	OVR	STR	AGI	ACC	AWR	PBK	RBK	INJ	STA
Alabama	71	97	97	65	74	82	97	99	92	80
Ole Miss	74	97	95	64	78	88	97	97	90	74
Ohio State	75	96	94	65	68	88	97	96	92	76
Alabama	59	96	94	65	72	85	95	99	90	76
LSU	70	94	93	62	68	84	98	96	86	78

Guard (G)

The two guards' (left and right) primary responsibility is to open holes inside for the running back to follow. Having guards with speed is also important if you plan on running options, sweeps, counters, and screens. They need to be able to get outside and set up the blocking for the play to be successful.

▲ *A highly rated guard (LG): #72 (Senior) from Oklahoma*

TEAM	NUMBER	OVR	STR	AGI	ACC	AWR	PBK	RBK	INJ	STA
Oklahoma	72	97	96	52	68	88	95	99	88	72
LSU	79	96	99	58	66	85	95	98	86	78
Ohio State	71	95	95	59	68	86	93	96	86	72
Oregon State	62	93	92	59	66	85	91	96	87	82
Wisconsin	63	92	90	56	65	88	94	94	86	82

Defensive Tackle (DT, NT)

If the defense runs a 4-3 front, then there are two defensive tackles. If the defense runs a 3-4 scheme, then the solitary tackle is known as the nose tackle. In the 4-3 scheme, the defensive tackle's main purpose is to stop the run, but there are some that can put pressure on the quarterback. In a 3-4 scheme, the nose tackle's only job is to occupy the interior offensive linemen, so that the inside linebackers can go after the ball carrier.

▲ *A highly ranked defensive tackle: #47 (Senior) from Iowa*

TEAM	NUMBER	OVR	STR	AGI	SPD	ACC	AWR	TAK	INJ	STA
Iowa	47	96	85	72	70	78	90	89	94	83
Auburn	94	95	90	65	73	88	82	84	89	78
Georgia	95	95	90	68	67	80	86	87	89	78
USC	75	95	89	68	69	80	84	89	86	78
Oklahoma	96	94	93	65	68	74	82	87	87	80

Player Positions

▲ A highly ranked defensive end (DE):
#95 (Junior) from USF

Defensive End (DE)

Your base defense will determine the type of defensive ends the team requires for their scheme. If you play a 4-3 front, having two defensive ends that can rush the pass rusher is a must. If you play 3-4 fronts, then having two run stoppers is a must. Normally the right end is a better pass rusher than the left end.

TEAM	NUMBER	OVR	STR	AGI	SPD	ACC	AWR	TAK	INJ	STA
USF	95	97	74	84	89	96	74	80	82	78
LSU	93	96	90	72	77	80	84	83	89	87
Georgia Tech	93	96	82	78	83	88	72	82	90	89
Ohio State	87	95	84	82	85	88	72	76	89	84
Ole Miss	92	95	89	76	78	82	76	80	92	82

▲ A highly ranked middle linebacker:
#33 (Senior) from Ohio State

Middle Linebacker (MLB)

The middle linebacker is the heart and soul of the defense. Just like the quarterback on the offensive side of the ball, the MLB calls the plays for the defense. Outside of calling the plays, his primary job is to stop the run. He should have the speed to go sideline to sideline. He is often called upon to spy the opposing team's quarterback.

TEAM	NUMBER	OVR	STR	AGI	SPD	ACC	AWR	TAK	INJ	STA
Ohio State	33	99	82	88	89	96	94	96	92	94
USC	58	96	88	86	87	88	85	92	92	88
South Carolina	52	95	84	80	83	90	89	92	91	91
Florida	51	94	78	82	85	88	85	96	91	86
Georgia	33	94	78	90	89	96	86	92	78	86

▲ A highly ranked outside linebacker:
#45 (Senior) from Penn State

Outside Linebacker (OLB)

The right outside linebacker (WIL) tends to be a better pass rusher than the left outside linebacker (SAM). If you were to look at the outside linebacker's speed ratings for each team, you will notice that in most cases, the WIL is faster than the SAM. Not only can outside linebackers rush the quarterback, but they also must be able to drop pass coverage.

TEAM	NUMBER	OVR	STR	AGI	SPD	ACC	AWR	TAK	INJ	STA
Penn State	45	96	76	86	87	90	88	86	90	90
Ohio State	1	96	80	86	87	92	84	87	84	90
Boston College	16	95	78	84	85	88	88	88	80	91
USC	10	94	76	86	86	88	86	86	85	88
Cal	7	93	78	84	85	86	82	85	93	84

Cornerback (CB)

The Cornerback's primary responsibility is to cover the opposing offensive team's receivers. Most cornerbacks are the team's fastest defensive players. They use their speed to keep up with the man they are covering. Cornerbacks tend to struggle a bit in run support because of their size. In some blitz schemes, they will be asked to blitz the quarterback from the outside.

TEAM	NUMBER	OVR	AGI	SPD	ACC	AWR	TAK	JMP	INJ	STA
Ohio State	2	96	90	93	95	90	70	90	92	94
Cincinnati	21	94	92	94	94	92	62	89	84	90
Georgia	2	94	94	94	97	88	68	88	84	87
Illinois	1	94	93	95	96	88	68	89	87	87
Virginia Tech	1	94	95	95	93	80	66	89	90	92

▲ A highly ranked cornerback: #2 (Senior) from Ohio State

Free Safety (FS)

The free safety's primary job is to prevent the deep pass play. This especially holds true if the defensive coverage called is Cover 1 or Cover 3. He usually has less speed than a cornerback, but typically has more speed than the strong safety. Free safeties are also used to blitz and help in run support.

TEAM	NUMBER	OVR	AGI	SPD	ACC	AWR	TAK	JMP	INJ	STA
USC	2	96	89	94	93	82	80	89	89	92
Missouri	1	96	88	91	90	82	74	86	90	86
Oklahoma	5	96	88	92	92	86	80	87	91	85
Virginia Tech	17	95	88	92	90	85	76	87	89	91
LSU	27	94	88	92	91	84	72	87	90	89

▲ A highly ranked free safety: #2 (Junior) from USC

Strong Safety (SS)

His primary responsibility is run support. In some defensive schemes, he is considered an extra linebacker because he lines up close to the line of scrimmage. A good example of this type of scheme is the 46 Bear. Strong safeties are also used to drop back in pass coverage and often are in charge of calling out the coverage assignments.

TEAM	NUMBER	OVR	AGI	SPD	ACC	AWR	TAK	JMP	INJ	STA
Florida State	3	97	88	92	92	85	82	91	93	93
Clemson	25	95	89	91	92	84	76	88	94	91
Tennessee	14	94	91	95	95	78	72	93	93	84
UCF	29	92	87	91	88	80	80	89	89	89
Georgia	5	92	88	90	87	84	80	89	86	85

▲ A highly ranked strong safety: #3 (Junior) from Florida State

Player Positions

▲ A highly ranked kicker:
#28 (Sophomore) from Arizona State

Kicker (K)

The kicker has two jobs: kick field goals and kick the ball off when his team scores, at the beginning of the game or at the half. Kickers need to have strong legs and an accurate stroke. They often are called upon to kick a game winning field goal as the clock counts down.

TEAM	NUMBER	OVR	AGI	SPD	ACC	AWR	KPW	KAC	INJ	STA
Arizona State	28	95	65	65	70	68	93	94	88	85
Indiana	18	92	68	70	70	81	88	94	86	85
LSU	6	90	65	68	70	84	90	91	92	86
Wake Forest	38	90	65	70	70	76	92	90	91	88
UCLA	15	89	68	74	74	68	95	88	93	90
South Carolina	14	87	68	72	74	76	90	90	91	87

▲ A highly ranked punter:
#47 (Senior) from Tennessee

Punter (P)

The punter's job is to punt the ball away if the offense is unable to pick up a first down. Much like a kicker, they need to have power in their legs and be accurate. Having a punter with these two attributes is critical due to the importance of field position. Punters at times may be asked to pass or run the ball if a trick play is called.

TEAM	NUMBER	OVR	AGI	SPD	ACC	AWR	KPW	KAC	INJ	STA
Tennessee	47	94	70	72	74	82	91	92	92	86
Oklahoma State	18	94	65	68	72	76	93	91	82	85
Texas A&M	16	93	59	59	59	84	92	90	88	86
Ball State	35	89	68	68	70	64	92	90	89	80
UCLA	17	88	65	68	72	72	92	88	91	91

AP Images/Laizure Photo

Taking Control

The best *NCAA Football 09* players are constantly working on their mastery of the controls. In a game between two players with good play calling skills, the game often comes down to who is better on the stick.

If you are a first-time player, the sheer number of controller options can become overwhelming to you. If you get stuck, the Controller Layout settings (available from the Pause menu or in the Setting section) display all of the buttons and what they do in a concise manner.

Preplay menus also give you a leg up on remembering all the options available to you presnap. Once you master these controls, you can hide them so you can see more of the field.

This section of the guide breaks down the controls in detail as well as providing expert hints on when and where to use each one.

Offense: General Controls

SPRINT

Xbox 360: *RT (pull & hold)*
PS3: *R2 button (hold)*

▲ *Sprinting to open field*

No matter what side of the ball you are playing on in *NCAA Football 09*, the Sprint button is the control you will most often use. Below we take a look at some of the situations you will want to use the Sprint button in:

Offense

1. Sprint through an open hole before it closes or use the Sprint button to get the ball carrier outside quickly on toss and sweeps. Don't outrun your blockers. New players often tend to do this and it causes them frustration because they are not able to establish a solid run game.

2. If a pass play doesn't develop, use the Sprint button to take off and run with your QB. Teams with fast quarterbacks give you another dimension on offense.

3. Option plays or run plays (QB Wrap) designed for the quarterback to keep the ball himself are situations when the Sprint button may be used. The same advice applies here; don't outrun the blocking.

4. If you have good user stick control, learning to use the Sprint button after taking control of the receiver can turn an ordinary pass play into a big pass play. While the ball is in the air, take control of the receiver and use the Sprint button to gain separation from the defender in coverage.

Defense

1. Use the Sprint button to get into position quicker to make a play on the ball carrier.

2. While in control of a defender, use the Sprint button to manually apply pressure on the quarterback.

3. After the ball is thrown, take control of a defender and use the Sprint button to catch up with the receiver to make a play on the ball.

SWITCH PLAYERS

Xbox 360: *B button*
PS3: *Circle button*

Another common player control used on offense is the Switch player button.

1. On offense, this control is used to switch between run blockers and motion eligible receivers. Either press the B button each time you want to switch to another player or hold the B button down and press left/right on the left stick to switch between the players.

2. You can also use the Switch Players button to take control of your receiver once the ball is in the air. Use this feature to cut underneath defenders and grab otherwise uncatchable passes.

CALL TIMEOUT

Xbox 360: *Back button*
PS3: *SELECT button*

▲ *New! Interactive Timeouts*

Calling timeout is not only important as far as refreshing your player's fatigue levels, but it also gives you a chance to coach your players on offense or defense. See the section on Interactive Timeouts for more information.

COACH CAM

Xbox 360: *RT + Right Thumbstick Up/Down/Left/Right*
PS3: *R2 + Right Thumbstick Up/Down/Left/Right*

▲ *Coach Cam — Actual Play*

▲ *Coach Cam — Bluff Play (left)*

▲ *Coach Cam — Bluff Play (right)*

▲ *Coach Cam — Performance Levels*

The pre-snap Coach Cam also has a new look to it. Not only can you view the actual play art by holding RT and pressing up on the Right Stick (R2 and Right Stick Up for PS3), but you also have the ability to bluff your opponent by pressing left or right.

In most cases, pressing left is a run play, and pressing right is a pass play. By pressing

down on the Right Thumbstick, you can view your player Composure and see if any of them are "In the Zone".

On defense the same holds true. By holding RT and pressing up on the Right Thumbstick, (R2 and Right Thumbstick Up for PS3) you can view the actual play art. Press left or right to show them a fake play.

This feature is really nice when playing head-to-head games because if you forget what play, pass routes, or pass coverages were called, you now can view

them without giving away the actual play.

QUICK REPLAY

Xbox 360: *RB and LB buttons*
PS3: *R1 and L1 buttons*

Activating the Quick Replay button allows you to jump right to Instant Replay without having to go through the Pause menu. You can now relive your great play instantly!

Offense: Line of Scrimmage

SNAP THE BALL

Xbox 360: *A button*
PS3: *X button*

▲ *Getting ready for the snap*

You can't start the play until you snap the ball.

FAKE SNAP

Xbox 360: *RB button*
PS3: *R1 button*

▲ *Fake Snap to draw the defense offside*

If your opponent is good at jumping the snap or if you want to try to draw your opponent offside, then you'll want to make liberal

use of the Fake Snap. Be warned that using it too much may end up causing one of your offensive linemen to false start.

QUIET/PUMP UP THE CROWD

Xbox 360 | PS3: *Click the Left Thumbstick*

If the crowd is getting too loud while on offense, you can quiet the crowd down some by clicking the Left Thumbstick. When you are on defense, you can pump up the crowd and make it harder for your opponent to get the play off, make hot routes, or call audibles. Keep in mind this feature only works for the home team.

SEND MAN IN MOTION

▲ *Putting a player in motion*

Sending a man in motion has many benefits to your offense production. If you are not using motion, you should seriously consider implementing it into your offense. Here are few reasons why motion should be used on a frequent basis:

1. Makes it easier to get good pre-snap reads of the defense.
2. Forces your opponent to make adjustments on defense.
3. Creates new formations on the fly.
4. Creates new route combinations on the fly.
5. Enables you to get run or pass blockers in position at the point of attack.

To send a receiver in motion, press the B button or Circle (PS3) to cycle through receivers. Once the proper player is selected press left/right on the left stick to send him in motion in that direction.

FLIP RUN DIRECTION

Xbox 360 | PS3: *Move the Right Thumbstick in the opposite direction of your run play to flip.*

Knowing how to change the run play's direction will allow you to exploit weak spots in the defensive front. In addition, you can avoid situations where linebacker/line shifts have taken away your blocking advantage.

For example, your play call has the ball carrier running to the left. If your opponent has overloaded that side with multiple defenders, you don't want to run where the defense is strongest. Instead, flip the run direction of the play to the right where the run defense is weaker. This greatly increases the chances of the play's success.

Offense: Hurry Up Offense »»

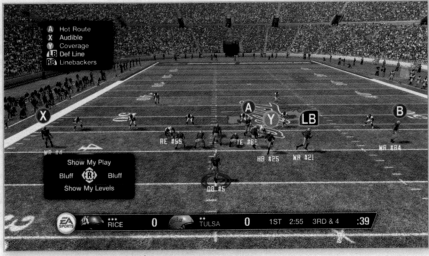

▲ Going into Hurry Up Mode

College football teams tend to use the hurry up offense more than their counterparts in the NFL. Before implementing the hurry up offense, there are some basic controls you need to know.

HURRY TO THE LINE OF SCRIMMAGE

Xbox360: *Y button* | **PS3:** *Triangle* (hold after the whistle)

This control hurries the offense back to the line of scrimmage. It only takes a few seconds, so be ready to snap the ball as soon as they are set.

SPIKE THE BALL

Xbox360: *X button* | **PS3:** *Square* (hold after the whistle)

▲ Stopping the clock

If you need to kill the clock during any part of the game, consider spiking the ball. It will cost you a down, but it prevents the clock from ticking off those precious seconds you may need to win the game.

FAKE SPIKE PLAY

Xbox360: *B button* | **PS3:** *Circle* (hold after the whistle)

▲ Running the Fake Spike Play

This works pretty much the same as spike the ball, but with one difference. Instead of spiking the ball, the quarterback fakes the spike and then is able to throw a pass or run the ball. You can use this technique to fool your opponent into relaxing thinking you are killing the clock. Just be careful with it, because there are not a lot of throwing options.

ADVANTAGES OF RUNNING THE NO HUDDLE OFFENSE

1. It makes it hard for the defense to substitute personnel groupings and rotate fresh players.

2. The no huddle can help the offense get into a rhythm if things aren't initially going too well.

3. It allows the offense to control the tempo of the game. Another benefit is that it gives you more time at the line of scrimmage to survey the defense and change the play/routes if necessary.

4. The No Huddle allows you to run more plays on offense, which could add up to more scoring opportunities!

Note: Using No Huddle Against a Human Opponent. *If you decide to use the no huddle offense as your base offensive scheme, understand some players may have issue with you, especially if you play in an Online Dynasty league. Make sure you understand your league's rules before you start. However, no one will complain if you go No Huddle before the end of the half or game.*

Offense: Lead Blocking

▲ *Using the Lead Blocking Control*

Lead Blocking Control allows you to take control of a blocker while the CPU controls your running back. Once you have made contact with a defender, control switches back to the running back so that you can dart into the space cleared by your blocker.

At the line of scrimmage, press the B button (circle on PS3) to cycle through the available players. You can select a blocking back, lineman, tight end, or even wide receiver. Once you have the correct player selected, press the LB button (L1 on PS3) to active Lead Blocking Control.

After the snap, you will control your selected blocker until he engages a defender. You can flick up on the Right Thumbstick to attempt a pancake block. If you are successful, your blocker can flatten the defender with a highlight reel block. Remember, size matters. Don't expect to run over a linebacker or defensive lineman if you are using a wide receiver to block.

▲ *A crushing pancake block*

In instances where your blocker is out matched size-wise, flick the Right Thumbstick down to execute a cut block. Your blocker will go low and attempt to cut the legs out from under the defender. If things go your way, you can take him right out of the play.

▲ *Cutting his legs out from under him*

For toss plays and outside runs, taking control of the fullback is ideal. You can get out in front of your halfback to lead the charge, or pick up any defenders that might shoot through the line and hit your back behind the line of scrimmage.

You can also use your fullback when running inside plays like HB Blast or HB Slam from two back formations. Get right up in the hole and look for the nearest defender to lay a hat on.

▲ *The FB leads the way*

When running the ball from singleback sets, use one of the linemen that doesn't have a defensive lineman lined up right in front of him. You can often pull your guard and smack the outside linebacker on outside runs.

In this sequence we take RT #76 and get him out into space against a smaller linebacker.

▲ *Our LT lines up his target...*

We flick the Right Thumbstick up and level him with a crushing pancake block. Our tackle goes looking for another defender while we run to daylight with our halfback.

▲ *And leaves him in the dust*

JUMP/HURDLE

Xbox 360: *Y button (tap)*
PS3: *Triangle button (tap)*

 The HB hurdles over the defender

Use the Jump/Hurdle button to leap over defenders while they are on the ground. If you see a defender moving in and anticipate a low tackle, you can use the hurdle button to go over him for extra yards. Watch out though, if he goes high you might lay the ball down on the turf.

SPIN

Xbox 360: *B button (tap for quick spin, hold for a power spin or move the Right Thumbstick in a circular motion)*
PS3: *Circle button (tap for quick spin, hold for a power spin or move the Right Thumbstick in circular motion)*

 A tricky spin move

The key to pulling off a successful spin move is to use it when a defender is approaching you from a poor angle. Right before the defender tries to make the tackle, spin to the direction opposite to the one you are running. If you time things right, the defenders will be grabbing nothing but air.

Another common way to use the spin move is when a defender is near one of your run blockers. Perform the move properly and you can get the run blocker to block the defender while spinning away. The highlight stick can also be used to get the ball carrier to

spin away from a would-be tackler. This move is context sensitive so you don't always know what he'll do.

DIVE/QB SLIDE

Xbox 360: *X button (tap)*
PS3: *Square button (tap)*

 The HB dives over the top for six

The Dive/QB slide button is used to pick up extra yardage before being tackled or to keep the quarterback from getting injured. When down near the goal line, use the dive button to jump over the top of the pile for a touchdown.

If you scramble out of the pocket and are unable to get out of bounds, tap the Dive button to perform a QB slide and protect that most important asset.

STIFF ARM

Xbox 360: *A button (hold)*
PS3: *X button (hold)*

The stiff arm is a great way to break tackles, but can lead to fumbles if overused. The higher the ball carrier's stiff arm rating is, the better the chance he has at breaking tackles. You can also tap this button to switch the ball to your other hand. When breaking down the sideline, you'll want the ball on the same side as the line so fumbles will go out of bounds instead of into the field of play.

PROTECT THE BALL

Xbox 360: *RB button (hold)*
PS3: *R1 button (hold)*

Believe it or not, many players forget about using the protect ball button to avoid fumbles. If your ball carriers are putting the ball on the ground, then your best option is to protect the

 Putting two hands on the ball

ball. This is key in short yardage and end of game situations where a turnover would be critical.

PITCH THE BALL

Xbox 360: *LT button*
PS3: *L2 button*

Use the pitch button to lateral the ball on option plays. Just be careful not to pitch it at the wrong time, or you risk fumbling the ball.

JUKE

Xbox 360 | PS3: *Right Thumbstick left, right, or down*

The Juke move allows you to fake defenders right out of their shoes. The key to pulling off a juke move is to catch the defender at a bad angle and at full speed. You want the ball carrier to be facing straight down field before executing the juke move. Once the ball carrier pulls off the juke move get going forward again...don't hesitate. More often than not, players who first pick up the controller will get carried away with the juke move. However, once you get the timing down, it is a spectacular move to use in one-on-one open field situations.

HIGHLIGHT STICK

One of the better additions to the NCAA Football franchise over the years has been the highlight stick. Pressing up on the Right Thumbstick causes ball carriers to perform different types of moves depending on their abilities. Some will try to run over defenders, while others will make more evasive moves. The top tier ball carriers can do both.

Offense: QB Option

The option controls are simple to learn, but to be a true option stud takes some serious reps. Let's start out with the option basics.

Georgia Tech is one of the few teams that run Flexbone and Wishbone option plays as a base for their offense. We will use them to break down the option controls in this section of the guide.

FULLBACK HANDOFF

Xbox 360: *A button* (hold)
PS3: *X button* (hold)

▲ *Handing it to the Fullback*

On triple option play calls, the QB will take a step back after the snap and place the ball in the FB's gut. If you want the FB to keep the ball and run the dive play up the middle, simply hold down the A button (X on PS3) as the QB and Fullback meet.

The QB will hand the ball to the back for a quick hitter up the middle. You'll want to use this control to keep the defense honest and force them to guard the middle of the field.

▲ *The Fullback breaks into the hole*

As you come up to the line of scrimmage, take a look at the defensive front. First count the number of defensive linemen. Against a 3-4 defense, the FB dive is very effective. However, against a 5-2 defense you will struggle. Also take a look at the spacing between the linemen. If the line is spread, then you can almost guarantee a good gain on the dive. If the line is pinched, look elsewhere as your FB is going to get stuffed at the point of attack.

THE PITCH

Xbox 360: *LT button*
PS3: *L2 button*

▲ *The QB gets to the edge of the line*

Last year, you could make amazing pitches as your QB was hovering inches above the ground and in the grasp of the defense. Not so in *NCAA Football 09*. You'll need to get rid of the ball earlier if you want to hit the pitch man. You can make the pitch by pressing the LT button (L2 on PS3). In this sequence, the QB sees that he is shut down and can't make the edge of the line.

He waits as long as possible and then pitches to the HB who has plenty of open space to turn the corner and break down the sideline.

▲ *With no room to run, the QB pitches*

Note: *In* NCAA Football 09, *there are several different styles of option play you can run:*

Speed Options *get the QB and the HB to the corner as quickly as possible.*
Power Option *involves one back leading out as a blocker while the other back and QB run the option together.*
Triple Option *involves a potential fake/handoff to the FB, followed by an option sequence between the QB and another back.*
Slot Option *allows the QB to run the option with a speedy wide receiver. Be sure to use packages to get your fastest receiver in the formation as the pitch man.*

FAKE PITCH

Xbox 360: *LB button*
PS3: *L1 button*

▲ *The fake pitch draws the linebacker...*

Getting the timing down for the Fake Pitch can be a bit tricky, but it will pay big dividends if you can pull it off. With the Fake Pitch, you are trying to make the pursuing defenders think that you are about to toss it out to your back. You are hoping that he will hesitate in his pursuit of your QB so that you can cut it up inside and get a positive gain.

In this screenshot you can see that #1 is closing in on our QB. We fake the pitch to our trailing back (#20).

He hesitates and takes a step towards our halfback. This is all we need to cut the ball inside of him and get into the secondary.

▲ *...enabling the QB to get more yards*

Be sure to get into practice mode and work on this move. You won't use it a lot as most defenders do a good job at keeping to their assignments, but when you do break it out you can get a huge gain!

Offense: Passing

THROW TO A RECEIVER

Xbox 360: *X, A, B, Y, LB*
(hold for a bullet, tap for lob)
PS3: *Square, X, Circle, Triangle, L1*
(hold for a bullet, tap for lob)

▲ *Dropping back to pass*

Press the button corresponding to a receiver's icon to throw him a pass. For a bullet pass, hold the receiver's pass icon button down. For a lob pass, tap the receiver's pass icon button. Most of the time you will want to use the bullet pass. It gets the ball to the receiver quicker and helps cut down on the chances that the pass will be picked off. You will go with the lob pass most typically on deep balls. By getting a lot of air under the ball, a speedy receiver can often outrun the defender covering him. This also gives you a better opportunity to take control of the receiver and move him into position for the catch.

THROW BALL AWAY

Xbox 360: *RB button* **PS3:** *R1 button*

▲ *When in doubt, throw it away*

When you are under pressure and there are no receivers open, it's best to throw the ball away. Be sure you are outside of the tackles or you will be called for intentional grounding.

PUMP FAKE

Xbox 360 | PS3: *Right Thumbstick*

Top players will tell you that using the pump fake will get receivers open deep more often than not. In *NCAA Football 09*, you can press the Right Thumbstick in any direction and the quarterback will act as if he is going to pass the ball. New to this year's game is the ability to pump fake while on the run.

TUCK AND RUN

Xbox 360: *RT button (hold)*
PS3: *R2 button (hold)*

▲ *Get what you can*

If no receivers are open down the field, you can take off and run with the quarterback by holding down the Sprint button. Not all quarterbacks have the speed to do much damage, but any positive yardage beats a sack. Be sure to get down on the ground by sliding if you can't get out of bounds. Something else to consider is calling a pass play where all your receivers go deep (a good example is the Hail Mary). Once the ball is snapped, watch to see if any defenders are in QB Spy or QB Contain. If the way is clear, let your receivers draw the coverage deep and take off. This only works well against man coverage.

Offense: Catching

If you want to become an elite player in *NCAA Football 09*, then you need to learn how to user catch on both offense and defense. There are several types of user catch animations that can be triggered based on player ratings, the way the ball is thrown, and the position the receiver is in as the catch is being made. In this section of the book, we take a look at some of the more common user catches found in the game.

SWITCH PLAYER

Xbox 360: *B button*
PS3: *Circle button*

▲ *Switch receiver*

The key controlling your receiver is to switch to him the moment the ball is thrown. The longer you wait, the harder it will become to make a user catch. To switch to take control of your receiver, press the B button on the 360 or Circle button for the PS3.

CATCH

Xbox 360: *Y button*
PS3: *Triangle button*

▲ *Going up for the catch*

One of the biggest advantages of the user catch over letting the CPU controlled receiver make the catch is if the ball is thrown off target, you still get the receiver in position to make the grab. By taking control of the receiver, you can manually make adjust-

ments to catch the ball that the CPU controlled receiver would not make. Hold down the Y button on 360 or Triangle button on PS3 to make the grab.

DIVING CATCH

Xbox 360: *Y button*
PS3: *Triangle button*

▲ *Diving catch*

Not many players use the dive button to make a catch. It's very hard to make the catch since your timing must be perfect. The diving catch is best performed on out routes where you are just a bit short of the ball. In general, you are better off sticking with more traditional catches.

STRAFE CATCH

Xbox 360: *LT button*
PS3: *L2 button*

One of the more popular ways to catch the ball in *NCAA Football 08* was to use the strafe catch. Take control of your receiver and hold down the Ⓛ button (Ⓛ2 on PS3). If your timing is spot on, the receiver will turn towards the ball and make the catch. This takes some practice to pull off, so don't expect to get the timing down right away. You will want to spend some time in practice mode getting it down just right.

SPECTACULAR CATCH

Receivers with high spectacular catch ratings (90 or above) can make grabs that other receivers cannot make. You can execute a spectacular catch by either letting the CPU receiver make the catch or manually taking control of the receiver. If you decide to take

▲ *A spectacular catch*

control of the receiver, hold down the catch/jump button. If you get the right timing down, the receiver will sky up in the air to make the catch. Be warned, safeties will wind up for the big hit to knock the ball out. Often this will cause the receiver to drop the pass or even get injured.

USER CATCH ON DEFENSE

▲ *A great defensive catch*

User catching on defense works pretty much the same as on offense. Look for the icon on the ground to see where the ball is projected to land. Take control of the defender and move him near the area. Use the catch/jump button to pick the pass off. Also consider using the strafe button to square the defender up. Once you become accustomed to controlling defenders when the ball is up in the air, you will find your pass defense much improved. If you are playing against a human opponent with good user catch skills, don't let him abuse your defense by not taking control of your defenders and battling right back for the ball.

There will be instances where the Swat button will be more helpful on defense as it will allow you to get a hand on passes that the Catch button will not.

Spend time in practice mode to get a feel for how close you have to be to the ball to make a defensive catch attempt.

Offense: Hot Routes

Using hot routes is a must if you want to become a top player, even if you only use them a few times a game. Hot routes give you several advantages including:

1. Hot Routes allow you to exploit holes in the pass coverage based on your pre-snap reads.
2. You can create new pass route combinations on the fly.
3. Hot routes such as the fly route can be used to clear out room for routes underneath.

To activate a Hot Route, first press the hot route button (360: Y Button, PS3: Triangle Button). Next, press the button matching the icon on the receiver you wish to change. Now you can press either stick in one of four different directions to select the route you wish him to run.

FLY

Xbox 360 | PS3: *Press up on the Left Thumbstick*

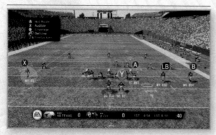

▲ *Fly Route*

Of all the hot routes in the game, the fly (streak) is probably the most used because of its big play potential.

CURL

Xbox 360 | PS3: *Press down on the Left Thumbstick*

▲ *Curl Route*

The curl route is best used against normal man or soft zone coverage.

IN/OUT

Xbox 360 | PS3: *Press left or right on the Left Thumbstick*

▲ *In Route*

The in route works well against normal man coverage. Look for the receiver once he breaks inside. The out route is very effective against normal man coverage and can also be used against soft zone coverage.

FADE

Xbox 360 | PS3: *Press up on the Right Thumbstick*

▲ *Fade Route*

The fade route is an excellent route to go deep with. It also is one of the easier routes in the game to User Catch.

DRAG

Xbox 360 | PS3: *Press down on the Right Thumbstick*

The drag route is another hot route that should become part of your arsenal. It works against man and most zone coverages. It doesn't always pick up a lot of yardage, but is a low risk throw.

SLANT

Xbox 360 | PS3: *Press left/right on the Right Thumbstick*

▲ *Slant Route*

The slant works best when the defense calls a blitz. It doesn't matter if man or zone coverage is called, just throw the ball in the area the defender vacates.

PASS BLOCK

Xbox 360: *LT or RT buttons*
PS3: *L1 or R1 buttons*

If it looks like the defense has called a blitz and you don't have enough pass blockers to cover all the defenders rushing the quarterback, leave one or two receivers in to pass block. This especially holds true when you want to go deep.

SMART ROUTES

Xbox 360: *RB button*
PS3: *R1 button*

▲ *Smart Route*

Smart routes are used when a particular pass route is short of the first down marker or goal line. For instance, your receiver is running a curl route, but the route falls short of the first down marker.

Offense: Slide Protection

▲ Slide Protect Left

USING SLIDE PROTECTION

Xbox 360: *To call for slide protection, pull the LT button and then press left, right, down, or up on the left stick.*
PS3: *To call for slide protection, pull the L2 button and press left, right, down, or up on the left stick.*

Brand new to the Xbox 360/PS3 versions of *NCAA Football 09* is slide protection. Slide protection enables the player on offense to control the blocking technique his offensive line uses. The line can be assigned to slide to the left, right, pinch, or aggressively pass block. To call for normal pass protection, press the B button (360) or Circle button for (PS3). For those of you who have played *NCAA Football* games on PS2/Xbox, you know how important slide protection is to countering enhanced blitz set ups. With slide protection now in the game, you can expect to see more cat-and-mouse games between two human opponents.

USING SLIDE PROTECTION

Slide Protect Left: If the defense looks to be overloading the left side of the offensive line, use slide protect to the left to block for the quarterback. It's a good idea to have

▲ Slide Protect Right

at least one back blocking to the right side as well to pick up any blitzers that might come from that direction.

Slide Protect Right: The same concept holds true with slide protect to the right. If the defense looks to be overloading the right side of the offensive line, use slide protect to the right to counter the blitz. Keep one back blocking to the left to help protect the QB's blind side.

PINCH

▲ Slide Protect Pinch

If the defense looks to be bringing heat up the middle A and B Gaps, having the offensive line pinch will keep the pressure from getting to the QB. Watch out for pressure coming off

both edges. With the left and right tackles pinching in, the defensive ends may have a clear path to the QB.

AGGRESSIVE SLIDE PROTECT

▲ Aggressive Slide Protect

When aggressive slide protection is used, the offensive line doesn't drop far back to block the defenders rushing the quarterback. Instead they stay near the line of scrimmage and aggressively try to keep the pass rushers from getting past them.

Getty Images

Defense: Line of Scrimmage

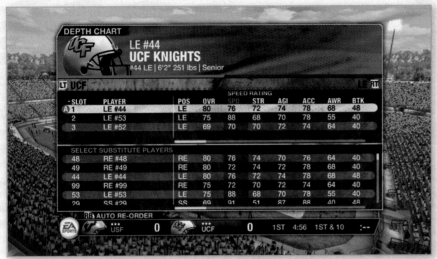

▲ Default Starting LE

Some players are quick snappers, while others take their time.

Linebackers can be used as well to jump the snap. The same principles apply.

Be careful not to jump the snap before the ball is actually snapped. If you cross the line of scrimmage or touch an offensive player, it's a five yard penalty.

Jumping the snap can also be used to disrupt the running game.

PUMP UP THE CROWD

Xbox 360 | PS3:
Click the Left Thumbstick

▲ Pump up the crowd

There are a few controls that you should know about while at the line of scrimmage on defense. Both of the controls listed in this section can have an impact on the outcome of the play.

JUMP THE SNAP

Xbox 360: *Press the LT button*
PS3: *Press the L2 button*

▲ A faster LE

Being able to time the snap is a great way to get pressure on the quarterback while in control of a defensive end or linebacker. It takes practice to get the jump snap control down, but once you get it you can really disrupt the opposing offense's passing or running game.

The faster the defensive linemen, the better the chance that you will be able to jump the snap and get to the quarterback. If there is a lineman down on the depth chart that is considerably faster than the starter, consider putting him in as we do with the UCF Knights left end.

The default starter's speed is 76. Not bad,

but UCF's number 2 left end has an 88 speed rating. 12 points can make a lot difference when using jump the snap to put pressure on the quarterback.

We time the snap and are able to get a jump on the right tackle.

This allows us to go straight after the quarterback and make the sack.

QUICK SNAP TIPS

▲ The DE bursts past his blocker

▲ QB Sack!

Timing the snap count is everything. When playing against a human, try to get a feel for when your opponent likes to snap the ball.

If you're the home team and your opponent is in a critical third or fourth down situation, try pumping up the crowd to make it more difficult. The more you press the pump up the crowd button, the louder your fans and the stadium will get. The quarterback will have a harder time calling out audibles and the offensive coach cam play art will get squiggly, making it hard to tell what pass routes are being run.

Defense: Pursuit/Tackling

The Penn State Linebacker makes the tackle

DIVE

Xbox 360: *X button*
PS3: *Square button*

The main reason for using the dive button is to make a tackle on the ball carrier. When you get near the ball carrier, press the dive button. The defender will attempt to make a tackle.

Another use of the dive button is to make a game saving play on the ball while it is in the air. This takes some skill to perfect, but it can be the difference between giving up six points or holding the offense to a field goal.

STRIP BALL

Xbox 360: *A button*
(while ball carrier has the ball)
PS3: *X button*
(while ball carrier has the ball)

Using the strip ball function can be a high risk/high reward move. You can either cause a fumble or miss a sure tackle and let the ball carrier escape. We suggest only using this when you know there are more defenders in the area to make the tackle just in case you miss.

STRAFE

Xbox 360: *LT button (pull and hold)*
PS3: *L2 button (pull and hold)*

Strafing into position

Making the play

Use the strafe button to spy the QB, create stunts on the defensive line, get squared up with a ball carrier, or cover receivers coming across the middle of the field. In these two screen shots, we are in control of the LB and are lined up to deliver a punishing hit on the running back.

BIG SWAT

Xbox 360: *A button*
(while ball is in the air)
PS3: *X button (while ball is in the air)*

Use the Swat Ball button to get the defender up in the air to defend the pass. The key is learning where to position the defender and then timing when to go up in the air. If you are able to learn to use the Big Swat, it will make it much more difficult for your opponent to throw deep passes.

A great way to learn how to use the Big Swat is to have a friend play offense, and throw deep passes. While the ball is up in the air take control of the defender closest to the receiver and press the A button (X button for PS3). If you don't have a friend who can help you with the Big Swat, call the Hail Mary, and let the CPU controlled quarterback throw deep passes. Call Cover 2 zones, so that way it forces you to take control of one of the safeties deep to defend the pass. If you want to control a cornerback, call Cover 0 defenses where there is no safety help deep.

BIG HIT

Xbox 360: *Right Thumbstick Up*
PS3: *Right Thumbstick Up*

Lining up for a Big Hit

The Big Hit is a defensive move that allows the defender to deliver bone-crushing hits on the receiver. The Bit Hit can be used to knock the ball loose as receivers are coming down with the catch. By timing your hits, you can make it very hard for the opposing offense to complete passes over the middle or make high spectacular catches.

The key to delivering a Big Hit is to use the strafe button to line up your defender. Use the Right Thumbstick to activate the hit.

Defense: Line Moves »

▲ The DE looks to overpower the lineman

▲ Success! He is free to go after the QB

In the third screen shot, we break off the pass blocker and go straight after the quarterback.

HANDS UP/ BAT THE BALL

Xbox 360: *Y button*
PS3: *Triangle button*

For those of you who like to control defensive linemen to put pressure on the QB, there are a few different types of moves that can be used to blow by offensive linemen or bat the pass down. In this section of the guide, we take a look at those moves and how they work.

FINESSE MOVE

Xbox 360: *LB button*
PS3: *L1 button*

▲ The DE is engaged by the blocker

▲ Putting our hands up

POWER/BULL RUSH

Xbox 360: *RB button*
PS3: *R1 button*

▲ A successful Bull Rush

The power/bull move is used to run over offensive linemen. If the defender has a high enough power move rating, he can use it to power/bull rush the offensive lineman he is engaged with.

The offensive lineman has stepped out to engage our pass rusher. We use the power/bull rush move to get by him and go after the quarterback.

▲ He starts his spin move

Use the finesse move to spin your defender away from the offensive lineman. Your defender may also use the swim move. The higher the defender's finesse move rating is, the better the chance he has of spinning out of the block.

In the first screenshot, the offensive lineman has his arms locked onto us.

In the second shot, we have hit the finesse move button. Notice we have started to spin around the pass blocker.

▲ Batting the ball down

In a perfect world, getting to the quarterback for a sack is what every defensive lineman craves. However, we all know that's not going to happen every time. If the defensive lineman can't get to the quarterback, his next best option is to bat the pass down. In *NCAA Football 09* this can be achieved by pressing the hands up/bat button.

If the ball is thrown near the defensive lineman, there is a good chance he will be able to bat the pass down.

In the first screen, notice the quarterback is making the throw. We press the hands up/bat button. Our defensive lineman jumps up in the air.

In the second screenshot, we are able to knock the ball down for an incomplete pass.

Defense: Hot Routes

Back again for another season are individual defensive hot routes. These routes enable you to change the defensive assignment of an individual player on the fly. There are a total of 8 adjustments that can be made. In this section of the strategy guide, we take a look at each one of them.

HOW DEFENSIVE HOT ROUTES WORK

To call a defensive hot route, tap the switch player or hold the switch play button and press the left stick up/down or left/right until your desired defender is selected. Press the A button (X on PS3) to activate the defensive hot route options.

HOOK ZONE (YELLOW CIRCLE)

Xbox 360 | PS3:
Press up on the Left Thumbstick

▲ *Hook Zone*

The defender will drop back in a hook zone. This coverage is good at defending passes over the short middle of the field. If your opponent is beating you with drags, slants, crosses, or circle routes, this is a good coverage to call.

QB CONTAIN (BLACK ARROW)

Xbox 360 | PS3:
Press down on the Left Thumbstick

When playing against a quarterback who has the ability to scramble, consider putting a defender or two in QB Contain on both sides of the field. This forces the quarterback to stay in the pocket. To put a defender in QB Contain, press down on the Left Thumbstick.

▲ *QB Contain*

MAN COVERAGE (RED LINE)

Xbox 360 | PS3: *Press left on the Left Thumbstick, then the receiver's icon*

▲ *Man Coverage*

There are some receivers in the game that may need some extra attention to prevent them from getting the ball. By pressing left on the Left Thumbstick followed by the receiver's icon, you can put man coverage on him.

BUZZ ZONE (PURPLE CIRCLE)

Xbox 360 | PS3:
Press right on the Left Thumbstick

Most players that use buzz zones use them to defend against corner routes. They also can be used to defend the flats, since the defenders play near the sideline. To have a defender drop into a buzz zone, press right on the Left Thumbstick.

DEEP ZONE (BLUE)

Xbox 360 | PS3:
Press up on the Right Thumbstick

Deep zone hot routes are used to take away the deep pass. If your opponent likes to throw bombs, you may consider dropping

a few extra defenders deep to take away his bread and butter. To put a defender in deep zone, press up on the Right Thumbstick.

BLITZ (ORANGE ARROW)

Xbox 360 | PS3:
Press down on the Right Thumbstick

▲ *Blitz Hot Route*

By blitzing defenders that are not already assigned to blitz, you can create schemes on the fly to stop both run and pass plays. Just remember that this will leave holes in the pass coverage. To send a defender on a blitz, press down on the Right Thumbstick.

QB SPY (ORANGE CIRCLE)

Xbox 360 | PS3:
Press left on the Right Thumbstick

This is another defensive hot route that can be used to counter scrambling quarterbacks. The QB Spy hot route can also be used to defend short passes over the middle of the field. To put a defender in QB Spy, press left on the Right Thumbstick.

FLAT ZONE (DARK BLUE)

Xbox 360 | PS3:
Press right on the Right Thumbstick

If the opposing offense is attacking the flat areas, consider hot routing a defender into flat coverage. Flat zones can also be used to defend screens or prevent the quarterback from taking off. To put a defender in flat coverage, press right on the Right Thumbstick.

Note: *To cancel a defensive hot route, press the B button for Xbox 360 or the Circle button for the PS3.*

Defense: Coverage Audibles ≫

▲ *Faking the SS Blitz*

SHOW BLITZ COVERAGE AUDIBLE

This audible drops an extra defender (strong safety) down in the box to defend the run or bring pressure. It also can be used to trick the player on offense into thinking blitz, when really no blitz has been called. The downside of this coverage is that it can be exploited deep since the strong safety has farther to go to get into coverage.

MAN SHIFT COVERAGE AUDIBLE

Using the Man Shift Coverage Audible will put the defenders in better position to cover their assignment. Be careful not to overuse the Man Shift Coverage Audible. Against the CPU it is fine to use whenever you want, but against a human opponent it will give away your coverage.

LOOSE COVERAGE AUDIBLE

Loose coverage forces the corners to play off the receivers by giving them a 7 yard cushion. Loose coverage is good to use in long passing situations when you know your opponent has to throw deep routes to get a first down. Quick Outs will eat this type of coverage up unless the corners are playing the flats. If it is 3rd and 4, don't use this type of cover-

▲ *Loose Coverage*

age. Use normal or Bump-N-Run instead.

TIGHT COVERAGE AUDIBLE *(ALSO KNOWN AS BUMP-N-RUN)*

▲ *Tight Coverage*

If you are playing against the CPU, you won't see this coverage, unless the defenders are playing the flats or a play like Cover 1 Press has been called. When playing against a human opponent expect to see a heavy dose of tight coverage, especially when a blitz is called. It's a good idea to find pass plays to beat this type of coverage and have them in your audibles.

SAFETY SHADE LEFT/RIGHT

▲ *Safeties shaded to the right*

This coverage is generally used to cheat the safeties to the left or right side of the field to help cover an elite receiver. For example, if an elite receiver is lined up on the left side of the field, you can cheat the safeties to the left so they don't have to cover as much ground to guard him. It makes it more difficult to pass to him since the safeties are in better position.

SAFETY SHADE INSIDE/OUT

▲ *Safeties Spread Out*

▲ *Safeties in Tight*

Shading safeties inside isn't used that much because most players don't want to give up the big pass play on the outside. However, if your opponent is killing you with deep post or seam routes down the middle of the field, have the safeties play inside.

Another popular coverage tactic is to have the safeties play farther out to help defend against the deep pass, particularly streaks, corners, and post corner routes.

Defense: Linebacker Audibles

Shifting the linebackers can put them in position to shut down the inside or outside run. You can also shift them into better pass coverage, or give them better pass rush angles for going after the QB. In this section of the guide, we take a look at the defensive linebacker audibles available in *NCAA Football 09*.

HOW LINEBACKER AUDIBLES WORK

To call a linebacker audible, press the linebacker audible button (RB for 360, R1 for PS3), then use one of the following controls:

SPREAD LINEBACKERS

Xbox 360 | PS3:
Press up on the Left Thumbstick

▲ *Linebackers spread out*

One of the more common uses for spreading the linebackers out is to help defend against option or toss plays. Spreading the linebackers out also puts them in better position to rush the quarterback from the outside.

PINCH LINEBACKERS IN

Xbox 360 | PS3:
Press down on the Left Thumbstick

▲ *Linebackers pinched*

If your opponent has an effective inside run game, consider pinching the linebackers. This puts them in better position to defend the

inside run. A and B gap blitz set ups can also be created by pinching the linebackers.

SHIFT LINEBACKERS LEFT

Xbox 360 | PS3:
Press left on the Left Thumbstick

▲ *Linebackers shifted left*

Shifting the linebackers to the left creates an overload that often favors the defense. The offense normally does not have enough pass blockers to counter the pass rush. At least one defender should be able to get through, provided that enough defenders are rushing the quarterback.

SHIFT LINEBACKERS RIGHT

Xbox 360 | PS3:
Press right on the Left Thumbstick

▲ *Linebackers shifted right*

The same can be said of shifting linebackers to the right. Overloads can be created to bring pressure on the quarterback. The offense may not have enough pass blockers to keep at least one pass rusher from getting to the quarterback.

SEND ALL LINEBACKERS ON A BLITZ

Xbox 360 | PS3:
Press down on the Right Thumbstick

▲ *All Linebackers blitzing*

This sends all the linebackers on the field on a blitz. If you are looking to bring instant pressure on the quarterback, this is a great tactic to use. Just don't get carried away with it, because a smart player on offense will look to beat it by throwing quick passes over the middle.

ALL LINEBACKERS IN ZONE

Xbox 360 | PS3:
Press up on the Right Thumbstick

▲ *All Linebackers in zone*

This puts all the linebackers on the field in zone coverage. For instance, if two linebackers are blitzing, and you want to call off the blitz, press the linebacker shift button, and then up on the Right Thumbstick. Both linebackers will now play hook zones.

Note: *To cancel any linebacker shift, press the B button for the Xbox 360 or Circle button for the PS3.*

Defense: Line Audibles

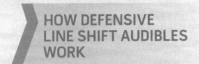

DEFENSIVE LINE SHIFTS

Being able to control the trenches is key to winning football games. Thankfully *NCAA Football 09* gives players several tools to work with while in control of the defensive line. Let's take a look at each one of those tools and how to maximize their use.

HOW DEFENSIVE LINE SHIFT AUDIBLES WORK

To call a linebacker audible, press the linebacker audible button (RB for Xbox 360, R1 for PS3), then use one of the following controls:

SHIFT LEFT

Xbox 360 | PS3:
Press left on the Left Thumbstick

▲ *Defensive line shifted left*

Shifting the defensive line to the left creates an overload on the left side of the offensive line. Often the offense won't have enough pass blockers to keep the defense from getting some type of pressure. It also can be used to defend toss and option plays to the right side of the offensive line.

SHIFT RIGHT

Xbox 360 | PS3:
Press right on the Left Thumbstick

▲ *Defensive line shifted right*

Shifting the defensive line to the right does the same as shifting to the left; only it creates an overload to the right side of the offensive line. Another benefit to shifting the defensive line to the left or right is it puts a defensive tackle over the center. This often frees up the middle linebacker to make plays.

SPREAD

Xbox 360 | PS3:
Press up on the Left Thumbstick

▲ *Spreading the defensive line*

Spreading the defensive line puts the defensive ends in better position to blow up sweeps and option plays. It also gives the defensive ends better pass rush angles for attacking the quarterback.

PINCH

Xbox 360 | PS3:
Press down on the Left Thumbstick

▲ *Defensive line pinched*

Pinching the defensive linemen helps defend against power running plays. It also increases the inside pass rush because all the defensive linemen are lined up tighter.

CRASH LEFT/ MIDDLE/RIGHT

Xbox 360 | PS3: *Press left/down/right on the Right Thumbstick*

▲ *Defensive line crashing right*

▲ *Defensive line crashing middle*

Crashing the defensive line left, down, or right creates different angles for the defensive linemen to defend the run or pass. You will want to experiment with this because there are ways to create enhanced blitz schemes that allow linebackers and defensive backs to shoot through gaps to blow up the run or put pressure on the quarterback.

OUTSIDE RUSH CONTAIN

Xbox 360 | PS3:
Press up on the Right Thumbstick

▲ *Outside rush*

Use this control to contain quarterbacks in the pocket. This works best if the defensive line is spread out and then given an outside rush contain assignment.

Getty Images/Doug Pensinger

Special Teams

▲ Lining up for a Field Goal attampt

The offensive and defensive sides of the ball have a huge impact on the game, but special teams also play an important role. Many a game has come down to a last second field goal to determine the winner. Kickers and punters possessing strong legs can help control the starting field position of the opposition.

KICKING/PUNTING THE BALL

▲ The Kick Meter

Kicking the ball is fairly simple in *NCAA Football 09* once you get the kicking mechanics down. To adjust the kick's height and direction, move the Left Thumbstick up/down and left/right.

To adjust the power and accuracy of the kick, press down on the Right Thumbstick to start the kick and then press up on the stick when the meter reaches the top. While the power meter is going up, move the Right Thumbstick left or right to adjust the accuracy of the kick.

ABANDON KICKS/PUNTS (AFTER SNAP)

▲ Preparing to punt

If for some reason you want to abandon a kick or punt, you can press the LT button (L2 button on PS3) after the ball is snapped. Be aware that your chance of picking up a first down or scoring is greatly reduced by trying it this way. You are better off having your offense run a special team fake run or pass play on the field rather than trying to pick up a first down by abandoning the kick.

▲ Abandoning the kick

FAKE KICKS/PUNTS

Trick plays on special teams are a big part of the excitement of college football. There is nothing more demoralizing to the opposing team than stopping an opponent's offense only to have them get a first down on a special teams trick play. In *NCAA Football 09*, there are a few trick plays that can be used to keep your opponent on his toes.

EXAMPLE OF HOW TO RUN A TRICK PLAY

▲ The Max Protect Pass

The Max Protect Pass is a perfect example of a good special team trick play that can be used to swing the tide of the game in your direction.

▲ Executing the fake

Instead of punting, he drops back to pass. The SS, who is lined up on the left, is running a flat route.

▲ The SS gets open

We spot him wide open in the flat and throw a bullet pass his way.

We make the catch and take off down the field for a first down.

Returning Kicks/Punts

▲ Using our blockers

▲ Now is the time to Sprint

Another momentum changer that can happen while on special teams is returning a kick or punt for a touchdown. How many times have you seen the kick or punt team kick the ball away from a dangerous return man? They would rather kick the ball short on a kickoff, or punt the ball out of bounds than let a return man take the rock all the way back for six. If you are able to follow blocks and look for opening holes, you too can force your opponent to kick away from you.

KICK RETURN

The key to a successful kick return is getting behind your blockers and waiting to see what holes open up. Many players think they

need to press the Sprint button down as soon they get the ball. That's usually not the best option. If you wait for the blocks to set up, and then press the Sprint button, you will find yourself picking up more yards when returning kicks.

PUNT RETURN

A common tactic that is used during punt returns is to take control of a player on the line of scrimmage and drop him back before the ball is punted. Once the ball is up in the air, look to block a defender as he races down the field to make a tackle. Once the punt returner makes the catch, take control of him and start looking for holes. The same applies to kick

returns; don't use the Sprint button as soon as the catch is made. Wait for the blocks to set up before using it.

FIELD GOAL KICK RETURNS

▲ Preparing to return a Field Goal

Brand new to *NCAA Football 09* is the ability to return missed field goals. We like to call FG Safe Zone. Once on the field, we take control of the receiver on the right and drop him back. If the kick looks like it's going to be short, we get him in position to make a catch. Once the catch is made, we look to break outside to one of the sidelines. The downside of trying to return field goals is there is no guarantee that you will be able to make it back past the line of scrimmage where the kick attempt occurred. If this happens you end up losing field position, so keep this in mind any time you decide to return a field goal kick.

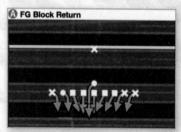

▲ FG Block Return

The FG Safe Zone play gives you decent coverage against fakes, but doesn't get any pressure after the kicker.

If you are pretty confident that your opponent will be kicking the ball, but still want to give yourself an opportunity at a return, call the FG Block Return play.

This plays sends 10 men after the ball with one player back waiting on a potential return.

Gameplay Features

The NCAA Football 09 team introduced a host of new features to the game this season. Home Field Advantage has arrived on the Next Gen consoles and changes the way the game is played in a big way. You'll notice a distinct difference between playing in the friendly confines of your own stadium versus going on the road into a hostile environment. It is important that you have a set of go-to plays that you know inside and out, as you will rarely be able to view your on-field play art at a place like The Swamp.

Everything from Icing the Kicker to rattled QBs is covered in the game. Custom stadium sounds allow you to personalize your home venue and Interactive Timeouts allow you to prepare your team to handle their jobs on the field. This section of the guide will prep you on what you need to know about these new features.

Home Field Advantage

▲ Play Art Confusion

If you have ever been to a college football game at a big time school, then you know the impact that home field advantage can have on a team. Places like The Swamp, The Horseshoe, and Lane Stadium are packed with screaming fans on Saturday afternoons. These environments can be very intimidating for visiting teams and have a definite effect on the outcome of the game.

PLAY ART

NCAA Football 09 models Home Field Advantage (HFA) with a number of gameplay features. The HFA factor is focused around the concept of composure. When the game starts out in a hostile environment, the play art will be shown with a bunch of squiggly lines.

If you are able to sustain a good drive, the lines will go back to normal and you'll see the standard play art. Throw an interception or have a couple of failed drives and the squiggly lines will be back.

COMPOSURE

▲ In the Zone

Pull up the Coach's Cam and then press down on the Right Thumbstick. You'll be able to see your player performance levels. Players with a white icon are neutral. Player's with blue icons are rattled. Players that turn orange are starting to get hot.

String together enough good plays and your player will get "In the Zone." Players who are in the zone will have red pulsing icons. Your players will see an attribute increase while they are in the zone. Your backs will break more tackles, your receivers will make spectacular catches and your quarterbacks will complete passes with deadly accuracy.

▲ Unstoppable!

QB QUIZ

▲ QB Quiz – Screen 1

Make a mistake by throwing an interception, and the EA SPORTS QB Quiz will pop up. QB Quiz allows you to see 4 screen shots of the last play. You will have the opportunity to read the coverage again, and pick which one of three plays at the bottom of the quiz matches that coverage.

▲ QB Quiz – Screen 2

▲ Correct, Composure Gained!

You don't have to view all 4 pictures. If you choose the correct play, you will regain some of your QB's composure. If you can pick the correct play after only viewing 1 or 2 of the screens you will regain more composure. Choose wrong and you lose composure.

Interactive Timeouts

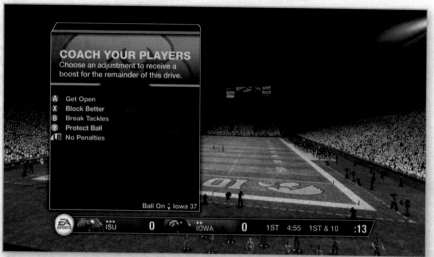

▲ Interactive Timeout – Offense

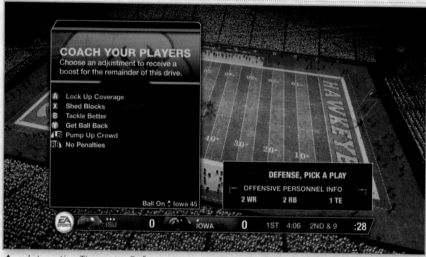

▲ Interactive Timeout – Defense

On defense there are five adjustments that can be used to help improve your team's abilities during the remainder of the current drive. They are as follows:

1. Lock Up Coverage: Use this adjustment to encourage your defensive backs to lock down the opposing receivers during obvious passing downs.

2. Shed Blocks: This adjustment can be used on both run and passing downs. If a run is called, the defenders have a better chance of shedding blockers and getting to the ball carrier. If a pass play is called, blitzing defenders can shed blocks and get to the quarterback quicker.

3. Tackle Better: If your opponent has a tough running back to bring down, use this adjustment to give your defenders a better chance of making the tackle.

4. Get Ball Quick: This adjustment can be used to try to get the ball back during a run or pass play. If a run play is called, the defenders will try to strip the ball away from the ball carrier. If a pass play is called, the defenders will aggressively go after the pick.

5. No Penalties: Before the ball is snapped on a crucial down, consider selecting this option to remind your team to keep it clean and avoid flags.

Note: *Interactive Timeout selections can be cancelled out by your opponent's choices. If you choose Get Open and your opponent chooses Lock Up Coverage, then the coaching points will void each other out.*

OFFENSE TIMEOUT

The new Interactive Timeouts feature gives you the opportunity to coach up your team and make adjustments.

On offense one of the following five coaching points can be made to improve your team's abilities during the remainder of the current drive. They are as follows:

1. Get Open: Use this adjustment to improve your receivers' ability to get open.

2. Block Better: If your offensive line is not blocking very well, this adjustment will help improve their blocking.

3. Break Tackles: This adjustment is used to improve the ball carrier's ability to break tackles.

4. Protect Ball: If you are down near the goal line or you are running out the clock late in the game, use this adjustment to encourage your players to hold onto the ball.

5. No Penalties: Before the ball is snapped on a crucial down, consider selecting this option to remind your team to keep it clean and avoid flags.

Formation Audibles

ICE THE KICKER

▲ *Icing the Kicker*

There are few things as thrilling, and nerve wracking as the game winning field goal. The Miami-FSU series has been decided by a missed field goal five different times since 1991. These types of kicks are tougher than normal, and *NCAA Football 09* goes the extra mile to portray these stressful moments in as realistic a manner as possible.

The Ice the Kicker feature is triggered when the following criteria are met:

1. There is 10 seconds or less left in the game

2. It is a game winning or game tying field goal attempt

3. The defense calls a timeout (CPU will always call a timeout when 1 and 2 are met)

You will notice that the kicking meter is "iced over." The accuracy meter is smaller and

▲ *The kick is away...*

your controller will rumble. You will be placed at a different camera angle that makes getting the kick direction right a little more difficult. Also a slow motion camera angle will prolong the agony of the moment.

FORMATION AUDIBLES

▲ *Formation Audibles – Offense*

Formation audibles give you a much needed play call option. Each set that you call on offense or defense will have four different plays that you can call using the option button and the Right Thumbstick.

On offense you will have plays that fall

▲ *Formation Audibles – Defense*

under the following categories:

Up – Quick Pass   **Right** – Deep Pass
Down – Run   **Left** – PA Pass

On defense you will have plays that fall under the following categories:

Up – Man   **Right** – Cover 2
Down – Blitz   **Left** – Cover 3

Learn the plays that you have available to you for the formations that you most often run. You don't want to call these plays from the play call screen. This way you give yourself the most options possible at the line of scrimmage. If you see that your original play was a bad call, make a quick change using the Formation Audibles feature. If you set up your standard audibles to be from the same formation, you could conceivably have nine plays available to you from your favorite formation.

▲ *Game Winner, or Wide Right V?*

Custom Sounds/Bluff Play

BLUFF PLAY OPTION

Playing against the CPU can be a lot of fun, but nothing beats the thrill of head-to-head competition. Having your best buddy sit next to you while you wear him out in *NCAA Football 09* is just about as fun as it gets.

However, there are two problems:

1. Your buddy can see your play call screen and your play choice.

2. What do you do if you want to see your coach cam play art?

Fortunately, EA SPORTS has made some changes to the game to make head-to-head play work better. First off, you have four buttons you can choose on the playcall screen instead of just one. Now your opponent can't see which specific play you have selected.

▲ *New Playcall Screen*

You can also trick your opponent by bluffing on the Playcalling screen. Once you press A (X on the PS3) to call your play, keep holding A down and move the Left Thumbstick to scroll through other plays and throw your opponent off.

Many online players struggle when they play head-to-head because they can't see their play art. Bluff play art allows you to see your play art and throw a monkey wrench into your opponent's game at the same time.

Start by holding down the coach's cam

▲ *Show your opponent a fake play*

button to bring up your four options. Pushing up on the Right Thumbstick shows your actual play art. Right/Left shows fake plays from the same formation. This lets you see your art without letting the defense know your exact play. Down on the Right Thumbstick shows the performance levels of your players.

CUSTOM STADIUM SOUNDS

▲ *Custom stadium sounds*

Use your personal audio collection to set up your own custom in-game atmosphere. Set your playlist to trigger whenever one of over 20 user-defined situations occurs on the field. We've listed the different custom situations below:

- ☐ Field Goal Kick is Successful
- ☐ PAT is Successful
- ☐ 2 Point Conversion is Successful
- ☐ Touchdown
- ☐ Safety
- ☐ Defense on 3rd Down
- ☐ Defense on 4th Down
- ☐ Kickoff
- ☐ Timeout - Home Town
- ☐ Timeout - Away Team
- ☐ Start of 3rd Quarter
- ☐ Tackle for Loss/Sack
- ☐ Defensive Stop on 3rd Down
- ☐ Defensive Stop on 4th Down
- ☐ Turnover
- ☐ Defense Takes the Field After Kick Return
- ☐ 3rd Down Conversion is Successful
- ☐ 4th Down Conversion is Successful
- ☐ 1st Down Conversion on 1st or 2nd Down
- ☐ Field Goal Miss by Opponent
- ☐ Challenged Play
- ☐ Start of 4th Quarter
- ☐ Penalty on the Away Team

Playbook Styles

College football is unique because of the multitude of styles that you see from teams. Watch an NFL game and you more or less see everybody do the same things. In a college game you will see one team come out in Shotgun all game and another roll out in the Flexbone for every series.

NCAA Football 09 captures these differences in detail. The game is packed with hundreds of formations and literally thousands of different plays. Calling the right plays in the right situations may be the most important skill to master.

This section of the guide breaks down the most common offensive styles in the game, and gives you an example play for each one. You will learn the key formation groups with an explanation of the key personnel, and the purpose for each one. This section also provides diagrams of the most common formations and their sets so you can get a quick visual of how they are arranged.

Offensive Styles

SHOTGUN SPREAD OPTION OFFENSE

By spreading out the field with four and five receiver sets while in the Shotgun, the defense is forced to adjust their personnel based on what the offense has on the field. Making the defense's task even more difficult is the fact that the offense can run or pass from the Spread Option Offense. Florida's Urban Meyer is often associated with Spread Option Offense because of his success with Utah and Florida.

SHOTGUN 5WR TRIO QB WRAP JET SWEEP

▲ *The Slot receiver comes in motion*

The Shotgun 5WR Trio QB Wrap Jet Sweep has five receivers spread out. Two are lined up on the left, while three are lined up on the right. The far left receiver is sent in auto motion to the right.

▲ *The QB can hand it off...*

Once the ball is snapped, the quarterback has the option to hand the ball to the receiver

▲ *...or keep it for himself*

in motion, or he can keep it himself. What the defense does before and after the snap will determine where he goes with the ball.

If he decides to keep the ball he will follow his blockers and look to pick up yardage.

WEST COAST OFFENSE

The West Coast Offense (WCO) is an offensive system that places a greater emphasis on passing than on running. By throwing short, higher percentage passes it allows the receivers to use their athleticism and speed to pick up yardage after the catch. Bill Walsh created the offense back while he was an assistant coach with the Bengals in the 1960's. Having a highly accurate quarterback who is able to find the open receiver is a high priority when running the West Coast Offense.

ACE SLOT INSIDE CROSS

▲ *Surveying the field*

The Ace Slot Inside Cross is a good example of a West Coast Offense play that you will find in the game. With the slot receiver and tight end running crossing routes underneath, one of them is almost always open against man or zone coverage.

▲ *Look for crossing routes*

Look for them to get open as they cross each other over the short middle.

Once you spot one open, throw a bullet pass. Expect to pick up 5-12 yards with this play.

PRO STYLE OFFENSE

The Pro Style Offense is based off of traditional offenses run by professional teams. Generally the Pro Style Offense has one quarterback, two receivers, two running backs, and one tight end. The I Form Normal, Strong I Normal, and Weak I Normal are all good examples of Pro Style Offensive formations. The scheme is known for its simple run blocking schemes and timing pass routes principles. What makes this offensive scheme so effective is that when scouted, it looks confusing, but it is actually simple for the teams that run it.

I FORM NORMAL PA SCISSORS

▲ *Trying to fool the defense*

After establishing the inside run game out of the I Form Normal, the PA Scissors has potential for a big play down the field.

If the safeties bite on the play action, there is a good chance that the flanker will be wide open as he breaks to the post.

▲ *Hit the flat route*

If he is not open, the quarterback should look to hit the fullback in the flat or dump the ball off to the halfback once he curls back towards the quarterback.

PISTOL OFFENSE

The Pistol offense takes advantage of the best parts of lining up directly behind the center and lining up in the shotgun. This allows the offense to run or pass the ball while still having a running back line up directly behind the quarterback. In 2005, Nevada's Head Coach Chris Ault came up with the Pistol Offense in part because he wanted to be able to have a threat of a power run offense, but also because he wanted to be able to throw the ball with success.

PISTOL 4WR TRIPS SMASH

▲ Lining up in the pistol

The Pistol 4WR Trips Smash is an excellent passing concept to attack all types of pass coverages. With the slot receiver running a corner route and the flanker running a curl route, one of them should be able to get open.

If the defense is playing a soft zone such as Cover 4, look to throw to the flanker.

▲ The QB fires it downfield

▲ Complete for a first down

If the defense is playing Cover 1 or Cover 3, look to throw to the slot once he breaks to the corner.

OPTION RUN

▲ Attacking with the Option

The Option Run relies on two common principles: the first is being able to read the defensive alignment and the second is having at least two ball carriers. Option run plays are normally called double or triple option. With so many potential ball carriers on any given play, the defense is often overwhelmed. Here is a list of the more common option run formations:

- ☐ Wishbone
- ☐ Flexbone I Form Spread
- ☐ Flexbone Wide Triple Counter Option

▲ HB #22 finds plenty of running room

The Air Force Playbook has some really nice Flexbone option plays; one of which is the Triple Counter Option. This play has the wingback on the left coming in auto motion to the right.

Once the ball is snapped, the quarterback has the option to hand the ball off to the fullback, keep it himself, or pitch the ball to the trailing wingback.

If the quarterback feels like he going to be tackled, he can pitch the ball at the last second. If the pitch is timed right, there is often a lot of room to run the ball outside and down the sideline.

SPREAD OFFENSE

The spread offense employs four and five receiver sets. Typically the sets are either balanced with an equal number of receivers on both sides, or unbalanced with more receivers on one side than the other. Some think that the spread offense is all about passing the ball, but that's not always the case. Spreading the defense out not only opens up passing lanes, it also helps open up bigger running lanes for running backs to get through.

SHOTGUN TRIPS HB WK QUICK SLANTS

▲ Standing tall in the pocket

Because the spread offense sends four to five receivers out on pass routes, there is not always time to throw deep, especially when a blitz is called. Plays such as the Shotgun Trips HB Wk Quick Slants are a good example of spread pass plays that get the ball out of the quarterback's hands and into a speedy receiver's grasp.

▲ Get rid of it quickly

Look for one of the receivers running a slant route over the middle.

If the ball is thrown on time, there is big potential to pick up solid yardage.

Offensive Styles continued...

AIR RAID

The Air Raid offensive scheme is all about spreading the ball out to multiple receivers. This prevents the defense from keying in on one or two receivers. Teams like Texas Tech that run the Air Raid offense like to spread the field out by running four and five receiver sets. They look to throw early and often, usually by throwing high percentage passes, although they will look to go deep on occasion. There are several playbooks in NCAA Football 09 that are geared toward the Air Raid offense.

SHOTGUN DOUBLE FLEX SLOT OUT

▲ The HB Angle route

Throwing to the running back out of the backfield is one of the key characteristics of the Air Raid Offense. One of the key routes that running backs run from this offensive scheme is the angle route. The Shotgun Double Flex has the running back working an angle route. This route works well against both man and zone coverage.

▲ Completing the pass

Once the ball is snapped, he will act as if he is going towards the sideline.

He then will break over the middle and get open. It's at this point that we throw him a bullet pass.

FLEXBONE

The Flexbone offensive scheme isn't used as much in college football as it once was. It is mostly known as a run-oriented scheme, but it does have passing plays as well. The Flexbone has three running backs lined up in the back-field. Add in the quarterback and you have a very difficult set to defend. The most common play run from the Flexbone is the triple option. The play has three running options: quarterback, fullback, and wingback.

FLEXBONE WIDE QUICK OPTION

▲ The QB attacks the edge of the line

▲ Take the pitch down the sideline

Another run play in the Flexbone Wide that we like besides the triple option is the quick option. This play is highly effective when the defense is playing man coverage. The key to this play is flipping it to the same side as the receiver. You will be surprised by the amount of yardage that can be picked up.

The quarterback has the option to keep the ball himself or he can pitch it to the trailing wingback.

We found that by pitching the ball to the wingback, we often have a lot of room to run the rock to the outside.

ONE BACK

The One Back offense typically is a balanced offense with the running back lined up directly behind the quarterback. The running back may also line up on the left or right side of the quarterback. With an extra tight end or wide receiver in place of the fullback, you have better speed and hands for the running and passing game. Two of the more common one back offensive formations are the Ace Big and Ace Slot.

ACE BIG HB STRETCH

▲ The HB looks for an open lane

▲ He bursts into the open field

Zone running plays have become a very popular way to move the ball on the ground from one back formations. The Ace Big HB Stretch is a good example of a zone running play that is very effective from the One Back offense. In the first screen shot, the quarterback sprints to the spot of the handoff, while not tipping off whether it's pass or run.

Once the ball is handed off to the running back, we look to follow our run blocks.

Once to the outside, we press down on the Sprint button and find plenty of daylight.

Offensive Formations

The team at EA SPORTS spends thousands of man-hours researching and developing the playbooks each year for the NCAA Football franchise. On average, the team watches 5 games of each of the 120 FBS teams to get a feel for how they run their offense and what sets they use. They then work diligently to replicate what they see on the field as best as possible in the game. In this section of the guide, we will give you an overview of the most common formations.

ACE

The Ace (also known as Singleback or One Back) features one running back lined up directly behind the QB. Teams such as USC, Oregon State, and UTEP have plenty of Ace formations to choose from. Formations such as the Ace Jumbo and Big are solid run formations. The Ace Slot and Slot Strong are good balanced formations to pass and run from. The Ace Spread and Spread Flex have plenty of firepower for those who like to air it out.

EMPTY

There is only one Empty formation in *NCAA Football 09* and that's the Empty Trips. It can be found in the One Back, USC, UTEP, and Washington State playbooks. This formation has 12 (11 pass, 1 run) plays to choose from. There are five receivers that go out on pass routes. It is best to run pass plays that have short and intermediate pass routes because there normally won't be much time to sit in the pocket. Some of the better plays to run are the FL Drag, Smash Fork, and Tight Screen.

MOST COMMON **EMPTY** SET

Trips

FAR

The Far is considered a West Coast Offensive set. In *NCAA Football 09*, there is only one set to be found and that's Far Pro. The fullback lines up directly behind the quarterback, while the halfback lines up on the left side of the fullback. There are two receivers split out wide. The Far Pro can be found in only one playbook; the West Coast. A few plays to check out are the Double Swing, HB Sweep, and TE Post.

MOST COMMON **FAR** SET

Pro

FLEXBONE

The Flexbone has three running backs lined up in the backfield with the quarterback. There are two wingbacks and one fullback. Navy and Air Force are two playbooks you will want to consider running if you like run plays from the Flexbone. The Flexbone is best known for double and triple option plays. If you feel the need to pass, two plays to consider using are the Flexbone-Normal Curl Flats and Flexbone-Split Slot Wheel.

MOST COMMON **ACE** SETS

4WR Trips   Jumbo   Spread   Twin TE Slot

Big Flip   Normal Slot   Tight Slots   Twin TE

Big Twins   Slot Flex   Trey Open   Wing Trips

Big Wing   Slot Strong   Trio   Y Trips

Big   Slot   Trips TE

Bunch   Spread Flex   Trips

MOST COMMON **FLEXBONE** SETS

Normal   Trips

Slot   Twins

Split   Wide

Tight

Offensive Formations continued...

FULL HOUSE

There is only one Full House formation in the game: the Normal Wide. It can be found in the Georgia Tech and Navy playbooks. This formation has three running backs lined up in the backfield with the quarterback. With this alignment, the Full House Wide is well equipped to run and pass from. Run plays such as the FB Slam, HB Slam, and HB Sweep are all solid choices to pound your opponent into submission. Pass plays such as the PA Middle and WR DBL Shake will keep your opponent from stacking the box to stop the run.

MOST COMMON **FULL HOUSE** SET

Normal Wide

I-FORM

One of the more traditional sets in the game is the I-Form. There are 11 I-Form formations that can be found in the game. The I-Form Normal is the most common as it can be found in several playbooks. The I-Form gets its name because the fullback and halfback line up directly behind the quarterback, thus creating the "I". I-Form formations can have two tight ends and some can have three receivers lined up on the field. Some of the I-Form formations you will want to check out if you like to run the ball are the Big, Twins, and Twin TE Wing.

PISTOL

One of our personal favorite formations in the game is the Pistol. Lining up a few yards behind the center helps defeat the inside pass rush. Throw in the fact that that the running back lines up behind the quarterback, and you can still have a traditional rushing attack. There is a wide variety of balanced, run, and passing sets to choose from. If you are interested in running the Pistol, the Nevada playbook is by far the best choice.

POWER I

The Power I is a variation of the I-Form. The fullback and halfback line up behind the quarterback, forming an "I" with an extra running back lined off to the left side of the fullback. This gives the Power I that extra fuel to power the rushing attack. The only Power I formation in the game is the Power I Weak. It can be found in the Run Balance playbook.

MOST COMMON **POWER I** SET

Weak

MOST COMMON **I-FORM** SETS

PRO/SPLIT BACK

The Pro/Split Back is another popular West Coast Offensive set that mostly relies on short passing routes to move the ball. There are also some solid run plays to choose from. There are a total of three Pro/Split Formations in the game. The Split Pro and Normal can be found in the Notre Dame, Tulane, and West Coast playbooks. The Split Backs 3WR can be found in two playbooks: Balanced and South Carolina.

MOST COMMON **PRO/SPLIT BACK** SET

MOST COMMON **PISTOL** SETS

SHOTGUN

Of all the sets in the game, the Shotgun gets the most attention, and appropriately so. With so many teams running spread option and spread passing attacks, it's no wonder that the playbooks in the game are dominated with Shotgun formations. Unlike professional football teams, college teams will also run from the Shotgun. Missouri, Oregon, and North Texas all rely heavily on Shotgun formations to move the ball through the air and ground. Florida, SMU and Illinois are a few other Shotgun playbooks to check out.

STRONG I

The Strong I has the fullback lined up on the strong side of the quarterback. The idea is to give him better run blocking angles and make him more of a threat out of the backfield as a receiver. There are a total of 9 Strong I Formations in *NCAA Football 09*. The Strong Normal, I Twins, and Twin TE are some of the more common ones found in the game.

MOST COMMON STRONG I SETS

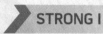

I-Normal | Tight

I-Twins | Twin TE

H Pro | Twin

H Twins | Y-Trips

Normal

MOST COMMON SHOTGUN SETS

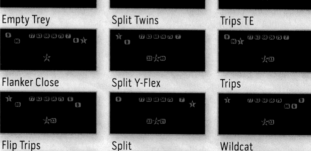

4WR Spread	Ace Twins Wk	Normal Wing TE	Spread
4WR Trey Str	Ace Twins	Normal Y-Slot	Tight
4WR Trio Str	Ace Wing Wk	Normal	Trio HB Wk
4WR Trio	Ace Wing	Slot F Trips	Trips HB Wk
4WR	Ace	Slot Strong	Trips Open Str
5-Wide Tiger	Bunch HB Str	Split Offset	Trips Open
5WR Bunch	Double Flex	Split Slot	Trips Over
5WR Flex Trey	Empty Trey	Split Twins	Trips TE
5WR Flex Trio	Flanker Close	Split Y-Flex	Trips
5WR Trey	Flip Trips	Split	Wildcat
5WR Trio	Gator Heavy	Spread Flex Wk	Wing Trio Wk
5WR Trips	Normal Flex Wk	Spread Flex	Wing Trips
5WR	Normal HB Wk	Spread HB Wk	Y-Trips HB

Offensive Formations continued...

WEAK I

The Weak I in a sense is the same as the Strong I, the only difference is the fullback lines up on the weak side of the quarterback. The running game may not be as strong since the tight end is lined up on the opposite side of the fullback. That's not to say the running game can't be established from the Weak I, but it will be somewhat harder. Passing the ball from the Weak I is a better choice in our opinion.

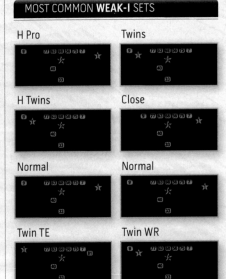

MOST COMMON **WEAK-I** SETS

H Pro
Twins
H Twins
Close
Normal
Normal
Twin TE
Twin WR

WISHBONE

With three running backs in the backfield forming what looks like a wishbone, you have one of the better rushing sets in the game. There are plenty of option plays to be found within the three Wishbone formations. The Navy playbook has all three of them: Normal, Tight, and Wide. There are a few good pass plays you can use to keep the defense from stacking the line of scrimmage. The option pass in particular is a good choice.

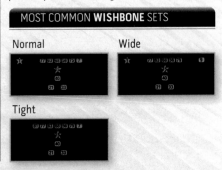

MOST COMMON **WISHBONE** SETS

Normal
Wide
Tight

Reading Offensive Diagrams

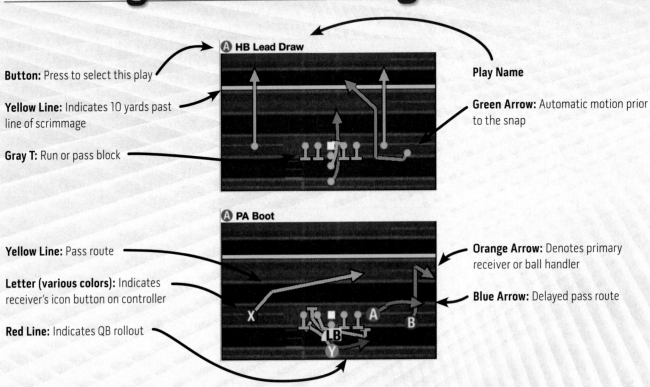

Ⓐ HB Lead Draw

Button: Press to select this play

Yellow Line: Indicates 10 yards past line of scrimmage

Gray T: Run or pass block

Play Name

Green Arrow: Automatic motion prior to the snap

Ⓐ PA Boot

Yellow Line: Pass route

Letter (various colors): Indicates receiver's icon button on controller

Red Line: Indicates QB rollout

Orange Arrow: Denotes primary receiver or ball handler

Blue Arrow: Delayed pass route

Defensive Formations

3-4

The 3-4 is a defense that has three defensive linemen, four linebackers, and four defensive backs. The 3-4 is good to use if you have a better set of linebackers than D-linemen. The idea of having 4 linebackers is to give you more speed on defense. The strength of the 3-4 is in stopping the outside run. You will also get good coverage against short passes with the extra LB. The weakness of the 3-4 is that it struggles against the inside run, and you will not get a lot of pressure from your line. You will want to blitz more to add pressure if you decide to use the 3-4.

MOST COMMON 3-4 SETS

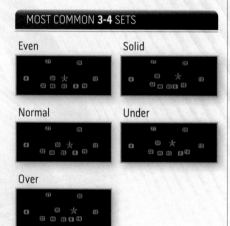

4-3

The base 4-3 defense is good against the inside running game and gives you a strong pass rush from your four down linemen. The ROLB (Will) is generally the team's fastest linebacker. He should be able to blitz from his side and put heat on the QB. The 4-3 is the most used defensive set in the game.

MOST COMMON 4-3 SETS

4-4

The 4-4 is intended to stop runs to the outside, and shut down the short passing game. The 4-4 uses four down linemen, four linebackers, two cornerbacks, and a safety. With eight to nine men in the box, the 4-4 defense can shut down most run plays. Stunts are another frequent element of a 4-4 defensive scheme.

MOST COMMON 4-4 SET

Normal

5-2

The 5-2 consists of a nose guard, two defensive tackles and two defensive ends. It is intended mainly to be a run defense. However, it can be effective against short to medium pass routes. The only problem with 5-2 defenses is that they expose the defensive backs more than the other standard defenses in *NCAA Football 09*. For this reason, the coverage deep is weaker than we like to have. Consider running the 5-2 inside the red zone or if your team's secondary is superior to the offense's receivers.

MOST COMMON 5-2 SET

Normal

NICKEL

The Nickel defense has four D-linemen, two linebackers and 5 defensive backs. The Nickel defense is used as a pass defense, but because you still have 2 linebackers you can use it against the run. You will want your four best pass rushers on the defensive line. Your two best cover Linebackers should be in the nickel as well. The 5th DB (Nickelback) should be your third best cover back. The object of the

nickel defense is to get enough speed on the field to cover multiple receivers.

MOST COMMON NICKEL SETS

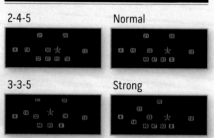

3-3-5

There are several 3-3-5 formations in *NCAA Football 09*. One of these formations is the 3-3-5 Stack. It puts two strong safeties up near the line of scrimmage. This provides the defense with eight men in the box. It presents good run support inside and out, while providing adequate coverage. Because there are so many defenders in the box, it makes it difficult for the offensive line to determine who is blitzing. It also confuses the QB because linemen drop back in zone coverage, while linebackers and defensive backs rush the QB.

MOST COMMON 3-3-5 SETS

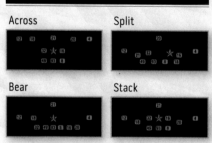

4-2-5

Technically you could call the 4-2-5 a nickel defense since it uses five defensive backs on the field. The secondary consists of two cornerbacks, one free safety, and two strong safety types who'll usually play closer to the line of scrimmage as linebackers. The 4-2-5 defense as played in college and high school football is intended to be an eight man front

Defensive Formations continued...

defense along the lines of the 4-4. The primary difference between the 4-2-5 and 4-4 defense is that you're replacing the two outside linebackers in the 4-4 with strong safety type players. You're able to defend passing formations much better as you have five defensive backs in the game. The two strong safeties also allow the defense to easily get into multiple eight man fronts.

MOST COMMON 4-2-5 SETS

Bear   Over   Normal   Under

DIME

The Dime defense brings in a 6th DB and replaces the Linebackers. This gives you four defensive linemen, 1 linebacker, and 6 defensive backs. The Dime defense is mostly used against 4WR and 5WR sets when you know the offense is going to pass. When using the Dime defense you are sacrificing the run defense to be able to stop the pass.

MOST COMMON DIME SETS

Normal

3-2-6

The 3-2-6 has three defensive linemen, two linebackers, and six defensive backs. The main difference between Dime and 3-2-6 is the Dime has four down linemen and one linebacker, while the 3-2-6 has three down linemen and linebackers. The Dime can add a little more pressure without a blitz being called since it has four down linemen. On the other hand, the 3-2-6 has better pass coverage since an extra linebacker replaces a defensive lineman. The 3-2-6 also provides better run support than the Dime and Quarter 3 Deep.

MOST COMMON 3-2-6 SET

Normal

QUARTER 3 DEEP

The Quarter 3 Deep has three defensive linemen, one linebacker, and seven defensive backs. The free safety, free safety #2, and the strong safety all play deep. Based on their alignment, this formation should be strictly used for pass defense. However, through some creative set ups, it can also be used to stop the run.

MOST COMMON QUARTER 3 DEEP SET

Normal

Reading Defensive Diagrams

Button: Press to select this play
Defensive Play Name
Light Blue Bubble: Deep Zone
Yellow Bubble: Hook Zone
Dark Blue Bubble: Flat Zone

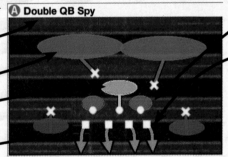
Ⓐ Double QB Spy

Orange Bubble: QB Spy
Orange Arrow: Blitz Assignment
Red Line (not shown): Man Coverage
Purple Bubble (not shown): Buzz Zone
Gray Arrow (not shown): Contain Rush

Getty Images/Kevin Terrell

Team Rosters

NCAA Football 09 is packed with all 120 FBS football squads. Eleven different conferences are represented as well as the independent teams like Notre Dame. Trying to sort through and scout each of these teams is a daunting task for anyone that picks up the game.

This section of the guide does just that. First, each team has a Report Card that provides their overall, offensive and defensive ratings. Below the grades are prestige ratings and a quick recap of the team's 2007 season.

Comprehensive depth charts are provided for each team, including starters and back up players. Overall ratings are provided for each player and the team's impact players are designated as well. These ratings are based on the Xbox 360 and PS3 versions of the game. They may differ slightly from other platforms as the Next Gen consoles have additional ratings categories for each player.

One final bit of key information is located at the bottom of each team capsule: the offensive playbook sets. This comes in handy for players that are searching to find that "perfect playbook."

AIR FORCE
Falcons

Conference: **Mountain West**
Location: **Colorado Springs, CO**

REPORT CARD AND PRESTIGE

64 Overall **68** Offense **69** Defense

PRESTIGE RATINGS
Overall ★★
Coach Good
Academic Great

2007 SEASON RECAP
- 9-4 overall record
- 6-2 conference record
- Lost Armed Forces Bowl

DEFENSIVE DEPTH CHART AND SCOUTING REPORT

Conservative 3-4 Defense
AI Playcall Tendency: 45% defend run, 55% defend pass

	FS		MLB	MLB	LOLB		SS	
	78 #23	81 #32	72 #45	73 #48	76 #36		85 #34	
74 #6	76 #29	69 #37	61 #47	72 #31	66 #92		67 #30	77 #8
70 #18	79 #91		74 #76		80 #95			70 #20
62 #24	71 #90		67 #65		79 #93			64 #1
CB	RE		DT		LE			CB

■ IMPACT PLAYERS   ■ LIKELY STARTERS

OFFENSIVE DEPTH CHART AND SCOUTING REPORT

Aggressive Balanced Offense
AI Playcall Tendency: 60% run, 40% pass

K	WR	LT	LG	C	RG	RT	TE	WR	P
75 KPW	69 #26	79 #79	81 #57	77 #63	77 #62	73 #60	86 #88	74 #81	62 KPW
87 KAC	68 #80	75 #70	70 #64	65 #65	69 #67	70 #78	71 #85	68 #19	84 KAC
85 #13		FB		QB1	QB2		HB		78 #98
		78 #25		75 THP / 85 THA / 78 #14	68 THP / 82 THA / 74 #7		81 #2		
		64 #40					76 #22		

■ IMPACT PLAYERS   ■ LIKELY STARTERS

TEAM OFFENSIVE PLAYBOOK

Ace-Big	I-Form-Normal	Shotgun-Normal
Ace-Big Flip	I-Form-Slot	Shotgun-Split
Ace-Big Twins	I-Form-Tight	Shotgun-Split Offset
Ace-Y-Trips	I-Form-Twin TE	Shotgun-Split Slot
Flexbone-Normal	I-Form-Twins	Shotgun-Spread Flex
Flexbone-Wide	Shotgun-Ace	Shotgun-Y-Trips

AKRON
Zips

Conference: **MAC (East)**
Location: **Akron, OH**

REPORT CARD AND PRESTIGE

72 Overall **75** Offense **73** Defense

PRESTIGE RATINGS
Overall ★★
Coach Fair
Academic Fair

2007 SEASON RECAP
- 4-8 overall record
- 3-5 conference record
- 6th in MAC East

DEFENSIVE DEPTH CHART AND SCOUTING REPORT

Neutral 3-3-5 Defense
AI Playcall Tendency: 59% defend run, 41% defend pass

	SS	ROLB	MLB	FS	LOLB		SS	
	81 #54		84 #21		71 #27		78 #1	
77 #2	74 #20	60 #49	82 #30	75 #28	70 #23		69 #40	75 #6
73 #11	77 #94		84 #92		88 #56			70 #18
70 #25	75 #45		69 #91		77 #95			69 #22
CB	RE		DT		LE			CB

■ IMPACT PLAYERS   ■ LIKELY STARTERS

OFFENSIVE DEPTH CHART AND SCOUTING REPORT

Conservative Spread Offense
AI Playcall Tendency: 50% run, 50% pass

K	WR	LT	LG	C	RG	RT	TE	WR	P
76 KPW	79 #17	82 #74	80 #71	75 #51	79 #78	77 #75	78 #83	83 #1	75 KPW
89 KAC	76 #81	73 #69	77 #79	73 #72	68 #73	75 #77	72 #8	78 #4	85 KAC
85 #45		FB		QB1	QB2		HB		86 #38
		82 #32		79 THP / 88 THA / 78 #11	73 THP / 89 THA / 82 #14		82 #24		
		78 #33					81 #7		

■ IMPACT PLAYERS   ■ LIKELY STARTERS

TEAM OFFENSIVE PLAYBOOK

I-Form-Tight	Shotgun-Ace Twins Wk	Shotgun-Split Twins
I-Form-Y-Trips	Shotgun-Normal	Shotgun-Split Y-Flex
Shotgun-4WR Trio	Shotgun-Normal HB Wk	Shotgun-Spread
Shotgun-4WR Trio Str	Shotgun-Normal Y-Slot	Shotgun-Trio HB Wk
Shotgun-5WR Trio	Shotgun-Split	Shotgun-Y-Trips
Shotgun-Ace	Shotgun-Split Slot	Shotgun-Y-Trips HB Wk

ALABAMA
Crimson Tide

Conference: **SEC (West)**
Location: **Tuscaloosa, AL**

REPORT CARD AND PRESTIGE

84	88	82
Overall	Offense	Defense

PRESTIGE RATINGS
Overall ★★★★★
Coach Elite
Academic Very Good

2007 SEASON RECAP
- 7-6 overall record
- 4-4 conference record
- Won Independence Bowl

DEFENSIVE DEPTH CHART AND SCOUTING REPORT

Neutral 4-3 Defense
AI Playcall Tendency: 38% defend run, 62% defend pass

	CB	RE	DT	DT	LE	CB
Starter	81 #24	84 #96	82 #97	82 #60	88 #93	81 #16
Backup	79 #9	79 #98	78 #72	79 #79	86 #95	79 #3

	FS	ROLB	MLB	LOLB	SS
Starter	93 #49	82 #13	81 #25	82 #47	82 #26
Backup	80 #28	80 #51	73 #32	77 #48	75 #31 / 81 #35

■ IMPACT PLAYERS ■ LIKELY STARTERS

OFFENSIVE DEPTH CHART AND SCOUTING REPORT

Neutral Balanced Offense
AI Playcall Tendency: 50% run, 50% pass

	K	WR	LT	LG	C	RG	RT	TE	WR	P
	72 KPW	85 #9	97 #71	92 #76	83 #70	87 #78	96 #59	80 #88	86 #80	79 KPW
	88 KAC	80 #11	75 #74	80 #73	77 #77	78 #79	78 #83	80 #81	86 #81	91 KAC
	82 #99									82 #97

	FB	QB1	QB2	HB
THP	78 #25	87	78	85 #29
THA	64 #40	89	89	85 #38
		87 #14	84 #12	

■ IMPACT PLAYERS ■ LIKELY STARTERS

TEAM OFFENSIVE PLAYBOOK

Ace-Big	Ace-Twin TE	Shotgun-Double Flex
Ace-Big Twins	Ace-Twin TE Slot	Shotgun-Empty Trey
Ace-Big Wing	Ace-Y-Trips	Shotgun-Normal Flex
Ace-Bunch	I-Form-Twin TE	Shotgun-Split Y-Flex
Ace-Slot Flex	I-Form-Twins	Shotgun-Wing Trips
Ace-Spread	Shotgun-4WR Trio	Shotgun-Y-Trips HB Wk

ARIZONA
Wildcats

Conference: **PAC-10**
Location: **Tucson, AZ**

REPORT CARD AND PRESTIGE

84	86	82
Overall	Offense	Defense

PRESTIGE RATINGS
Overall ★★★
Coach Very Good
Academic Very Good

2007 SEASON RECAP
- 5-7 overall record
- 4-5 conference record
- 6th in PAC-10

DEFENSIVE DEPTH CHART AND SCOUTING REPORT

Aggressive 4-3 Defense
AI Playcall Tendency: 42% defend run, 58% defend pass

	CB	RE	DT	DT	LE	CB
Starter	81 #23	81 #44	80 #3	84 #46	91 #97	80 #2
Backup	78 #11	79 #42	78 #60	79 #94	77 #83	70 #24

	FS	ROLB	MLB	LOLB	SS
Starter	82 #32	82 #15	86 #33	85 #25	81 #20
Backup	80 #34	80 #41	72 #39	76 #8	78 #31 / 85 #6

■ IMPACT PLAYERS ■ LIKELY STARTERS

OFFENSIVE DEPTH CHART AND SCOUTING REPORT

Aggressive Spread Offense
AI Playcall Tendency: 53% run, 47% pass

	K	WR	LT	LG	C	RG	RT	TE	WR	P
	65 KPW	84 #4	81 #67	81 #74	77 #54	82 #68	94 #77	80 #48	88 #10	67 KPW
	85 KAC	77 #11	80 #78	77 #64	77 #50	81 #75	80 #73	78 #88	78 #84	88 KAC
	80 #13									78 #47

	FB	QB1	QB2	HB
THP	80 #35	88	77	88 #30
THA	75 #45	91	88	82 #5
		86 #7	84 #17	

■ IMPACT PLAYERS ■ LIKELY STARTERS

TEAM OFFENSIVE PLAYBOOK

Ace-Big	Shotgun-4WR Trio	Shotgun-Spread Flex
Ace-Slot	Shotgun-Double Flex	Shotgun-Spread Flex Wk
Ace-Twin TE	Shotgun-Normal	Shotgun-Spread HB Wk
Ace-Y-Trips	Shotgun-Split	Shotgun-Trips HB Wk
I-Form-Normal	Shotgun-Split Slot	Shotgun-Y-Trips
I-Form-Tight	Shotgun-Split Y-Flex	Strong-Normal

ARIZONA STATE
Sun Devils

Conference: **PAC-10**
Location: **Tempe, AZ**

REPORT CARD AND PRESTIGE

86	88	87
Overall	Offense	Defense

PRESTIGE RATINGS
Overall ★★★★
Coach Great
Academic Good

2007 SEASON RECAP
- 10-3 overall record
- 7-2 conference record
- Lost Holiday Bowl

DEFENSIVE DEPTH CHART AND SCOUTING REPORT

Neutral 4-3 Defense
AI Playcall Tendency: 53% defend run, 47% defend pass

85 #7 / 88 #25		85 #52		84 #44 / 88 #14	
80 #32	77 #15 / 75 #12 (FS ROLB)	74 #45 (MLB)		79 #41 / 83 #22 (LOLB SS)	83 #5
75 #17	89 #58	82 #92	88 #90	87 #97	75 #13
70 #27 (CB)	81 #95 (RE)	75 #99 (DT)	75 #46 (DT)	81 #54 (LE)	72 #6 (CB)

■ IMPACT PLAYERS   ■ LIKELY STARTERS

OFFENSIVE DEPTH CHART AND SCOUTING REPORT

Neutral Spread Offense
AI Playcall Tendency: 50% run, 50% pass

K	WR	LT	LG	C	RG	RT	TE	WR
95 KPW	88 #13	77 #59	80 #62	78 #56	80 #63	77 #75	77 #84	89 #1
93 KAC	80 #16	75 #73	80 #67	73 #52	73 #79	70 #70	77 #80	82 #6
94 #28				QB1 92 THP 93 THA 92 #12	QB2 78 THP 88 THA 85 #15		HB 91 #24 / 82 #31	

■ IMPACT PLAYERS   ■ LIKELY STARTERS

TEAM OFFENSIVE PLAYBOOK

Ace-Big	Ace-Trey Open	Shotgun-5WR Trey
Ace-Big Twins	Ace-Trips	Shotgun-Bunch HB Str
Ace-Big Wing	Ace-Twin TE	Shotgun-Normal
Ace-Bunch	Ace-Twin TE Slot	Shotgun-Normal HB Wk
Ace-Jumbo	Ace-Y-Trips	Shotgun-Trips TE
Ace-Slot	Shotgun-4WR Trey Str	Shotgun-Y-Trips HB Wk

ARKANSAS
Razorbacks

Conference: **SEC (West)**
Location: **Fayetteville, AR**

REPORT CARD AND PRESTIGE

79	79	82
Overall	Offense	Defense

PRESTIGE RATINGS
Overall ★★★★
Coach Excellent
Academic Good

2007 SEASON RECAP
- 8-5 overall record
- 4-4 conference record
- Lost Cotton Bowl

DEFENSIVE DEPTH CHART AND SCOUTING REPORT

Conservative 4-3 Defense
AI Playcall Tendency: 56% defend run, 44% defend pass

83 #35 / 82 #45		79 #47		91 #44 / 78 #32	
79 #29	76 #39 / 80 #38 (FS ROLB)	73 #36 (MLB)		83 #42 / 70 #42 (LOLB SS)	87 #27
73 #17	87 #40	79 #93	80 #90	88 #96	78 #33
(CB)	86 #97 (RE)	73 #98 (DT)	74 #65 (DT)	79 #99 (LE)	64 #1 (CB)

■ IMPACT PLAYERS   ■ LIKELY STARTERS

OFFENSIVE DEPTH CHART AND SCOUTING REPORT

Aggressive Balanced Offense
AI Playcall Tendency: 50% run, 50% pass

K	WR	LT	LG	C	RG	RT	TE	WR	P
59 KPW	82 #88	81 #78	81 #66	92 #63	78 #65	77 #62	80 #82	84 #2	75 KPW
84 KAC	79 #18	76 #73	68 #64	74 #58	68 #60	76 #78	77 #80	82 #1	84 KAC
78 #7		FB 78 #36		QB1 82 THP 87 THA 89 #11	QB2 82 THP 96 THA 87 #15		HB 82 #21 / 82 #26		87 #50

■ IMPACT PLAYERS   ■ LIKELY STARTERS

TEAM OFFENSIVE PLAYBOOK

Ace-Big	I-Form-Normal	Shotgun-Split Slot
Ace-Slot	I-Form-Twin TE	Shotgun-Spread HB Wk
Ace-Spread	I-Form-Twins	Shotgun-Trio HB Wk
Ace-Twin TE	Shotgun-5WR Trio	Shotgun-Y-Trips
Ace-Twin TE Slot	Shotgun-Normal Flex	Strong-Normal
Ace-Y-Trips	Shotgun-Normal Flex Wk	Weak-Normal

ARKANSAS STATE
Indians

Conference: **Sun Belt**
Location: **Jonesboro, AR**

REPORT CARD AND PRESTIGE

62	**73**	**60**
Overall	Offense	Defense

PRESTIGE RATINGS
Overall ★
Coach Fair
Academic Good

2007 SEASON RECAP
- 5-7 overall record
- 3-4 conference record
- 5th in the Sun Belt

DEFENSIVE DEPTH CHART AND SCOUTING REPORT

Conservative 4-3 Defense
AI Playcall Tendency: 48% defend run, 52% defend pass

	FS	ROLB	MLB		LOLB	SS	
	73 #39	68 #51	78 #40		69 #46	74 #26	
74 #13	70 #32	67 #45	71 #29		55 #23	67 #33	75 #8

CB	RE	DT	DT	LE	CB
74 #19	76 #44	71 #99	71 #90	78 #98	74 #20
61 #35	72 #54	63 #93	70 #97	69 #52	73 #15

■ IMPACT PLAYERS   ■ LIKELY STARTERS

OFFENSIVE DEPTH CHART AND SCOUTING REPORT

Neutral Balanced Offense
AI Playcall Tendency: 52% run, 48% pass

K	WR	LT	LG	C	RG	RT	TE	WR	P
57 KPW	75 #14	85 #63	74 #60	75 #55	72 #59	72 #64	78 #85	76 #82	63 KPW
77 KAC	71 #9	72 #71	74 #62	71 #75	71 #61	71 #71	75 #87	73 #6	84 KAC
83 #89									79 #11

FB	QB1	QB2	HB
73 #34	81 THP	76 THP	86 #2
71 #43	86 THA	88 THA	74 #25
	86 #1	82 #17	

■ IMPACT PLAYERS   ■ LIKELY STARTERS

TEAM OFFENSIVE PLAYBOOK

Ace-Big	I-Form-Slot Flex	Shotgun-Double Flex
Ace-Big Twins	I-Form-Tight	Shotgun-Normal Flex
Ace-Slot Flex	I-Form-Twins	Shotgun-Spread Flex
Ace-Twin TE Slot	I-Form-Y-Trips	Shotgun-Spread Flex Wk
Ace-Y-Trips	Shotgun-4WR Trio Str	Shotgun-Trio HB Wk
I-Form-Normal	Shotgun-Ace	Shotgun-Y-Trips

ARMY
Black Knights

Conference: **Independent**
Location: **West Point, NY**

REPORT CARD AND PRESTIGE

60	**66**	**60**
Overall	Offense	Defense

PRESTIGE RATINGS
Overall ★
Coach Fair
Academic Great

2007 SEASON RECAP
- 3-9 overall record
- 1st season under new coach

DEFENSIVE DEPTH CHART AND SCOUTING REPORT

Conservative 4-3 Defense
AI Playcall Tendency: 40% defend run, 60% defend pass

	FS	ROLB	MLB		LOLB	SS	
	73 #9	72 #70	75 #46		77 #42	71 #19	
68 #2	70 #18	70 #50	73 #52		70 #43	68 #26	77 #3

CB	RE	DT	DT	LE	CB
63 #8	75 #49	76 #93	78 #99	74 #92	64 #5
60 #16	70 #97	65 #94	65 #90	69 #77	60 #28

■ IMPACT PLAYERS   ■ LIKELY STARTERS

OFFENSIVE DEPTH CHART AND SCOUTING REPORT

Conservative Balanced Offense
AI Playcall Tendency: 50% run, 50% pass

K	WR	LT	LG	C	RG	RT	TE	WR	P
56 KPW	75 #10	76 #75	79 #79	73 #73	73 #93	73 #63	71 #88	80 #8	62 KPW
84 KAC	68 #17	73 #67	72 #70	70 #54	69 #68	73 #77	68 #84	73 #36	82 KAC
76 #10									82 #47

FB	QB1	QB2	HB
62 #30	78 THP	70 THP	79 #27
59 #44	86 THA	87 THA	77 #9
	87 #16	76 #12	

■ IMPACT PLAYERS   ■ LIKELY STARTERS

TEAM OFFENSIVE PLAYBOOK

Ace-4WR Trips	I-Form-Normal	Shotgun-Split Slot
Ace-Big	I-Form-Slot Flex	Shotgun-Trips
Ace-Slot	I-Form-Tight	Shotgun-Y-Trips
Ace-Spread	I-Form-Twins	Strong-Normal
Ace-Trips	Shotgun-Double Flex	Strong-Twins
Ace-Y-Trips	Shotgun-Normal	Weak-Twins

AUBURN
Tigers
Conference: **SEC (West)**
Location: **Auburn, AL**

BALL STATE
Cardinals
Conference: **MAC (West)**
Location: **Muncie, IN**

REPORT CARD AND PRESTIGE

84	83	87
Overall	Offense	Defense

PRESTIGE RATINGS
Overall ★★★★★
Coach Excellent
Academic Very Good

2007 SEASON RECAP
- 9-4 overall record
- 5-3 conference record
- Won Chick-fil-A Bowl

REPORT CARD AND PRESTIGE

69	79	64
Overall	Offense	Defense

PRESTIGE RATINGS
Overall ★
Coach Fair
Academic Good

2007 SEASON RECAP
- 7-6 overall record
- 5-2 conference record
- Lost International Bowl

DEFENSIVE DEPTH CHART AND SCOUTING REPORT

Neutral 4-3 Defense
AI Playcall Tendency: 53% defend run, 47% defend pass

	FS	ROLB	MLB	LOLB	SS	
	83 #2	81 #46	84 #10	90 #59	81 #4	
81 #6	80 #26	78 #47	80 #55	83 #56	72 #28	85 #8
74 #11	88 #42	80 #91	95 #94	90 #52		74 #25
72 #29	85 #49	76 #98	79 #93	80 #45		72 #23
CB	RE	DT	DT	LE		CB

■ IMPACT PLAYERS   ■ LIKELY STARTERS

DEFENSIVE DEPTH CHART AND SCOUTING REPORT

Neutral 3-4 Defense
AI Playcall Tendency: 47% defend run, 53% defend pass

	FS	ROLB	MLB	MLB	LOLB	SS	
	68 #25	77 #49	76 #48	78 #11	75 #99	78 #38	
77 #3	67 #32	72 #55	55 #54	72 #42	68 #30	69 #10	81 #12
76 #15	76 #85		74 #65		74 #56		77 #8
70 #19	75 #91		69 #64		74 #90		76 #34
CB	RE		DT		LE		CB

■ IMPACT PLAYERS   ■ LIKELY STARTERS

OFFENSIVE DEPTH CHART AND SCOUTING REPORT

Neutral Spread Offense
AI Playcall Tendency: 50% run, 50% pass

K	WR	LT	LG	C	RG	RT	TE	WR	P
60 KPW	85 #84	79 #50	86 #71	82 #68	79 #76	81 #73	75 #83	88 #80	73 KPW
76 KAC	84 #23	79 #75	79 #57	74 #66	78 #53	71 #58	72 #5	85 #3	87 KAC
86 #18		FB	QB1	QB2			HB		84 #21
		72 #30	82 THP 88 THA 84 #16	77 THP 86 THA 84 #12			90 #44 / 89 #1		

FB 72 #30
QB1 82 THP / 88 THA / 84 #16
QB2 77 THP / 86 THA / 84 #12
HB 90 #44 / 89 #1

■ IMPACT PLAYERS   ■ LIKELY STARTERS

OFFENSIVE DEPTH CHART AND SCOUTING REPORT

Conservative Spread Offense
AI Playcall Tendency: 47% run, 53% pass

K	WR	LT	LG	C	RG	RT	TE	WR	P
72 KPW	81 #81	85 #79	75 #73	86 #52	75 #51	82 #71	81 #88	83 #86	89 KPW
86 KAC	71 #83	74 #58	67 #74	77 #70	72 #66	66 #78	73 #82	74 #80	92 KAC
85 #29		FB	QB1	QB2			HB		90 #35

FB 67 #38
QB1 87 THP / 93 THA / 92 #13
QB2 77 THP / 89 THA / 88 #17
HB 81 #33 / 78 #2

■ IMPACT PLAYERS   ■ LIKELY STARTERS

TEAM OFFENSIVE PLAYBOOK

Ace-Big	Shotgun-Double Flex	Shotgun-Spread Flex
Ace-Trips	Shotgun-Flanker Close	Shotgun-Spread Flex Wk
Shotgun-4WR Trey Str	Shotgun-Normal	Shotgun-Trips HB Wk
Shotgun-5WR Trey	Shotgun-Normal Y-Slot	Shotgun-Trips Open
Shotgun-Ace Wing	Shotgun-Split Slot	Shotgun-Trips Open Str
Shotgun-Ace Wing Wk	Shotgun-Split Y-Flex	Shotgun-Y-Trips HB Wk

TEAM OFFENSIVE PLAYBOOK

Ace-Big	Ace-Y-Trips	Shotgun-Ace Twins
Ace-Big Twins	Pistol-Ace	Shotgun-Double Flex
Ace-Bunch	Pistol-Twin TE	Shotgun-Normal Flex
Ace-Jumbo	Pistol-Twin TE Slot	Shotgun-Spread
Ace-Twin TE	Pistol-Y-Trips	Shotgun-Y-Trips
Ace-Twin TE Slot	Shotgun-Ace	Shotgun-Y-Trips HB Wk

BAYLOR
Bears

Conference: **Big 12 (South)**
Location: **Waco, TX**

REPORT CARD AND PRESTIGE

67	70	71
Overall	Offense	Defense

PRESTIGE RATINGS
Overall ★★
Coach Good
Academic Very Good

2007 SEASON RECAP
- 3-9 overall record
- 0-8 conference record
- 6th in Big 12 South

DEFENSIVE DEPTH CHART AND SCOUTING REPORT

Conservative 4-3 Defense
AI Playcall Tendency: 52% defend run, 48% defend pass

	FS ROLB	MLB	LOLB SS	
	77 #21 / 73 #12	82 #41	75 #51 / 78 #4	
76 #26	76 #30 / 65 #50	75 #33	75 #8 / 64 #28	79 #27
72 #24	83 #49	79 #91	83 #88	73 #29
67 #31	75 #94	77 #97 / 71 #99	77 #10	70 #16
CB	RE	DT DT	LE	CB

■ IMPACT PLAYERS   ■ LIKELY STARTERS

OFFENSIVE DEPTH CHART AND SCOUTING REPORT

Aggressive Spread Offense
AI Playcall Tendency: 48% run, 52% pass

K	WR	LT	LG	C	RG	RT	TE	WR	P
74 KPW	83 #13	76 #70	70 #60	71 #55	78 #61	78 #71	77 #14	84 #4	68 KPW
85 KAC	81 #23	75 #72	69 #65	68 #67	75 #74	75 #75	68 #17	81 #3	85 KAC
87 #43									80 #38

QB1	QB2		HB
79 THP 89 THA 84 #6	76 THP 89 THA 80 #10		78 #25 / 76 #32

■ IMPACT PLAYERS   ■ LIKELY STARTERS

TEAM OFFENSIVE PLAYBOOK

Ace-Big Twins	Shotgun-4WR Trey Str	Shotgun-Spread
Ace-Slot	Shotgun-5WR Trey	Shotgun-Spread Flex
Ace-Y-Trips	Shotgun-Double Flex	Shotgun-Trips
Flexbone-Trips	Shotgun-Normal HB Wk	Shotgun-Trips HB Wk
I-Form-Slot	Shotgun-Normal Wing TE	Shotgun-Y-Trips
I-Form-Twins	Shotgun-Split Slot	Strong-Twin TE

BOISE STATE
Broncos

Conference: **WAC**
Location: **Boise, ID**

REPORT CARD AND PRESTIGE

77	81	76
Overall	Offense	Defense

PRESTIGE RATINGS
Overall ★★★★
Coach Great
Academic Good

2007 SEASON RECAP
- 10-3 overall record
- 7-1 conference record
- Lost Hawaii Bowl

DEFENSIVE DEPTH CHART AND SCOUTING REPORT

Conservative 4-3 Defense
AI Playcall Tendency: 39% defend run, 61% defend pass

	FS ROLB	MLB	LOLB SS	
	79 #23 / 83 #43	76 #51	83 #24 / 78 #36	
75 #38	75 #87 / 82 #18	76 #56	83 #30 / 70 #29	84 #1
71 #33	88 #93	78 #67 / 78 #74	80 #53	74 #17
64 #31	75 #96	68 #90 / 77 #94	68 #91	66 #28
CB	RE	DT DT	LE	CB

■ IMPACT PLAYERS   ■ LIKELY STARTERS

OFFENSIVE DEPTH CHART AND SCOUTING REPORT

Neutral West Coast Offense
AI Playcall Tendency: 48% run, 52% pass

K	WR	LT	LG	C	RG	RT	TE	WR	P
86 KPW	79 #89	81 #77	81 #76	78 #58	86 #60	81 #61	75 #82	84 #19	70 KPW
88 KAC	77 #21	77 #73	72 #70	75 #78	76 #57	74 #72	74 #88	78 #87	87 KAC
92 #35									82 #49

FB	QB1	QB2	HB
71 #40	83 THP 88 THA 85 #3	78 THP 90 THA 85 #7	93 #41 / 75 #27

■ IMPACT PLAYERS   ■ LIKELY STARTERS

TEAM OFFENSIVE PLAYBOOK

Ace-Big	I-Form-Normal	Shotgun-Split Y-Flex
Ace-Big Twins	I-Form-Twin TE	Shotgun-Y-Trips HB Wk
Ace-Bunch	I-Form-Twins	Strong-Normal
Ace-Slot	Shotgun-5WR Trey	Strong-Tight
Ace-Twin TE Slot	Shotgun-Double Flex	Strong-Y-Trips
Ace-Y-Trips	Shotgun-Normal	Weak-Normal

BOSTON COLLEGE
Eagles
Conference: **ACC (Atlantic)**
Location: **Chestnut Hill, MA**

REPORT CARD AND PRESTIGE

77	77	80
Overall	Offense	Defense

PRESTIGE RATINGS
Overall ★★★★
Coach Very Good
Academic Excellent

2007 SEASON RECAP
- 11-3 overall record
- 6-2 conference record
- Won Champs Sports Bowl

DEFENSIVE DEPTH CHART AND SCOUTING REPORT

Conservative 4-3 Defense
AI Playcall Tendency: 53% defend run, 47% defend pass

	83 #8	95 #16		74 #34		90 #94	82 #19	
76 #20	79 #45 FS	84 #35 ROLB		70 #39 MLB		82 #7 LOLB	75 #21 SS	78 #9
71 #4	80 #92		82 #54	83 #60		85 #98		73 #31
71 #27 CB	79 #97 RE		66 #72 DT	72 #52 DT		80 #86 LE		71 #17 CB

■ IMPACT PLAYERS   ■ LIKELY STARTERS

OFFENSIVE DEPTH CHART AND SCOUTING REPORT

Neutral West Coast Offense
AI Playcall Tendency: 50% run, 50% pass

K	WR	LT	LG	C	RG	RT	TE	WR	P
69 KPW	82 #18	84 #74	86 #73	79 #65	74 #91	77 #66	81 #80	84 #2	77 KPW
88 KAC	77 #11	74 #72	81 #70	77 #62	73 #64	71 #71	72 #88	78 #82	87 KAC
82 #23		FB 71 #36		QB1 81 THP 87 THA 85 #10	QB2 75 THP 90 THA 80 #13		HB 80 #1 / 75 #6		86 #83

■ IMPACT PLAYERS   ■ LIKELY STARTERS

TEAM OFFENSIVE PLAYBOOK

Ace-Big	I-Form-Twins	Shotgun-Wing Trips
Ace-Slot Flex	Shotgun-5WR Trips	Shotgun-Wing Trips Wk
Ace-Twin TE Slot	Shotgun-Normal	Shotgun-Y-Trips
Ace-Y-Trips	Shotgun-Split Y-Flex	Strong-Normal
I-Form-Normal	Shotgun-Spread Flex	Weak-Normal
I-Form-Twin TE	Shotgun-Wing Trio Wk	Weak-Twins

BOWLING GREEN
Falcons
Conference: **MAC (East)**
Location: **Bowling Green, OH**

REPORT CARD AND PRESTIGE

74	73	80
Overall	Offense	Defense

PRESTIGE RATINGS
Overall ★★
Coach Fair
Academic Good

2007 SEASON RECAP
- 8-5 overall record
- 6-2 conference record
- Lost GMAC Bowl

DEFENSIVE DEPTH CHART AND SCOUTING REPORT

Conservative 4-3 Defense
AI Playcall Tendency: 60% defend run, 40% defend pass

	84 #24	75 #37		80 #44		86 #30	90 #25	
81 #2	72 #4 FS	71 #53 ROLB		72 #43 MLB		69 #52 LOLB	67 #10 SS	86 #21
70 #23	88 #99		78 #90	79 #95		82 #40		72 #26
63 #28 CB	82 #47 RE		72 #77 DT	76 #63 DT		81 #58 LE		68 #31 CB

■ IMPACT PLAYERS   ■ LIKELY STARTERS

OFFENSIVE DEPTH CHART AND SCOUTING REPORT

Neutral Spread Offense
AI Playcall Tendency: 45% run, 55% pass

K	WR	LT	LG	C	RG	RT	TE	WR	P
81 KPW	82 #1	76 #76	76 #75	75 #46	75 #55	75 #74	74 #89	83 #7	80 KPW
87 KAC	76 #83	75 #66	73 #70	73 #87	65 #62	73 #60	67 #91	80 #3	87 KAC
88 #41				QB1 82 THP 88 THA 87 #13	QB2 73 THP 87 THA 78 #11		HB 80 #1 / 75 #6		87 #26

■ IMPACT PLAYERS   ■ LIKELY STARTERS

TEAM OFFENSIVE PLAYBOOK

Ace-Twin TE	Shotgun-Normal Wing TE	Shotgun-Trips HB Wk
Ace-Y-Trips	Shotgun-Normal Y-Slot	Shotgun-Trips Open
Shotgun-4WR Trio	Shotgun-Spread	Shotgun-Trips Open Str
Shotgun-5WR Trio	Shotgun-Spread Flex	Shotgun-Wing Trips
Shotgun-5WR Trips	Shotgun-Spread HB Wk	Shotgun-Wing Trips Wk
Shotgun-Bunch HB Str	Shotgun-Trips	

BUFFALO
Bulls

Conference: **MAC (East)**
Location: **Buffalo, NY**

REPORT CARD AND PRESTIGE

67	**77**	**62**
Overall	Offense	Defense

PRESTIGE RATINGS
Overall ★
Coach Fair
Academic Good

2007 SEASON RECAP
- 5-7 overall record
- 5-3 conference record
- 3rd in the MAC East

DEFENSIVE DEPTH CHART AND SCOUTING REPORT

Conservative 4-3 Defense
AI Playcall Tendency: 41% defend run, 59% defend pass

	FS	ROLB		MLB		LOLB	SS	
Row 1	82 #30	68 #26		68 #53		73 #44	80 #7	
Row 2	66 #49	69 #51		68 #41		73 #34	69 #43	72 #25

	CB	RE		DT	DT	LE		CB
Row 1	70 #16	74 #52		74 #74	80 #95	78 #48		70 #12
Row 2	68 #22	74 #60		68 #63	68 #92	72 #56		62 #19

■ IMPACT PLAYERS ■ LIKELY STARTERS

OFFENSIVE DEPTH CHART AND SCOUTING REPORT

Conservative Balanced Offense
AI Playcall Tendency: 45% run, 55% pass

K	WR	LT	LG	C	RG	RT	TE	WR	P
75 KPW	79 #88	79 #70	77 #73	73 #79	74 #75	76 #77	71 #45	83 #18	67 KPW
87 KAC	72 #3	70 #72	73 #57	71 #66	71 #76	69 #78	71 #82	79 #21	87 KAC
87 #39									82 #11

FB	QB1	QB2	HB
75 #32	86 THP	68 THP	85 #19
67 #29	86 THA	84 THA	78 #28
	92 #16	76 #17	

■ IMPACT PLAYERS ■ LIKELY STARTERS

TEAM OFFENSIVE PLAYBOOK

Ace-Big	I-Form-Tight	Shotgun-Split
Ace-Slot	I-Form-Twin TE	Shotgun-Split Y-Flex
Ace-Twin TE	I-Form-Twins	Shotgun-Spread Flex
Ace-Twin TE Slot	Shotgun-5WR Trey	Shotgun-Wing Trips
Ace-Y-Trips	Shotgun-Double Flex	Weak-Normal
I-Form-Normal	Shotgun-Normal Flex Wk	Weak-Twin TE

BYU
Cougars

Conference: **Mountain West**
Location: **Provo UT**

REPORT CARD AND PRESTIGE

79	**88**	**73**
Overall	Offense	Defense

PRESTIGE RATINGS
Overall ★★★★
Coach Great
Academic Great

2007 SEASON RECAP
- 11-2 overall record
- 8-0 conference record
- Won Las Vegas Bowl

DEFENSIVE DEPTH CHART AND SCOUTING REPORT

Aggressive 3-4 Defense
AI Playcall Tendency: 33% defend run, 67% defend pass

	FS	ROLB		MLB	MLB		LOLB	SS	
Row 1	78 #16	84 #43		80 #35	81 #42		84 #39	74 #23	
Row 2	71 #30	71 #57		65 #59	69 #47		76 #54	71 #20	76 #4

	CB	RE		DT		LE		CB
Row 1	69 #25	90 #84		80 #56		83 #99		67 #21
Row 2	67 #17	78 #41		76 #71		80 #92		66 #24

■ IMPACT PLAYERS ■ LIKELY STARTERS

OFFENSIVE DEPTH CHART AND SCOUTING REPORT

Aggressive Spread Offense
AI Playcall Tendency: 40% run, 60% pass

K	WR	LT	LG	C	RG	RT	TE	WR	P
72 KPW	83 #3	91 #65	87 #76	82 #53	85 #74	85 #68	79 #80	85 #9	76 KPW
88 KAC	77 #2	75 #64	79 #66	73 #70	73 #73	76 #72	77 #37	79 #87	95 KAC
84 #38									78 #26

FB	QB1	QB2	HB
86 #1	89 THP	80 THP	87 #45
	89 THA	88 THA	72 #10
	90 #15	86 #6	

■ IMPACT PLAYERS ■ LIKELY STARTERS

TEAM OFFENSIVE PLAYBOOK

Ace-Spread	Shotgun-4WR Trey Str	Shotgun-Split Y-Flex
Ace-Twin TE	Shotgun-Double Flex	Shotgun-Spread Flex
I-Form-Normal	Shotgun-Normal Y-Slot	Shotgun-Spread Flex Wk
I-Form-Slot Flex	Shotgun-Split	Shotgun-Trips HB Wk
I-Form-Tight	Shotgun-Split Slot	Shotgun-Trips Open
I-Form-Twins	Shotgun-Split Twins	Weak-H Twins

CAL
Golden Bears

Conference: **PAC-10**
Location: **Berkeley, CA**

REPORT CARD AND PRESTIGE

81 Overall   **79** Offense   **85** Defense

PRESTIGE RATINGS
Overall ★★★★★
Coach Excellent
Academic Elite

2007 SEASON RECAP
- 7-6 overall record
- 3-6 conference record
- Won Armed Forces Bowl

DEFENSIVE DEPTH CHART AND SCOUTING REPORT

Aggressive 4-3 Defense
AI Playcall Tendency: 45% defend run, 55% defend pass

	80 #25	93 #7	90 #1	86 #56	79 #2	
84 #26	80 #6 FS	75 #53 ROLB	66 #10 MLB	78 #18 LOLB	77 #29 SS	85 #5
77 #27	80 #44		81 #91	86 #98	84 #94	77 #24
75 #17 CB	74 #92 RE		77 #99 DT	78 #76 DT	68 #97 LE	77 #21 CB

■ IMPACT PLAYERS   ■ LIKELY STARTERS

OFFENSIVE DEPTH CHART AND SCOUTING REPORT

Aggressive West Coast Offense
AI Playcall Tendency: 48% run, 52% pass

K	WR	LT	LG	C	RG	RT	TE		WR	P
67 KPW	77 #8	83 #58	72 #71	95 #51	89 #55	84 #79	76 #81		81 #85	74 KPW
80 KAC	76 #83	80 #50	71 #57	85 #54	79 #75	81 #76	73 #5		77 #80	89 KAC
85 #34		FB		QB1	QB2		HB			84 #19
		77 #23		90 THP 96 THA 91 #6	86 THP 89 THA 90 #13		81 #21 78 #4			

■ IMPACT PLAYERS   ■ LIKELY STARTERS

TEAM OFFENSIVE PLAYBOOK

Ace-Big	Shotgun-4WR Trio	Strong-Normal
Ace-Big Twins	Shotgun-Ace	Strong-Twin TE
Ace-Bunch	Shotgun-Bunch HB Str	Strong-Twins
Ace-Slot Flex	Shotgun-Normal Flex Wk	Strong-Y-Trips
Ace-Twin TE	Shotgun-Split Y-Flex	Weak-Normal
I-Form-Twins	Shotgun-Y-Trips	Weak-Twins

CENTRAL MICHIGAN
Chippewas

Conference: **MAC (West)**
Location: **Mt. Pleasant, MI**

REPORT CARD AND PRESTIGE

72 Overall   **81** Offense   **66** Defense

PRESTIGE RATINGS
Overall ★★
Coach Fair
Academic Fair

2007 SEASON RECAP
- 8-6 overall record
- 6-1 conference record
- Lost Motor City Bowl

DEFENSIVE DEPTH CHART AND SCOUTING REPORT

Conservative 4-3 Defense
AI Playcall Tendency: 49% defend run, 51% defend pass

	73 #31	76 #20	80 #43	77 #26	76 #12	
79 #4	68 #24 FS	75 #33 ROLB	73 #46 MLB	66 #58 LOLB	65 #44 SS	80 #19
71 #14	80 #95		68 #79	73 #51	78 #98	72 #22
68 #9 CB	75 #15 RE		66 #92 DT	68 #47 DT	70 #54 LE	68 #26 CB

■ IMPACT PLAYERS   ■ LIKELY STARTERS

OFFENSIVE DEPTH CHART AND SCOUTING REPORT

Aggressive Spread Offense
AI Playcall Tendency: 50% run, 50% pass

K	WR	LT	LG	C	RG	RT	TE		WR	P
56 KPW	83 #27	81 #74	75 #66	74 #57	71 #75	73 #77	70 #86		88 #7	66 KPW
80 KAC	73 #1	65 #73	67 #99	74 #63	66 #76	71 #64	63 #86		76 #16	85 KAC
80 #36		FB		QB1	QB2		HB			80 #96
		72 #21 65 #48		91 THP 88 THA 90 #13	74 THP 86 THA 82 #18		87 #28 81 #3			

■ IMPACT PLAYERS   ■ LIKELY STARTERS

TEAM OFFENSIVE PLAYBOOK

Ace-Big	Shotgun-Bunch HB Str	Shotgun-Spread HB Wk
Ace-Slot	Shotgun-Normal	Shotgun-Trio HB Wk
Ace-Spread	Shotgun-Normal Flex Wk	Shotgun-Trips HB Wk
Ace-Y-Trips	Shotgun-Normal HB Wk	Shotgun-Trips Open Str
Shotgun-5WR Trio	Shotgun-Normal Y-Slot	Shotgun-Y-Trips
Shotgun-5WR Trips	Shotgun-Split Slot	Shotgun-Y-Trips HB Wk

CINCINNATI
Bearcats

Conference: **Big East**
Location: **Cincinnati, OH**

REPORT CARD AND PRESTIGE

84	81	89
Overall	Offense	Defense

PRESTIGE RATINGS
Overall ★★★
Coach Good
Academic Good

2007 SEASON RECAP
- 10-3 overall record
- 4-3 conference record
- Won PapaJohns.com Bowl

DEFENSIVE DEPTH CHART AND SCOUTING REPORT

Conservative 4-3 Defense
AI Playcall Tendency: 36% defend run, 64% defend pass

CB		FS	ROLB		MLB		LOLB	SS			CB
		80 #25	87 #50		82 #45		87 #42	86 #18			
86 #6		72 #4	83 #3		62 #9		66 #49	78 #17		94 #21	
75 #32		87 #89			83 #67	88 #95		88 #10		81 #19	
72 #14		76 #94			78 #40	78 #90		68 #7		73 #26	

Bottom labels: CB | RE | DT | DT | LE | CB

■ IMPACT PLAYERS ■ LIKELY STARTERS

OFFENSIVE DEPTH CHART AND SCOUTING REPORT

Aggressive Spread Offense
AI Playcall Tendency: 50% run, 50% pass

K	WR	LT	LG	C	RG	RT	TE	WR	P
72 KPW	85 #85	82 #79	82 #76	79 #56	77 #60	83 #71	83 #83	87 #16	72 KPW
87 KAC	80 #87	68 #59	75 #63	75 #69	74 #70	71 #68	72 #19	82 #1	86 KAC
84 #97									84 #47

FB: 73 #35
QB1: 87 THP / 90 THA / 90 #4
QB2: 84 THP / 95 THA / 84 #3
HB: 80 #20 / 78 #22

■ IMPACT PLAYERS ■ LIKELY STARTERS

TEAM OFFENSIVE PLAYBOOK

Ace-Big	Shotgun-Ace	Shotgun-Spread HB Wk
Ace-Slot	Shotgun-Ace Twins	Shotgun-Trips
Ace-Twin TE	Shotgun-Ace Twins Wk	Shotgun-Trips HB Wk
Ace-Twin TE Slot	Shotgun-Bunch HB Str	Shotgun-Trips Over
Shotgun-5WR Trio	Shotgun-Normal	Shotgun-Y-Trips
Shotgun-5WR Trips	Shotgun-Normal Y-Slot	Strong-Normal

CLEMSON
Tigers

Conference: **ACC (Atlantic)**
Location: **Clemson, SC**

REPORT CARD AND PRESTIGE

89	90	92
Overall	Offense	Defense

PRESTIGE RATINGS
Overall ★★★★
Coach Great
Academic Great

2007 SEASON RECAP
- 9-4 overall record
- 5-3 conference record
- Lost Chick-fil-A Bowl

DEFENSIVE DEPTH CHART AND SCOUTING REPORT

Conservative 4-3 Defense
AI Playcall Tendency: 51% defend run, 49% defend pass

CB		FS	ROLB		MLB		LOLB	SS			CB
		92 #22	89 #33		80 #45		84 #44	95 #25			
85 #38		78 #35	83 #5		79 #47		78 #17	82 #2		87 #18	
78 #12		91 #7			87 #91	87 #97		87 #93		79 #36	
74 #42		81 #90			80 #98	83 #8		82 #96		77 #29	

Bottom labels: CB | RE | DT | DT | LE | CB

■ IMPACT PLAYERS ■ LIKELY STARTERS

OFFENSIVE DEPTH CHART AND SCOUTING REPORT

Aggressive Spread Offense
AI Playcall Tendency: 52% run, 48% pass

K	WR	LT	LG	C	RG	RT	TE	WR	P
81 KPW	85 #13	80 #50	78 #73	77 #62	84 #71	80 #61	76 #84	92 #80	75 KPW
94 KAC	77 #21	79 #76	78 #70	76 #65	79 #55	78 #72	76 #86	82 #6	87 KAC
84 #19									84 #49

FB: 76 #27 / 72 #30
QB1: 90 THP / 93 THA / 91 #10
QB2: 82 THP / 88 THA / 86 #3
HB: 95 #1 / 95 #28

■ IMPACT PLAYERS ■ LIKELY STARTERS

TEAM OFFENSIVE PLAYBOOK

Ace-4WR Trips	Ace-Twin TE	Shotgun-Split Slot
Ace-Big	Ace-Twin TE Slot	Shotgun-Trips HB Wk
Ace-Jumbo	Ace-Y-Trips	Shotgun-Trips Over
Ace-Slot	Shotgun-Double Flex	Shotgun-Wing Trips Wk
Ace-Spread	Shotgun-Normal HB Wk	Shotgun-Y-Trips HB Wk
Ace-Trips	Shotgun-Split	Strong-H Pro

COLORADO
Buffaloes

Conference: **Big 12 (North)**
Location: **Boulder, CO**

REPORT CARD AND PRESTIGE

79 Overall **81** Offense **80** Defense

PRESTIGE RATINGS
Overall ★★★★
Coach Very Good
Academic Very Good

2007 SEASON RECAP
- 6-7 overall record
- 4-4 conference record
- Lost Independence Bowl

DEFENSIVE DEPTH CHART AND SCOUTING REPORT

Conservative 4-3 Defense
AI Playcall Tendency: 43% defend run, 57% defend pass

85 #15 / 82 #52	84 #45	87 #40 / 76 #9	
76 #23 / 81 #24 FS ROLB	76 #57 MLB	79 #50 / 69 #41 LOLB SS	79 #42
77 #29			
75 #6	82 #90	85 #94 / 85 #86	92 #91	75 #3
68 #46 CB	73 #99 RE	76 #78 / 76 #97 DT DT	75 #96 LE	73 #18 CB

■ IMPACT PLAYERS ■ LIKELY STARTERS

OFFENSIVE DEPTH CHART AND SCOUTING REPORT

Neutral Balanced Offense
AI Playcall Tendency: 50% run, 50% pass

K	WR	LT	LG	C	RG	RT	TE	WR	P
48 KPW	84 #21	75 #61	77 #70	85 #75	81 #72	78 #73	80 #87	85 #4	84 KPW
82 KAC	77 #81	66 #71	75 #51	71 #56	74 #66	75 #68	73 #85	78 #9	93 KAC
74 #2									85 #14

FB: 73 #41 / 63 #32
QB1: 84 THP 88 THA 88 #7
QB2: 74 THP 86 THA 86 #3
HB: 85 #20 / 82 #8

■ IMPACT PLAYERS ■ LIKELY STARTERS

TEAM OFFENSIVE PLAYBOOK

Ace-Big | Shotgun-5WR Trips | Shotgun-Split Slot
Ace-Slot | Shotgun-Ace | Shotgun-Spread HB Wk
Ace-Twin TE | Shotgun-Ace Twins Wk | Shotgun-Trips
Ace-Twin TE Slot | Shotgun-Bunch HB Str | Shotgun-Trips HB Wk
I-Form-Normal | Shotgun-Normal | Shotgun-Trips Over
Shotgun-5WR Trio | Shotgun-Normal Y-Slot | Shotgun-Y-Trips

COLORADO STATE
Rams

Conference: **Mountain West**
Location: **Fort Collins, CO**

REPORT CARD AND PRESTIGE

72 Overall **75** Offense **76** Defense

PRESTIGE RATINGS
Overall ★★★
Coach Good
Academic Very Good

2007 SEASON RECAP
- 3-9 overall record
- 2-6 conference record
- 8th in the Mountain West

DEFENSIVE DEPTH CHART AND SCOUTING REPORT

Conservative 4-3 Defense
AI Playcall Tendency: 43% defend run, 57% defend pass

85 #20 / 80 #56	84 #51	80 #55 / 75 #13	
76 #15 / 70 #9 FS ROLB	64 #6 MLB	76 #42 / 67 #31 LOLB SS	73 #2
73 #4			
72 #11	82 #96	77 #62 / 85 #45	91 #91	72 #35
# CB	77 #24 RE	75 #66 / 75 #97 DT DT	73 #61 LE	64 #22 CB

■ IMPACT PLAYERS ■ LIKELY STARTERS

OFFENSIVE DEPTH CHART AND SCOUTING REPORT

Conservative Balanced Offense
AI Playcall Tendency: 56% run, 44% pass

K	WR	LT	LG	C	RG	RT	TE	WR	P
51 KPW	74 #84	78 #53	82 #60	78 #57	77 #74	80 #78	83 #80	79 #31	62 KPW
87 KAC	73 #4	78 #75	76 #55	77 #52	74 #77	73 #76	77 #88	73 #3	85 KAC
70 #37									78 #48

FB: 71 #36 / 62 #49
QB1: 78 THP 88 THA 82 #15
QB2: 76 THP 87 THA 86 #18
HB: 88 #34 / 87 #5

■ IMPACT PLAYERS ■ LIKELY STARTERS

TEAM OFFENSIVE PLAYBOOK

Ace-Big | Ace-Twin TE Slot | Shotgun-Split Slot
Ace-Big Twins | Ace-Y-Trips | Shotgun-Spread HB Wk
Ace-Jumbo | I-Form-Normal | Shotgun-Y-Trips HB Wk
Ace-Slot | I-Form-Slot Flex | Strong-H Pro
Ace-Trips | I-Form-Twin TE | Weak-H Pro
Ace-Twin TE | I-Form-Twins | Weak-H Twins

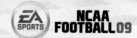

CONNECTICUT
Huskies

Conference: **Big East**
Location: **East Hartford, CT**

REPORT CARD AND PRESTIGE

74 Overall **77** Offense **73** Defense

PRESTIGE RATINGS
Overall ★★★
Coach Great
Academic Great

2007 SEASON RECAP
- 9-4 overall record
- 5-2 conference record
- Lost Meineke Bowl

DEFENSIVE DEPTH CHART AND SCOUTING REPORT

Neutral 4-3 Defense
AI Playcall Tendency: 53% defend run, 47% defend pass

■ IMPACT PLAYERS   ■ LIKELY STARTERS

OFFENSIVE DEPTH CHART AND SCOUTING REPORT

Neutral Balanced Offense
AI Playcall Tendency: 50% run, 50% pass

■ IMPACT PLAYERS   ■ LIKELY STARTERS

TEAM OFFENSIVE PLAYBOOK

Ace-Big	I-Form-Normal	Shotgun-Normal HB Wk
Ace-Big Twins	I-Form-Tight	Shotgun-Spread
Ace-Bunch	I-Form-Twins	Shotgun-Trips HB Wk
Ace-Slot	I-Form-Y-Trips	Shotgun-Trips Over
Ace-Twin TE Slot	Shotgun-Ace	Shotgun-Y-Trips
Ace-Y-Trips	Shotgun-Flanker Close	Weak-Normal

DUKE
Blue Devils

Conference: **ACC (Coastal)**
Location: **Durham, NC**

REPORT CARD AND PRESTIGE

77 Overall **81** Offense **76** Defense

PRESTIGE RATINGS
Overall ★★
Coach Very Good
Academic Elite

2007 SEASON RECAP
- 1-11 overall record
- 0-8 conference record
- 6th in ACC Coastal

DEFENSIVE DEPTH CHART AND SCOUTING REPORT

Conservative 4-3 Defense
AI Playcall Tendency: 56% defend run, 44% defend pass

■ IMPACT PLAYERS   ■ LIKELY STARTERS

OFFENSIVE DEPTH CHART AND SCOUTING REPORT

Conservative Balanced Offense
AI Playcall Tendency: 50% run, 50% pass

■ IMPACT PLAYERS   ■ LIKELY STARTERS

TEAM OFFENSIVE PLAYBOOK

Ace-Big	Ace-Y-Trips	Shotgun-Split Slot
Ace-Big Twins	I-Form-Normal	Shotgun-Spread Flex Wk
Ace-Bunch	I-Form-Tight	Shotgun-Trips HB Wk
Ace-Slot	I-Form-Twin TE	Shotgun-Y-Trips
Ace-Twin TE	I-Form-Twins	Strong-H Twins
Ace-Twin TE Slot	Shotgun-Normal	Weak-H Twins

EASTERN MICHIGAN
Eagles
Conference: **MAC (West)**
Location: **Ypsilanti, MI**

REPORT CARD AND PRESTIGE

64 Overall   **68** Offense   **69** Defense

PRESTIGE RATINGS
Overall ★
Coach Fair
Academic Good

2007 SEASON RECAP
- 4-8 overall record
- 3-4 conference record
- 4th in the MAC West

DEFENSIVE DEPTH CHART AND SCOUTING REPORT

Conservative 4-3 Defense
AI Playcall Tendency: 53% defend run, 47% defend pass

	FS	ROLB	MLB	LOLB	SS	
	77 #23	69 #25	86 #44	79 #20	78 #21	
	75 #31	69 #29	64 #55	71 #52	77 #10	75 #30

	CB	RE	DT	DT	LE	CB
	74 #34					
	71 #28	78 #5	67 #93	81 #91	77 #46	72 #24
	65 #37	69 #97	61 #96	66 #92	73 #56	69 #19

■ IMPACT PLAYERS   ■ LIKELY STARTERS

OFFENSIVE DEPTH CHART AND SCOUTING REPORT

Conservative Spread Offense
AI Playcall Tendency: 50% run, 50% pass

K	WR	LT	LG	C	RG	RT	TE	WR	P
76 KPW	75 #15	79 #50	81 #60	68 #61	75 #64	74 #65	74 #17	79 #8	59 KPW
88 KAC	72 #18	72 #69	73 #74	67 #54	70 #72	68 #78	71 #89	74 #87	85 KAC
85 #33									76 #66

FB	QB1	QB2	HB
60 #49	82 THP 89 THA 82 #7	74 THP 86 THA 82 #11	79 #3 / 72 #22

■ IMPACT PLAYERS   ■ LIKELY STARTERS

TEAM OFFENSIVE PLAYBOOK

Ace-Big	Shotgun-5WR	Shotgun-Trips HB Wk
Ace-Big Twins	Shotgun-Ace Wing Wk	Shotgun-Trips Over
Ace-Trips	Shotgun-Normal	Shotgun-Wing Trips
Ace-Twin TE	Shotgun-Normal HB Wk	Shotgun-Wing Trips Wk
I-Form-Normal	Shotgun-Split Slot	Shotgun-Y-Trips
I-Form-Tight	Shotgun-Spread	Shotgun-Y-Trips HB Wk

ECU
Pirates
Conference: **C-USA (East)**
Location: **Greenville, NC**

REPORT CARD AND PRESTIGE

72 Overall   **75** Offense   **76** Defense

PRESTIGE RATINGS
Overall ★ ★ ★
Coach Good
Academic Good

2007 SEASON RECAP
- 8-5 overall record
- 6-2 conference record
- Won Hawaii Bowl

DEFENSIVE DEPTH CHART AND SCOUTING REPORT

Neutral 4-3 Defense
AI Playcall Tendency: 60% defend run, 40% defend pass

	FS	ROLB	MLB	LOLB	SS	
	78 #4	79 #50	82 #55	77 #31	78 #9	
	68 #2	78 #49	48 #40	76 #34	78 #20	80 #35

CB	RE	DT	DT	LE	CB
77 #23					
72 #13	93 #92	77 #90	81 #98	84 #41	73 #21
62 #26	83 #95	69 #97	70 #79	83 #53	65 #22

■ IMPACT PLAYERS   ■ LIKELY STARTERS

OFFENSIVE DEPTH CHART AND SCOUTING REPORT

Conservative Spread Offense
AI Playcall Tendency: 50% run, 50% pass

K	WR	LT	LG	C	RG	RT	TE	WR	P
53 KPW	76 #17	79 #78	77 #60	76 #72	87 #70	78 #74	76 #3	85 #10	63 KPW
72 KAC	73 #84	71 #62	74 #75	75 #67	82 #54	76 #66	74 #87	74 #80	89 KAC
84 #30									76 #5

FB	QB1	QB2	HB
65 #45	84 THP 86 THA 80 #15	81 THP 90 THA 82 #14	80 #24 / 77 #25

■ IMPACT PLAYERS   ■ LIKELY STARTERS

TEAM OFFENSIVE PLAYBOOK

Ace-Big	Shotgun-4WR Trio	Shotgun-Spread Flex
Ace-Big Twins	Shotgun-5WR Trio	Shotgun-Spread Flex Wk
Ace-Bunch	Shotgun-Ace Twins	Shotgun-Trips Over
Ace-Slot	Shotgun-Normal	Shotgun-Y-Trips HB Wk
I-Form-Normal	Shotgun-Split Twins	Strong-Twins
I-Form-Twins	Shotgun-Split Y-Flex	Weak-Twins

FIU
Golden Panthers

Conference: **Sun Belt**
Location: **Miami, FL**

REPORT CARD AND PRESTIGE

67	70	66
Overall	Offense	Defense

PRESTIGE RATINGS
Overall ★
Coach Fair
Academic Very Good

2007 SEASON RECAP
- 1-11 overall record
- 1-6 conference record
- 8th in the Sun Belt

DEFENSIVE DEPTH CHART AND SCOUTING REPORT

Conservative 4-3 Defense
AI Playcall Tendency: 43% defend run, 57% defend pass

	FS	ROLB	MLB	LOLB	SS	
	76 #11	81 #53	75 #3	81 #44	77 #6	
	73 #38	75 #87	71 #13	73 #33	65 #23	
73 #26						76 #17

	CB	RE	DT	DT	LE	CB
	70 #40	77 #98	72 #95	74 #94	78 #96	72 #29
	65 #24	74 #91	69 #97	71 #99	74 #93	69 #21

■ IMPACT PLAYERS   ■ LIKELY STARTERS

OFFENSIVE DEPTH CHART AND SCOUTING REPORT

Conservative Spread Offense
AI Playcall Tendency: 48% run, 52% pass

K	WR	LT	LG	C	RG	RT	TE	WR	P
72 KPW	74 #5	75 #58	72 #65	74 #76	72 #50	78 #78	77 #89	75 #9	71 KPW
84 KAC	72 #16	72 #77	69 #71	72 #64	70 #72	76 #79	67 #85	73 #84	88 KAC
84 #10									80 #41

	FB	QB1	QB2	HB	
	76 #27	85 THP 88 THA 84 #14	74 THP 85 THA 82 #12	81 #32	
	63 #35			80 #3	

■ IMPACT PLAYERS   ■ LIKELY STARTERS

TEAM OFFENSIVE PLAYBOOK

Ace-Big	I-Form-Twins	Shotgun-Bunch HB Str
Ace-Bunch	I-Form-Y-Trips	Shotgun-Normal
Ace-Twin TE	Shotgun-4WR Trey Str	Shotgun-Spread
Ace-Twin TE Slot	Shotgun-4WR Trio Str	Shotgun-Spread Flex Wk
I-Form-Normal	Shotgun-5WR Trio	Shotgun-Trio HB Wk
I-Form-Twin TE	Shotgun-Ace	Shotgun-Y-Trips HB Wk

FLORIDA
Gators

Conference: **SEC (East)**
Location: **Gainesville, FL**

REPORT CARD AND PRESTIGE

94	96	94
Overall	Offense	Defense

PRESTIGE RATINGS
Overall ★★★★★
Coach Elite
Academic Excellent

2007 SEASON RECAP
- 9-4 overall record
- 5-3 conference record
- Lost Capital One Bowl

DEFENSIVE DEPTH CHART AND SCOUTING REPORT

Neutral 4-3 Defense
AI Playcall Tendency: 48% defend run, 52% defend pass

	FS	ROLB	MLB	LOLB	SS	
	88 #21	93 #32	94 #51	86 #16	87 #20	
	84 #31	90 #41	76 #30	82 #40	83 #18	
85 #4						87 #12

	CB	RE	DT	DT	LE	CB
	81 #29	90 #49	86 #47	89 #93	90 #8	82 #14
	77 #28	87 #90	80 #72	82 #95	79 #98	80 #23

■ IMPACT PLAYERS   ■ LIKELY STARTERS

OFFENSIVE DEPTH CHART AND SCOUTING REPORT

Aggressive Spread Offense
AI Playcall Tendency: 50% run, 50% pass

K	WR	LT	LG	C	RG	RT	TE	WR	P
76 KPW	87 #9	86 #77	91 #63	83 #68	92 #56	87 #75	87 #7	96 #1	80 KPW
94 KAC	85 #86	72 #64	80 #66	81 #55	81 #74	83 #57	83 #81	85 #6	90 KAC
82 #25									85 #17

	FB	QB1	QB2	HB	
	69 #40	99 THP 97 THA 93 #15	84 THP 93 THA 84 #13	87 #21	
				85 #25	

■ IMPACT PLAYERS   ■ LIKELY STARTERS

TEAM OFFENSIVE PLAYBOOK

Ace-Big	Shotgun-Flip Trips	Shotgun-Tight
Ace-Twin TE Slot	Shotgun-Gator Heavy	Shotgun-Trio HB Wk
I-Form-Twins	Shotgun-Normal	Shotgun-Trips
Shotgun-5WR Trio	Shotgun-Slot F Trips	Shotgun-Wing Trio Wk
Shotgun-Ace	Shotgun-Split Slot	Shotgun-Y-Trips HB Wk
Shotgun-Empty Trey	Shotgun-Spread	

FLORIDA ATLANTIC
Owls
Conference: **Sun Belt**
Location: **Boca Raton, FL**

REPORT CARD AND PRESTIGE

72	77	71
Overall	Offense	Defense

PRESTIGE RATINGS
Overall ★★
Coach Good
Academic Fair

2007 SEASON RECAP
- 8-5 overall record
- 6-1 conference record
- Won New Orleans Bowl

DEFENSIVE DEPTH CHART AND SCOUTING REPORT

Neutral 4-3 Defense
AI Playcall Tendency: 43% defend run, 57% defend pass

	FS	ROLB		MLB		LOLB	SS	
	80 #3	80 #61		78 #56		82 #50	74 #4	
	68 #37	76 #47		70 #44		77 #49	67 #10	
74 #26								80 #5
70 #21	77 #94		75 #95	79 #92		80 #98		71 #9
65 #23	75 #54		65 #90	71 #96		69 #58		68 #35
CB	RE		DT	DT		LE		CB

■ IMPACT PLAYERS   ■ LIKELY STARTERS

OFFENSIVE DEPTH CHART AND SCOUTING REPORT

Aggressive West Coast Offense
AI Playcall Tendency: 48% run, 52% pass

K	WR	LT	LG	C	RG	RT	TE	WR	P
68 KPW	80 #1	75 #65	72 #64	79 #68	79 #72	75 #57	79 #88	83 #16	62 KPW
82 KAC	76 #80	69 #70	72 #79	73 #51	73 #73	75 #71	74 #87	77 #7	88 KAC
84 #34		FB		QB1	QB2		HB		76 #22
		85 #46		83 THP 91 THA 87 #11	72 THP 87 THA 84 #12		83 #20		
							81 #32		

■ IMPACT PLAYERS   ■ LIKELY STARTERS

TEAM OFFENSIVE PLAYBOOK

Ace-Big	I-Form-Tight	Shotgun-Normal HB Wk
Ace-Big Twins	I-Form-Twins	Shotgun-Split Y-Flex
Ace-Spread Flex	I-Form-Y-Trips	Shotgun-Trips Over
Ace-Y-Trips	Shotgun-5WR Trey	Shotgun-Y-Trips HB Wk
I-Form-Normal	Shotgun-Ace	Strong-Normal
I-Form-Slot Flex	Shotgun-Double Flex	Weak-Twins

FLORIDA STATE
Seminoles
Conference: **ACC (Atlantic)**
Location: **Tallahassee, FL**

REPORT CARD AND PRESTIGE

94	92	99
Overall	Offense	Defense

PRESTIGE RATINGS
Overall ★★★★★
Coach Elite
Academic Good

2007 SEASON RECAP
- 7-6 overall record
- 4-4 conference record
- Lost Music City Bowl

DEFENSIVE DEPTH CHART AND SCOUTING REPORT

Neutral 4-3 Defense
AI Playcall Tendency: 42% defend run, 58% defend pass

	FS	ROLB		MLB		LOLB	SS	
	87 #24	92 #7		92 #30		91 #36	97 #3	
	84 #20	81 #46		83 #13		84 #41	81 #47	
89 #4								90 #21
79 #27	95 #99		87 #72	91 #54		84 #95		86 #29
78 #28	88 #97		80 #58	82 #94		80 #49		78 #15
CB	RE		DT	DT		LE		CB

■ IMPACT PLAYERS   ■ LIKELY STARTERS

OFFENSIVE DEPTH CHART AND SCOUTING REPORT

Neutral Balanced Offense
AI Playcall Tendency: 48% run, 52% pass

WR	LT	LG	C	RG	RT	TE	WR	P
89 #18	86 #62	81 #71	85 #60	82 #75	84 #76	84 #87	92 #5	79 KPW
82 #9	76 #73	70 #69	75 #63	77 #57	80 #70	77 #88	86 #89	89 KAC
	FB		QB1	QB2		HB		84 #43
	85 #35		86 THP 89 THA 84 #11	86 THP 89 THA 89 #14		92 #6		
	81 #42					84 #3		

■ IMPACT PLAYERS   ■ LIKELY STARTERS

TEAM OFFENSIVE PLAYBOOK

Ace-Big	I-Form-Normal	Shotgun-Ace Twins
Ace-Big Twins	I-Form-Twin TE	Shotgun-Normal Flex Wk
Ace-Bunch	I-Form-Twins	Shotgun-Split Slot
Ace-Slot Flex	I-Form-Y-Trips	Shotgun-Spread Flex
Ace-Twin TE Slot	Shotgun-4WR Trio	Shotgun-Y-Trips HB Wk
Ace-Y-Trips	Shotgun-4WR Trio Str	Weak-Normal

FRESNO STATE
Bulldogs

Conference: **WAC**
Location: **Fresno, CA**

REPORT CARD AND PRESTIGE

74 Overall **81** Offense **69** Defense

PRESTIGE RATINGS
Overall ★★★
Coach Very Good
Academic Good

2007 SEASON RECAP
- 9-4 overall record
- 6-2 conference record
- Won Humanitarian Bowl

DEFENSIVE DEPTH CHART AND SCOUTING REPORT

Neutral 4-3 Defense
AI Playcall Tendency: 53% defend run, 47% defend pass

	FS	ROLB	MLB	LOLB	SS	
	87 #19 / 78 #32		78 #54		75 #30 / 75 #3	
	82 #23 / 73 #33		63 #51		64 #53 / 63 #36	
75 #38						76 #8

	CB	RE	DT	DT	LE	CB
72 #4		80 #41	74 #50 / 78 #94		79 #96	75 #28
69 #31		75 #27	65 #97 / 72 #99		76 #59	70 #46

■ IMPACT PLAYERS ■ LIKELY STARTERS

OFFENSIVE DEPTH CHART AND SCOUTING REPORT

Conservative Balanced Offense
AI Playcall Tendency: 50% run, 50% pass

K	WR	LT	LG	C	RG	RT	TE	WR	P
65 KPW	81 #6	88 #72	88 #62	83 #76	79 #69	82 #73	84 #85	82 #5	70 KPW
85 KAC	74 #13	73 #60	76 #65	73 #66	77 #61	74 #79	76 #45	76 #2	86 KAC
82 #35									82 #42

	FB	QB1	QB2	HB	
	82 #22	86 THP #50	74 THP #44	81 #21	
	73 #49	91 THA / 87 #7	90 THA / 84 #15	80 #1	

■ IMPACT PLAYERS ■ LIKELY STARTERS

TEAM OFFENSIVE PLAYBOOK

- Ace-Big
- Ace-Big Twins
- Ace-Bunch
- Ace-Slot Flex
- Ace-Twin TE Slot
- Ace-Y-Trips
- I-Form-Normal
- I-Form-Slot Flex
- I-Form-Twin TE
- I-Form-Twins
- Shotgun-5WR Trio
- Shotgun-Double Flex
- Shotgun-Normal
- Shotgun-Spread Flex Wk
- Shotgun-Y-Trips
- Strong-Normal
- Strong-Twin TE
- Weak-Normal

GEORGIA
Bulldogs

Conference: **SEC (East)**
Location: **Athens, GA**

REPORT CARD AND PRESTIGE

99 Overall **99** Offense **99** Defense

PRESTIGE RATINGS
Overall ★★★★★
Coach Excellent
Academic Great

2007 SEASON RECAP
- 11-2 overall record
- 6-2 conference record
- Won Sugar Bowl

DEFENSIVE DEPTH CHART AND SCOUTING REPORT

Aggressive 4-3 Defense
AI Playcall Tendency: 43% defend run, 57% defend pass

	FS	ROLB	MLB	LOLB	SS	
	89 #9 / 86 #37		94 #33		86 #51 / 92 #5	
	82 #10 / 80 #53		84 #44		84 #52 / 77 #31	
91 #23						94 #2

	CB	RE	DT	DT	LE	CB
80 #11		88 #55	89 #56 / 95 #95		88 #41	84 #3
73 #25		78 #57	82 #85 / 87 #91		81 #58	77 #21

■ IMPACT PLAYERS ■ LIKELY STARTERS

OFFENSIVE DEPTH CHART AND SCOUTING REPORT

Neutral Balanced Offense
AI Playcall Tendency: 49% run, 51% pass

K	WR	LT	LG	C	RG	RT	TE	WR	P
77 KPW	87 #88	93 #77	86 #71	87 #63	87 #60	84 #75	89 #86	92 #1	80 KPW
90 KAC	85 #85	80 #78	77 #54	77 #74	81 #79	82 #72	78 #87	85 #16	88 KAC
87 #23									85 #32

	FB	QB1	QB2	HB	
	85 #36	93 THP #56	85 THP #44	96 #24	
	79 #48	96 THA / 91 #7	89 THA / 91 #14	86 #4	

■ IMPACT PLAYERS ■ LIKELY STARTERS

TEAM OFFENSIVE PLAYBOOK

- Ace-Big
- Ace-Bunch
- Ace-Slot Flex
- Ace-Twin TE Slot
- Ace-Y-Trips
- I-Form-Normal
- I-Form-Slot Flex
- I-Form-Tight
- I-Form-Twin TE
- I-Form-Twins
- I-Form-Y-Trips
- Shotgun-Normal
- Shotgun-Normal Flex Wk
- Shotgun-Normal HB Wk
- Shotgun-Split Slot
- Shotgun-Split Y-Flex
- Shotgun-Trips Over
- Shotgun-Y-Trips HB Wk

GEORGIA TECH
Yellow Jackets
Conference: **ACC (Coastal)**
Location: **Atlanta, GA**

REPORT CARD AND PRESTIGE

81 Overall   **81** Offense   **87** Defense

PRESTIGE RATINGS
Overall ★★★★
Coach Very Good
Academic Excellent

2007 SEASON RECAP
- 7-6 overall record
- 4-4 conference record
- Lost Humanitarian Bowl

DEFENSIVE DEPTH CHART AND SCOUTING REPORT

Neutral 4-3 Defense
AI Playcall Tendency: 38% defend run, 62% defend pass

FS	ROLB	MLB	LOLB	SS	
81 #47	84 #57	82 #17	90 #52	81 #1	
75 #48	81 #12	73 #56	76 #29	77 #27	85 #32

CB	RE	DT	DT	LE	CB
83 #10	96 #93	90 #94	93 #96	82 #91	78 #26
77 #7	79 #97	77 #98	81 #99	79 #92	73 #2
69 #21					

■ IMPACT PLAYERS   ■ LIKELY STARTERS

OFFENSIVE DEPTH CHART AND SCOUTING REPORT

Conservative Flexbone Offense
AI Playcall Tendency: 68% run, 32% pass

K	WR	LT	LG	C	RG	RT	TE	WR	P
77 KPW	82 #89	91 #64	79 #82	78 #74	78 #68	83 #71	80 #81	84 #5	63 KPW
96 KAC	79 #88	84 #53	76 #77	74 #62	77 #63	78 #65	64 #36	81 #8	86 KAC
80 #12									80 #31

FB	QB1	QB2	HB
82 #38	84 THP 87 THA 84 #14	83 THP 88 THA 84 #19	83 #20
76 #46			81 #21

■ IMPACT PLAYERS   ■ LIKELY STARTERS

TEAM OFFENSIVE PLAYBOOK

Flexbone-Normal	Flexbone-Wide	JumboT-Big
Flexbone-Slot	FullHouse-Normal Wide	Wishbone-Normal
Flexbone-Split	I-Form-3WR	Wishbone-Tight
Flexbone-Tight	I-Form-Normal	Wishbone-Wide
Flexbone-Trips	I-Form-Twin TE Wing	
Flexbone-Twins	I-Form-Twin WR	

HAWAII
Warriors
Conference: **WAC**
Location: **Honolulu, HI**

REPORT CARD AND PRESTIGE

77 Overall   **75** Offense   **80** Defense

PRESTIGE RATINGS
Overall ★★★★
Coach Good
Academic Good

2007 SEASON RECAP
- 12-1 overall record
- 8-0 conference record
- Lost Sugar Bowl

DEFENSIVE DEPTH CHART AND SCOUTING REPORT

Aggressive 4-3 Defense
AI Playcall Tendency: 60% defend run, 40% defend pass

FS	ROLB	MLB	LOLB	SS	
82 #24	90 #44	84 #17	79 #8	84 #35	
77 #30	84 #53	58 #41	73 #59	74 #7	86 #3
75 #12					

CB	RE	DT	DT	LE	CB
72 #28	78 #96	83 #93	85 #71	80 #70	72 #29
71 #31	75 #91	76 #92	81 #94	75 #95	71 #2

■ IMPACT PLAYERS   ■ LIKELY STARTERS

OFFENSIVE DEPTH CHART AND SCOUTING REPORT

Neutral Spread Offense
AI Playcall Tendency: 30% run, 70% pass

K	WR	LT	LG	C	RG	RT	TE	WR
78 KPW	79 #89	86 #62	76 #63	83 #55	83 #50	85 #78	70 #1	79 #5
89 KAC	75 #25	74 #68	75 #74	78 #51	81 #64	77 #76		76 #26
86 #86								

QB1	QB2	HB
83 THP 89 THA 92 #6	80 THP 89 THA 92 #6	83 #21
		81 #4

■ IMPACT PLAYERS   ■ LIKELY STARTERS

TEAM OFFENSIVE PLAYBOOK

Ace-4WR Trips	Shotgun-Double Flex	Shotgun-Tight
Ace-Spread	Shotgun-Flanker Close	Shotgun-Trips
Shotgun-4WR	Shotgun-Normal Y-Slot	Shotgun-Trips HB Wk
Shotgun-4WR Trio	Shotgun-Spread	Shotgun-Trips Open
Shotgun-5WR Trips	Shotgun-Spread Flex Wk	Shotgun-Trips Open Str
Shotgun-Bunch HB Str	Shotgun-Spread HB Wk	Shotgun-Wing Trips

HOUSTON
Cougars
Conference: C-USA (West)
Location: Houston, TX

REPORT CARD AND PRESTIGE

74 Overall **73** Offense **82** Defense

PRESTIGE RATINGS
Overall ★★
Coach Good
Academic Good

2007 SEASON RECAP
- 8-5 overall record
- 6-2 conference record
- Lost Texas Bowl

DEFENSIVE DEPTH CHART AND SCOUTING REPORT

Neutral 4-3 Defense
AI Playcall Tendency: 33% defend run, 67% defend pass

	86 #5	83 #27	84 #34	82 #7	87 #28	
78 #8	78 #23	80 #30 FS ROLB	81 #4 MLB	74 #55	75 #32 LOLB SS	80 #21
67 #13	90 #53		85 #91	87 #90	77 #96	68 #35
62 #29 CB	78 #93 RE		79 #92	80 #56 DT DT	76 #33 LE	66 #17 CB

■ IMPACT PLAYERS ■ LIKELY STARTERS

OFFENSIVE DEPTH CHART AND SCOUTING REPORT

Aggressive Spread Offense
AI Playcall Tendency: 45% run, 55% pass

K	WR	LT	LG	C	RG	RT	TE	WR	P
68 KPW	76 #10	89 #74	79 #79	78 #57	78 #64	76 #59	81 #87	78 #8	70 KPW
82 KAC	74 #82	67 #71	72 #70	72 #65	78 #75	73 #60	67 #18	75 #19	92 KAC
85 #14		FB		QB1	QB2		HB		76 #80
		68 #44		84 THP 88 THA 88 #7	79 THP 87 THA 86 #15		76 #6		
		65 #36					75 #20		

■ IMPACT PLAYERS ■ LIKELY STARTERS

TEAM OFFENSIVE PLAYBOOK

- Ace-4WR Trips
- Ace-Big Flip
- Ace-Spread Flex
- I-Form-Normal
- Shotgun-4WR Trey Str
- Shotgun-Double Flex
- Shotgun-Normal Flex Wk
- Shotgun-Split
- Shotgun-Split Slot
- Shotgun-Split Y-Flex
- Shotgun-Spread Flex
- Shotgun-Spread Flex Wk
- Shotgun-Trips
- Shotgun-Trips HB Wk
- Shotgun-Trips Open
- Shotgun-Trips Open Str
- Shotgun-Wing Trio Wk
- Weak-H Pro

IDAHO
Vandals
Conference: WAC
Location: Moscow, ID

REPORT CARD AND PRESTIGE

60 Overall **66** Offense **60** Defense

PRESTIGE RATINGS
Overall ★
Coach Fair
Academic Good

2007 SEASON RECAP
- 1-11 overall record
- 0-8 conference record
- 9th in the WAC

DEFENSIVE DEPTH CHART AND SCOUTING REPORT

Aggressive 4-3 Defense
AI Playcall Tendency: 43% defend run, 57% defend pass

	77 #10	75 #41	69 #13	73 #46	68 #36	
72 #4	72 #6	70 #23 FS ROLB	56 #45 MLB	68 #44	62 #58 LOLB SS	78 #34
63 #39	77 #48		68 #54	76 #90	77 #98	69 #3
	77 #57 CB RE		66 #40	68 #43 DT DT	72 #95 LE	61 #26 CB

■ IMPACT PLAYERS ■ LIKELY STARTERS

OFFENSIVE DEPTH CHART AND SCOUTING REPORT

Conservative Spread Offense
AI Playcall Tendency: 50% run, 50% pass

K	WR	LT	LG	C	RG	RT	TE	WR	P
61 KPW	75 #84	74 #71	78 #77	80 #72	75 #62	74 #65	71 #65	79 #22	54 KPW
84 KAC	71 #2	66 #66	66 #74	70 #69	68 #67	69 #79	69 #89	72 #81	82 KAC
78 #19		FB		QB1	QB2		HB		76 #14
		69 #35		74 THP 87 THA 84 #10	74 THP 85 THA 80 #17		79 #3		
							78 #28		

■ IMPACT PLAYERS ■ LIKELY STARTERS

TEAM OFFENSIVE PLAYBOOK

- Ace-Big
- Ace-Big Twins
- Ace-Bunch
- Ace-Jumbo
- Ace-Slot
- Ace-Spread
- Ace-Trips
- Ace-Twin TE
- Ace-Twin TE Slot
- Ace-Y-Trips
- Shotgun-4WR Trey Str
- Shotgun-5WR Trio
- Shotgun-Normal
- Shotgun-Normal HB Wk
- Shotgun-Split Slot
- Shotgun-Spread Flex
- Shotgun-Trips TE
- Shotgun-Y-Trips

ILLINOIS
Fighting Illini

Conference: **Big Ten**
Location: **Champaign, IL**

REPORT CARD AND PRESTIGE

81 Overall   **81** Offense   **85** Defense

PRESTIGE RATINGS
Overall ★★★
Coach Good
Academic Excellent

2007 SEASON RECAP
- 9-4 overall record
- 6-2 conference record
- Lost Rose Bowl

DEFENSIVE DEPTH CHART AND SCOUTING REPORT

Aggressive 4-3 Defense
AI Playcall Tendency: 44% defend run, 56% defend pass

	81 #24	78 #2	84 #43	89 #44	83 #27	
80 #28	78 #20	76 #41	74 #55	78 #45	70 #31	94 #1
		FS ROLB	MLB	LOLB SS		
75 #14	84 #95		85 #68	86 #94	89 #91	79 #15
74 #23	81 #81		81 #92	81 #56	82 #82	75 #18
CB	RE		DT	DT	LE	CB

■ IMPACT PLAYERS   ■ LIKELY STARTERS

OFFENSIVE DEPTH CHART AND SCOUTING REPORT

Neutral Spread Offense
AI Playcall Tendency: 55% run, 45% pass

K	WR	LT	LG	C	RG	RT	TE	WR	P
56 KPW	82 #26	76 #78	82 #74	90 #60	82 #52	80 #79	80 #17	93 #9	67 KPW
90 KAC	81 #13	76 #76	71 #63	74 #62	78 #77	80 #66	76 #89	82 #21	90 KAC
72 #35		FB	QB1	QB2			HB		76 #87
		80 #30	86 THP 91 THA 82 #7	82 THP 89 THA 86 #10			77 #22 76 #5		

■ IMPACT PLAYERS   ■ LIKELY STARTERS

TEAM OFFENSIVE PLAYBOOK

Ace-Slot
Ace-Y-Trips
I-Form-Normal
I-Form-Slot
I-Form-Tight
Shotgun-4WR Trio

Shotgun-4WR Trio Str
Shotgun-5WR Trips
Shotgun-Normal
Shotgun-Normal HB Wk
Shotgun-Normal Y-Slot
Shotgun-Split Slot

Shotgun-Spread HB Wk
Shotgun-Trips
Shotgun-Trips HB Wk
Shotgun-Trips Open Str
Shotgun-Y-Trips
Shotgun-Y-Trips HB Wk

INDIANA
Hoosiers

Conference: **Big Ten**
Location: **Bloomington, IN**

REPORT CARD AND PRESTIGE

79 Overall   **81** Offense   **82** Defense

PRESTIGE RATINGS
Overall ★★★
Coach Good
Academic Great

2007 SEASON RECAP
- 7-6 overall record
- 3-5 conference record
- Lost Insight Bowl

DEFENSIVE DEPTH CHART AND SCOUTING REPORT

Conservative 4-3 Defense
AI Playcall Tendency: 60% defend run, 40% defend pass

	86 #8	81 #34	77 #46	90 #56	85 #20	
78 #17	71 #33	80 #25	75 #43	72 #50	74 #26	80 #16
		FS ROLB	MLB	LOLB SS		
76 #23	93 #92		80 #55	80 #62	84 #57	76 #18
68 #21	78 #93		76 #97	77 #51	78 #49	74 #4
CB	RE		DT	DT	LE	CB

■ IMPACT PLAYERS   ■ LIKELY STARTERS

OFFENSIVE DEPTH CHART AND SCOUTING REPORT

Conservative Spread Offense
AI Playcall Tendency: 50% run, 50% pass

K	WR	LT	LG	C	RG	RT	TE	WR	P
92 KPW	80 #7	80 #76	81 #72	80 #71	83 #79	80 #68	71 #87	84 #6	66 KPW
88 KAC	79 #13	77 #52	78 #64	73 #67	80 #77	76 #74	68 #41	79 #19	88 KAC
94 #18			QB1	QB2			HB		78 #12
			90 THP 88 THA 86 #15	77 THP 88 THA 86 #4			85 #2 81 #27		

■ IMPACT PLAYERS   ■ LIKELY STARTERS

TEAM OFFENSIVE PLAYBOOK

Ace-Big
Ace-Big Twins
Ace-Twin TE Slot
Ace-Y-Trips
Shotgun-4WR Trio
Shotgun-4WR Trio Str

Shotgun-5WR Trio
Shotgun-Ace Wing Wk
Shotgun-Normal
Shotgun-Normal HB Wk
Shotgun-Normal Wing TE
Shotgun-Spread Flex

Shotgun-Spread Flex Wk
Shotgun-Trips Over
Shotgun-Trips TE
Shotgun-Wildcat
Shotgun-Y-Trips
Shotgun-Y-Trips HB Wk

IOWA
Hawkeyes

Conference: **Big Ten**
Location: **Iowa City, IA**

IOWA STATE
Cyclones

Conference: **Big 12 (North)**
Location: **Ames, IA**

REPORT CARD AND PRESTIGE

74	**79**	**73**
Overall	Offense	Defense

PRESTIGE RATINGS
Overall ★★★
Coach Excellent
Academic Great

2007 SEASON RECAP
- 6-6 overall record
- 4-4 conference record
- 6th in Big Ten

REPORT CARD AND PRESTIGE

72	**73**	**76**
Overall	Offense	Defense

PRESTIGE RATINGS
Overall ★★★
Coach Good
Academic Very Good

2007 SEASON RECAP
- 3-9 overall record
- 2-6 conference record
- 6th in Big 12 North

DEFENSIVE DEPTH CHART AND SCOUTING REPORT

Conservative 4-3 Defense
AI Playcall Tendency: 33% defend run, 67% defend pass

	FS	ROLB		MLB		LOLB	SS	
	78 #14	76 #33		71 #55		86 #49	81 #2	
75 #4	78 #30	74 #42		68 #57		72 #87	74 #9	79 #29
74 #16	79 #94		93 #53	96 #47		80 #46		75 #34
65 #35	79 #98		74 #95	79 #59		79 #96		72 #23
CB	RE		DT	DT		LE		CB

DEFENSIVE DEPTH CHART AND SCOUTING REPORT

Neutral 4-3 Defense
AI Playcall Tendency: 53% defend run, 47% defend pass

	FS	ROLB		MLB		LOLB	SS	
	87 #2	72 #32		77 #54		79 #14	84 #8	
81 #11	76 #20	61 #52		73 #43		75 #24	74 #23	82 #12
71 #26	84 #29		70 #62	77 #85		84 #47		74 #17
67 #28	78 #55		69 #56	69 #96		79 #25		69 #21
CB	RE		DT	DT		LE		CB

■ IMPACT PLAYERS   ■ LIKELY STARTERS

OFFENSIVE DEPTH CHART AND SCOUTING REPORT

Conservative Balanced Offense
AI Playcall Tendency: 50% run, 50% pass

K	WR	LT	LG	C	RG	RT	TE	WR	P
74 KPW	79 #15	80 #79	77 #74	85 #52	90 #71	80 #60	83 #83	84 #80	84 KPW
87 KAC	76 #22	76 #52	77 #63	78 #58	75 #61	77 #75	85 #81	76 #86	91 KAC
85 #1									87 #5

FB	QB1	QB2	HB
76 #38	86 THP	76 THP	80 #23
68 #36	89 THA	87 THA	80 #28
	85 #6	82 #12	

OFFENSIVE DEPTH CHART AND SCOUTING REPORT

Conservative Balanced Offense
AI Playcall Tendency: 52% run, 48% pass

K	WR	LT	LG	C	RG	RT	TE	WR	P
54 KPW	77 #85	83 #75	79 #73	76 #60	81 #63	78 #63	72 #84	85 #5	82 KPW
82 KAC	76 #82	67 #67	78 #66	70 #52	74 #77	74 #74	69 #88	76 #81	91 KAC
78 #36									84 #13

FB	QB1	QB2	HB
71 #29	78 THP	74 THP	82 #22
68 #49	92 THA	86 THA	82 #3
	82 #4	82 #7	

■ IMPACT PLAYERS   ■ LIKELY STARTERS

TEAM OFFENSIVE PLAYBOOK

Ace-Big	I-Form-Normal	Shotgun-Y-Trips
Ace-Big Twins	I-Form-Tight	Shotgun-Y-Trips HB Wk
Ace-Slot	I-Form-Twin TE	Strong-Normal
Ace-Twin TE	I-Form-Twins	Strong-Twins
Ace-Twin TE Slot	Shotgun-Normal	Weak-Normal
Ace-Y-Trips	Shotgun-Normal HB Wk	Weak-Twins

TEAM OFFENSIVE PLAYBOOK

Ace-Big	Shotgun-5WR	Shotgun-Wing Trips
Ace-Slot	Shotgun-Normal	Shotgun-Y-Trips
Ace-Y-Trips	Shotgun-Normal HB Wk	Strong-Normal
I-Form-Normal	Shotgun-Split Slot	Strong-Twins
I-Form-Slot Flex	Shotgun-Spread Flex	Weak-Normal
I-Form-Twin TE	Shotgun-Trips TE	Weak-Twins

KANSAS
Jayhawks
Conference: **Big 12 (North)**
Location: **Lawrence, KS**

REPORT CARD AND PRESTIGE

77	81	78
Overall	Offense	Defense

PRESTIGE RATINGS
Overall ★★★
Coach Good
Academic Very Good

2007 SEASON RECAP
- 12-1 overall record
- 7-1 conference record
- Won Orange Bowl

DEFENSIVE DEPTH CHART AND SCOUTING REPORT

Aggressive 4-3 Defense
AI Playcall Tendency: 60% defend run, 40% defend pass

FS	ROLB	MLB	LOLB	SS	
82 #25	84 #12	82 #8	84 #40	78 #37	
81 #46	82 #51	70 #45	75 #58	73 #36	81 #16

CB	RE	DT	DT	LE	CB
77 #24					
75 #20	86 #81	75 #99	80 #94	85 #87	76 #4
73 #32	77 #91	72 #96	73 #72	77 #47	74 #2

■ IMPACT PLAYERS   ■ LIKELY STARTERS

OFFENSIVE DEPTH CHART AND SCOUTING REPORT

Aggressive Spread Offense
AI Playcall Tendency: 48% run, 52% pass

K	WR	LT	LG	C	RG	RT	TE	WR	P
67 KPW	79 #85	77 #75	83 #66	84 #50	84 #79	79 #63	78 #87	79 #88	69 KPW
82 KAC	76 #9	75 #70	74 #78	69 #77	72 #62	77 #60	75 #82	78 #13	89 KAC
84 #14									78 #13

FB	QB1	QB2	HB
71 #31	92 THP 88 THA 94 #5	80 THP 87 THA 85 #10	83 #1 / 82 #22

■ IMPACT PLAYERS   ■ LIKELY STARTERS

TEAM OFFENSIVE PLAYBOOK

Ace-Bunch
Ace-Slot
Ace-Y-Trips
I-Form-Slot Flex
Shotgun-4WR Trey Str
Shotgun-5WR Flex Trio

Shotgun-Bunch HB Str
Shotgun-Double Flex
Shotgun-Normal
Shotgun-Normal HB Wk
Shotgun-Normal Y-Slot
Shotgun-Split Slot

Shotgun-Split Y-Flex
Shotgun-Spread Flex
Shotgun-Spread Flex Wk
Shotgun-Trips HB Wk
Shotgun-Wing Trips
Shotgun-Y-Trips HB Wk

KANSAS STATE
Wildcats
Conference: **Big 12 (North)**
Location: **Manhattan, KS**

REPORT CARD AND PRESTIGE

81	81	85
Overall	Offense	Defense

PRESTIGE RATINGS
Overall ★★★
Coach Good
Academic Very Good

2007 SEASON RECAP
- 5-7 overall record
- 3-5 conference record
- 4th in Big 12 North

DEFENSIVE DEPTH CHART AND SCOUTING REPORT

Neutral 3-4 Defense
AI Playcall Tendency: 42% defend run, 58% defend pass

FS	ROLB	MLB	MLB	LOLB	SS	
84 #30	88 #90	78 #59	81 #39	87 #19	83 #21	
81 #36	80 #42	75 #53	76 #52	84 #10	80 #20	82 #23

CB	RE	DT	LE	CB
80 #9				
78 #25	94 #98	80 #92	84 #95	78 #4
75 #26	71 #56	77 #93	79 #97	76 #22

■ IMPACT PLAYERS   ■ LIKELY STARTERS

OFFENSIVE DEPTH CHART AND SCOUTING REPORT

Conservative West Coast Offense
AI Playcall Tendency: 50% run, 50% pass

K	WR	LT	LG	C	RG	RT	TE	WR	P
77 KPW	83 #17	82 #71	83 #76	89 #79	86 #73	80 #63	79 #85	83 #18	77 KPW
85 KAC	81 #88	80 #78	74 #62	80 #68	78 #75	78 #64	75 #80	82 #87	89 KAC
88 #16									84 #97

FB	QB1	QB2	HB
68 #44	90 THP 93 THA 89 #1	77 THP 86 THA 84 #14	82 #9 / 75 #37

■ IMPACT PLAYERS   ■ LIKELY STARTERS

TEAM OFFENSIVE PLAYBOOK

Ace-Big
Ace-Bunch
Ace-Jumbo
Ace-Slot
Ace-Twin TE
Ace-Twin TE Slot

Ace-Y-Trips
I-Form-Tight
I-Form-Twins
Shotgun-4WR Trey Str
Shotgun-Bunch HB Str
Shotgun-Double Flex

Shotgun-Empty Trey
Shotgun-Normal
Shotgun-Split
Shotgun-Split Y-Flex
Shotgun-Y-Trips
Strong-Twins

KENT STATE
Golden Flashes
Conference: **MAC (East)**
Location: **Kent, OH**

REPORT CARD AND PRESTIGE

72	77	71
Overall	Offense	Defense

PRESTIGE RATINGS
Overall ★
Coach Fair
Academic Good

2007 SEASON RECAP
- 3-9 overall record
- 1-7 conference record
- 7th in the MAC East

DEFENSIVE DEPTH CHART AND SCOUTING REPORT

Conservative 4-3 Defense
AI Playcall Tendency: 39% defend run, 61% defend pass

■ IMPACT PLAYERS   ■ LIKELY STARTERS

OFFENSIVE DEPTH CHART AND SCOUTING REPORT

Conservative Spread Offense
AI Playcall Tendency: 50% run, 50% pass

■ IMPACT PLAYERS   ■ LIKELY STARTERS

TEAM OFFENSIVE PLAYBOOK

Ace-Big	Shotgun-Double Flex	Shotgun-Trips Over
Ace-Big Twins	Shotgun-Normal HB Wk	Shotgun-Trips TE
Ace-Slot	Shotgun-Normal Y-Slot	Shotgun-Y-Trips HB Wk
Ace-Twin TE	Shotgun-Spread HB Wk	Strong-H Pro
Ace-Y-Trips	Shotgun-Trips	Weak-H Pro
Shotgun-5WR	Shotgun-Trips HB Wk	Weak-H Twins

KENTUCKY
Wildcats
Conference: **SEC (East)**
Location: **Lexington, KY**

REPORT CARD AND PRESTIGE

77	77	82
Overall	Offense	Defense

PRESTIGE RATINGS
Overall ★★★
Coach Very Good
Academic Very Good

2007 SEASON RECAP
- 8-5 overall record
- 3-5 conference record
- Won Music City Bowl

DEFENSIVE DEPTH CHART AND SCOUTING REPORT

Aggressive 4-3 Defense
AI Playcall Tendency: 60% defend run, 40% defend pass

■ IMPACT PLAYERS   ■ LIKELY STARTERS

OFFENSIVE DEPTH CHART AND SCOUTING REPORT

Neutral Balanced Offense
AI Playcall Tendency: 48% run, 52% pass

■ IMPACT PLAYERS   ■ LIKELY STARTERS

TEAM OFFENSIVE PLAYBOOK

Ace-4WR Trips	I-Form-Tight	Shotgun-Trips
Ace-Bunch	I-Form-Twins	Shotgun-Trips Over
Ace-Slot	Shotgun-Normal HB Wk	Shotgun-Wing Trips Wk
Ace-Y-Trips	Shotgun-Split Slot	Shotgun-Y-Trips
I-Form-Normal	Shotgun-Split Twins	Strong-Normal
I-Form-Slot Flex	Shotgun-Spread Flex	Strong-Tight

LOUISIANA TECH
Bulldogs
Conference: **WAC**
Location: **Ruston, LA**

REPORT CARD AND PRESTIGE

69 Overall | **75** Offense | **71** Defense

PRESTIGE RATINGS
Overall ★★
Coach Fair
Academic Very Good

2007 SEASON RECAP
- 5-7 overall record
- 4-4 conference record
- 5th in the WAC

DEFENSIVE DEPTH CHART AND SCOUTING REPORT

Neutral 4-3 Defense
AI Playcall Tendency: 52% defend run, 48% defend pass

	89 #34	82 #37		83 #58		75 #55	82 #25	
	72 #4	57 #48		61 #30		74 #42	70 #31	
73 #38	FS	ROLB		MLB		LOLB	SS	78 #35
69 #11	76 #85		73 #5	74 #94		75 #97		69 #27
60 #15	70 #91		68 #86	73 #95		75 #90		66 #28
CB	RE		DT	DT		LE		CB

■ IMPACT PLAYERS ■ LIKELY STARTERS

OFFENSIVE DEPTH CHART AND SCOUTING REPORT

Conservative Spread Offense
AI Playcall Tendency: 47% run, 53% pass

K	WR	LT	LG	C	RG	RT	TE	WR	P
65 KPW	81 #6	77 #74	77 #62	74 #60	75 #67	74 #76	79 #49	82 #82	72 KPW
84 KAC	76 #19	75 #78	72 #66	66 #69		73 #77	79 #47	80 #81	87 KAC
82 #33		FB		QB1	QB2		HB		82 #17
		80 #43		81 THP 90 THA 94 #15	80 THP 88 THA 85 #11		84 #23		
		66 #39					81 #20		

■ IMPACT PLAYERS ■ LIKELY STARTERS

TEAM OFFENSIVE PLAYBOOK

Ace-Big	Shotgun-Empty Trey	Shotgun-Trips HB Wk
Ace-Slot	Shotgun-Normal	Shotgun-Wing Trips
Ace-Twin TE	Shotgun-Normal HB Wk	Shotgun-Y-Trips
Ace-Y-Trips	Shotgun-Split Slot	Strong-H Pro
I-Form-Normal	Shotgun-Spread HB Wk	Strong-H Twins
Shotgun-5WR Trio	Shotgun-Trips	Weak-H Pro

LOUISVILLE
Cardinals
Conference: **Big East**
Location: **Louisville, KY**

REPORT CARD AND PRESTIGE

79 Overall | **81** Offense | **76** Defense

PRESTIGE RATINGS
Overall ★★★★
Coach Very Good
Academic Good

2007 SEASON RECAP
- 6-6 overall record
- 3-4 conference record
- 6th in Big East

DEFENSIVE DEPTH CHART AND SCOUTING REPORT

Neutral 4-3 Defense
AI Playcall Tendency: 46% defend run, 54% defend pass

	87 #34	78 #31		77 #57		80 #5	79 #10	
	80 #21	78 #90		71 #50		76 #43	79 #2	
79 #19	FS	ROLB		MLB		LOLB	SS	81 #9
77 #36	79 #93		83 #94	87 #99		87 #99		77 #4
74 #67	78 #55		79 #91	80 #56		80 #56		74 #44
CB	RE		DT	DT		LE		CB

■ IMPACT PLAYERS ■ LIKELY STARTERS

OFFENSIVE DEPTH CHART AND SCOUTING REPORT

Aggressive Balanced Offense
AI Playcall Tendency: 47% run, 53% pass

K	WR	LT	LG	C	RG	RT	TE	WR
54 KPW	81 #9	87 #68	76 #75	92 #77	79 #71	80 #78	74 #43	84 #84
74 KAC	81 #3	72 #55	73 #79	79 #62	74 #72	77 #74	72 #81	81 #26
82 #17		FB		QB1	QB2		HB	
		84 #32		89 THP 95 THA 89 #14	79 THP 86 THA 85 #15		84 #24	
		75 #48					81 #30	

■ IMPACT PLAYERS ■ LIKELY STARTERS

TEAM OFFENSIVE PLAYBOOK

Ace-4WR Trips	I-Form-Normal	Shotgun-Split
Ace-Big	I-Form-Tight	Shotgun-Spread Flex Wk
Ace-Slot	I-Form-Twins	Shotgun-Trips HB Wk
Ace-Spread	Shotgun-Ace Twins	Shotgun-Y-Trips HB Wk
Ace-Twin TE	Shotgun-Double Flex	Strong-Normal
Ace-Y-Trips	Shotgun-Normal	Weak-Normal

LSU (LOUISIANA STATE)
Tigers
Conference: **SEC (West)**
Location: **Baton Rouge, LA**

REPORT CARD AND PRESTIGE

91 Overall **88** Offense **96** Defense

PRESTIGE RATINGS
Overall ★★★★★★
Coach Excellent
Academic Good

2007 SEASON RECAP
- 12-2 overall record
- 6-2 conference record
- FBS National Champions

DEFENSIVE DEPTH CHART AND SCOUTING REPORT

Aggressive 4-3 Defense
AI Playcall Tendency: 59% defend run, 41% defend pass

		FS	ROLB		MLB		LOLB	SS	
		94 #27 / 89 #11		93 #48		85 #56 / 89 #24			
		85 #44 / 79 #50		81 #54		78 #52 / 85 #3		84 #29	

CB	RE		DT	DT		LE		CB
82 #45	94 #49		87 #99	93 #97		96 #93		82 #4
81 #33	86 #90		79 #92	85 #91		83 #47		78 #28

■ IMPACT PLAYERS   ■ LIKELY STARTERS

OFFENSIVE DEPTH CHART AND SCOUTING REPORT

Aggressive Balanced Offense
AI Playcall Tendency: 50% run, 50% pass

K	WR	LT	LG	C	RG	RT	TE	WR	P
90 KPW / 90 KAC / 91 #6	87 #2 / 85 #87	94 #70 / 76 #76	96 #79 / 82 #77	92 #74 / 87 #63	84 #65 / 76 #72	78 #78 / 73 #66	87 #82 / 77 #41	91 #1 / 85 #80	69 KPW / 88 KAC / 80 #30

FB: 78 #45 / 75 #55
QB1: 79 THP / 90 THA / 84 #14
QB2: 78 THP / 91 THA / 84 #12
HB: 89 #5 / 88 #32

■ IMPACT PLAYERS   ■ LIKELY STARTERS

TEAM OFFENSIVE PLAYBOOK

Ace-Big, Ace-Bunch, Ace-Slot, Ace-Twin TE, Ace-Y-Trips, I-Form-Normal, I-Form-Slot Flex, I-Form-Tight, I-Form-Twin TE, I-Form-Twins, I-Form-Y-Trips, Pistol-Ace, Shotgun-4WR Trio Str, Shotgun-5WR Trio, Shotgun-Normal HB Wk, Shotgun-Normal Wing TE, Shotgun-Spread, Strong-Normal

---

MARSHALL
Thundering Herd
Conference: **C-USA (East)**
Location: **Huntington, WV**

REPORT CARD AND PRESTIGE

72 Overall **75** Offense **73** Defense

PRESTIGE RATINGS
Overall ★★★
Coach Good
Academic Very Good

2007 SEASON RECAP
- 3-9 overall record
- 3-5 conference record
- Lost Emerald Bowl

DEFENSIVE DEPTH CHART AND SCOUTING REPORT

Neutral 4-3 Defense
AI Playcall Tendency: 30% defend run, 70% defend pass

		FS	ROLB		MLB		LOLB	SS	
		79 #4 / 82 #30		79 #45		80 #21 / 82 #19			
76 #20		76 #29 / 72 #27		70 #33		73 #55 / 77 #6		77 #11	

CB	RE		DT	DT		LE		CB
76 #8	86 #96		77 #95	79 #58		80 #46		76 #14
73 #25	71 #93		71 #50	72 #91		77 #90		75 #37

■ IMPACT PLAYERS   ■ LIKELY STARTERS

OFFENSIVE DEPTH CHART AND SCOUTING REPORT

Neutral Spread Offense
AI Playcall Tendency: 50% run, 50% pass

K	WR	LT	LG	C	RG	RT	TE	WR	P
66 KPW / 88 KAC / 80 #82	82 #1 / 80 #22	79 #76 / 74 #78	74 #61 / 73 #71	75 #62 / 72 #68	73 #65 / 66 #75	80 #79 / 72 #66	85 #85 / 76 #16	82 #24 / 80 #80	65 KPW / 86 KAC / 80 #4

FB: 76 #83 / 68 #43
QB1: 76 THP / 89 THA / 85 #12
QB2: 75 THP / 85 THA / 87 #9
HB: 82 #28 / 82 #5

■ IMPACT PLAYERS   ■ LIKELY STARTERS

TEAM OFFENSIVE PLAYBOOK

Ace-Big, Ace-Big Twins, Ace-Jumbo, Ace-Slot, Ace-Spread, Ace-Trips, Ace-Twin TE, Ace-Twin TE Slot, Ace-Y-Trips, Shotgun-4WR Trey Str, Shotgun-5WR Trey, Shotgun-Ace Twins Wk, Shotgun-Double Flex, Shotgun-Normal Flex Wk, Shotgun-Spread, Shotgun-Spread Flex Wk, Shotgun-Trips Over, Shotgun-Y-Trips

MARYLAND
Terrapins

Conference: **ACC (Atlantic)**
Location: **College Park, MD**

REPORT CARD AND PRESTIGE

81	**81**	**85**
Overall	Offense	Defense

PRESTIGE RATINGS
Overall ★★★
Coach Great
Academic Very Good

2007 SEASON RECAP
- 6-7 overall record
- 3-5 conference record
- 5th in ACC Atlantic

DEFENSIVE DEPTH CHART AND SCOUTING REPORT

Aggressive 3-4 Defense
AI Playcall Tendency: 48% defend run, 52% defend pass

89 #1	83 #54		78 #44	84 #34		84 #48	83 #29	
83 #20	77 #52		72 #58	77 #33		75 #27	71 #4	86 #2
FS	ROLB		MLB	MLB		LOLB	SS	
82 #6	83 #91		85 #40			89 #55	80 #9	
79 #25	81 #57		78 #97			82 #51	77 #28	
CB	RE		DT			LE	CB	

■ IMPACT PLAYERS   ■ LIKELY STARTERS

OFFENSIVE DEPTH CHART AND SCOUTING REPORT

Neutral Balanced Offense
AI Playcall Tendency: 52% run, 48% pass

K	WR	LT	LG	C	RG	RT	TE	WR	P
78 KPW	83 #17	79 #77	86 #76	80 #60	77 #67	87 #75	77 #13	93 #8	72 KPW
92 KAC	79 #18	76 #74	73 #70	72 #65	74 #72	72 #66	75 #86	82 #84	89 KAC
84 #39									80 #35

FB	QB1	QB2	HB
78 #38	81 THP 91 THA 82 #19	80 THP 89 THA 85 #10	83 #23
72 #30			81 #5

■ IMPACT PLAYERS   ■ LIKELY STARTERS

TEAM OFFENSIVE PLAYBOOK

Ace-Big	I-Form-Tight	Shotgun-Split
Ace-Big Twins	I-Form-Twin TE	Shotgun-Spread Flex
Ace-Slot	I-Form-Y-Trips	Shotgun-Spread HB Wk
Ace-Twin TE	Shotgun-5WR Trips	Shotgun-Wing Trips
Ace-Y-Trips	Shotgun-Ace	Strong-Normal
I-Form-Normal	Shotgun-Normal HB Wk	Weak-Twin TE

MEMPHIS
Tigers

Conference: **C-USA (East)**
Location: **Memphis, TN**

REPORT CARD AND PRESTIGE

69	**75**	**69**
Overall	Offense	Defense

PRESTIGE RATINGS
Overall ★★★
Coach Fair
Academic Fair

2007 SEASON RECAP
- 7-6 overall record
- 6-2 conference record
- Lost New Orleans Bowl

DEFENSIVE DEPTH CHART AND SCOUTING REPORT

Neutral 4-3 Defense
AI Playcall Tendency: 52% defend run, 48% defend pass

82 #2	80 #59		69 #51			73 #90	80 #8	
69 #9	71 #48		68 #50			70 #25	69 #39	
72 #16	FS	ROLB		MLB		LOLB	SS	78 #21
70 #27	79 #41		77 #60	80 #53		82 #94	72 #7	
65 #4	77 #83		74 #97	76 #99		72 #96	69 #46	
CB	RE		DT	DT		LE	CB	

■ IMPACT PLAYERS   ■ LIKELY STARTERS

OFFENSIVE DEPTH CHART AND SCOUTING REPORT

Neutral Spread Offense
AI Playcall Tendency: 49% run, 51% pass

K	WR	LT	LG	C	RG	RT	TE	WR	P
74 KPW	84 #89	76 #55	75 #54	84 #57	74 #77	79 #71	79 #13	87 #22	78 KPW
87 KAC	78 #2	72 #79	73 #64	73 #61	73 #70	76 #68	74 #85	80 #80	88 KAC
84 #43									85 #49

FB	QB1	QB2	HB
71 #35	80 THP 89 THA 85 #8	77 THP 86 THA 84 #10	78 #26
			78 #3

■ IMPACT PLAYERS   ■ LIKELY STARTERS

TEAM OFFENSIVE PLAYBOOK

Ace-Big	I-Form-Y-Trips	Shotgun-Spread Flex
Ace-Slot	Shotgun-4WR Trey Str	Shotgun-Spread Flex Wk
Ace-Trips	Shotgun-5WR Trey	Shotgun-Trips HB Wk
Ace-Y-Trips	Shotgun-Normal	Shotgun-Trips TE
I-Form-Normal	Shotgun-Normal HB Wk	Shotgun-Y-Trips
I-Form-Slot Flex	Shotgun-Split Slot	Shotgun-Y-Trips HB Wk

MIAMI (FLA.)
Hurricanes
Conference: **ACC (Coastal)**
Location: **Miami, FL**

REPORT CARD AND PRESTIGE

86	**83**	**92**
Overall	Offense	Defense

PRESTIGE RATINGS
Overall ★ ★ ★ ★ ★
Coach Great
Academic Excellent

2007 SEASON RECAP
- 5-7 overall record
- 2-6 conference record
- 5th in ACC Coastal

DEFENSIVE DEPTH CHART AND SCOUTING REPORT

Aggressive 4-3 Defense
AI Playcall Tendency: 56% defend run, 44% defend pass

91 #35	88 #50		83 #3		91 #44	92 #6	
87 #26	85 #48		80 #11		86 #51	80 #39	84 #8
FS	ROLB		MLB		LOLB	SS	
82 #22							
80 #24	85 #49		84 #99	86 #96	94 #94	81 #27	
79 #13	79 #90		82 #91	83 #93	88 #57	79 #1	
CB	RE		DT	DT	LE	CB	

■ IMPACT PLAYERS   ■ LIKELY STARTERS

OFFENSIVE DEPTH CHART AND SCOUTING REPORT

Conservative Balanced Offense
AI Playcall Tendency: 50% run, 50% pass

K	WR	LT	LG	C	RG	RT	TE	WR	P
55 KPW	84 #82	90 #64	81 #74	85 #70	81 #61	86 #77	81 #18	85 #83	69 KPW
80 KAC	82 #4	84 #76	79 #65	76 #66	79 #68	82 #67	80 #88	83 #85	85 KAC
80 #40		FB		QB1	QB2		HB		85 #25
		73 #30		82 THP 89 THA 85 #9	78 THP 89 THA 84 #12		88 #2 / 87 #5		

■ IMPACT PLAYERS   ■ LIKELY STARTERS

TEAM OFFENSIVE PLAYBOOK

Ace-Big	Ace-Twin TE	Shotgun-Normal Flex Wk
Ace-Big Twins	Ace-Twin TE Slot	Shotgun-Spread Flex
Ace-Bunch	Ace-Y-Trips	Shotgun-Spread Flex Wk
Ace-Jumbo	I-Form-Normal	Shotgun-Wing Trio Wk
Ace-Slot Flex	Shotgun-4WR Trio Str	Shotgun-Y-Trips
Ace-Spread	Shotgun-Normal Flex	Shotgun-Y-Trips HB Wk

MIAMI (OHIO)
RedHawks
Conference: **MAC (East)**
Location: **Oxford, OH**

REPORT CARD AND PRESTIGE

72	**75**	**73**
Overall	Offense	Defense

PRESTIGE RATINGS
Overall ★ ★
Coach Fair
Academic Very Good

2007 SEASON RECAP
- 6-7 overall record
- 5-2 conference record
- 2nd in the MAC East

DEFENSIVE DEPTH CHART AND SCOUTING REPORT

Neutral 4-3 Defense
AI Playcall Tendency: 52% defend run, 48% defend pass

79 #22	84 #9		82 #48		80 #44	81 #6	
75 #23	68 #32		70 #20		72 #47	73 #15	79 #3
FS	ROLB		MLB		LOLB	SS	
74 #26							
72 #16	85 #99		73 #98	75 #93	80 #51	73 #30	
62 #29	72 #21		69 #65	73 #90	69 #85	67 #25	
CB	RE		DT	DT	LE	CB	

■ IMPACT PLAYERS   ■ LIKELY STARTERS

OFFENSIVE DEPTH CHART AND SCOUTING REPORT

Neutral Spread Offense
AI Playcall Tendency: 49% run, 51% pass

K	WR	LT	LG	C	RG	RT	TE	WR	P
70 KPW	80 #2	78 #55	88 #68	76 #52	75 #75	78 #76	77 #80	81 #1	72 KPW
90 KAC	74 #9	68 #71	71 #77	73 #56	68 #79	67 #63	77 #83	76 #11	87 KAC
80 #19				QB1	QB2		HB		82 #4
				81 THP 89 THA 86 #12	73 THP 89 THA 84 #7		80 #10 / 78 #34		

■ IMPACT PLAYERS   ■ LIKELY STARTERS

TEAM OFFENSIVE PLAYBOOK

Ace-Big	Shotgun-Normal	Shotgun-Trips HB Wk
Ace-Big Twins	Shotgun-Split	Shotgun-Trips Over
Ace-Twin TE	Shotgun-Split Slot	Shotgun-Trips TE
Ace-Twin TE Slot	Shotgun-Spread	Shotgun-Y-Trips HB Wk
Ace-Y-Trips	Shotgun-Spread Flex Wk	Strong-Normal
I-Form-Slot Flex	Shotgun-Trips	Weak-Twins

MICHIGAN
Wolverines

Conference: **Big Ten**
Location: **Ann Arbor, MI**

REPORT CARD AND PRESTIGE

84 Overall | **81** Offense | **89** Defense

PRESTIGE RATINGS
Overall ★★★★★★
Coach Excellent
Academic Elite

2007 SEASON RECAP
- 9-4 overall record
- 6-2 conference record
- Won Capital One Bowl

DEFENSIVE DEPTH CHART AND SCOUTING REPORT

Aggressive 4-3 Defense
AI Playcall Tendency: 44% defend run, 56% defend pass

	FS	ROLB	MLB	LOLB	SS	
	90 #27 / 77 #44		84 #47	82 #46 / 83 #3		
	75 #40 / 77 #59		81 #49	77 #57 / 83 #5		
87 #14						90 #3
	CB	RE	DT DT	LE		CB
79 #35	93 #90	81 #93 / 89 #67	90 #55	82 #2	
75 #30	74 #89	79 #91 / 80 #97	85 #99	77 #29	

■ IMPACT PLAYERS   ■ LIKELY STARTERS

OFFENSIVE DEPTH CHART AND SCOUTING REPORT

Neutral Spread Offense
AI Playcall Tendency: 52% run, 48% pass

K	WR	LT	LG	C	RG	RT	TE	WR	P
58 KPW	82 #21	86 #52	83 #75	80 #62	83 #60	83 #60	82 #85	86 #13	82 KPW
82 KAC	79 #22	76 #74	69 #50	77 #56	78 #77	78 #77	80 #83	82 #17	95 KAC
80 #84		FB		QB1	QB2		HB		80 #41
		76 #32		77 THP 89 THA 84 #15	74 THP 88 THA 82 #8		89 #4		
							86 #23		

■ IMPACT PLAYERS   ■ LIKELY STARTERS

TEAM OFFENSIVE PLAYBOOK

Ace-Big Twins | Shotgun-5WR Trio | Shotgun-Spread
Ace-Spread | Shotgun-5WR Trips | Shotgun-Spread HB Wk
Ace-Y-Trips | Shotgun-Empty Trey | Shotgun-Trips
I-Form-Slot Flex | Shotgun-Normal HB Wk | Shotgun-Trips HB Wk
I-Form-Tight | Shotgun-Split Slot | Shotgun-Trips Open Str
I-Form-Y-Trips | Shotgun-Split Twins | Shotgun-Y-Trips HB Wk

MICHIGAN STATE
Spartans

Conference: **Big Ten**
Location: **East Lansing, MI**

REPORT CARD AND PRESTIGE

79 Overall | **83** Offense | **78** Defense

PRESTIGE RATINGS
Overall ★★★
Coach Very Good
Academic Great

2007 SEASON RECAP
- 7-6 overall record
- 3-5 conference record
- Lost Champs Sports Bowl

DEFENSIVE DEPTH CHART AND SCOUTING REPORT

Conservative 4-3 Defense
AI Playcall Tendency: 54% defend run, 46% defend pass

	FS	ROLB	MLB	LOLB	SS	
	82 #40 / 82 #43		75 #55	83 #53 / 87 #21		
	78 #33 / 75 #41		69 #44	77 #36 / 69 #32		
77 #31						84 #38
	CB	RE	DT DT	LE		CB
74 #5	82 #47	80 #97 / 81 #93	81 #58	76 #37	
67 #34	75 #91	68 #96 / 77 #80	80 #49	72 #29	

■ IMPACT PLAYERS   ■ LIKELY STARTERS

OFFENSIVE DEPTH CHART AND SCOUTING REPORT

Conservative Balanced Offense
AI Playcall Tendency: 53% run, 47% pass

K	WR	LT	LG	C	RG	RT	TE	WR	P
78 KPW	80 #84	78 #57	89 #73	82 #65	89 #64	84 #79	76 #83	82 #2	71 KPW
90 KAC	76 #4	73 #77	77 #67	69 #60	75 #62	73 #69	65 #85	80 #1	91 KAC
85 #14		FB		QB1	QB2		HB		78 #18
		78 #45		87 THP 89 THA 86 #7	74 THP 92 THA 84 #17		91 #23		
		75 #35					85 #20		

■ IMPACT PLAYERS   ■ LIKELY STARTERS

TEAM OFFENSIVE PLAYBOOK

Ace-Big | I-Form-Tight | Shotgun-Split Y-Flex
Ace-Big Twins | I-Form-Twin TE | Shotgun-Spread HB Wk
Ace-Slot | I-Form-Twins | Shotgun-Y-Trips HB Wk
Ace-Trips | Shotgun-5WR Trips | Strong-Normal
Ace-Twin TE Slot | Shotgun-Bunch HB Str | Strong-Twins
I-Form-Normal | Shotgun-Normal | Weak-Normal

MIDDLE TENNESSEE
Blue Raiders

Conference: **Sun Belt**
Location: **Murfreesboro, TN**

REPORT CARD AND PRESTIGE

67	**73**	**69**
Overall	Offense	Defense

PRESTIGE RATINGS
Overall ★
Coach Fair
Academic Fair

2007 SEASON RECAP
- 5-7 overall record
- 4-3 conference record
- 4th in the Sun Belt

DEFENSIVE DEPTH CHART AND SCOUTING REPORT

Conservative 4-3 Defense
AI Playcall Tendency: 52% defend run, 48% defend pass

	FS	ROLB		MLB		LOLB	SS	
	68 #28	82 #29		77 #44		73 #55	74 #8	
	67 #20	73 #27		63 #54		73 #32	62 #33	
77 #7								78 #11

	CB	RE		DT	DT		LE		CB
	70 #26	88 #56		77 #95	83 #78		79 #98		76 #24
	68 #6	74 #49		76 #47	77 #90		74 #51		70 #29

■ IMPACT PLAYERS ■ LIKELY STARTERS

OFFENSIVE DEPTH CHART AND SCOUTING REPORT

Neutral Balanced Offense
AI Playcall Tendency: 50% run, 50% pass

K	WR	LT	LG	C	RG	RT	TE	WR	P
50 KPW	81 #13	78 #72	82 #76	71 #71	72 #75	71 #74	77 #82	82 #17	60 KPW
85 KAC	75 #83	66 #78	67 #50	66 #63	70 #62	67 #69	71 #16	77 #84	85 KAC
74 #39									78 #37

		FB		QB1	QB2		HB		
		71 #42		81 THP	80 THP		79 #2		
		72 #34		88 THA	86 THA		77 #21		
				85 #12	84 #9				

■ IMPACT PLAYERS ■ LIKELY STARTERS

TEAM OFFENSIVE PLAYBOOK

Ace-Big	I-Form-Twin TE	Shotgun-Spread Flex Wk
Ace-Slot	I-Form-Y-Trips	Shotgun-Trips
Ace-Twin TE	Shotgun-5WR Trey	Shotgun-Trips Over
Ace-Y-Trips	Shotgun-Ace Twins Wk	Shotgun-Y-Trips HB Wk
I-Form-Normal	Shotgun-Normal HB Wk	Strong-Normal
I-Form-Slot Flex	Shotgun-Split Slot	Strong-Y-Trips

MINNESOTA
Golden Gophers

Conference: **Big Ten**
Location: **Minneapolis, MN**

REPORT CARD AND PRESTIGE

77	**79**	**76**
Overall	Offense	Defense

PRESTIGE RATINGS
Overall ★ ★ ★
Coach Good
Academic Very Good

2007 SEASON RECAP
- 1-11 overall record
- 0-8 conference record
- 11th in Big Ten

DEFENSIVE DEPTH CHART AND SCOUTING REPORT

Aggressive 4-3 Defense
AI Playcall Tendency: 45% defend run, 55% defend pass

	FS	ROLB		MLB		LOLB	SS	
	82 #27	78 #28		85 #44		81 #56	79 #26	
	77 #23	76 #39		82 #6		76 #59	75 #25	
								84 #7

	CB	RE		DT	DT		LE		CB
	78 #29	83 #30		79 #99	82 #58		82 #93		77 #2
	71 #21	81 #91		69 #94	71 #51		81 #96		68 #20

■ IMPACT PLAYERS ■ LIKELY STARTERS

OFFENSIVE DEPTH CHART AND SCOUTING REPORT

Aggressive Spread Offense
AI Playcall Tendency: 48% run, 52% pass

K	WR	LT	LG	C	RG	RT	TE	WR	P
71 KPW	80 #81	79 #73	79 #74	80 #52	80 #53	74 #76	83 #82	85 #7	84 KPW
84 KAC	78 #6	70 #72	76 #66	70 #61	75 #75	66 #63	80 #86	79 #30	89 KAC
85 #36									87 #41

		FB		QB1	QB2		HB		
		74 #35		84 THP	80 THP		84 #22		
				90 THA	88 THA		80 #25		
				82 #8	84 #17				

■ IMPACT PLAYERS ■ LIKELY STARTERS

TEAM OFFENSIVE PLAYBOOK

Ace-Big	Shotgun-Normal HB Wk	Shotgun-Trips
Ace-Wing Trips	Shotgun-Normal Wing TE	Shotgun-Trips HB Wk
Shotgun-4WR	Shotgun-Normal Y-Slot	Shotgun-Trips TE
Shotgun-4WR Trio Str	Shotgun-Split Slot	Shotgun-Wing Trips
Shotgun-5WR Flex Trio	Shotgun-Spread HB Wk	Shotgun-Y-Trips
Shotgun-Bunch HB Str	Shotgun-Tight	Strong-Y-Trips

MISSISSIPPI STATE
Bulldogs

Conference: **SEC (West)**
Location: **Starkville, MS**

REPORT CARD AND PRESTIGE

74	75	78
Overall	Offense	Defense

PRESTIGE RATINGS
Overall ★★★
Coach   Good
Academic Good

2007 SEASON RECAP
- 8-5 overall record
- 4-4 conference record
- Won Liberty Bowl

DEFENSIVE DEPTH CHART AND SCOUTING REPORT

Aggressive 4-3 Defense
AI Playcall Tendency: 41% defend run, 59% defend pass

	FS / ROLB	MLB	LOLB / SS	
	93 #3 / 77 #10	79 #22	75 #41 / 81 #8	
78 #28	79 #31 / 70 #52	76 #36	75 #34 / 81 #1	82 #7
CB / RE		DT DT	LE / CB	
74 #18	79 #93	83 #95 / 84 #94	88 #39	78 #23
67 #21	77 #97	78 #56 / 79 #90	84 #92	70 #20

■ IMPACT PLAYERS ■ LIKELY STARTERS

OFFENSIVE DEPTH CHART AND SCOUTING REPORT

Conservative West Coast Offense
AI Playcall Tendency: 55% run, 45% pass

K	WR	LT	LG	C	RG	RT	TE	WR	P
69 KPW	78 #89	80 #77	83 #77	76 #58	82 #58	79 #79	70 #85	79 #87	85 KPW
85 KAC	74 #81	76 #76	80 #63	75 #66	75 #66	70 #73	69 #82	75 #15	90 KAC
84 #37									87 #43

FB	QB1	QB2	HB
85 #35	83 THP / 86 THA / 87 #13	76 THP / 85 THA / 80 #11	83 #24
77 #38			82 #29

■ IMPACT PLAYERS ■ LIKELY STARTERS

TEAM OFFENSIVE PLAYBOOK

- Ace-Big
- Ace-Bunch
- Ace-Slot Flex
- Ace-Twin TE Slot
- Ace-Y-Trips
- I-Form-Normal
- I-Form-Tight
- I-Form-Twin TE
- I-Form-Twins
- Shotgun-Normal Flex
- Shotgun-Split
- Shotgun-Split Slot
- Shotgun-Split Y-Flex
- Shotgun-Trips
- Shotgun-Wing Trips
- Shotgun-Y-Trips HB Wk
- Strong-Normal
- Weak-Twins

MISSOURI
Tigers

Conference: **Big 12 (North)**
Location: **Columbia, MO**

REPORT CARD AND PRESTIGE

94	96	92
Overall	Offense	Defense

PRESTIGE RATINGS
Overall ★★★★
Coach   Very Good
Academic Very Good

2007 SEASON RECAP
- 12-2 overall record
- 7-1 conference record
- Won Cotton Bowl

DEFENSIVE DEPTH CHART AND SCOUTING REPORT

Neutral 4-3 Defense
AI Playcall Tendency: 56% defend run, 44% defend pass

	FS / ROLB	MLB	LOLB / SS	
	96 #1 / 92 #12	89 #34	87 #5 / 86 #8	
81 #15	87 #4 / 70 #6	74 #33	81 #30 / 71 #36	84 #19
CB / RE		DT DT	LE / CB	
75 #22	94 #38	81 #96 / 86 #94	88 #48	80 #21
65 #31	85 #39	74 #78 / 80 #92	84 #47	74 #20

■ IMPACT PLAYERS ■ LIKELY STARTERS

OFFENSIVE DEPTH CHART AND SCOUTING REPORT

Aggressive Spread Offense
AI Playcall Tendency: 40% run, 60% pass

K	WR	LT	LG	C	RG	RT	TE	WR	P
81 KPW	86 #4	91 #68	87 #76	77 #62	87 #78	90 #61	95 #45	94 #9	65 KPW
91 KAC	82 #2	76 #72	72 #71	72 #67	77 #56	75 #75	77 #87	84 #84	86 KAC
86 #99									80 #36

FB	QB1	QB2	HB
78 #43	97 THP / 90 THA / 97 #10	85 THP / 92 THA / 97 #10	87 #1
			82 #26

■ IMPACT PLAYERS ■ LIKELY STARTERS

TEAM OFFENSIVE PLAYBOOK

- Ace-Big
- Pistol-Twin TE Slot
- Shotgun-5WR
- Shotgun-5WR Bunch
- Shotgun-5WR Trio
- Shotgun-5WR Trips
- Shotgun-Bunch HB Str
- Shotgun-Normal Wing TE
- Shotgun-Normal Y-Slot
- Shotgun-Split Slot
- Shotgun-Spread
- Shotgun-Spread HB Wk
- Shotgun-Trio HB Wk
- Shotgun-Trips
- Shotgun-Trips HB Wk
- Shotgun-Trips Open
- Shotgun-Trips Open Str
- Shotgun-Wing Trips

NAVY

Midshipmen
Conference: **Independent**
Location: **Annapolis, MD**

REPORT CARD AND PRESTIGE

72 Overall **77** Offense **71** Defense

PRESTIGE RATINGS
Overall ★★
Coach Fair
Academic Great

2007 SEASON RECAP
- 8-5 overall record
- Lost Poinsettia Bowl

DEFENSIVE DEPTH CHART AND SCOUTING REPORT

Conservative 3-4 Defense
AI Playcall Tendency: 52% defend run, 48% defend pass

	FS	ROLB	MLB	MLB	LOLB	SS	
	79 #17	76 #49	73 #44	75 #51	75 #5	78 #8	
	75 #25	72 #46	64 #52	67 #50	74 #34	69 #32	
78 #11							82 #18

CB	RE	DT	LE	CB
71 #15	80 #59	80 #99	85 #38	73 #1
64 #22	78 #97	69 #91	74 #77	68 #3

■ IMPACT PLAYERS   ■ LIKELY STARTERS

OFFENSIVE DEPTH CHART AND SCOUTING REPORT

Neutral Flexbone Offense
AI Playcall Tendency: 75% run, 25% pass

K	WR	LT	LG	C	RG	RT	TE	WR	P
52 KPW	75 #24	76 #60	82 #72	81 #68	78 #67	79 #75	76 #86	78 #89	60 KPW
74 KAC	68 #84	74 #59	74 #64	78 #53	78 #79	72 #65	70 #85	70 #85	84 KAC
80 #19									78 #35

FB	QB1	QB2	HB
93 #36	84 THP	71 THP	85 #26
75 #45	84 THA	84 THA	77 #29
	80 #10	76 #4	

■ IMPACT PLAYERS   ■ LIKELY STARTERS

TEAM OFFENSIVE PLAYBOOK

Flexbone-Normal	Flexbone-Wide	JumboT-Big
Flexbone-Slot	FullHouse-Normal Wide	Wishbone-Normal
Flexbone-Split	I-Form-3WR	Wishbone-Tight
Flexbone-Tight	I-Form-Normal	Wishbone-Wide
Flexbone-Trips	I-Form-Twin TE Wing	
Flexbone-Twins	I-Form-Twin WR	

NC (NORTH CAROLINA) STATE

Wolfpack
Conference: **ACC (Atlantic)**
Location: **Raleigh, NC**

REPORT CARD AND PRESTIGE

77 Overall **79** Offense **78** Defense

PRESTIGE RATINGS
Overall ★★★
Coach Very Good
Academic Very Good

2007 SEASON RECAP
- 5-7 overall record
- 3-5 conference record
- 6th in ACC Atlantic

DEFENSIVE DEPTH CHART AND SCOUTING REPORT

Neutral 4-3 Defense
AI Playcall Tendency: 45% defend run, 55% defend pass

	FS	ROLB	MLB	LOLB	SS	
	84 #14	80 #47	79 #44	84 #56	82 #4	
	80 #22	79 #34	75 #40	75 #46	76 #35	
74 #21						83 #30

CB	RE	DT	DT	LE	CB
72 #23	85 #96	81 #93	83 #49	89 #97	74 #20
65 #25	77 #11	79 #92	80 #98	77 #62	70 #33

■ IMPACT PLAYERS   ■ LIKELY STARTERS

OFFENSIVE DEPTH CHART AND SCOUTING REPORT

Neutral West Coast Offense
AI Playcall Tendency: 50% run, 50% pass

K	WR	LT	LG	C	RG	RT	TE	WR	P
66 KPW	79 #15	79 #70	78 #91	79 #74	86 #76	79 #60	82 #83	85 #80	76 KPW
82 KAC	77 #86	79 #73	77 #66	77 #78	73 #75	77 #50	82 #84	79 #82	87 KAC
84 #36									84 #26

FB	QB1	QB2	HB
70 #39	83 THP	82 THP	86 #29
64 #34	90 THA	91 THA	86 #24
	84 #7	85 #12	

■ IMPACT PLAYERS   ■ LIKELY STARTERS

TEAM OFFENSIVE PLAYBOOK

Ace-Big	Ace-Y-Trips	Shotgun-Normal HB Wk
Ace-Big Twins	I-Form-Normal	Shotgun-Split
Ace-Slot	I-Form-Tight	Shotgun-Spread Flex Wk
Ace-Trips	I-Form-Twin TE	Shotgun-Y-Trips
Ace-Twin TE	I-Form-Twins	Shotgun-Y-Trips HB Wk
Ace-Twin TE Slot	Shotgun-Normal	Strong-Normal

NEBRASKA
Cornhuskers
Conference: **Big 12 (North)**
Location: **Lincoln, NE**

REPORT CARD AND PRESTIGE

81	88	80
Overall	Offense	Defense

PRESTIGE RATINGS
Overall ★ ★ ★ ★ ★
Coach Very Good
Academic Very Good

2007 SEASON RECAP
- 5-7 overall record
- 2-6 conference record
- 5th in Big 12 North

DEFENSIVE DEPTH CHART AND SCOUTING REPORT

Aggressive 4-3 Defense
AI Playcall Tendency: 54% defend run, 46% defend pass

	80 #3	78 #6	81 #52		80 #53	85 #4	
	75 #17	76 #36	77 #45		79 #12	78 #28	83 #5
81 #14	FS	ROLB	MLB		LOLB	SS	
79 #26	86 #99	84 #93	86 #43		85 #98	80 #22	
68 #18	82 #88	78 #97	78 #56		77 #95	78 #21	
CB	RE	DT	DT		LE	CB	

■ IMPACT PLAYERS   ■ LIKELY STARTERS

OFFENSIVE DEPTH CHART AND SCOUTING REPORT

Aggressive West Coast Offense
AI Playcall Tendency: 50% run, 50% pass

K	WR	LT	LG	C	RG	RT	TE	WR	P
66 KPW	85 #17	92 #76	84 #62	78 #67	84 #70	78 #72	78 #89	86 #87	77 KPW
90 KAC	81 #4	82 #74	77 #65	74 #58	83 #73	75 #66	74 #3	82 #1	88 KAC
76 #20		FB	QB1	QB2			HB		84 #97
		84 #19	86 THP 89 THA 87 #12	78 THP 89 THA 87 #7			93 #5 / 86 #34		

■ IMPACT PLAYERS   ■ LIKELY STARTERS

TEAM OFFENSIVE PLAYBOOK

Ace-Big Twins	I-Form-Normal	Shotgun-Normal Flex Wk
Ace-Bunch	I-Form-Tight	Shotgun-Split Y-Flex
Ace-Slot Flex	I-Form-Twin TE	Shotgun-Y-Trips HB Wk
Ace-Twin TE	I-Form-Twins	Strong-Normal
Ace-Twin TE Slot	Shotgun-4WR Trey Str	Strong-Tight
Ace-Y-Trips	Shotgun-Double Flex	Weak-Twins

NEVADA
Wolf Pack
Conference: **WAC**
Location: **Reno, NV**

REPORT CARD AND PRESTIGE

69	77	69
Overall	Offense	Defense

PRESTIGE RATINGS
Overall ★ ★
Coach Good
Academic Good

2007 SEASON RECAP
- 6-7 overall record
- 4-4 conference record
- Lost New Mexico Bowl

DEFENSIVE DEPTH CHART AND SCOUTING REPORT

Neutral 4-3 Defense
AI Playcall Tendency: 55% defend run, 45% defend pass

	83 #49	79 #54	81 #30		71 #33	79 #17	
	78 #3	66 #55	74 #31		69 #43	77 #9	75 #21
73 #32	FS	ROLB	MLB		LOLB	SS	
73 #29	78 #90	75 #66	79 #95		79 #48	73 #38	
63 #42	78 #94	61 #97	72 #96		77 #99	70 #19	
CB	RE	DT	DT		LE	CB	

■ IMPACT PLAYERS   ■ LIKELY STARTERS

OFFENSIVE DEPTH CHART AND SCOUTING REPORT

Neutral Spread Offense
AI Playcall Tendency: 51% run, 49% pass

K	WR	LT	LG	C	RG	RT	TE	WR	P
67 KPW	84 #89	80 #50	80 #65	79 #61	78 #60	74 #73	69 #85	84 #4	64 KPW
76 KAC	76 #2	78 #76	77 #79	75 #63	77 #59	72 #64	66 #98	76 #12	84 KAC
90 #13		FB	QB1	QB2			HB		82 #19
		73 #34	84 THP 89 THA 88 #10	79 THP 90 THA 87 #8			82 #7 / 79 #24		

■ IMPACT PLAYERS   ■ LIKELY STARTERS

TEAM OFFENSIVE PLAYBOOK

Ace-Big	Pistol-Jumbo Wing	Pistol-Twin TE Slot
Pistol-4WR Trips	Pistol-Slot	Pistol-Y-Trips
Pistol-Ace	Pistol-Slot Flex	Shotgun-Ace Twins Wk
Pistol-Ace Twins	Pistol-Trio	Shotgun-Normal Flex
Pistol-Bunch	Pistol-Trips	Shotgun-Trips TE
Pistol-H Twins	Pistol-Twin TE	Shotgun-Y-Trips

NEW MEXICO
Lobos

Conference: **Mountain West**
Location: **Albuquerque, NM**

REPORT CARD AND PRESTIGE

67	75	66
Overall	Offense	Defense

PRESTIGE RATINGS
Overall ★★
Coach Good
Academic Good

2007 SEASON RECAP
- 9-4 overall record
- 5-3 conference record
- Won New Mexico Bowl

DEFENSIVE DEPTH CHART AND SCOUTING REPORT

Aggressive 3-3-5 Defense
AI Playcall Tendency: 54% defend run, 46% defend pass

■ IMPACT PLAYERS   ■ LIKELY STARTERS

OFFENSIVE DEPTH CHART AND SCOUTING REPORT

Aggressive Balanced Offense
AI Playcall Tendency: 49% run, 51% pass

■ IMPACT PLAYERS   ■ LIKELY STARTERS

TEAM OFFENSIVE PLAYBOOK

Ace-Big	Ace-Twin TE	Shotgun-Normal Flex
Ace-Bunch	Ace-Twin TE Slot	Shotgun-Split Y-Flex
Ace-Slot	Ace-Y-Trips	Shotgun-Trio HB Wk
Ace-Slot Flex	Shotgun-4WR Trio Str	Shotgun-Y-Trips
Ace-Spread Flex	Shotgun-5WR Flex Trio	Strong-H Pro
Ace-Trips	Shotgun-Double Flex	Weak-H Pro

NEW MEXICO STATE
Aggies

Conference: **WAC**
Location: **Las Cruces, NM**

REPORT CARD AND PRESTIGE

74	83	69
Overall	Offense	Defense

PRESTIGE RATINGS
Overall ★
Coach Good
Academic Fair

2007 SEASON RECAP
- 4-9 overall record
- 1-7 conference record
- 8th in the WAC

DEFENSIVE DEPTH CHART AND SCOUTING REPORT

Aggressive 3-3-5 Defense
AI Playcall Tendency: 53% defend run, 47% defend pass

■ IMPACT PLAYERS   ■ LIKELY STARTERS

OFFENSIVE DEPTH CHART AND SCOUTING REPORT

Aggressive Spread Offense
AI Playcall Tendency: 25% run, 75% pass

■ IMPACT PLAYERS   ■ LIKELY STARTERS

TEAM OFFENSIVE PLAYBOOK

Ace-Big	Shotgun-Empty Trey	Shotgun-Spread Flex
Ace-Slot	Shotgun-Normal Flex Wk	Shotgun-Spread Flex Wk
Ace-Trips	Shotgun-Split	Shotgun-Trips HB Wk
Ace-Y-Trips	Shotgun-Split Slot	Shotgun-Trips TE
Shotgun-5WR Trey	Shotgun-Split Twins	Shotgun-Y-Trips HB Wk
Shotgun-Bunch HB Str	Shotgun-Split Y-Flex	Strong-Normal

NORTH CAROLINA
Tar Heels

Conference: **ACC (Coastal)**
Location: **Chapel Hill, NC**

REPORT CARD AND PRESTIGE

79 79 80
Overall　Offense　Defense

PRESTIGE RATINGS
Overall　★ ★ ★
Coach　Great
Academic　Elite

2007 SEASON RECAP
- 4-8 overall record
- 3-5 conference record
- 4th in ACC Coastal

DEFENSIVE DEPTH CHART AND SCOUTING REPORT

Aggressive 4-3 Defense
AI Playcall Tendency: 43% defend run, 57% defend pass

	85 #27 / 84 #44	81 #41	83 #54 / 86 #31		
	83 #5 / 78 #53	75 #52	82 #51 / 76 #20		
80 #16	FS / ROLB	MLB	LOLB / SS		82 #42
77 #24	81 #40	82 #97 / 83 #9	84 #92		77 #23
74 #34	79 #94	76 #58 / 79 #96	78 #91		76 #26
CB	RE	DT / DT	LE		CB

■ IMPACT PLAYERS　■ LIKELY STARTERS

OFFENSIVE DEPTH CHART AND SCOUTING REPORT

Neutral Balanced Offense
AI Playcall Tendency: 51% run, 49% pass

WR	LT	LG	C	RG	RT	TE	WR	P
85 #1	80 #72	77 #76	81 #73	83 #79	80 #75	78 #17	86 #88	75 KPW
80 #3	77 #60	74 #65	77 #69	72 #77	71 #66	75 #86	85 #87	86 KAC
								84 #19

FB: 80 #4 / 69 #45
QB1: 83 THP / 90 THA / 86 #13
QB2: 81 THP / 88 THA / 82 #11
HB: 80 #26 / 80 #32

■ IMPACT PLAYERS　■ LIKELY STARTERS

TEAM OFFENSIVE PLAYBOOK

Ace-Big	Ace-Twin TE	Shotgun-Wing Trips
Ace-Big Twins	Ace-Twin TE Slot	Shotgun-Y-Trips HB Wk
Ace-Big Wing	Ace-Y-Trips	Strong-Normal
Ace-Bunch	I-Form-Twins	Strong-Twins
Ace-Slot	Shotgun-Normal	Weak-Normal
Ace-Trips	Shotgun-Split Y-Flex	Weak-Twins

NORTH TEXAS
Mean Green

Conference: **Sun Belt**
Location: **Denton, TX**

REPORT CARD AND PRESTIGE

69 75 69
Overall　Offense　Defense

PRESTIGE RATINGS
Overall　★ ★
Coach　Fair
Academic　Good

2007 SEASON RECAP
- 2-10 overall record
- 1-6 conference record
- 7th in the Sun Belt

DEFENSIVE DEPTH CHART AND SCOUTING REPORT

Conservative 4-3 Defense
AI Playcall Tendency: 41% defend run, 59% defend pass

	78 #16 / 78 #39	73 #44	79 #42 / 74 #13		
	76 #8 / 75 #59	63 #36	76 #40 / 63 #38		
79 #31	FS / ROLB	MLB	LOLB / SS		83 #22
74 #35	80 #48	73 #61 / 79 #9			75 #37
70 #23	79 #94	71 #95 / 65 #99			72 #21
CB	RE	DT / DT			CB

■ IMPACT PLAYERS　■ LIKELY STARTERS

OFFENSIVE DEPTH CHART AND SCOUTING REPORT

Neutral Spread Offense
AI Playcall Tendency: 45% run, 55% pass

K	WR	LT	LG	C	RG	RT	TE	WR	P
70 KPW	74 #82	73 #71	78 #57	80 #68	73 #64	80 #60	81 #92	91 #87	63 KPW
84 KAC	73 #80	71 #69	77 #67	72 #73	72 #74	70 #66	73 #83	74 #9	82 KAC
85 #49									82 #25

FB: 77 #30
QB1: 83 THP / 86 THA / 90 #15
QB2: 75 THP / 84 THA / 81 #7
HB: 77 #32 / 74 #26

■ IMPACT PLAYERS　■ LIKELY STARTERS

TEAM OFFENSIVE PLAYBOOK

Ace-Big	Shotgun-Ace Wing	Shotgun-Trips
Shotgun-5WR	Shotgun-Ace Wing Wk	Shotgun-Trips HB Wk
Shotgun-5WR Trio	Shotgun-Bunch HB Str	Shotgun-Trips Open
Shotgun-5WR Trips	Shotgun-Normal Y-Slot	Shotgun-Trips Open Str
Shotgun-Ace Twins	Shotgun-Spread	Shotgun-Y-Trips
Shotgun-Ace Twins Wk	Shotgun-Spread HB Wk	Shotgun-Y-Trips HB Wk

NORTHERN ILLINOIS
Huskies

Conference: **MAC (West)**
Location: **DeKalb, IL**

REPORT CARD AND PRESTIGE

77	79	78
Overall	Offense	Defense

PRESTIGE RATINGS
Overall ★★
Coach Fair
Academic Good

2007 SEASON RECAP
- 2-10 overall record
- 1-6 conference record
- 6th in the MAC West

DEFENSIVE DEPTH CHART AND SCOUTING REPORT

Neutral 4-3 Defense
AI Playcall Tendency: 55% defend run, 45% defend pass

	FS	ROLB		MLB		LOLB	SS	
	79 #24	81 #26		88 #53		86 #9	82 #37	
75 #36	75 #32	80 #42		73 #44		81 #57	71 #27	80 #2
71 #6	89 #51		74 #58	78 #69		83 #99		72 #1
69 #33	75 #92		69 #90	74 #98		80 #56		70 #30
CB	RE		DT	DT		LE		CB

■ IMPACT PLAYERS   ■ LIKELY STARTERS

OFFENSIVE DEPTH CHART AND SCOUTING REPORT

Conservative Balanced Offense
AI Playcall Tendency: 50% run, 50% pass

K	WR	LT	LG	C	RG	RT	TE	WR	P
51 KPW	83 #7	78 #66	79 #59	84 #50	81 #65	88 #60	72 #83	84 #85	73 KPW
76 KAC	77 #17	73 #71	75 #77	74 #74	78 #78	74 #64	68 #88	81 #5	68 KAC
80 #11									82 #18

	FB	QB1	QB2		HB	
	80 #91	82 THP 90 THA 85 #19	76 THP 88 THA 84 #1		85 #20 / 84 #21	

■ IMPACT PLAYERS   ■ LIKELY STARTERS

TEAM OFFENSIVE PLAYBOOK

Ace-Y-Trips	I-Form-Y-Trips	Shotgun-Trips HB Wk
I-Form-Normal	Pistol-Slot Flex	Shotgun-Trips Over
I-Form-Slot Flex	Shotgun-Ace	Shotgun-Y-Trips HB Wk
I-Form-Tight	Shotgun-Ace Twins Wk	Strong-Normal
I-Form-Twin TE	Shotgun-Split	Strong-Twin TE
I-Form-Twins	Shotgun-Trips	Strong-Y-Trips

NORTHWESTERN
Wildcats

Conference: **Big Ten**
Location: **Evanston, IL**

REPORT CARD AND PRESTIGE

81	86	82
Overall	Offense	Defense

PRESTIGE RATINGS
Overall ★★★
Coach Good
Academic Elite

2007 SEASON RECAP
- 6-6 overall record
- 3-5 conference record
- 10th in Big Ten

DEFENSIVE DEPTH CHART AND SCOUTING REPORT

Conservative 4-3 Defense
AI Playcall Tendency: 56% defend run, 44% defend pass

	FS	ROLB		MLB		LOLB	SS	
	85 #4	84 #36		81 #31		82 #46	82 #17	
79 #16	74 #32	73 #41		71 #50		77 #57	80 #37	85 #24
75 #28	86 #95		84 #79	85 #70		85 #99		75 #26
60 #22	68 #56		79 #62	82 #67		73 #94		68 #21
CB	RE		DT	DT		LE		CB

■ IMPACT PLAYERS   ■ LIKELY STARTERS

OFFENSIVE DEPTH CHART AND SCOUTING REPORT

Conservative Spread Offense
AI Playcall Tendency: 53% run, 47% pass

K	WR	LT	LG	C	RG	RT	TE	WR	P
69 KPW	86 #10	77 #68	77 #60	79 #52	81 #76	84 #78	75 #42	86 #9	70 KPW
86 KAC	80 #5	77 #63	74 #54	68 #93	79 #59	70 #73	72 #82	83 #8	82 KAC
82 #96									88 #1

	FB	QB1	QB2		HB	
	79 #44 / 68 #40	85 THP 88 THA 87 #18	77 THP 91 THA 80 #13		92 #19 / 83 #29	

■ IMPACT PLAYERS   ■ LIKELY STARTERS

TEAM OFFENSIVE PLAYBOOK

Ace-Spread	Shotgun-Normal HB Wk	Shotgun-Trips Open
Ace-Twin TE Slot	Shotgun-Normal Y-Slot	Shotgun-Trips Open Str
Ace-Y-Trips	Shotgun-Split Slot	Shotgun-Trips Over
I-Form-Tight	Shotgun-Spread HB Wk	Shotgun-Wing Trips
Shotgun-5WR	Shotgun-Trips	Shotgun-Wing Trips Wk
Shotgun-Normal	Shotgun-Trips HB Wk	Shotgun-Y-Trips

NOTRE DAME
Fighting Irish
Conference: **Independent**
Location: **Notre Dame, IN**

OHIO
Bobcats
Conference: **MAC (East)**
Location: **Athens, OH**

REPORT CARD AND PRESTIGE

81	83	82
Overall	Offense	Defense

PRESTIGE RATINGS
Overall ★★★★★★
Coach Elite
Academic Elite

2007 SEASON RECAP
- 3-9 overall record
- Snapped 43 game winning streak against Navy

REPORT CARD AND PRESTIGE

67	66	73
Overall	Offense	Defense

PRESTIGE RATINGS
Overall ★★
Coach Great
Academic Great

2007 SEASON RECAP
- 6-6 overall record
- 4-4 conference record
- 4th in the MAC East

DEFENSIVE DEPTH CHART AND SCOUTING REPORT

Aggressive 3-4 Defense
AI Playcall Tendency: 38% defend run, 62% defend pass

	FS	ROLB	MLB	MLB	LOLB	SS	
	87 #27	80 #58	81 #49	89 #40	80 #56	80 #28	
	78 #29	77 #42	79 #50	80 #41	80 #57	79 #31	

	CB	RE	DT	LE	CB
	82 #2	86 #94	84 #95	86 #90	84 #20
	79 #4	76 #91	78 #54	83 #53	79 #8

DEFENSIVE DEPTH CHART AND SCOUTING REPORT

Neutral 4-3 Defense
AI Playcall Tendency: 52% defend run, 48% defend pass

	FS	ROLB	MLB	LOLB	SS	
	80 #23	81 #32	72 #47	81 #35	82 #34	
77 #9	78 #42	79 #48	68 #52	77 #19	78 #6	80 #24

	CB	RE	DT	DT	LE	CB
	71 #4	81 #54	76 #96	79 #95	86 #90	71 #12
	69 #22	69 #92	65 #53	70 #62	81 #97	69 #30

■ IMPACT PLAYERS   ■ LIKELY STARTERS

OFFENSIVE DEPTH CHART AND SCOUTING REPORT

Conservative Balanced Offense
AI Playcall Tendency: 50% run, 50% pass

K	WR	LT	LG	C	RG	RT	TE	WR	P
67 KPW	81 #18	87 #72	81 #67	85 #51	85 #55	94 #74	82 #88	81 #23	68 KPW
84 KAC	80 #11	75 #70	81 #77	77 #63	79 #59	77 #75	80 #83	80 #82	88 KAC
84 #14									78 #43

	FB	QB1	QB2		HB	
	85 #44	85 THP #92 THA #87 #7	82 THP #89 THA #88 #13		86 #34	
	80 #32				84 #5	

OFFENSIVE DEPTH CHART AND SCOUTING REPORT

Conservative Balanced Offense
AI Playcall Tendency: 55% run, 45% pass

K	WR	LT	LG	C	RG	RT	TE	WR	P
43 KPW	72 #11	76 #74	78 #76	81 #66	75 #61	73 #73	75 #84	78 #23	74 KPW
74 KAC	68 #80	75 #68	67 #63	77 #58	72 #57	73 #60	72 #81	71 #7	86 KAC
78 #17									84 #43

	FB	QB1	QB2		HB	
	74 #39	78 THP #89 THA #84 #8	72 THP #86 THA #82 #3		77 #21	
	72 #40				76 #2	

■ IMPACT PLAYERS   ■ LIKELY STARTERS

■ IMPACT PLAYERS   ■ LIKELY STARTERS

TEAM OFFENSIVE PLAYBOOK

Ace-Big Twins	Ace-Y-Trips	Shotgun-Split Slot
Ace-Jumbo	I-Form-Normal	Shotgun-Spread HB Wk
Ace-Slot	I-Form-Tight	Shotgun-Trips HB Wk
Ace-Spread	I-Form-Twin TE	Shotgun-Y-Trips HB Wk
Ace-Twin TE	I-Form-Twins	Split-Pro
Ace-Twin TE Slot	Shotgun-Normal	Weak-Normal

TEAM OFFENSIVE PLAYBOOK

Ace-Big	I-Form-Tight	Shotgun-Normal Flex
Ace-Big Twins	I-Form-Twin TE	Shotgun-Normal Flex Wk
Ace-Slot Flex	I-Form-Twins	Shotgun-Spread
Ace-Twin TE Slot	I-Form-Y-Trips	Shotgun-Trips Over
Ace-Y-Trips	Shotgun-4WR Trio	Shotgun-Y-Trips HB Wk
I-Form-Normal	Shotgun-Ace	Strong-Normal

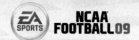

OHIO STATE
Buckeyes
Conference: **Big Ten**
Location: **Columbus, OH**

OKLAHOMA
Sooners
Conference: **Big 12 (South)**
Location: **Norman, OK**

REPORT CARD AND PRESTIGE

99	99	99
Overall	Offense	Defense

PRESTIGE RATINGS
Overall ★★★★★★
Coach Elite
Academic Excellent

2007 SEASON RECAP
- 11-2 overall record
- 7-1 conference record
- 2nd Straight BCS

REPORT CARD AND PRESTIGE

96	99	94
Overall	Offense	Defense

PRESTIGE RATINGS
Overall ★★★★★★
Coach Elite
Academic Very Good

2007 SEASON RECAP
- 11-3 overall record
- 6-2 conference record
- Lost Fiesta Bowl

DEFENSIVE DEPTH CHART AND SCOUTING REPORT

Aggressive 4-3 Defense
AI Playcall Tendency: 58% defend run, 42% defend pass

FS	ROLB	MLB	LOLB	SS	
90 #21	96 #1	99 #33	88 #51	86 #4	
91 #20	83 #23	80 #55	84 #38	81 #26	83 #3	96 #2
CB	RE	DT	DT	LE	CB
83 #13	86 #97	87 #92	88 #72	95 #87	85 #5
79 #11	84 #9	85 #84	87 #93	85 #90	80 #29

■ IMPACT PLAYERS   ■ LIKELY STARTERS

DEFENSIVE DEPTH CHART AND SCOUTING REPORT

Aggressive 4-3 Defense
AI Playcall Tendency: 41% defend run, 59% defend pass

FS	ROLB	MLB	LOLB	SS	
96 #5	85 #28	86 #8	88 #22	90 #11	
84 #15	84 #6	77 #42	71 #30	86 #10	84 #7	86 #2
CB	RE	DT	DT	LE	CB
78 #3	88 #98	88 #97	94 #96	94 #33	79 #21
74 #26	84 #44	82 #89	86 #93	88 #95	74 #32

■ IMPACT PLAYERS   ■ LIKELY STARTERS

OFFENSIVE DEPTH CHART AND SCOUTING REPORT

Neutral Balanced Offense
AI Playcall Tendency: 55% run, 45% pass

K	WR	LT	LG	C	RG	RT	TE	WR	P
78 KPW	88 #9	96 #75	95 #71	92 #64	85 #63	83 #70	90 #80	92 #80	87 KPW
87 KAC	81 #83	83 #74	88 #74		83 #77	82 #50	86 #4	86 #4	89 KAC
90 #20		FB		QB1	QB2		HB		89 #15
		81 #43		89 THP	85 THP		97 #28		
				94 THA	89 THA		88 #3		
				90 #17	86 #7				

■ IMPACT PLAYERS   ■ LIKELY STARTERS

OFFENSIVE DEPTH CHART AND SCOUTING REPORT

Aggressive Balanced Offense
AI Playcall Tendency: 50% run, 50% pass

K	WR	LT	LG	C	RG	RT	TE	WR	P
73 KPW	87 #1	94 #79	97 #72	93 #50	86 #73	88 #76	92 #18	91 #9	71 KPW
90 KAC	86 #84	80 #75	81 #63	79 #54	82 #74	79 #71	82 #83	87 #80	88 KAC
84 #95		FB		QB1	QB2		HB		80 #13
		83 #34		94 THP	83 THP		91 #7		
				93 THA	90 THA		89 #29		
				95 #14	87 #15				

■ IMPACT PLAYERS   ■ LIKELY STARTERS

TEAM OFFENSIVE PLAYBOOK

Ace-Big Twins	Ace-Y-Trips	I-Form-Y-Trips
Ace-Bunch	I-Form-Normal	Shotgun-4WR Trio Str
Ace-Jumbo	I-Form-Slot Flex	Shotgun-5WR Flex Trio
Ace-Slot	I-Form-Tight	Shotgun-Normal
Ace-Twin TE	I-Form-Twin TE	Shotgun-Split Slot
Ace-Twin TE Slot	I-Form-Twins	Shotgun-Y-Trips HB Wk

TEAM OFFENSIVE PLAYBOOK

Ace-Bunch	I-Form-Normal	Shotgun-Normal HB Wk
Ace-Slot	I-Form-Slot Flex	Shotgun-Spread HB Wk
Ace-Spread	I-Form-Tight	Shotgun-Trips
Ace-Twin TE	I-Form-Twin TE	Shotgun-Trips Over
Ace-Twin TE Slot	I-Form-Twins	Shotgun-Wing Trips Wk
Ace-Y-Trips	Shotgun-Normal	Shotgun-Y-Trips

OKLAHOMA STATE
Cowboys

Conference: **Big 12 (South)**
Location: **Stillwater, OK**

REPORT CARD AND PRESTIGE

79 Overall   **83** Offense   **80** Defense

PRESTIGE RATINGS
Overall ★★★
Coach Good
Academic Good

2007 SEASON RECAP
- 7-6 overall record
- 4-4 conference record
- Won Insight Bowl

DEFENSIVE DEPTH CHART AND SCOUTING REPORT

Aggressive 4-3 Defense
AI Playcall Tendency: 33% defend run, 67% defend pass

83 #6 / 77 #26		79 #4		81 #41 / 83 #20
78 #25 / 67 #58 (FS/ROLB)		74 #42 (MLB)		79 #54 / 76 #31 (LOLB/SS)	86 #17
83 #16	83 #91	81 #92 / 85 #96		85 #98	79 #23
78 #11	78 #97	76 #95 / 79 #90		73 #99	77 #7
74 #28 (CB)	(RE)	(DT) (DT)		(LE)	(CB)

■ IMPACT PLAYERS   ■ LIKELY STARTERS

OFFENSIVE DEPTH CHART AND SCOUTING REPORT

Neutral Spread Offense
AI Playcall Tendency: 55% run, 45% pass

K	WR	LT	LG	C	RG	RT	TE	WR	P
76 KPW	79 #83	89 #76	86 #54	87 #63	84 #65	85 #60	93 #87	81 #9	94 KPW
89 KAC	75 #84	82 #78	73 #67	71 #74	75 #52	78 #71	73 #80	79 #1	93 KAC
86 #21									91 #18

FB	QB1	QB2	HB
69 #48	87 THP / 88 THA / 85 #11	79 THP / 89 THA / 84 #3	85 #5 / 84 #2

■ IMPACT PLAYERS   ■ LIKELY STARTERS

TEAM OFFENSIVE PLAYBOOK

Ace-Big	I-Form-Twins	Shotgun-Split Twins
Ace-Big Twins	Shotgun-4WR Trio	Shotgun-Spread Flex Wk
Ace-Bunch	Shotgun-4WR Trio Str	Shotgun-Trips TE
Ace-Y-Trips	Shotgun-Ace Twins Wk	Shotgun-Y-Trips
I-Form-Normal	Shotgun-Normal	Shotgun-Y-Trips HB Wk
I-Form-Tight	Shotgun-Split Slot	Strong-Normal

OLE MISS
Rebels

Conference: **SEC (West)**
Location: **Oxford, MS**

REPORT CARD AND PRESTIGE

84 Overall   **86** Offense   **87** Defense

PRESTIGE RATINGS
Overall ★★★
Coach Very Good
Academic Good

2007 SEASON RECAP
- 3-9 overall record
- 0-8 conference record
- 6th in the SEC West

DEFENSIVE DEPTH CHART AND SCOUTING REPORT

Conservative 4-3 Defense
AI Playcall Tendency: 60% defend run, 40% defend pass

84 #1 / 85 #45		82 #47		83 #11 / 88 #13
78 #20 / 85 #42 (FS/ROLB)		77 #41 (MLB)		80 #95 / 66 #17 (LOLB/SS)	79 #18
79 #5	94 #86	86 #98		95 #92	78 #12
76 #24	83 #40	82 #99 / 72 #54		74 #97	75 #22
75 #21 (CB)	(RE)	(DT) (DT)		(LE)	(CB)

■ IMPACT PLAYERS   ■ LIKELY STARTERS

OFFENSIVE DEPTH CHART AND SCOUTING REPORT

Conservative Balanced Offense
AI Playcall Tendency: 53% run, 47% pass

K	WR	LT	LG	C	RG	RT	TE	WR	P
83 KPW	86 #2	97 #74	79 #75	75 #63	88 #77	80 #79	80 #78	87 #3	75 KPW
92 KAC	82 #65	81 #71	79 #67	74 #76	71 #50	77 #82	72	84 #8	87 KAC
85 #93									84 #36

FB	QB1	QB2	HB
85 #44 / 70 #32	84 THP / 93 THA / 86 #4	78 THP / 91 THA / 84 #17	86 #25 / 82 #33

■ IMPACT PLAYERS   ■ LIKELY STARTERS

TEAM OFFENSIVE PLAYBOOK

Ace-Big	I-Form-Normal	Shotgun-Split Slot
Ace-Big Twins	I-Form-Slot Flex	Shotgun-Spread Flex
Ace-Big Wing	I-Form-Twin TE	Shotgun-Wildcat
Ace-Slot	I-Form-Twins	Shotgun-Wing Trips Wk
Ace-Twin TE Slot	Shotgun-Normal HB Wk	Shotgun-Y-Trips HB Wk
Ace-Y-Trips	Shotgun-Split	Strong-H Pro

OREGON
Ducks

Conference: **PAC-10**
Location: **Eugene, OR**

REPORT CARD AND PRESTIGE

81 Overall **81** Offense **82** Defense

PRESTIGE RATINGS
Overall ★★★★
Coach Great
Academic Very Good

2007 SEASON RECAP
- 9-4 overall record
- 5-4 conference record
- Won Sun Bowl

DEFENSIVE DEPTH CHART AND SCOUTING REPORT

Aggressive 4-3 Defense
AI Playcall Tendency: 42% defend run, 58% defend pass

79 #27	82 #25	83 #40		90 #13	90 #15	
79 #44	81 #35	73 #55		76 #26	62 #29	86 #6
81 #32	FS ROLB	MLB		LOLB SS		
76 #17	80 #43	82 #97	86 #56	83 #49		76 #1
73 #18	79 #58	78 #95	81 #91	78 #39		74 #2
CB	RE	DT	DT	LE		CB

■ IMPACT PLAYERS ■ LIKELY STARTERS

OFFENSIVE DEPTH CHART AND SCOUTING REPORT

Aggressive Spread Offense
AI Playcall Tendency: 50% run, 50% pass

K	WR	LT	LG	C	RG	RT	TE	WR	P
82 KPW	85 #6	91 #57	82 #51	95 #60	84 #63	85 #78	86 #83	90 #4	69 KPW
91 KAC	80 #23	75 #73	82 #69	77 #71	70 #76	76 #74	78 #81	81 #89	89 KAC
85 #85		FB		QB1	QB2		HB		80 #26
		66 #46		76 THP	75 THP		84 #44		
				89 THA	89 THA		83 #24		
				86 #12	78 #9				

■ IMPACT PLAYERS ■ LIKELY STARTERS

TEAM OFFENSIVE PLAYBOOK

Pistol-Y-Trips	Shotgun-Normal Wing TE	Shotgun-Trio HB Wk
Shotgun-4WR Trio	Shotgun-Split Slot	Shotgun-Wing Trio Wk
Shotgun-4WR Trio Str	Shotgun-Spread	Shotgun-Wing Trips
Shotgun-5WR Trio	Shotgun-Spread Flex	Shotgun-Wing Trips Wk
Shotgun-Ace	Shotgun-Spread Flex Wk	Shotgun-Y-Trips
Shotgun-Normal	Shotgun-Spread HB Wk	Shotgun-Y-Trips HB Wk

OREGON STATE
Beavers

Conference: **PAC-10**
Location: **Norman, OK**

REPORT CARD AND PRESTIGE

77 Overall **75** Offense **80** Defense

PRESTIGE RATINGS
Overall ★★★★
Coach Very Good
Academic Good

2007 SEASON RECAP
- 9-4 overall record
- 6-3 conference record
- Won Emerald Bowl

DEFENSIVE DEPTH CHART AND SCOUTING REPORT

Neutral 4-3 Defense
AI Playcall Tendency: 54% defend run, 46% defend pass

84 #9	84 #12	79 #41		82 #1	84 #23	
74 #4	78 #59	72 #33		77 #6	81 #44	84 #26
83 #36	FS ROLB	MLB		LOLB SS		
	82 #90	79 #60	81 #99	85 #91		78 #21
76 #2	79 #58	73 #92	77 #97	81 #74		61 #17
CB	RE	DT	DT	LE		CB

■ IMPACT PLAYERS ■ LIKELY STARTERS

OFFENSIVE DEPTH CHART AND SCOUTING REPORT

Neutral Balanced Offense
AI Playcall Tendency: 51% run, 49% pass

K	WR	LT	LG	C	RG	RT	TE	WR	P
61 KPW	79 #7	84 #76	93 #62	79 #60	78 #73	78 #66	79 #81	80 #2	70 KPW
78 KAC	76 #67	74 #61	79 #51	79 #65	78 #54	76 #88	76 #88	78 #15	86 KAC
84 #27		FB		QB1	QB2		HB		82 #18
		76 #24		85 THP	78 THP		78 #28		
				94 THA	60 THA		77 #34		
				88 #5	86 #3				

■ IMPACT PLAYERS ■ LIKELY STARTERS

TEAM OFFENSIVE PLAYBOOK

Ace-Big	Ace-Trey Open	Shotgun-Normal
Ace-Big Twins	Ace-Trips	Shotgun-Trio HB Wk
Ace-Big Wing	Ace-Twin TE	Shotgun-Wing Trio Wk
Ace-Bunch	Ace-Twin TE Slot	Shotgun-Wing Trips Wk
Ace-Jumbo	Ace-Wing Trips	Shotgun-Y-Trips HB Wk
Ace-Slot	Ace-Y-Trips	Weak-Normal

PENN STATE
Nittany Lions
Conference: **Big Ten**
Location: **University Park, PA**

REPORT CARD AND PRESTIGE

91 Overall **88** Offense **94** Defense

PRESTIGE RATINGS
Overall ★★★★★
Coach Elite
Academic Elite

2007 SEASON RECAP
- 9-4 overall record
- 4-4 conference record
- Won Alamo Bowl

DEFENSIVE DEPTH CHART AND SCOUTING REPORT

Conservative 4-3 Defense
AI Playcall Tendency: 59% defend run, 41% defend pass

FS	ROLB	MLB	LOLB	SS
90 #11 / 90 #46		84 #5		96 #45 / 87 #7
82 #34 / 82 #34		81 #58		78 #43 / 79 #26

CB	RE	DT	DT	LE	CB
86 #10	90 #48	85 #85	85 #91	94 #47	90 #1
75 #20	86 #59	78 #97	79 #55	86 #57	76 #6

■ IMPACT PLAYERS   ■ LIKELY STARTERS

OFFENSIVE DEPTH CHART AND SCOUTING REPORT

Conservative Balanced Offense
AI Playcall Tendency: 52% run, 48% pass

K	WR	LT	LG	C	RG	RT	TE	WR	P
83 KPW	89 #3	85 #76	87 #64	92 #57	82 #50	84 #73	83 #82	92 #2	71 KPW
85 KAC	83 #9	77 #75	77 #77	74 #62	81 #65	81 #79	76 #41	84 #24	84 KAC
91 #23									84 #41

FB	QB1	QB2	HB
78 #33	85 THP / 92 THA / 85 #17	81 THP / 90 THA / 85 #7	84 #22 / 78 #25

■ IMPACT PLAYERS   ■ LIKELY STARTERS

TEAM OFFENSIVE PLAYBOOK

Ace-Bunch	I-Form-Slot Flex	Shotgun-Split
Ace-Slot	I-Form-Tight	Shotgun-Split Y-Flex
Ace-Trey Open	I-Form-Twins	Shotgun-Spread
Ace-Twin TE Slot	Shotgun-4WR Trey Str	Shotgun-Y-Trips
Ace-Y-Trips	Shotgun-Empty Trey	Strong-H Pro
I-Form-Normal	Shotgun-Normal HB Wk	Weak-H Twins

PITTSBURGH
Panthers
Conference: **Big East**
Location: **Pittsburgh, PA**

REPORT CARD AND PRESTIGE

79 Overall **88** Offense **76** Defense

PRESTIGE RATINGS
Overall ★★★★
Coach Very Good
Academic Excellent

2007 SEASON RECAP
- 5-7 overall record
- 3-4 conference record
- 7th in Big East

DEFENSIVE DEPTH CHART AND SCOUTING REPORT

Aggressive 4-3 Defense
AI Playcall Tendency: 41% defend run, 59% defend pass

FS	ROLB	MLB	LOLB	SS	
78 #21 / 79 #15		88 #40		84 #96 / 77 #20	
76 #28 / 73 #44		70 #6		82 #2 / 68 #38	79 #7

CB	RE	DT	DT	LE	CB
78 #36					
74 #26	82 #99	80 #51	84 #50	81 #97	78 #17
71 #35	80 #91	76 #93	77 #95	76 #94	74 #23

■ IMPACT PLAYERS   ■ LIKELY STARTERS

OFFENSIVE DEPTH CHART AND SCOUTING REPORT

Neutral West Coast Offense
AI Playcall Tendency: 54% run, 46% pass

K	WR	LT	LG	C	RG	RT	TE	WR	P
78 KPW	86 #81	80 #77	81 #55	78 #64	87 #56	78 #54	85 #80	87 #88	73 KPW
87 KAC	81 #84	79 #72	76 #70	73 #53	74 #71	77 #62	71 #85	83 #10	86 KAC
86 #37									84 #18

FB	QB1	QB2	HB
87 #30 / 77 #32	83 THP / 90 THA / 89 #19	79 THP / 89 THA / 86 #11	92 #25 / 83 #34

■ IMPACT PLAYERS   ■ LIKELY STARTERS

TEAM OFFENSIVE PLAYBOOK

Ace-Big	I-Form-Normal	Shotgun-Wing Trips
Ace-Bunch	I-Form-Tight	Shotgun-Y-Trips HB Wk
Ace-Slot	I-Form-Twins	Strong-Normal
Ace-Spread	Shotgun-Normal	Strong-Tight
Ace-Twin TE Slot	Shotgun-Spread	Weak-Normal
Ace-Y-Trips	Shotgun-Spread Flex Wk	Weak-Twins

PURDUE
Boilermakers

Conference: **Big Ten**
Location: **West Lafayette, IN**

REPORT CARD AND PRESTIGE

84	86	82
Overall	Offense	Defense

PRESTIGE RATINGS
Overall ★★★★
Coach Very Good
Academic Great

2007 SEASON RECAP
- 8-5 overall record
- 3-5 conference record
- Won Motor City Bowl

DEFENSIVE DEPTH CHART AND SCOUTING REPORT

Conservative 4-3 Defense
AI Playcall Tendency: 56% defend run, 44% defend pass

Position	Starter	Backup
CB	82 #35	73 #4
FS	86 #7	81 #31
ROLB	81 #29	79 #46
RE	78 #97	78 #49
MLB	83 #27	74 #56
DT	81 #90	79 #79
DT	84 #71	80 #92
LOLB	93 #42	79 #57
SS	85 #2	81 #43
LE	85 #95	75 #93
CB	83 #10	79 #15 / 69 #8

■ IMPACT PLAYERS ■ LIKELY STARTERS

OFFENSIVE DEPTH CHART AND SCOUTING REPORT

Neutral Spread Offense
AI Playcall Tendency: 45% run, 55% pass

Position	Starter	Backup
K	77 KPW / 92 KAC / 82 #13	
WR	82 #6	75 #83
LT	90 #74	76 #63
LG	80 #75	74 #76
C	81 #78	74 #55
RG	84 #50	83 #72
RT	85 #61	84 #51
TE	79 #85	74 #80
WR	85 #21	79 #19
FB	77 #44	
QB1	90 THP / 92 THA / 89 #12	
QB2	84 THP / 88 THA / 85 #14	
HB	89 #24	86 #33

■ IMPACT PLAYERS ■ LIKELY STARTERS

TEAM OFFENSIVE PLAYBOOK

Ace-Big	Shotgun-5WR Trio	Shotgun-Spread Flex
Ace-Slot	Shotgun-Bunch HB Str	Shotgun-Trio HB Wk
Ace-Twin TE	Shotgun-Normal	Shotgun-Trips HB Wk
Ace-Twin TE Slot	Shotgun-Normal HB Wk	Shotgun-Y-Trips
Ace-Y-Trips	Shotgun-Split Slot	Shotgun-Y-Trips HB Wk
Shotgun-4WR Trio Str	Shotgun-Spread	Strong-Normal

RICE
Owls

Conference: **C-USA (West)**
Location: **Houston, TX**

REPORT CARD AND PRESTIGE

77	81	76
Overall	Offense	Defense

PRESTIGE RATINGS
Overall ★★
Coach Fair
Academic Elite

2007 SEASON RECAP
- 3-9 overall record
- 3-5 conference record
- 4th in C-USA West

DEFENSIVE DEPTH CHART AND SCOUTING REPORT

Conservative 4-2-5 Defense
AI Playcall Tendency: 52% defend run, 48% defend pass

Position	Starter	Backup
CB	72 #2	66 #26
SS	84 #34 / 83 #9	74 #29
ROLB	84 #30	70 #47
RE	82 #55	70 #88
FS	78 #20	...
DT	73 #91	69 #97
DT	74 #74	70 #89
MLB	84 #36	77 #31
SS	79 #32	74 #44 / 79 #15
LE	80 #13	75 #90
CB	67 #24	63 #38

■ IMPACT PLAYERS ■ LIKELY STARTERS

OFFENSIVE DEPTH CHART AND SCOUTING REPORT

Aggressive Spread Offense
AI Playcall Tendency: 40% run, 60% pass

Position	Starter	Backup
K	63 KPW / 82 KAC / 82 #46	
WR	79 #7	76 #82
LT	76 #56	68 #79
LG	73 #60	40 #76
C	82 #73	73 #54
RG	76 #63	67 #72
RT	72 #75	72 #67
TE	81 #12	77 #84
WR	95 #81	78 #3
P	68 KPW / 87 KAC / 80 #1	
FB	69 #22	59 #49
QB1	91 THP / 89 THA / 90 #16	
QB2	78 THP / 85 THA / 80 #17	
HB	80 #28	79 #5

■ IMPACT PLAYERS ■ LIKELY STARTERS

TEAM OFFENSIVE PLAYBOOK

Ace-Big	Shotgun-Ace	Shotgun-Spread HB Wk
Ace-Slot	Shotgun-Ace Twins Wk	Shotgun-Tight
Pistol-Ace Twins	Shotgun-Bunch HB Str	Shotgun-Trips Open Str
Pistol-H Twins	Shotgun-Normal	Shotgun-Trips Over
Shotgun-4WR Trey Str	Shotgun-Normal HB Wk	Shotgun-Y-Trips
Shotgun-5WR Trey	Shotgun-Spread Flex	Shotgun-Y-Trips HB Wk

RUTGERS
Scarlet Knights
Conference: **Big East**
Location: **Piscataway, NJ**

REPORT CARD AND PRESTIGE

79	81	82
Overall	Offense	Defense

PRESTIGE RATINGS
Overall ★★★★
Coach Great
Academic Great

2007 SEASON RECAP
- 8-5 overall record
- 3-4 conference record
- Won International Bowl

DEFENSIVE DEPTH CHART AND SCOUTING REPORT

Aggressive 4-3 Defense
AI Playcall Tendency: 59% defend run, 41% defend pass

91 #36	84 #34		83 #44		82 #48	87 #6
73 #20	82 #51		74 #50		75 #17	78 #26	81 #25
FS	ROLB		MLB		LOLB	SS
79 #21						
70 #30	84 #92		79 #97	85 #90		81 #99	72 #35
66 #40	80 #31		77 #98	77 #95		77 #45	69 #41
CB	RE		DT	DT		LE	CB

■ IMPACT PLAYERS ■ LIKELY STARTERS

OFFENSIVE DEPTH CHART AND SCOUTING REPORT

Neutral Balanced Offense
AI Playcall Tendency: 50% run, 50% pass

K	WR	LT	LG	C	RG	RT	TE	WR	P
74 KPW	87 #88	80 #75	82 #78	79 #61	76 #60	82 #70	75 #89	88 #7	81 KPW
90 KAC	79 #5	72 #73	76 #76	78 #62	73 #74	75 #69	74 #3	81 #2	90 KAC
80 #12									84 #93
		FB		QB1	QB2		HB		
		76 #19		88 THP	81 THP		80 #8		
		73 #37		89 THA	88 THA		76 #24		
				91 #14	86 #15				

■ IMPACT PLAYERS ■ LIKELY STARTERS

TEAM OFFENSIVE PLAYBOOK

Ace-Big	I-Form-Slot Flex	Shotgun-Trips HB Wk
Ace-Bunch	I-Form-Tight	Shotgun-Y-Trips
Ace-Slot	Shotgun-5WR	Strong-Normal
Ace-Trips	Shotgun-Normal Flex	Strong-Tight
Ace-Twin TE Slot	Shotgun-Normal Y-Slot	Strong-Twins
I-Form-Normal	Shotgun-Split Slot	Weak-Twin TE

SAN DIEGO STATE
Aztecs
Conference: **Mountain West**
Location: **San Diego, CA**

REPORT CARD AND PRESTIGE

74	75	80
Overall	Offense	Defense

PRESTIGE RATINGS
Overall ★★
Coach Fair
Academic Very Good

2007 SEASON RECAP
- 4-8 overall record
- 3-5 conference record
- 6th in the Mountain West

DEFENSIVE DEPTH CHART AND SCOUTING REPORT

Aggressive 4-3 Defense
AI Playcall Tendency: 53% defend run, 47% defend pass

87 #40	84 #32		77 #35		86 #46	79 #2
81 #11	79 #34		73 #38		68 #31	78 #5	81 #6
FS	ROLB		MLB		LOLB	SS
79 #43						
69 #29	85 #92		77 #55	79 #66		86 #56	75 #28
64 #21	83 #90		69 #93	76 #96		83 #98	66 #39
CB	RE		DT	DT		LE	CB

■ IMPACT PLAYERS ■ LIKELY STARTERS

OFFENSIVE DEPTH CHART AND SCOUTING REPORT

Conservative Spread Offense
AI Playcall Tendency: 45% run, 55% pass

K	WR	LT	LG	C	RG	RT	TE	WR	P
64 KPW	81 #4	75 #74	77 #77	77 #50	86 #59	78 #73	77 #86	82 #1	66 KPW
78 KAC	80 #80	73 #72	76 #67	74 #60	71 #65	77 #79	77 #82	81 #19	88 KAC
86 #14									76 #13
		FB		QB1	QB2		HB		
		85 #23		78 THP	73 THP		83 #24		
		77 #38		89 THA	86 THA		83 #21		
				84 #9	87 #2				

■ IMPACT PLAYERS ■ LIKELY STARTERS

TEAM OFFENSIVE PLAYBOOK

Ace-Big	I-Form-Tight	Shotgun-Trips
Ace-Bunch	I-Form-Y-Trips	Shotgun-Trips Open Str
Ace-Slot	Shotgun-5WR	Shotgun-Trips Over
Ace-Trips	Shotgun-Normal Wing TE	Shotgun-Wing Trips
Ace-Twin TE Slot	Shotgun-Normal Y-Slot	Shotgun-Y-Trips HB Wk
I-Form-Normal	Shotgun-Split Slot	Strong-Normal

SAN JOSE STATE

Spartans

Conference: **WAC**
Location: **San Jose, CA**

REPORT CARD AND PRESTIGE

62	66	64
Overall	Offense	Defense

PRESTIGE RATINGS
Overall ★
Coach Very Good
Academic Good

2007 SEASON RECAP
- 5-7 overall record
- 4-4 conference record
- 6th in the WAC

DEFENSIVE DEPTH CHART AND SCOUTING REPORT

Neutral 3-4 Defense
AI Playcall Tendency: 43% defend run, 57% defend pass

	FS	ROLB	MLB	MLB	LOLB	SS
	74 #32	71 #31	71 #14		74 #57	75 #22
	70 #19	69 #48	69 #45	62 #26	71 #56	68 #36

	CB	RE	DT	LE	CB
	76 #29	84 #44	73 #96	80 #53	85 #4
	73 #16	77 #93	66 #99	71 #58	74 #30
	62 #37				72 #24

■ IMPACT PLAYERS   ■ LIKELY STARTERS

OFFENSIVE DEPTH CHART AND SCOUTING REPORT

Conservative West Coast Offense
AI Playcall Tendency: 46% run, 54% pass

	K	WR	LT	LG	C	RG	RT	TE	WR	P
	75 KPW	78 #6	71 #73	71 #65	71 #68	74 #72	82 #77	72 #9	81 #87	73 KPW
	90 KAC	74 #88	71 #64	69 #67	67 #79	72 #75	65 #59	67 #85	75 #80	87 KAC
	84 #10									82 #8

	FB	QB1	QB2	HB
	69 #43	77 THP	75 THP	75 #33
	65 #18	84 THA	85 THA	71 #21
		84 #15	84 #15	

■ IMPACT PLAYERS   ■ LIKELY STARTERS

TEAM OFFENSIVE PLAYBOOK

Ace-Big	I-Form-Twins	Shotgun-4WR Trio Str
Ace-Big Twins	I-Form-Y-Trips	Shotgun-5WR Trey
Ace-Twin TE Slot	Pistol-Bunch	Shotgun-5WR Trio
I-Form-Normal	Pistol-Slot	Shotgun-5WR Trips
I-Form-Slot Flex	Pistol-Y-Trips	Shotgun-Normal HB Wk
I-Form-Tight	Shotgun-4WR Trey Str	Shotgun-Y-Trips HB Wk

SMU (SOUTHERN METHODIST)

Mustangs

Conference: **C-USA (West)**
Location: **Dallas, TX**

REPORT CARD AND PRESTIGE

69	73	71
Overall	Offense	Defense

PRESTIGE RATINGS
Overall ★
Coach Very Good
Academic Great

2007 SEASON RECAP
- 1-11 overall record
- 0-8 conference record
- 6th in C-USA West

DEFENSIVE DEPTH CHART AND SCOUTING REPORT

Neutral 4-3 Defense
AI Playcall Tendency: 53% defend run, 47% defend pass

	FS	ROLB	MLB	LOLB	SS
	84 #6	72 #34	79 #27	80 #52	74 #41
	72 #35	68 #36	68 #39	73 #54	66 #32

	CB	RE	DT	DT	LE	CB
	76 #10	79 #70	74 #93	76 #46	92 #40	76 #7
	70 #25	62 #97	68 #95	73 #99	81 #94	73 #21
						70 #12

■ IMPACT PLAYERS   ■ LIKELY STARTERS

OFFENSIVE DEPTH CHART AND SCOUTING REPORT

Aggressive Spread Offense
AI Playcall Tendency: 20% run, 80% pass

	K	WR	LT	LG	C	RG	RT	TE	WR	P
	85 KPW	77 #5	69 #72	73 #74	76 #51	71 #68	73 #82	86 #86	80 #17	71 KPW
	91 KAC	72 #26	68 #71	72 #67	73 #59	62 #77	72 #9	74 #89	74 #9	85 KAC
	87 #15									84 #11

	FB	QB1	QB2	HB
	73 #45	79 THP	70 THP	85 #8
		88 THA	86 THA	80 #20
		82 #12	80 #14	

■ IMPACT PLAYERS   ■ LIKELY STARTERS

TEAM OFFENSIVE PLAYBOOK

Ace-4WR Trips	Shotgun-Double Flex	Shotgun-Tight
Ace-Spread	Shotgun-Flanker Close	Shotgun-Trips
Shotgun-4WR	Shotgun-Normal Y-Slot	Shotgun-Trips HB Wk
Shotgun-4WR Trio	Shotgun-Spread	Shotgun-Trips Open
Shotgun-5WR Trips	Shotgun-Spread Flex Wk	Shotgun-Trips Open Str
Shotgun-Bunch HB Str	Shotgun-Spread HB Wk	Shotgun-Wing Trips

SOUTH CAROLINA
Gamecocks
Conference: **SEC (East)**
Location: **Columbia, SC**

REPORT CARD AND PRESTIGE

89	86	92
Overall	Offense	Defense

PRESTIGE RATINGS
Overall ★★
Coach Elite
Academic Very Good

2007 SEASON RECAP
- 6-6 overall record
- 3-5 conference record
- 5th in the SEC East

DEFENSIVE DEPTH CHART AND SCOUTING REPORT

Aggressive 4-3 Defense
AI Playcall Tendency: 31% defend run, 69% defend pass

	85 #32	84 #49		95 #52		91 #45	83 #21		
	79 #26	77 #12		82 #53		87 #30	76 #24		89 #5
85 #1	FS	ROLB		MLB		LOLB	SS		
78 #3	86 #41		84 #91	84 #79		92 #40		81 #36	
76 #27	84 #83		81 #95	82 #97		81 #42		77 #10	
CB	RE		DT	DT		LE		CB	

■ IMPACT PLAYERS   ■ LIKELY STARTERS

OFFENSIVE DEPTH CHART AND SCOUTING REPORT

Aggressive Balanced Offense
AI Playcall Tendency: 45% run, 55% pass

K	WR	LT	LG	C	RG	RT	TE	WR	P
87 KPW	81 #17	87 #77	83 #72	82 #70	84 #57	89 #78	81 #84	92 #11	69 KPW
90 KAC	80 #9	84 #75	81 #64	76 #65	81 #74	67 #68	75 #44	81 #82	85 KAC
90 #14									82 #87

			FB	QB1	QB2		HB	
			77 #47	82 THP	79 THP		90 #25	
				89 THA	91 THA		83 #22	
				90 #7	84 #5			

■ IMPACT PLAYERS   ■ LIKELY STARTERS

TEAM OFFENSIVE PLAYBOOK

Ace-Big	I-Form-Twin WR	Split Backs-3WR
Ace-Normal Slot	Shotgun-4WR Spread	Strong-Normal
Ace-Slot Strong	Shotgun-4WR Trey Str	
Ace-Spread	Shotgun-5-Wide Tiger	
Ace-Trio	Shotgun-Normal Flex	
I-Form-Normal	Shotgun-Slot Strong	

SOUTHERN MISS
Golden Eagles
Conference: **C-USA (East)**
Location: **Hattiesburg, MS**

REPORT CARD AND PRESTIGE

72	79	71
Overall	Offense	Defense

PRESTIGE RATINGS
Overall ★★★
Coach Good
Academic Good

2007 SEASON RECAP
- 7-6 overall record
- 5-3 conference record
- Lost PapaJohns.com Bowl

DEFENSIVE DEPTH CHART AND SCOUTING REPORT

Aggressive 4-3 Defense
AI Playcall Tendency: 60% defend run, 40% defend pass

	79 #18	83 #41		91 #24		76 #21	76 #8		
	74 #30	66 #54		70 #46		75 #48	70 #13		78 #39
77 #17	FS	ROLB		MLB		LOLB	SS		
75 #20	75 #45		75 #68	77 #95		78 #98		76 #7	
72 #28	74 #37		73 #97	75 #74		73 #91		73 #23	
CB	RE		DT	DT		LE		CB	

■ IMPACT PLAYERS   ■ LIKELY STARTERS

OFFENSIVE DEPTH CHART AND SCOUTING REPORT

Neutral Spread Offense
AI Playcall Tendency: 50% run, 50% pass

K	WR	LT	LG	C	RG	RT	TE	WR	P
74 KPW	79 #19	80 #72	80 #76	76 #59	78 #60	80 #66	87 #1	82 #82	74 KPW
89 KAC	74 #15	72 #65	72 #65	74 #63	76 #71	70 #70	71 #82	77 #86	90 KAC
84 #13									80 #3

			QB1	QB2		HB	
			76 THP	76 THP		91 #25	
			89 THA	88 THA		78 #34	
			81 #14	85 #12			

■ IMPACT PLAYERS   ■ LIKELY STARTERS

TEAM OFFENSIVE PLAYBOOK

Ace-Big	I-Form-Twins	Shotgun-Split Twins
Ace-Big Twins	Shotgun-4WR Trio	Shotgun-Spread Flex Wk
Ace-Bunch	Shotgun-4WR Trio Str	Shotgun-Trips TE
Ace-Y-Trips	Shotgun-Ace Twins Wk	Shotgun-Y-Trips
I-Form-Normal	Shotgun-Normal	Shotgun-Y-Trips HB Wk
I-Form-Tight	Shotgun-Split Slot	Strong-Normal

STANFORD
Cardinal

Conference: **PAC-10**
Location: **Stanford, CA**

REPORT CARD AND PRESTIGE

74	79	76
Overall	Offense	Defense

PRESTIGE RATINGS
Overall ★★★
Coach Good
Academic Elite

2007 SEASON RECAP
- 4-8 overall record
- 3-6 conference record
- 9th in the PAC-10

DEFENSIVE DEPTH CHART AND SCOUTING REPORT

Conservative 4-3 Defense
AI Playcall Tendency: 60% defend run, 40% defend pass

	80 #22	79 #43		79 #20		79 #44	79 #23	
	75 #32	76 #21		71 #50		64 #57	65 #46	
81 #24	FS	ROLB		MLB		LOLB	SS	85 #6
71 #12		80 #80		81 #99	87 #54		82 #91	73 #26
66 #29		72 #96		77 #74	77 #39		74 #98	70 #28
CB		RE		DT	DT		LE	CB

■ IMPACT PLAYERS ■ LIKELY STARTERS

OFFENSIVE DEPTH CHART AND SCOUTING REPORT

Neutral West Coast Offense
AI Playcall Tendency: 48% run, 52% pass

K	WR	LT	LG	C	RG	RT	TE	WR	P
64 KPW	78 #89	82 #76	81 #72	85 #60	77 #75	79 #63	83 #83	83 #9	69 KPW
82 KAC	75 #82	80 #67	80 #67	75 #70	71 #71	74 #61	77 #45	76 #10	90 KAC
82 #11		FB		QB1	QB2		HB		80 #45
		68 #48		82 THP	80 THP		87 #5		
				89 THA	91 THA		80 #7		
				86 #14	88 #13				

■ IMPACT PLAYERS ■ LIKELY STARTERS

TEAM OFFENSIVE PLAYBOOK

Ace-Big	Ace-Y-Trips	Shotgun-Bunch HB Str
Ace-Bunch	I-Form-Normal	Shotgun-Normal Flex
Ace-Trey Open	I-Form-Slot Flex	Shotgun-Spread Flex Wk
Ace-Twin TE	I-Form-Twin TE	Shotgun-Y-Trips
Ace-Twin TE Slot	I-Form-Twins	Strong-Normal
Ace-Wing Trips	Shotgun-Ace	Weak-H Twins

SYRACUSE
Orange

Conference: **Big East**
Location: **Syracuse, NY**

REPORT CARD AND PRESTIGE

72	73	78
Overall	Offense	Defense

PRESTIGE RATINGS
Overall ★★★
Coach Very Good
Academic Excellent

2007 SEASON RECAP
- 2-10 overall record
- 1-6 conference record
- 8th in Big East

DEFENSIVE DEPTH CHART AND SCOUTING REPORT

Aggressive 4-3 Defense
AI Playcall Tendency: 53% defend run, 47% defend pass

	81 #15	75 #50		81 #45		84 #46	81 #17	
	75 #20	69 #53		70 #48		71 #25	76 #34	
75 #35	FS	ROLB		MLB		LOLB	SS	75 #28
70 #27		86 #30		77 #95	89 #97		87 #94	73 #29
65 #21		74 #96		69 #55	71 #39		76 #92	67 #6
CB		RE		DT	DT		LE	CB

■ IMPACT PLAYERS ■ LIKELY STARTERS

OFFENSIVE DEPTH CHART AND SCOUTING REPORT

Neutral Balanced Offense
AI Playcall Tendency: 55% run, 45% pass

K	WR	LT	LG	C	RG	RT	TE	WR	P
74 KPW	78 #11	73 #77	72 #70	74 #60	90 #75	79 #64	68 #85	80 #1	85 KPW
84 KAC	75 #27	69 #59	69 #62	70 #79	79 #71	69 #78	67 #84	76 #10	92 KAC
87 #42		FB		QB1	QB2		HB		87 #47
		71 #43		81 THP	76 THP		82 #55		
				87 THA	84 THA		81 #3		
				84 #9	82 #4				

■ IMPACT PLAYERS ■ LIKELY STARTERS

TEAM OFFENSIVE PLAYBOOK

Ace-Big	Ace-Twin TE Slot	Shotgun-Spread HB Wk
Ace-Big Twins	Ace-Y-Trips	Shotgun-Y-Trips HB Wk
Ace-Jumbo	I-Form-Normal	Strong-H Pro
Ace-Slot	I-Form-Slot Flex	Weak-H Pro
Ace-Trips	I-Form-Twins	Weak-H Twins
Ace-Twin TE	Shotgun-Split Slot	

TCU (TEXAS CHRISTIAN)
Horned Frogs

Conference: **Mountain West**
Location: **Fort Worth, TX**

REPORT CARD AND PRESTIGE

79 Overall | **81** Offense | **78** Defense

PRESTIGE RATINGS
Overall ★★★
Coach Very Good
Academic Very Good

2007 SEASON RECAP
- 8-5 overall record
- 4-4 conference record
- Won Texas Bowl

DEFENSIVE DEPTH CHART AND SCOUTING REPORT

Aggressive 4-2-5 Defense
AI Playcall Tendency: 58% defend run, 42% defend pass

	76 #19	84 #4	90 #39	86 #29	
79 #28	75 #28 / 67 #58 (SS/ROLB)	78 #3 (FS)	72 #41 (MLB)	71 #31 (SS)	79 #20
74 #43	84 #42	79 #56 / 81 #69	84 #98		70 #25
67 #24 (CB)	84 #91 (RE)	77 #57 / 78 #55 (DT/DT)	75 #50 (LE)		67 #7 (CB)

■ IMPACT PLAYERS   ■ LIKELY STARTERS

OFFENSIVE DEPTH CHART AND SCOUTING REPORT

Neutral Balanced Offense
AI Playcall Tendency: 55% run, 45% pass

K	WR	LT	LG	C	RG	RT	TE	WR	P
63 KPW	83 #2	81 #70	80 #60	83 #75	85 #65	78 #79	81 #86	83 #1	67 KPW
88 KAC	78 #82	75 #50	78 #63	76 #76	73 #73	75 #78	70 #84	79 #85	86 KAC
80 #49		(FB) 79 #36		(QB1) 80 THP 86 THA 86 #14	(QB2) 79 THP 89 THA 80 #11		(HB) 90 #23 / 82 #24		80 #47

■ IMPACT PLAYERS   ■ LIKELY STARTERS

TEAM OFFENSIVE PLAYBOOK

Ace-Big	I-Form-Normal	Shotgun-Split Slot
Ace-Big Twins	I-Form-Tight	Shotgun-Spread HB Wk
Ace-Spread	I-Form-Y-Trips	Shotgun-Trips
Ace-Twin TE	Shotgun-5WR	Shotgun-Y-Trips
Ace-Twin TE Slot	Shotgun-Ace Twins Wk	Strong-Y-Trips
Ace-Y-Trips	Shotgun-Normal	Weak-Normal

TEMPLE
Owls

Conference: **MAC (East)**
Location: **Philadelphia, PA**

REPORT CARD AND PRESTIGE

69 Overall | **73** Offense | **69** Defense

PRESTIGE RATINGS
Overall ★
Coach Fair
Academic Good

2007 SEASON RECAP
- 4-8 overall record
- 4-4 conference record
- 5th in the MAC East

DEFENSIVE DEPTH CHART AND SCOUTING REPORT

Neutral 4-3 Defense
AI Playcall Tendency: 42% defend run, 58% defend pass

	77 #16 / 74 #56	80 #49	85 #46	83 #21	
71 #27	74 #25 / 73 #6 (FS/ROLB)	73 #38 (MLB)	80 #11 / 76 #29 (LOLB/SS)		72 #9
67 #24	75 #99	78 #92 / 81 #98	85 #93		70 #28
62 #20 (CB)	72 #45 (RE)	70 #91 / 71 #97 (DT/DT)	75 #52 (LE)		64 #2 (CB)

■ IMPACT PLAYERS   ■ LIKELY STARTERS

OFFENSIVE DEPTH CHART AND SCOUTING REPORT

Conservative Balanced Offense
AI Playcall Tendency: 55% run, 45% pass

K	WR	LT	LG	C	RG	RT	TE	WR	P
54 KPW	80 #22	79 #73	79 #70	84 #59	80 #97	78 #71	73 #88	82 #82	66 KPW
72 KAC	77 #3	73 #63	74 #74	73 #67	76 #57	77 #66	70 #86	77 #15	89 KAC
85 #47		(FB) 76 #5 / 65 #43		(QB1) 78 THP 87 THA 84 #13	(QB2) 76 THP 89 THA 86 #12		(HB) 80 #34 / 75 #23		78 #49

■ IMPACT PLAYERS   ■ LIKELY STARTERS

TEAM OFFENSIVE PLAYBOOK

Ace-Big	I-Form-Normal	Shotgun-Empty Trey
Ace-Big Twins	I-Form-Slot Flex	Shotgun-Normal Flex Wk
Ace-Slot	I-Form-Twin TE	Shotgun-Split Slot
Ace-Spread	I-Form-Twins	Shotgun-Split Twins
Ace-Twin TE Slot	I-Form-Y-Trips	Strong-Normal
Ace-Y-Trips	Shotgun-5WR Trey	Wishbone-Tight

TENNESSEE
Volunteers

Conference: **SEC (East)**
Location: **Knoxville, TN**

REPORT CARD AND PRESTIGE

89
Overall

88
Offense

92
Defense

PRESTIGE RATINGS
Overall ★★★★★
Coach Elite
Academic Very Good

2007 SEASON RECAP
- 10-4 overall record
- 6-2 conference record
- Won Outback Bowl

DEFENSIVE DEPTH CHART AND SCOUTING REPORT

Aggressive 4-3 Defense
AI Playcall Tendency: 44% defend run, 56% defend pass

	83 #41	91 #5		82 #35		87 #20	94 #14	
	80 #7	83 #43		78 #56		80 #11	77 #36	84 #37
	FS	ROLB		MLB		LOLB	SS	
83 #13	94 #91		85 #95	94 #98		88 #94		81 #24
80 #31	87 #46		78 #97	85 #55		86 #84		74 #21
74 #26	RE		DT	DT		LE		CB
CB								

■ IMPACT PLAYERS   ■ LIKELY STARTERS

OFFENSIVE DEPTH CHART AND SCOUTING REPORT

Neutral Balanced Offense
AI Playcall Tendency: 50% run, 50% pass

K	WR	LT	LG	C	RG	RT	TE	WR	P
83 KPW	85 #81	84 #79	81 #75	91 #50	84 #65	83 #78	79 #88	91 #12	94 KPW
92 KAC	83 #6	82 #72	79 #76	79 #66	83 #51	81 #70	79 #80	85 #21	91 KAC
86 #26									92 #47

FB	QB1	QB2	HB
79 #30	86 THP	76 THP	89 #27
70 #48	93 THA	91 THA	85 #2
	87 #8	87 #17	

■ IMPACT PLAYERS   ■ LIKELY STARTERS

TEAM OFFENSIVE PLAYBOOK

Ace-Big	Ace-Y-Trips	Shotgun-Split Slot
Ace-Big Twins	I-Form-Normal	Shotgun-Spread Flex Wk
Ace-Bunch	I-Form-Tight	Shotgun-Trips HB Wk
Ace-Slot	I-Form-Twin TE	Shotgun-Y-Trips
Ace-Twin TE	I-Form-Twins	Strong-H Pro
Ace-Twin TE Slot	Shotgun-Normal	Weak-H Twins

TEXAS
Longhorns

Conference: **Big 12 (South)**
Location: **Austin, TX**

REPORT CARD AND PRESTIGE

89
Overall

88
Offense

92
Defense

PRESTIGE RATINGS
Overall ★★★★★
Coach Elite
Academic Excellent

2007 SEASON RECAP
- 10-3 overall record
- 5-3 conference record
- Won Holiday Bowl

DEFENSIVE DEPTH CHART AND SCOUTING REPORT

Aggressive 4-3 Defense
AI Playcall Tendency: 56% defend run, 44% defend pass

	84 #5	87 #38		89 #44		85 #2	88 #19	
	77 #6	82 #53		83 #11		80 #16	79 #36	84 #7
	FS	ROLB		MLB		LOLB	SS	
83 #13	92 #32		80 #96	90 #99		91 #33		82 #3
79 #26	91 #98		76 #88	78 #90		86 #95		79 #8
78 #12	RE		DT	DT		LE		CB
CB								

■ IMPACT PLAYERS   ■ LIKELY STARTERS

OFFENSIVE DEPTH CHART AND SCOUTING REPORT

Neutral Balanced Offense
AI Playcall Tendency: 48% run, 52% pass

K	WR	LT	LG	C	RG	RT	TE	WR	P
82 KPW	84 #8	78 #78	86 #52	80 #66	89 #55	85 #74	81 #86	89 #6	82 KPW
91 KAC	79 #4	78 #72	82 #70	74 #60	81 #63	74 #54	74 #13	83 #14	93 KAC
87 #15									84 #17

FB	QB1	QB2	HB
93 #3	89 THP	81 THP	85 #2
72 #31	90 THA	90 THA	80 #30
	88 #12	80 #17	

■ IMPACT PLAYERS   ■ LIKELY STARTERS

TEAM OFFENSIVE PLAYBOOK

Ace-Big	Shotgun-5WR Flex Trey	Shotgun-Normal HB Wk
Ace-Big Twins	Shotgun-Ace	Shotgun-Split
Ace-Y-Trips	Shotgun-Ace Twins	Shotgun-Split Twins
I-Form-Normal	Shotgun-Ace Twins Wk	Shotgun-Y-Trips
I-Form-Tight	Shotgun-Empty Trey	Shotgun-Y-Trips HB Wk
I-Form-Twins	Shotgun-Normal	Strong-Normal

TEXAS A&M
Aggies
Conference: **Big 12 (South)**
Location: **College Station, TX**

REPORT CARD AND PRESTIGE

77 Overall | **79** Offense | **80** Defense

PRESTIGE RATINGS
Overall ★★★★★
Coach Very Good
Academic Excellent

2007 SEASON RECAP
- 7-6 overall record
- 4-4 conference record
- Lost Alamo Bowl

DEFENSIVE DEPTH CHART AND SCOUTING REPORT

Aggressive 4-3 Defense
AI Playcall Tendency: 43% defend run, 57% defend pass

87 #26	78 #25	78 #36	84 #46	84 #9	
75 #24	73 #15	72 #34	76 #44	72 #30	81 #4
FS	ROLB	MLB	LOLB	SS	
81 #18	84 #92	77 #84	82 #91	85 #49	80 #27
74 #16	80 #40	74 #70	75 #79	78 #93	63 #31
CB	RE	DT	DT	LE	CB

■ IMPACT PLAYERS ■ LIKELY STARTERS

OFFENSIVE DEPTH CHART AND SCOUTING REPORT

Neutral West Coast Offense
AI Playcall Tendency: 50% run, 50% pass

-K	WR	LT	LG	C	RG	RT	TE	WR	P
80 KPW	76 #5	79 #79	79 #76	73 #63	78 #61	80 #75	83 #81	77 #6	93 KPW
92 KAC	76 #12	72 #77	73 #72	70 #55	75 #74	72 #73	74 #86	76 #10	92 KAC
84 #7		FB		QB1	QB2		HB		90 #16
		73 #43		88 THP 89 THA 85 #7	80 THP 86 THA 80 #1		89 #3 86 #11		

■ IMPACT PLAYERS ■ LIKELY STARTERS

TEAM OFFENSIVE PLAYBOOK

Ace-Big	Ace-Y-Trips	Shotgun-Bunch HB Str
Ace-Bunch	I-Form-Normal	Shotgun-Normal Flex
Ace-Trey Open	I-Form-Slot Flex	Shotgun-Spread Flex Wk
Ace-Twin TE	I-Form-Twin TE	Shotgun-Y-Trips
Ace-Twin TE Slot	I-Form-Twins	Strong-Normal
Ace-Wing Trips	Shotgun-Ace	Weak-Twins

TEXAS TECH
Red Raiders
Conference: **Big 12 (South)**
Location: **Lubbock, TX**

REPORT CARD AND PRESTIGE

86 Overall | **92** Offense | **85** Defense

PRESTIGE RATINGS
Overall ★★★★
Coach Very Good
Academic Good

2007 SEASON RECAP
- 9-4 overall record
- 4-4 conference record
- Won Gator Bowl

DEFENSIVE DEPTH CHART AND SCOUTING REPORT

Aggressive 4-3 Defense
AI Playcall Tendency: 50% defend run, 50% defend pass

85 #7	87 #39	75 #52	85 #57	85 #86	
82 #10	79 #35	73 #41	75 #13	78 #23	88 #3
81 #1					
FS	ROLB	MLB	LOLB	SS	
77 #28	87 #84	80 #97	88 #91	84 #98	79 #31
74 #33	83 #48	75 #99	80 #93	80 #94	75 #21
CB	RE	DT	DT	LE	CB

■ IMPACT PLAYERS ■ LIKELY STARTERS

OFFENSIVE DEPTH CHART AND SCOUTING REPORT

Aggressive Spread Offense
AI Playcall Tendency: 20% run, 80% pass

K	WR	LT	LG	C	RG	RT	TE	WR	P
74 KPW	87 #12	89 #74	90 #65	81 #51	82 #76	80 #67	78 #80	96 #5	77 KPW
86 KAC	81 #83	76 #70	79 #71	75 #73	79 #78	72 #69	70 #87	86 #27	90 KAC
87 #19				QB1	QB2		HB		84 #45
				96 THP 90 THA 97 #6	78 THP 91 THA 86 #15		87 #2 81 #32		

■ IMPACT PLAYERS ■ LIKELY STARTERS

TEAM OFFENSIVE PLAYBOOK

Ace-4WR Trips	Shotgun-Split	Shotgun-Trips HB Wk
Ace-Big Flip	Shotgun-Split Slot	Shotgun-Trips Open
Ace-Spread Flex	Shotgun-Split Y-Flex	Shotgun-Trips Open Str
Shotgun-4WR Trey Str	Shotgun-Spread Flex	Shotgun-Wing Trio Wk
Shotgun-Double Flex	Shotgun-Spread Flex Wk	Strong-H Pro
Shotgun-Normal Flex Wk	Shotgun-Trips	Weak-H Pro

TOLEDO
Rockets

Conference: **MAC (West)**
Location: **Toledo, OH**

TROY
Trojans

Conference: **Sun Belt**
Location: **Troy, AL**

REPORT CARD AND PRESTIGE

67 Overall **75** Offense **66** Defense

PRESTIGE RATINGS
Overall ★★★
Coach Good
Academic Fair

2007 SEASON RECAP
- 5-7 overall record
- 3-5 conference record
- 5th in the MAC West

REPORT CARD AND PRESTIGE

72 Overall **70** Offense **78** Defense

PRESTIGE RATINGS
Overall ★★
Coach Good
Academic Fair

2007 SEASON RECAP
- 8-4 overall record
- 6-1 conference record
- 1st in the Sun Belt

DEFENSIVE DEPTH CHART AND SCOUTING REPORT

TOLEDO

Neutral 4-2-5 Defense
AI Playcall Tendency: 52% defend run, 48% defend pass

		SS	ROLB		FS		MLB	SS	
		78 #34			84 #28		76 #56	82 #8	
		70 #44	73 #36		73 #23		76 #54	69 #20	71 #3
73 #37									
66 #24		77 #57		74 #89	77 #98		73 #58	66 #35	
65 #30		76 #92		69 #99	71 #75		70 #41	65 #47	
CB		RE		DT	DT		LE	CB	

■ IMPACT PLAYERS   ■ LIKELY STARTERS

TROY

Neutral 4-3 Defense
AI Playcall Tendency: 42% defend run, 58% defend pass

	FS	ROLB		MLB		LOLB	SS	
84 #15	81 #43		81 #2		78 #50	81 #20	
76 #39	74 #44		64 #48		72 #46	80 #17	82 #12
76 #23							
75 #27	84 #90		76 #99	80 #92		90 #61	75 #36
73 #33	78 #54		66 #96	76 #95		73 #78	75 #37
CB	RE		DT	DT		LE	CB

■ IMPACT PLAYERS   ■ LIKELY STARTERS

OFFENSIVE DEPTH CHART AND SCOUTING REPORT

TOLEDO

Neutral Spread Offense
AI Playcall Tendency: 50% run, 50% pass

K	WR	LT	LG	C	RG	RT	TE	WR	P
76 KPW	81 #1	72 #74	79 #68	76 #50	76 #69	75 #62	75 #83	83 #88	69 KPW
82 KAC	72 #5	70 #65	76 #78	71 #55	75 #72	73 #76	67 #81	72 #80	87 KAC
90 #85									82 #2

	QB1	QB2		HB
	82 THP / 87 THA / 84 #19	75 THP / 84 THA / 80 #11		84 #22 / 75 #15

■ IMPACT PLAYERS   ■ LIKELY STARTERS

TROY

Neutral Spread Offense
AI Playcall Tendency: 48% run, 52% pass

WR	LT	LG	C	RG	RT	TE	WR	P
79 #81	81 #65	79 #68	78 #75	82 #67	79 #74	72 #45	79 #82	68 KPW
76 #1	76 #72	70 #73	71 #78	74 #69	72 #66	68 #84	77 #4	87 KAC
								82 #47

	FB	QB1	QB2	HB
	79 #40	76 THP / 86 THA / 84 #11	70 THP / 85 THA / 78 #16	81 #32 / 71 #28

■ IMPACT PLAYERS   ■ LIKELY STARTERS

TEAM OFFENSIVE PLAYBOOK

TOLEDO

Ace-Big	Ace-Twin TE	Shotgun-Double Flex
Ace-Big Twins	Ace-Twin TE Slot	Shotgun-Normal Flex Wk
Ace-Jumbo	Ace-Y-Trips	Shotgun-Spread
Ace-Slot	Shotgun-4WR Trey Str	Shotgun-Spread Flex Wk
Ace-Spread	Shotgun-5WR Trey	Shotgun-Trips Over
Ace-Trips	Shotgun-Ace Twins Wk	Shotgun-Y-Trips

TROY

Ace-Big	Shotgun-Double Flex	Shotgun-Spread Flex
Ace-Trips	Shotgun-Flanker Close	Shotgun-Spread Flex Wk
Shotgun-4WR Trey Str	Shotgun-Normal	Shotgun-Trips HB Wk
Shotgun-5WR Trey	Shotgun-Normal Y-Slot	Shotgun-Trips Open
Shotgun-Ace Wing	Shotgun-Split Slot	Shotgun-Trips Open Str
Shotgun-Ace Wing Wk	Shotgun-Split Y-Flex	Shotgun-Y-Trips HB Wk

TULANE
Green Wave

Conference: C-USA (West)
Location: New Orleans, LA

REPORT CARD AND PRESTIGE

67	70	66
Overall	Offense	Defense

PRESTIGE RATINGS
Overall ★★
Coach Good
Academic Excellent

2007 SEASON RECAP
- 4-8 overall record
- 3-5 conference record
- 3rd in C-USA West

DEFENSIVE DEPTH CHART AND SCOUTING REPORT

Conservative 4-3 Defense
AI Playcall Tendency: 42% defend run, 58% defend pass

	FS	ROLB	MLB	LOLB	SS	
	82 #33	77 #40	74 #34	72 #55	75 #24	
73 #1	73 #42	71 #44	69 #51	69 #41	69 #38	77 #12

CB	RE	DT	DT	LE	CB
72 #13	84 #90	75 #97	77 #98	78 #92	72 #12
62 #22	76 #94	68 #99	73 #96	75 #93	68 #8

■ IMPACT PLAYERS   ■ LIKELY STARTERS

OFFENSIVE DEPTH CHART AND SCOUTING REPORT

Aggressive West Coast Offense
AI Playcall Tendency: 52% run, 48% pass

K	WR	LT	LG	C	RG	RT	TE	WR	P
67 KPW	78 #83	77 #77	75 #76	83 #65	78 #68	78 #75	69 #88	82 #20	63 KPW
84 KAC	76 #15	73 #78	72 #62	74 #63	67 #59	69 #70	65 #80	77 #19	90 KAC
82 #47									74 #40

FB	QB1	QB2	HB
71 #36	82 THP	78 THP	76 #32
69 #49	86 THA	90 THA	64 #5
	86 #9	82 #4	

■ IMPACT PLAYERS   ■ LIKELY STARTERS

TEAM OFFENSIVE PLAYBOOK

Ace-Big	I-Form-Slot Flex	Shotgun-Trio HB Wk
Ace-Big Twins	I-Form-Tight	Shotgun-Trips HB Wk
Ace-Bunch	I-Form-Twins	Shotgun-Y-Trips HB Wk
Ace-Slot	I-Form-Y-Trips	Split-Pro
Ace-Y-Trips	Shotgun-Normal	Strong-Normal
I-Form-Normal	Shotgun-Spread Flex Wk	Weak-Twins

TULSA
Golden Hurricane

Conference: C-USA (West)
Location: Tulsa, OK

REPORT CARD AND PRESTIGE

74	77	73
Overall	Offense	Defense

PRESTIGE RATINGS
Overall ★★
Coach Fair
Academic Very Good

2007 SEASON RECAP
- 10-4 overall record
- 6-2 conference record
- Won GMAC Bowl

DEFENSIVE DEPTH CHART AND SCOUTING REPORT

Aggressive 3-3-5 Defense
AI Playcall Tendency: 41% defend run, 59% defend pass

	SS	ROLB	MLB	FS	LOLB	SS	
	77 #42		80 #24	78 #40	72 #46		
81 #10	66 #37	70 #43	76 #32	75 #19	71 #36	65 #41	78 #16

CB	RE	DT	LE	CB
77 #18	86 #8	83 #99	88 #93	77 #27
74 #4	73 #80	70 #98	77 #39	62 #5

■ IMPACT PLAYERS   ■ LIKELY STARTERS

OFFENSIVE DEPTH CHART AND SCOUTING REPORT

Aggressive Spread Offense
AI Playcall Tendency: 48% run, 52% pass

K	WR	LT	LG	C	RG	RT	TE	WR	P
83 KPW	81 #84	76 #77	73 #76	80 #65	76 #53	82 #70	74 #86	84 #4	67 KPW
88 KAC	79 #21	72 #75	71 #61	73 #60	73 #74	72 #78	68 #41	79 #83	85 KAC
88 #29									80 KAC
									35

FB	QB1	QB2	HB
79 #20	84 THP	83 THP	85 #25
78 #9	88 THA	91 THA	75 #22
	88 #5	87 #12	

■ IMPACT PLAYERS   ■ LIKELY STARTERS

TEAM OFFENSIVE PLAYBOOK

Ace-Big	Shotgun-Normal	Shotgun-Wildcat
Ace-Big Twins	Shotgun-Normal Wing TE	Shotgun-Wing Trips
Ace-Big Wing	Shotgun-Normal Y-Slot	Shotgun-Wing Trips Wk
Shotgun-4WR Trio	Shotgun-Split Slot	Shotgun-Y-Trips
Shotgun-4WR Trio Str	Shotgun-Spread Flex	Strong-H Pro
Shotgun-5WR Flex Trio	Shotgun-Spread Flex Wk	Weak-H Twins

UAB (ALABAMA-BIRMINGHAM)
Blazers
Conference: **C-USA (East)**
Location: **Birmingham, AL**

REPORT CARD AND PRESTIGE

69	70	71
Overall	Offense	Defense

PRESTIGE RATINGS
Overall ★
Coach Fair
Academic Good

2007 SEASON RECAP
- 2-10 overall record
- 1-7 conference record
- 6th in C-USA East

DEFENSIVE DEPTH CHART AND SCOUTING REPORT

Neutral 4-3 Defense
AI Playcall Tendency: 53% defend run, 47% defend pass

	FS	ROLB		MLB		LOLB	SS	
	83 #18	83 #51		77 #33		81 #45	81 #43	
	71 #25	70 #13		72 #3		80 #44	71 #47	
74 #4								83 #21
68 #8	76 #90		74 #98	76 #91		77 #87		69 #41
57 #19	73 #54		72 #97	72 #99		71 #95		58 #30
CB	RE		DT	DT		LE		CB

■ IMPACT PLAYERS   ■ LIKELY STARTERS

OFFENSIVE DEPTH CHART AND SCOUTING REPORT

Neutral Spread Offense
AI Playcall Tendency: 49% run, 51% pass

K	WR	LT	LG	C	RG	RT	TE	WR	P
51 KPW	75 #11	76 #71	75 #64	84 #53	77 #56	77 #55	75 #86	81 #7	70 KPW
74 KAC	74 #22	74 #67	67 #72	79 #63	73 #75	74 #70	74 #84	75 #1	90 KAC
80 #24									78 #94

QB1	QB2		HB
81 THP	75 THP		79 #40
88 THA	84 THA		78 #37
84 #5	84 #14		

■ IMPACT PLAYERS   ■ LIKELY STARTERS

TEAM OFFENSIVE PLAYBOOK

Ace-Big	I-Form-Normal	Shotgun-Spread HB Wk
Ace-Big Wing	Shotgun-4WR Trio	Shotgun-Trips
Ace-Slot	Shotgun-Normal	Shotgun-Trips HB Wk
Ace-Twin TE	Shotgun-Normal HB Wk	Shotgun-Trips TE
Ace-Twin TE Slot	Shotgun-Normal Y-Slot	Shotgun-Y-Trips
Ace-Y-Trips	Shotgun-Spread Flex	Shotgun-Y-Trips HB Wk

UCF (CENTRAL FLORIDA)
Golden Knights
Conference: **C-USA (East)**
Location: **Orlando, FL**

REPORT CARD AND PRESTIGE

77	75	85
Overall	Offense	Defense

PRESTIGE RATINGS
Overall ★★★
Coach Very Good
Academic Good

2007 SEASON RECAP
- 10-4 overall record
- 7-1 conference record
- Lost Liberty Bowl

DEFENSIVE DEPTH CHART AND SCOUTING REPORT

Conservative 4-3 Defense
AI Playcall Tendency: 55% defend run, 45% defend pass

	FS	ROLB		MLB		LOLB	SS	
	87 #45	81 #38		81 #54		81 #59	92 #29	
	81 #67	76 #56		72 #55		74 #57	74 #36	
89 #31								92 #19
77 #20	81 #49		79 #95	79 #98		81 #44		82 #22
CB	80 #48		74 #92	77 #97		76 #53		76 #23
CB	RE		DT	DT		LE		CB

■ IMPACT PLAYERS   ■ LIKELY STARTERS

OFFENSIVE DEPTH CHART AND SCOUTING REPORT

Conservative Balanced Offense
AI Playcall Tendency: 55% run, 45% pass

K	WR	LT	LG	C	RG	RT	TE	WR	P
62 KPW	81 #81	85 #78	78 #66	81 #62	80 #68	72 #72	76 #84	81 #5	70 KPW
84 KAC	77 #6	76 #75	75 #77	77 #73	73 #65	69 #76	69 #88	79 #3	88 KAC
80 #33									80 #41

FB	QB1	QB2		HB
76 #46	82 THP	75 THP		78 #30
	88 THA	92 THA		77 #34
	84 #2	86 #17		

■ IMPACT PLAYERS   ■ LIKELY STARTERS

TEAM OFFENSIVE PLAYBOOK

Ace-Big	Ace-Twin TE Slot	Shotgun-Normal Flex Wk
Ace-Big Twins	Ace-Y-Trips	Shotgun-Trips Over
Ace-Bunch	I-Form-Normal	Shotgun-Trips TE
Ace-Slot Flex	I-Form-Slot Flex	Shotgun-Wing Trio Wk
Ace-Trips	I-Form-Tight	Shotgun-Wing Trips Wk
Ace-Twin TE	I-Form-Y-Trips	Shotgun-Y-Trips HB Wk

UCLA
Bruins

Conference: **PAC-10**
Location: **Los Angeles, CA**

REPORT CARD AND PRESTIGE

81	**83**	**82**
Overall	Offense	Defense

PRESTIGE RATINGS
Overall ★★★★
Coach Excellent
Academic Excellent

2007 SEASON RECAP
- 6-7 overall record
- 5-4 conference record
- Lost Las Vegas Bowl

DEFENSIVE DEPTH CHART AND SCOUTING REPORT

Aggressive 4-3 Defense
AI Playcall Tendency: 42% defend run, 58% defend pass

	FS		MLB		LOLB	SS	
88 #27 / 85 #51	80 #38 / 81 #8		81 #12 / 75 #59		82 #54 / 85 #25	76 #53 / 77 #34	85 #1

CB	RE		DT	DT		LE	CB
80 #22	84 #39		83 #92	83 #50		88 #56	80 #21
76 #30	79 #47		73 #52	80 #90		87 #55	69 #7

■ IMPACT PLAYERS   ■ LIKELY STARTERS

OFFENSIVE DEPTH CHART AND SCOUTING REPORT

Neutral West Coast Offense
AI Playcall Tendency: 52% run, 48% pass

K	WR	LT	LG	C	RG	RT	TE	WR	P
89 KPW	82 #4	85 #78	82 #75	77 #51	83 #58	80 #72	81 #86	85 #19	88 KPW
95 KAC	77 #84	77 #73	75 #77	72 #50	70 #57	71 #68	79 #15	77 #80	92 KAC
88 #15									88 #17

FB	QB1	QB2		HB
77 #45	86 THP / 90 THA / 86 #12	83 THP / 94 THA / 86 #7		90 #36 / 83 #24
74 #44				

■ IMPACT PLAYERS   ■ LIKELY STARTERS

TEAM OFFENSIVE PLAYBOOK

Ace-Big	Ace-Y-Trips	Shotgun-Spread HB Wk
Ace-Big Twins	I-Form-Normal	Shotgun-Y-Trips HB Wk
Ace-Slot	I-Form-Slot Flex	Strong-Normal
Ace-Trips	I-Form-Twin TE	Strong-Twins
Ace-Twin TE	I-Form-Twins	Strong-Y-Trips
Ace-Twin TE Slot	Shotgun-Split Slot	Weak-Normal

UL LAFAYETTE
Ragin' Cajuns

Conference: **Sun Belt**
Location: **Lafayette, LA**

REPORT CARD AND PRESTIGE

69	**77**	**66**
Overall	Offense	Defense

PRESTIGE RATINGS
Overall ★
Coach Fair
Academic Fair

2007 SEASON RECAP
- 3-9 overall record
- 3-4 conference record
- 6th in the Sun Belt

DEFENSIVE DEPTH CHART AND SCOUTING REPORT

Conservative 4-3 Defense
AI Playcall Tendency: 38% defend run, 62% defend pass

	FS		MLB		LOLB	SS	
78 #30 / 75 #47	75 #36 / 74 #53		75 #43 / 68 #10		83 #41 / 76 #20	73 #40 / 69 #24	73 #13
69 #23							

CB	RE		DT	DT		LE	CB
68 #29	79 #93		78 #95	81 #96		77 #97	68 #27
67 #21	77 #92		69 #91	71 #99		71 #50	67 #3

■ IMPACT PLAYERS   ■ LIKELY STARTERS

OFFENSIVE DEPTH CHART AND SCOUTING REPORT

Conservative Spread Offense
AI Playcall Tendency: 51% run, 49% pass

K	WR	LT	LG	C	RG	RT	TE	WR	P
72 KPW	79 #5	78 #67	74 #75	85 #79	75 #60	74 #73	74 #88	82 #18	60 KPW
84 KAC	72 #15	74 #66	73 #78	65 #76	71 #61	62 #55	65 #86	74 #19	84 KAC
87 #48									78 #49

FB	QB1	QB2		HB
73 #45	82 THP / 87 THA / 84 #6	73 THP / 84 THA / 84 #11		89 #32 / 80 #31
68 #34				

■ IMPACT PLAYERS   ■ LIKELY STARTERS

TEAM OFFENSIVE PLAYBOOK

Shotgun-Ace	Shotgun-Normal Y-Slot	Shotgun-Trips TE
Shotgun-Ace Twins	Shotgun-Split Slot	Shotgun-Wing Trips Wk
Shotgun-Ace Wing Wk	Shotgun-Split Y-Flex	Shotgun-Y-Trips
Shotgun-Bunch HB Str	Shotgun-Spread HB Wk	Shotgun-Y-Trips HB Wk
Shotgun-Normal	Shotgun-Trips HB Wk	Strong-Normal
Shotgun-Normal HB Wk	Shotgun-Trips Open Str	Strong-Twins

UL MONROE
Indians

Conference: **Sun Belt**
Location: **Monroe, LA**

REPORT CARD AND PRESTIGE

67	75	66
Overall	Offense	Defense

PRESTIGE RATINGS
Overall ★
Coach Fair
Academic Fair

2007 SEASON RECAP
- 6-6 overall record
- 4-3 conference record
- 3rd in the Sun Belt

DEFENSIVE DEPTH CHART AND SCOUTING REPORT

Neutral 4-2-5 Defense
AI Playcall Tendency: 59% defend run, 41% defend pass

	SS	ROLB	FS	MLB	SS	
	75 #37	76 #32		73 #51	78 #19	
	76 #2 / 69 #42	71 #10		55 #52	74 #28	

CB	RE	DT	DT	LE	CB
77 #21	79 #43	78 #92	78 #99	77 #93	73 #38
69 #32	78 #58	76 #90	77 #98	76 #97	64 #27

■ IMPACT PLAYERS   ■ LIKELY STARTERS

OFFENSIVE DEPTH CHART AND SCOUTING REPORT

Neutral Spread Offense
AI Playcall Tendency: 52% run, 48% pass

K	WR	LT	LG	C	RG	RT	TE	WR	P
57 KPW	79 #18	75 #79	86 #70	75 #53	74 #71	75 #76	79 #15	80 #3	69 KPW
82 KAC	76 #6	70 #72	75 #74	72 #69	69 #65	73 #68	73 #88	76 #9	89 KAC
80 #85									78 #48

FB	QB1	QB2	HB
73 #33	84 THP 89 THA 82 #7	75 THP 86 THA 78 #12	80 #5 / 72 #25

■ IMPACT PLAYERS   ■ LIKELY STARTERS

TEAM OFFENSIVE PLAYBOOK

Ace-Big Twins	Shotgun-5WR Trio	Shotgun-Spread
Ace-Slot	Shotgun-Double Flex	Shotgun-Trips
Ace-Twin TE	Shotgun-Empty Trey	Shotgun-Trips HB Wk
Ace-Twin TE Slot	Shotgun-Normal	Shotgun-Trips TE
Ace-Y-Trips	Shotgun-Normal Flex Wk	Shotgun-Y-Trips
Shotgun-4WR Trio	Shotgun-Normal Wing TE	Shotgun-Y-Trips HB Wk

---

UNLV (NEVADA-LAS VEGAS)
Rebels

Conference: **Mountain West**
Location: **Las Vegas, NV**

REPORT CARD AND PRESTIGE

67	70	66
Overall	Offense	Defense

PRESTIGE RATINGS
Overall ★★
Coach Fair
Academic Fair

2007 SEASON RECAP
- 2-10 overall record
- 1-7 conference record
- 9th in the Mountain West

DEFENSIVE DEPTH CHART AND SCOUTING REPORT

Conservative 4-3 Defense
AI Playcall Tendency: 45% defend run, 55% defend pass

	FS	ROLB	MLB	LOLB	SS	
	80 #8 / 79 #33	76 #56		81 #14	70 #26	
74 #21	67 #36 / 73 #44	73 #51		66 #54	69 #35	77 #10

CB	RE	DT	DT	LE	CB
70 #1	76 #42	76 #93	77 #92	80 #94	71 #24
68 #29	72 #47	72 #97	73 #99	73 #91	70 #25

■ IMPACT PLAYERS   ■ LIKELY STARTERS

OFFENSIVE DEPTH CHART AND SCOUTING REPORT

Neutral Spread Offense
AI Playcall Tendency: 55% run, 45% pass

K	WR	LT	LG	C	RG	RT	TE	WR	P
64 KPW	82 #88	80 #75	80 #78	72 #66	81 #59	76 #73	70 #46	84 #80	67 KPW
82 KAC	74 #85	68 #67	76 #65	70 #50	68 #61	75 #79	66 #82	74 #17	86 KAC
82 #37									80 #26

QB1	QB2	HB
75 THP 84 THA 82 #2	75 THP 85 THA 80 #16	82 #4 / 80 #20

■ IMPACT PLAYERS   ■ LIKELY STARTERS

TEAM OFFENSIVE PLAYBOOK

Ace-Big	Shotgun-4WR Trio Str	Shotgun-Spread Flex
Ace-Big Twins	Shotgun-5WR Trio	Shotgun-Spread Flex Wk
Ace-Slot	Shotgun-Ace	Shotgun-Trio HB Wk
Ace-Trips	Shotgun-Bunch HB Str	Shotgun-Y-Trips
Shotgun-4WR Trey Str	Shotgun-Normal	Shotgun-Y-Trips HB Wk
Shotgun-4WR Trio	Shotgun-Split Slot	Strong-Tight

USC (SOUTHERN CALIFORNIA)
Trojans

Conference: **PAC-10**
Location: **Los Angeles, CA**

REPORT CARD AND PRESTIGE

94 Overall | **90** Offense | **99** Defense

PRESTIGE RATINGS
Overall ★ ★ ★ ★ ★ ★
Coach Elite
Academic Excellent

2007 SEASON RECAP
- 11-2 overall record
- 7-2 conference record
- Won Rose Bowl

DEFENSIVE DEPTH CHART AND SCOUTING REPORT

Aggressive 4-3 Defense
AI Playcall Tendency: 51% defend run, 49% defend pass

FS	ROLB		MLB		LOLB	SS	
96 #2	87 #43		96 #58		94 #10	92 #4	
89 #36	82 #6		82 #39		81 #42	87 #26	86 #7

CB	RE		DT	DT	LE		CB
85 #24	95 #84		83 #99	95 #75	83 #93		83 #22
81 #45	87 #81		78 #33	81 #98	81 #46		80 #15

■ IMPACT PLAYERS   ■ LIKELY STARTERS

OFFENSIVE DEPTH CHART AND SCOUTING REPORT

Aggressive West Coast Offense
AI Playcall Tendency: 50% run, 50% pass

K	WR	LT	LG	C	RG	RT	TE	WR	P
84 KPW	89 #7	81 #68	91 #53	83 #61	83 #74	88 #71	82 #86	91 #1	79 KPW
89 KAC	83 #8	80 #73	79 #66	77 #67	80 #56	82 #77	81 #88	85 #9	88 KAC
88 #18									85 #44

	FB	QB1	QB2		HB	
	81 #31	88 THP	84 THP		87 #4	
		95 THA	95 THA		87 #13	
		90 #6	87 #16			

■ IMPACT PLAYERS   ■ LIKELY STARTERS

TEAM OFFENSIVE PLAYBOOK

Ace-Big	Ace-Y-Trips	Shotgun-4WR
Ace-Big Twins	Empty-Trips	Strong-Normal
Ace-Bunch	I-Form-Normal	Strong-Twin TE
Ace-Slot Flex	I-Form-Tight	Strong-Twins
Ace-Twin TE	I-Form-Twin TE	Weak-Twin TE
Ace-Twin TE Slot	I-Form-Twins	Weak-Twins

USF (SOUTH FLORIDA)
Bulls

Conference: **Big East**
Location: **Tampa, FL**

REPORT CARD AND PRESTIGE

79 Overall | **81** Offense | **80** Defense

PRESTIGE RATINGS
Overall ★ ★ ★
Coach Good
Academic Good

2007 SEASON RECAP
- 9-4 overall record
- 4-3 conference record
- Lost Sun Bowl

DEFENSIVE DEPTH CHART AND SCOUTING REPORT

Aggressive 4-3 Defense
AI Playcall Tendency: 39% defend run, 61% defend pass

FS	ROLB		MLB		LOLB	SS	
82 #5	83 #57		81 #53		89 #27	81 #21	
77 #17	72 #51		74 #42		80 #43	79 #7	76 #3

CB	RE		DT	DT	LE		CB
75 #86	97 #95		77 #98	80 #44	84 #90		74 #31
72 #31	85 #49		72 #93	75 #97	81 #56		72 #6

■ IMPACT PLAYERS   ■ LIKELY STARTERS

OFFENSIVE DEPTH CHART AND SCOUTING REPORT

Neutral Spread Offense
AI Playcall Tendency: 49% run, 51% pass

K	WR	LT	LG	C	RG	RT	TE	WR	P
70 KPW	81 #89	78 #78	81 #65	78 #77	78 #61	77 #71	77 #9	82 #8	75 KPW
90 KAC	76 #85	70 #72	76 #55	74 #62	71 #66	75 #74	75 #82	77 #5	87 KAC
82 #27									84 #25

	FB	QB1	QB2		HB	
	75 #38	90 THP	81 THP		86 #26	
	60 #41	90 THA	88 THA		80 #30	
		86 #8	82 #15			

■ IMPACT PLAYERS   ■ LIKELY STARTERS

TEAM OFFENSIVE PLAYBOOK

Ace-Big	Shotgun-5WR Trio	Shotgun-Split Slot
Ace-Twin TE	Shotgun-Ace	Shotgun-Spread Flex
I-Form-Normal	Shotgun-Ace Wing Wk	Shotgun-Trio HB Wk
Shotgun-4WR Trey Str	Shotgun-Double Flex	Shotgun-Trips Open
Shotgun-4WR Trio	Shotgun-Normal Flex	Shotgun-Wing Trips Wk
Shotgun-4WR Trio Str	Shotgun-Normal Wing TE	Shotgun-Y-Trips

UTAH
Utes

Conference: **Mountain West**
Location: **Salt Lake City, UT**

REPORT CARD AND PRESTIGE

74	81	69
Overall	Offense	Defense

PRESTIGE RATINGS
Overall ★★★★
Coach Very Good
Academic Very Good

2007 SEASON RECAP
- 9-4 overall record
- 5-3 conference record
- Won Poinsettia Bowl

DEFENSIVE DEPTH CHART AND SCOUTING REPORT

Aggressive 4-3 Defense
AI Playcall Tendency: 42% defend run, 58% defend pass

	83 #17 / 81 #10	69 #20	75 #42 / 78 #12	
	74 #31 / 71 #53	66 #52	69 #59 / 74 #7	
78 #1	FS / ROLB	MLB	LOLB / SS	80 #4
73 #23	78 #11	76 #92 / 77 #43	81 #41	74 #25
68 #14	73 #90	73 #97 / 76 #98	73 #56	70 #29
CB	RE	DT / DT	LE	CB

■ IMPACT PLAYERS   ■ LIKELY STARTERS

OFFENSIVE DEPTH CHART AND SCOUTING REPORT

Neutral Spread Offense
AI Playcall Tendency: 50% run, 50% pass

K	WR	LT	LG	C	RG	RT	TE	WR	P
84 KPW	81 #88	81 #68	82 #72	79 #77	79 #66	81 #65	77 #37	83 #84	65 KPW
87 KAC	80 #81	79 #71	76 #74	71 #57	73 #55	75 #70	73 #45	81 #5	88 KAC
90 #35		FB		QB1	QB2		HB		76 #30
		77 #4		86 THP #...	73 THP		89 #6		
		68 #40		87 THA	84 THA		80 #24		
				88 #3	84 #19				

■ IMPACT PLAYERS   ■ LIKELY STARTERS

TEAM OFFENSIVE PLAYBOOK

Ace-Big	Shotgun-5WR Flex Trio	Shotgun-Spread Flex Wk
Ace-Bunch	Shotgun-Ace	Shotgun-Tight
Ace-Twin TE	Shotgun-Bunch HB Str	Shotgun-Wing Trips Wk
Ace-Twin TE Slot	Shotgun-Double Flex	Shotgun-Y-Trips
Ace-Y-Trips	Shotgun-Normal Flex	Strong-Normal
Shotgun-4WR Trey Str	Shotgun-Spread Flex	Strong-Y-Trips

UTAH STATE
Aggies

Conference: **WAC**
Location: **Logan, UT**

REPORT CARD AND PRESTIGE

60	60	69
Overall	Offense	Defense

PRESTIGE RATINGS
Overall ★
Coach Good
Academic Very Good

2007 SEASON RECAP
- 2-10 overall record
- 2-6 conference record
- 7th in the WAC

DEFENSIVE DEPTH CHART AND SCOUTING REPORT

Conservative 4-3 Defense
AI Playcall Tendency: 60% defend run, 40% defend pass

	75 #39 / 79 #45	82 #53	82 #31 / 77 #3	
	67 #2 / 78 #43	68 #20	74 #50 / 72 #10	
76 #23	FS / ROLB	MLB	LOLB / SS	78 #26
70 #25	78 #58	72 #57 / 72 #92	77 #46	71 #7
67 #22	74 #54	67 #95 / 71 #96	69 #77	69 #1
CB	RE	DT / DT	LE	CB

■ IMPACT PLAYERS   ■ LIKELY STARTERS

OFFENSIVE DEPTH CHART AND SCOUTING REPORT

Conservative Balanced Offense
AI Playcall Tendency: 55% run, 45% pass

K	WR	LT	LG	C	RG	RT	TE	WR	P
66 KPW	71 #17	74 #82	70 #69	75 #56	72 #79	75 #77	72 #86	74 #14	59 KPW
82 KAC	70 #85	73 #66	67 #62	70 #70	70 #61	70 #73	70 #83	71 #81	82 KAC
84 #16		FB		QB1	QB2		HB		82 #8
		65 #5		73 THP	70 THP		76 #2		
				85 THA	84 THA		73 #21		
				80 #15	76 #12				

■ IMPACT PLAYERS   ■ LIKELY STARTERS

TEAM OFFENSIVE PLAYBOOK

Ace-Big	I-Form-Tight	Shotgun-Spread
Ace-Big Twins	I-Form-Twins	Shotgun-Trips TE
Ace-Slot	Shotgun-Ace	Shotgun-Y-Trips
Ace-Trips	Shotgun-Empty Trey	Strong-Normal
Ace-Twin TE Slot	Shotgun-Normal	Strong-Tight
I-Form-Normal	Shotgun-Split Slot	Weak-Twins

UTEP (TEXAS at EL PASO)
Miners

Conference: C-USA (West)
Location: El Paso, TX

REPORT CARD AND PRESTIGE

72 Overall **75** Offense **73** Defense

PRESTIGE RATINGS
Overall ★★
Coach Very Good
Academic Fair

2007 SEASON RECAP
- 4-8 overall record
- 2-6 conference record
- 5th in C-USA West

DEFENSIVE DEPTH CHART AND SCOUTING REPORT

Aggressive 3-3-5 Defense
AI Playcall Tendency: 39% defend run, 61% defend pass

	71 #38	78 #5	87 #14		73 #7	80 #23		
	79 #26 SS	69 #27 ROLB	67 #52 MLB	82 #4 FS	71 #17 LOLB	62 #36 SS		
80 #2							79 #47	
79 #2	80 #96		83 #91		81 #56		74 #29	
73 #31 CB	80 #98 RE		78 #99 DT		75 #58 LE		68 #11 CB	

■ IMPACT PLAYERS   ■ LIKELY STARTERS

OFFENSIVE DEPTH CHART AND SCOUTING REPORT

Aggressive Spread Offense
AI Playcall Tendency: 48% run, 52% pass

K	WR	LT	LG	C	RG	RT	TE	WR	P
80 KPW	79 #2	85 #71	81 #78	89 #62	77 #65	75 #72	78 #87	84 #18	79 KPW
88 KAC	76 #7	72 #70	75 #74	75 #79	72 #64	72 #66	65 #86	78 #12	94 KAC
88 #10				QB1	QB2		HB		82 #15
				81 THP	75 THP		80 #34		
				86 THA	84 THA		80 #21		
				82 #10	78 #5				

■ IMPACT PLAYERS   ■ LIKELY STARTERS

TEAM OFFENSIVE PLAYBOOK

Ace-4WR Trips
Ace-Big
Ace-Big Twins
Ace-Slot
Ace-Spread
Ace-Trips

Ace-Twin TE
Ace-Twin TE Slot
Ace-Y-Trips
Empty-Trips
Shotgun-4WR
Shotgun-5WR

Shotgun-Normal HB Wk
Shotgun-Spread Flex
Shotgun-Spread HB Wk
Shotgun-Trips HB Wk
Shotgun-Wing Trips
Shotgun-Y-Trips HB Wk

VANDERBILT
Commodores

Conference: SEC (East)
Location: Nashville, TN

REPORT CARD AND PRESTIGE

72 Overall **75** Offense **71** Defense

PRESTIGE RATINGS
Overall ★★
Coach Good
Academic Excellent

2007 SEASON RECAP
- 5-7 overall record
- 2-6 conference record
- 6th in the SEC East

DEFENSIVE DEPTH CHART AND SCOUTING REPORT

Neutral 4-3 Defense
AI Playcall Tendency: 53% defend run, 47% defend pass

	79 #2	80 #35	74 #45		76 #91	86 #33		
76 #5	78 #41 FS	71 #52 ROLB	71 #30 MLB		75 #44 LOLB	76 #29 SS	80 #17	
75 #14	82 #96		75 #59	77 #98	83 #90		75 #20	
73 #25 CB	73 #89 RE		66 #62 DT	68 #99 DT	74 #93 LE		74 #6 CB	

■ IMPACT PLAYERS   ■ LIKELY STARTERS

OFFENSIVE DEPTH CHART AND SCOUTING REPORT

Neutral Spread Offense
AI Playcall Tendency: 50% run, 50% pass

K	WR	LT	LG	C	RG	RT	TE	WR	P
76 KPW	78 #7	80 #76	79 #73	79 #60	77 #70	76 #66	75 #85	81 #88	74 KPW
90 KAC	75 #4	73 #65	74 #61	72 #71	75 #79	73 #77	73 #82	75 #88	89 KAC
84 #8		FB		QB1	QB2		HB		82 #39
		71 #34		84 THP	83 THP		83 #31		
		69 #32		86 THA	88 THA		83 #21		
				84 #3	84 #9				

■ IMPACT PLAYERS   ■ LIKELY STARTERS

TEAM OFFENSIVE PLAYBOOK

Ace-Big
Ace-Big Twins
Ace-Slot Flex
Ace-Y-Trips
I-Form-Tight
Shotgun-4WR Trio

Shotgun-4WR Trio Str
Shotgun-5WR Flex Trio
Shotgun-Bunch HB Str
Shotgun-Double Flex
Shotgun-Normal Flex Wk
Shotgun-Normal HB Wk

Shotgun-Spread Flex Wk
Shotgun-Trips Open Str
Shotgun-Y-Trips
Shotgun-Y-Trips HB Wk
Strong-H Pro
Weak-H Pro

VIRGINIA
Cavaliers
Conference: **ACC (Coastal)**
Location: **Charlottesville, VA**

VIRGINIA TECH
Hokies
Conference: **ACC (Coastal)**
Location: **Blacksburg, VA**

REPORT CARD AND PRESTIGE

79	79	85
Overall	Offense	Defense

PRESTIGE RATINGS
Overall ★★★
Coach Very Good
Academic Elite

2007 SEASON RECAP
- 9-4 overall record
- 6-2 conference record
- Lost Gator Bowl

DEFENSIVE DEPTH CHART AND SCOUTING REPORT

Aggressive 3-4 Defense
AI Playcall Tendency: 42% defend run, 58% defend pass

	87 #22 / 84 #41	87 #57 / 89 #54	92 #51 / 80 #17			
	81 #29 / 79 #33 FS ROLB	70 #50 / 71 #49 MLB MLB	77 #12 / 76 #36 LOLB SS			
81 #28				84 #4		
80 #43	85 #93	85 #98	82 #99	81 #19		
77 #1 CB	73 #70 RE	70 #95 DT	79 #90 LE	77 #31 CB		

■ IMPACT PLAYERS ■ LIKELY STARTERS

OFFENSIVE DEPTH CHART AND SCOUTING REPORT

Conservative Balanced Offense
AI Playcall Tendency: 51% run, 49% pass

K	WR	LT	LG	C	RG	RT	TE	WR	P
61 KPW	81 #20	92 #75	77 #74	75 #64	77 #65	84 #61	79 #85	83 #80	58 KPW
86 KAC	77 #89	81 #76	76 #62	70 #72	77 #69	76 #78	75 #83	78 #81	86 KAC
78 #11		FB	QB1	QB2			HB		76 #14
		79 #31	81 THP 92 THA 86 #7	78 THP 91 THA 85 #15			85 #5 / 85 #37		

■ IMPACT PLAYERS ■ LIKELY STARTERS

TEAM OFFENSIVE PLAYBOOK

Ace-Big	Ace-Y-Trips	Shotgun-Ace
Ace-Big Twins	I-Form-Normal	Shotgun-Double Flex
Ace-Big Wing	I-Form-Tight	Shotgun-Normal
Ace-Bunch	I-Form-Twin TE	Shotgun-Split
Ace-Slot	I-Form-Twins	Shotgun-Split Twins
Ace-Twin TE	Shotgun-4WR Trey Str	Shotgun-Y-Trips HB Wk

REPORT CARD AND PRESTIGE

84	79	89
Overall	Offense	Defense

PRESTIGE RATINGS
Overall ★★★★★
Coach Excellent
Academic Great

2007 SEASON RECAP
- 11-3 overall record
- 7-1 conference record
- Lost Orange Bowl

DEFENSIVE DEPTH CHART AND SCOUTING REPORT

Aggressive 4-3 Defense
AI Playcall Tendency: 56% defend run, 44% defend pass

	95 #17 / 91 #41	84 #33	85 #45 / 79 #24	
	76 #37 / 81 #26 FS ROLB	75 #50 MLB	79 #89 / 74 #2 LOLB SS	
82 #21	87 #6	80 #95 / 82 #91	93 #90	94 #1
77 #9 CB	81 #82 RE	74 #96 / 78 #56 DT DT	84 #47 LE	82 #22 CB

■ IMPACT PLAYERS ■ LIKELY STARTERS

OFFENSIVE DEPTH CHART AND SCOUTING REPORT

Neutral Balanced Offense
AI Playcall Tendency: 55% run, 45% pass

K	WR	LT	LG	C	RG	RT	TE	WR	P
77 KPW	78 #80	83 #71	81 #67	85 #58	90 #70	76 #62	83 #18	77 #16	86 KPW
89 KAC	76 #14	83 #77	78 #76	77 #60	80 #66	74 #64	82 #8	76 #17	90 KAC
86 #6		FB	QB1	QB2			HB		88 #97
		71 #42 / 71 #44	85 THP 89 THA 87 #7	84 THP 91 THA 87 #5			88 #20 / 84 #34		

■ IMPACT PLAYERS ■ LIKELY STARTERS

TEAM OFFENSIVE PLAYBOOK

Ace-Big	I-Form-Normal	Shotgun-Split
Ace-Big Twins	I-Form-Tight	Shotgun-Split Twins
Ace-Slot Flex	I-Form-Twins	Shotgun-Split Y-Flex
Ace-Twin TE	Pistol-Slot Flex	Shotgun-Y-Trips HB Wk
Ace-Twin TE Slot	Shotgun-Double Flex	Strong-Normal
Ace-Y-Trips	Shotgun-Normal Flex Wk	Weak-Twins

WAKE FOREST
Demon Deacons

Conference: **ACC (Atlantic)**
Location: **Winston-Salem, NC**

REPORT CARD AND PRESTIGE

77 Overall **79** Offense **80** Defense

PRESTIGE RATINGS
Overall ★★★★
Coach Very Good
Academic Elite

2007 SEASON RECAP
- 9-4 overall record
- 5-3 conference record
- Won Meineke Bowl

DEFENSIVE DEPTH CHART AND SCOUTING REPORT

Neutral 4-3 Defense
AI Playcall Tendency: 53% defend run, 47% defend pass

	FS	ROLB	MLB	LOLB	SS	
	91 #10	78 #39	81 #43	88 #59	79 #9	
76 #17	64 #28	75 #63	75 #46	75 #47	76 #7	84 #2

CB	RE	DT	DT	LE	CB
75 #24	88 #93	77 #99	78 #96	86 #34	75 #29
62 #25	77 #97	75 #51	76 #91	84 #42	64 #1

■ IMPACT PLAYERS ■ LIKELY STARTERS

OFFENSIVE DEPTH CHART AND SCOUTING REPORT

Neutral Balanced Offense
AI Playcall Tendency: 57% run, 43% pass

K	WR	LT	LG	C	RG	RT	TE	WR	P
90 KPW	82 #88	81 #76	82 #72	79 #67	78 #61	85 #64	72 #85	83 #4	69 KPW
92 KAC	74 #36	75 #75	75 #78	71 #71	77 #65	73 #62	69 #84	77 #8	89 KAC
90 #38									80 #30

FB	QB1	QB2	HB
73 #35	87 THP	79 THP	81 #27
73 #44	89 THA	87 THA	80 #23
	87 #11	84 #6	

■ IMPACT PLAYERS ■ LIKELY STARTERS

TEAM OFFENSIVE PLAYBOOK

Ace-Big	Shotgun-Ace Twins Wk	Shotgun-Spread
Ace-Big Twins	Shotgun-Normal	Shotgun-Spread HB Wk
I-Form-Normal	Shotgun-Normal Flex Wk	Shotgun-Wing Trips
I-Form-Slot Flex	Shotgun-Normal HB Wk	Shotgun-Wing Trips Wk
I-Form-Tight	Shotgun-Split	Shotgun-Y-Trips
Shotgun-Ace	Shotgun-Split Slot	Shotgun-Y-Trips HB Wk

WASHINGTON
Huskies

Conference: **PAC-10**
Location: **Seattle, WA**

REPORT CARD AND PRESTIGE

79 Overall **81** Offense **80** Defense

PRESTIGE RATINGS
Overall ★★★
Coach Very Good
Academic Excellent

2007 SEASON RECAP
- 4-9 overall record
- 2-7 conference record
- 10th in the PAC-10

DEFENSIVE DEPTH CHART AND SCOUTING REPORT

Aggressive 4-3 Defense
AI Playcall Tendency: 53% defend run, 47% defend pass

	FS	ROLB	MLB	LOLB	SS	
	87 #26	92 #29	82 #59	87 #22	74 #45	
75 #21	83 #23	75 #24	76 #57	81 #9	73 #35	77 #16

CB	RE	DT	DT	LE	CB
72 #27	88 #66	78 #95	85 #99	82 #96	74 #25
65 #18	70 #50	72 #52	72 #91	78 #93	67 #2

■ IMPACT PLAYERS ■ LIKELY STARTERS

OFFENSIVE DEPTH CHART AND SCOUTING REPORT

Neutral Spread Offense
AI Playcall Tendency: 50% run, 50% pass

K	WR	LT	LG	C	RG	RT	TE	WR	P
84 KPW	77 #1	78 #76	81 #70	87 #58	81 #72	76 #65	81 #37	80 #16	72 KPW
94 KAC	71 #84	77 #79	75 #61	72 #62	77 #73	71 #63	80 #86	74 #87	87 KAC
84 #13									82 #12

FB	QB1	QB2	HB
87 #32	89 THP	72 THP	84 #24
71 #30	91 THA	84 THA	80 #6
	85 #10	78 #17	

■ IMPACT PLAYERS ■ LIKELY STARTERS

TEAM OFFENSIVE PLAYBOOK

Ace-Big	Shotgun-5WR	Shotgun-Trips HB Wk
Ace-Bunch	Shotgun-Ace	Shotgun-Trips TE
Ace-Twin TE Slot	Shotgun-Ace Twins Wk	Shotgun-Y-Trips
Ace-Y-Trips	Shotgun-Bunch HB Str	Shotgun-Y-Trips HB Wk
I-Form-Normal	Shotgun-Normal	Strong-Y-Trips
I-Form-Tight	Shotgun-Split Y-Flex	Weak-Normal

WASHINGTON STATE
Cougars

Conference: PAC-10
Location: Pullman, WA

REPORT CARD AND PRESTIGE

77	77	78
Overall	Offense	Defense

PRESTIGE RATINGS
Overall ★★★
Coach Fair
Academic Very Good

2007 SEASON RECAP
- 5-7 overall record
- 3-6 conference record
- 8th in the PAC-10

DEFENSIVE DEPTH CHART AND SCOUTING REPORT

Neutral 4-3 Defense
AI Playcall Tendency: 40% defend run, 60% defend pass

	FS	ROLB		MLB		LOLB	SS	
	78 #26	83 #49		88 #52		80 #38	79 #18	
	74 #25	72 #51		68 #50		74 #53	71 #13	
77 #39								78 #21
70 #29	92 #45		77 #96	83 #92		81 #95		74 #34
69 #37	83 #97		71 #74	72 #77		80 #93		70 #3
CB	RE		DT	DT		LE		CB

■ IMPACT PLAYERS   ■ LIKELY STARTERS

OFFENSIVE DEPTH CHART AND SCOUTING REPORT

Aggressive Spread Offense
AI Playcall Tendency: 50% run, 50% pass

WR	LT	LG	C	RG	RT	TE	WR	P
79 #85	81 #55	76 #73	85 #69	83 #60	77 #76	73 #80	88 #4	76 KPW
75 #86	76 #67	71 #79	76 #64	74 #56	76 #66	69 #48	77 #15	88 KAC
	FB		QB1	QB2		HB		82 #8
	65 #33		82 THP 88 THA 88 #17	78 THP 90 THA 84 #9		83 #31 79 #34		

■ IMPACT PLAYERS   ■ LIKELY STARTERS

TEAM OFFENSIVE PLAYBOOK

Ace-Big	Empty-Trips	Shotgun-Split Slot
Ace-Big Twins	Shotgun-5WR Trey	Shotgun-Spread Flex
Ace-Slot	Shotgun-Bunch HB Str	Shotgun-Spread HB Wk
Ace-Tight Slots	Shotgun-Double Flex	Shotgun-Trips
Ace-Trips	Shotgun-Normal	Shotgun-Trips HB Wk
Ace-Twin TE Slot	Shotgun-Normal HB Wk	Shotgun-Y-Trips

WEST VIRGINIA
Mountaineers

Conference: Big East
Location: Morgantown, WV

REPORT CARD AND PRESTIGE

84	90	80
Overall	Offense	Defense

PRESTIGE RATINGS
Overall ★★★★★
Coach Good
Academic Good

2007 SEASON RECAP
- 11-2 overall record
- 5-2 conference record
- Won Fiesta Bowl

DEFENSIVE DEPTH CHART AND SCOUTING REPORT

Aggressive 3-3-5 Defense
AI Playcall Tendency: 46% defend run, 54% defend pass

	SS	ROLB		MLB	FS		LOLB	SS	
	87 #44		86 #47	87 #8		85 #30	77 #15	
	76 #37	78 #49		68 #42	75 #20		82 #45	75 #29	
79 #24								77 #9
75 #4	78 #92		84 #93			84 #99		75 #17
69 #28	73 #84		77 #96			83 #91		64 #33
CB	RE		DT			LE		CB

■ IMPACT PLAYERS   ■ LIKELY STARTERS

OFFENSIVE DEPTH CHART AND SCOUTING REPORT

Neutral Spread Offense
AI Playcall Tendency: 60% run, 40% pass

K	WR	LT	LG	C	RG	RT	TE	WR	P
83 KPW	83 #83	88 #62	90 #79	82 #68	90 #73	86 #66	71 #86	85 #21	77 KPW
89 KAC	77 #22	76 #67	83 #75	73 #61	73 #71	73 #56	70 #85	78 #4	90 KAC
88 #40		FB		QB1	QB2		HB		82 #37
		66 #47		97 THP 94 THA 88 #5	86 THP 89 THA 84 #16		90 #7 78 #26		

■ IMPACT PLAYERS   ■ LIKELY STARTERS

TEAM OFFENSIVE PLAYBOOK

Ace-Big Twins	Shotgun-5WR Trio	Shotgun-Spread
Ace-Spread	Shotgun-5WR Trips	Shotgun-Spread HB Wk
Ace-Y-Trips	Shotgun-Empty Trey	Shotgun-Trips
I-Form-Slot Flex	Shotgun-Normal HB Wk	Shotgun-Trips HB Wk
I-Form-Tight	Shotgun-Split Slot	Shotgun-Trips Open Str
I-Form-Y-Trips	Shotgun-Split Twins	Shotgun-Y-Trips HB Wk

WESTERN KENTUCKY
Hilltoppers

Conference: **Independent**
Location: **Bowling Green, KY**

REPORT CARD AND PRESTIGE

60	68	60
Overall	Offense	Defense

PRESTIGE RATINGS
Overall ★
Coach Fair
Academic Good

2007 SEASON RECAP
- 7-5 overall record
- 1st season in NCAA Division I (FBS)

DEFENSIVE DEPTH CHART AND SCOUTING REPORT

Conservative 3-4 Defense
AI Playcall Tendency: 35% defend run, 65% defend pass

	FS		ROLB	MLB	MLB		LOLB	SS	
	73 #23	72 #48		68 #42	76 #25		79 #6	70 #30	
	64 #19	71 #36		63 #53	66 #49		67 #38	67 #31	
71 #9									75 #2
67 #18	72 #92		74 #59			76 #90		70 #21	
62 #28	72 #95		68 #98			69 #96		64 #32	
CB	RE		DT			LE		CB	

■ IMPACT PLAYERS ■ LIKELY STARTERS

OFFENSIVE DEPTH CHART AND SCOUTING REPORT

Neutral Spread Offense
AI Playcall Tendency: 45% run, 55% pass

K	WR	LT	LG	C	RG	RT	TE	WR	P
61 KPW	74 #86	73 #68	78 #70	76 #72	78 #64	71 #73	71 #89	79 #11	69 KPW
78 KAC	71 #22	72 #67	71 #65	74 #71	71 #76	69 #74	66 #43	73 #81	87 KAC
82 #86									80 #44

	FB	QB1	QB2	HB	
	73 #33	78 THP 88 THA 82 #7	78 THP 87 THA 84 #3	80 #1	
	67 #40			74 #28	

■ IMPACT PLAYERS ■ LIKELY STARTERS

TEAM OFFENSIVE PLAYBOOK

Ace-Big	Shotgun-5WR Trey	Shotgun-Split Slot
I-Form-Twins	Shotgun-Ace Wing Wk	Shotgun-Spread
Shotgun-4WR Trey Str	Shotgun-Double Flex	Shotgun-Spread Flex
Shotgun-4WR Trio	Shotgun-Empty Trey	Shotgun-Wing Trips
Shotgun-4WR Trio Str	Shotgun-Normal HB Wk	Shotgun-Y-Trips
Shotgun-5WR Flex Trio	Shotgun-Normal Wing TE	Shotgun-Y-Trips HB Wk

---

WESTERN MICHIGAN
Broncos

Conference: **MAC (West)**
Location: **Kalamazoo, MI**

REPORT CARD AND PRESTIGE

79	77	85
Overall	Offense	Defense

PRESTIGE RATINGS
Overall ★
Coach Good
Academic Good

2007 SEASON RECAP
- 5-7 overall record
- 3-4 conference record
- 3rd in the MAC West

DEFENSIVE DEPTH CHART AND SCOUTING REPORT

Neutral 4-3 Defense
AI Playcall Tendency: 32% defend run, 68% defend pass

	FS		ROLB	MLB		LOLB	SS	
	87 #9	80 #35		80 #59		89 #43	86 #26	
	78 #15	72 #29		69 #53		68 #51	71 #27	
78 #39								82 #1
69 #25	85 #90		87 #68	88 #99		88 #54		73 #46
65 #7	78 #48		72 #98	73 #91		74 #93		66 #14
CB	RE		DT	DT		LE		CB

■ IMPACT PLAYERS ■ LIKELY STARTERS

OFFENSIVE DEPTH CHART AND SCOUTING REPORT

Neutral Balanced Offense
AI Playcall Tendency: 48% run, 52% pass

K	WR	LT	LG	C	RG	RT	TE	WR	P
51 KPW	75 #4	78 #67	75 #65	78 #63	72 #61	76 #72	82 #82	87 #27	62 KPW
76 KAC	74 #11	78 #56	74 #77	68 #60	69 #79	74 #76	74 #84	75 #83	89 KAC
80 #66									76 #37

	QB1	QB2	HB	
	87 THP 89 THA 90 #3	69 THP 84 THA 78 #18	83 #2	
			80 #40	

■ IMPACT PLAYERS ■ LIKELY STARTERS

TEAM OFFENSIVE PLAYBOOK

Ace-Big	Ace-Twin TE Slot	Shotgun-Double Flex
Ace-Big Twins	Ace-Y-Trips	Shotgun-Normal Flex Wk
Ace-Bunch	I-Form-Normal	Shotgun-Split Slot
Ace-Slot Flex	I-Form-Slot Flex	Shotgun-Y-Trips
Ace-Spread	I-Form-Twins	Strong-Normal
Ace-Trips	Shotgun-5WR Flex Trio	Weak-Normal

WISCONSIN
Badgers

Conference: **Big Ten**
Location: **Madison, WI**

REPORT CARD AND PRESTIGE

89	**92**	**89**
Overall	Offense	Defense

PRESTIGE RATINGS
Overall ★ ★ ★ ★
Coach Great
Academic Excellent

2007 SEASON RECAP
- 9-4 overall record
- 5-3 conference record
- Lost Outback Bowl

DEFENSIVE DEPTH CHART AND SCOUTING REPORT

Aggressive 4-3 Defense
AI Playcall Tendency: 41% defend run, 59% defend pass

94 #25	**93** #2	**83** #52	**88** #11	**81** #8	
88 #22	**84** #49	**79** #48	**80** #47	**71** #39	**86** #17
	FS / ROLB	MLB	LOLB / SS		
70 #7	**94** #92	**79** #54 / **91** #91	**82** #99		**73** #23
67 #4	**86** #93	**68** #98 / **78** #90	**81** #59		**68** #21
CB	RE	DT / DT	LE		CB

■ IMPACT PLAYERS ■ LIKELY STARTERS

OFFENSIVE DEPTH CHART AND SCOUTING REPORT

Neutral Balanced Offense
AI Playcall Tendency: 55% run, 45% pass

K	WR	LT	LG	C	RG	RT	TE	WR	P
72 KPW	**81** #6	**86** #78	**87** #75	**85** #58	**92** #63	**86** #71	**94** #9	**86** #84	**76** KPW
86 KAC	**78** #8	**82** #67	**78** #79	**73** #62	**74** #76	**72** #86	**72** #86	**78** #2	**88** KAC
85 #96		FB	QB1	QB2			HB		**86** #95
		89 #44	**86** THP #90 THA #89 #4	**80** THP #89 THA #87 #18			**93** #39		
		75 #34					**87** #5		

■ IMPACT PLAYERS ■ LIKELY STARTERS

TEAM OFFENSIVE PLAYBOOK

Ace-Big	Ace-Wing Trips	I-Form-Twins
Ace-Big Twins	Ace-Y-Trips	Shotgun-Split Y-Flex
Ace-Bunch	I-Form-Normal	Strong-Normal
Ace-Slot Flex	I-Form-Slot Flex	Strong-Y-Trips
Ace-Twin TE	I-Form-Tight	Weak-Normal
Ace-Twin TE Slot	I-Form-Twin TE	Weak-Twin TE

WYOMING
Cowboys

Conference: **Mountain West**
Location: **Laramie, WY**

REPORT CARD AND PRESTIGE

62	**70**	**62**
Overall	Offense	Defense

PRESTIGE RATINGS
Overall ★ ★
Coach Good
Academic Good

2007 SEASON RECAP
- 5-7 overall record
- 2-6 conference record
- 7th in the Mountain West

DEFENSIVE DEPTH CHART AND SCOUTING REPORT

Aggressive 3-4 Defense
AI Playcall Tendency: 53% defend run, 47% defend pass

80 #1	**71** #55	**64** #52 / **78** #29	**73** #36	**75** #27	
67 #24	**69** #6	**64** #59 / **64** #43	**69** #15	**74** #23	**72** #2
	FS / ROLB	MLB / MLB	LOLB / SS		
71 #9	**79** #98	**76** #91	**77** #95		**71** #12
69 #4	**77** #47	**72** #94	**75** #48		**67** #17
CB	RE	DT	LE		CB

■ IMPACT PLAYERS ■ LIKELY STARTERS

OFFENSIVE DEPTH CHART AND SCOUTING REPORT

Conservative Spread Offense
AI Playcall Tendency: 50% run, 50% pass

K	WR	LT	LG	C	RG	RT	TE	WR	P
63 KPW	**73** #81	**71** #71	**76** #75	**77** #77	**75** #70	**79** #76	**75** #87	**74** #15	**60** KPW
84 KAC	**71** #13	**67** #78	**75** #67	**71** #66	**71** #57	**68** #72	**72** #85	**72** #33	**84** KAC
80 #21		FB	QB1	QB2			HB		**78** #40
		68 #42	**83** THP #92 THA #86 #16	**81** THP #89 THA #86 #9			**82** #5		
		64 #44					**81** #31		

■ IMPACT PLAYERS ■ LIKELY STARTERS

TEAM OFFENSIVE PLAYBOOK

Ace-Big	Ace-Y-Trips	Shotgun-Split Slot
Ace-Big Twins	Shotgun-4WR Trio	Shotgun-Spread HB Wk
Ace-Bunch	Shotgun-4WR Trio Str	Shotgun-Y-Trips HB Wk
Ace-Slot Flex	Shotgun-Ace Twins	Strong-H Pro
Ace-Spread	Shotgun-Double Flex	Strong-H Twins
Ace-Twin TE	Shotgun-Normal Flex	Weak-H Pro

Advanced Strategy

NCAA Football 09 does an excellent job of portraying the X's and O's of college football. There can be a lot to swallow for new and old players alike. You have to be able to create pass protection schemes so you will have time to get your plays off.

You'll need to be able to understand different defensive fronts and how to attack them in the running game. As the virtual QB, it falls on you to understand Cover 3, Cover 2 and Cover 1 defense. Not only that, but you need to know how to attack each one.

On defense, you'll need schemes you can use to get after the quarterback. You must be able to defend the inside and outside run, and shut down the passing game.

In this section of the guide, we teach you how to do all of these things and then some. We'll then break down the Top 20 teams in the game, and give you some of our favorite offensive and defensive plays.

We finish things off with insider secrets to recruiting and instructions on how to run your own Online Dynasty.

Top 20 Teams

TEAM REPORT CARD AND PRESTIGE

GEORGIA
Bulldogs

Conference: **SEC (East)**
Location: **Athens, GA**
Overall Prestige: ★ ★ ★ ★ ★
Coach Prestige: **Excellent**
Academic Prestige: **Great**

Overall	**99**
Offense	**99**
Defense	**99**

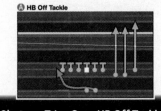

TEAM INTRODUCTION

Georgia rolls into *NCAA Football 09* as the number one ranked team. They are stacked on both sides of the ball and have plenty of weapons at their disposal. Pound the ball with HB #24 early and often. Georgia's playbook is based around a Pro Style offense with plenty of variety so be unpredictable with your playcalling.

MLB #33 can be used to control the middle of the field. Move him all over and attack from a variety of different angles. Shift the line where possible to keep him clean so that he can make stops in the run game.

IMPACT PLAYERS

HB #24 Sophomore (RS)	OVR 96	SPD 94	AGI 97	BTK 91

MLB #33 Senior (RS)	OVR 94	SPD 89	AWR 86	TAK 92

QB #7 Junior	OVR 93	SPD 74	THP 96	THA 91

KEY PLAYS

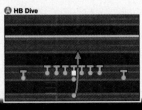

Ace Big HB Dive

You can pound the rock right into the heart of the defense with this play. Aim for the Center/Guard gap and blast away.

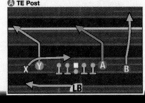

Ace Slot Flex TE Post

This play floods the left side of the field. Look for your TE on the post and then check down to the back if he is covered.

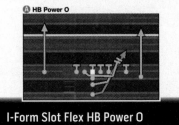

I-Form Slot Flex HB Power O

Follow your pulling LG and FB through the hole. If your slot receiver gets a good seal on the linebacker, spin it outside.

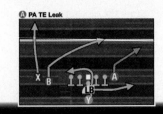

I-From Twins PA TE Leak

Once you've established the run with HB #24, you can sell this fake and get your receivers open. Look for the TE on the corner first.

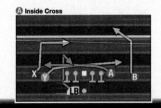

Shotgun Normal HB Wk Inside Cross

The crossing routes over the middle just tear up man coverage. You can also wait for them to clear the zone and hit the HB on the delay route.

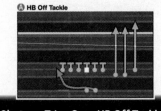

Shotgun Trips Over HB Off Tackle

The idea behind this play is to overload one side, and then hit the weak side with your HB. This play works great against man coverage.

Top 20 Teams

TEAM REPORT CARD AND PRESTIGE

OKLAHOMA
Sooners

Conference: **Big 12 (South)**
Location: **Norman, OK**
Overall Prestige: ★ ★ ★ ★ ★ ★
Coach Prestige: **Elite**
Academic Prestige: **Very Good**

Overall	**96**
Offense	**99**
Defense	**94**

TEAM INTRODUCTION

The Oklahoma Sooners team is built to score points. With one of the best offensive lines in the game, you'll have plenty of time in the pocket to throw and plenty of holes to run through with your impact HB #7.

With a solid receiving corp and a strong TE, Oklahoma can run a wide-open passing attack and throw at will. Experiment with some no-huddle-plays to put the defense on its heels and punish them with your playmakers.

The Sooner defensive line is stout, especially the left side of the line. Shift your line to their side so they can get an outside rush lane while you blitz FS #5 from the opposite side of the field.

IMPACT PLAYERS

FS #5 Senior	OVR 96	SPD 92	AWR 86	TAK 80

QB #14 Sophomore (RS)	OVR 94	SPD 72	THP 93	THA 95

HB #7 Sophomore (RS)	OVR 91	SPD 93	AGI 97	BTK 90

KEY PLAYS

Ace Twin TE Slot X Curl

The outside left receivers will cross over, usually causing some hesitation from the cornerbacks. The out route is an automatic gainer if they freeze up.

Ace Spread Flanker Dig

The two deep routes on the left will force the safety to choose a man, leaving the other receiver in 1-on-1 coverage.

I-Form Twin TE Weak Iso

This is basic power running at its best. Follow your Fullback into the hole, but be willing to pop it outside if the opportunity presents itself.

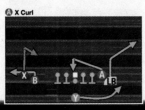

I-Form Normal PA Scissors

The Scissors route will again put the deep safety to the test. You have four routes going to the right side that will chew up zone.

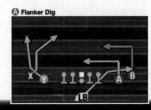

Shotgun Y-Trips PA Read

If you have success running from shotgun, you'll get the defense to bite on the play fake. Look for the deep out if you get man coverage.

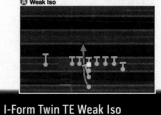

Shotgun Wing Trips Wk Z Spot

The Trips receiver bunch on the right side will create natural picks and rubs for your receivers. Against man coverage one of them will be open.

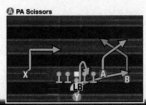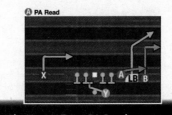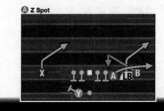

Top 20 Teams

TEAM REPORT CARD AND PRESTIGE

OHIO STATE
Buckeyes

Conference:	**Big Ten**
Location:	**Columbus, OH**
Overall Prestige:	★ ★ ★ ★ ★
Coach Prestige:	**Elite**
Academic Prestige:	**Excellent**

Overall **99**

Offense **99**

Defense **99**

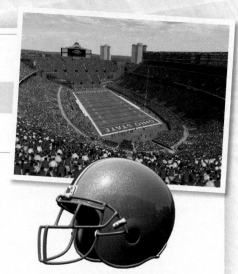

TEAM INTRODUCTION

The Ohio State Buckeyes are a deep and experienced team. The offense should remain a pretty straightforward affair, but don't be afraid to mix in a bit of spread here and there to keep the defense honest.

HB#28 is a stud and should be the focal point of your offense. His true bread and but-ter is going to be between the tackles. He has an impressive break tackle rating so expect him to knock over his share of defenders.

On defense you can't ask for much more than MLB #33. Quite simply, he is the best linebacker in *NCAA Football 09*. Move him all over the field, get him after the quarterback and generally use him to wreak havoc.

IMPACT PLAYERS

MLB #33 Senior	OVR	SPD	AWR	TAK
	99	89	94	96

HB #28 Junior	OVR	SPD	AGI	BTK
	97	92	90	99

CB #2 Senior	OVR	SPD	ACC	AWR
	96	93	95	90

KEY PLAYS

Ace Jumbo HB Stretch

Start to the outside and look for a cutback lane. There isn't a designated hole so you can free-lance a bit.

Ace Twin TE Slot HB Power O

Follow your LG and TE to the right side of the line. You'll be getting a kick out block from your extra TE that should open up running room.

I-Form Tight TE Flat

Throwing from a running set can be an effective change of pace. If your receivers are covered, the delay route will often come open for you.

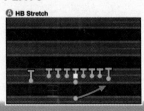

I-Form Slot Flex X Post

Plays with two levels of crossing routes coming over the middle are tough to defend. If the mid-dle gets clogged up, look for the HB in the flat.

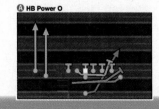

Shotgun Split Slot 46 Z Cross

Safe high percentage routes abound in this play. It puts pressure on both flats. Consider running two HBs in this set instead of a FB.

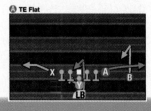

Shotgun 4WR Trio Str HB Draw

After you spread the defense out and throw on them for a while, you can hit the HB Draw. HB #28 will be hard for smaller DBs to tackle.

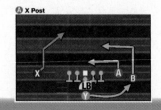

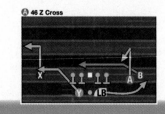

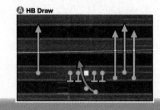

Top 20 Teams

TEAM REPORT CARD AND PRESTIGE

USC (SOUTHERN CALIFORNIA)
Trojans

Conference: **PAC-10**
Location: **Los Angeles, CA**
Overall Prestige: ★ ★ ★ ★ ★
Coach Prestige: **Elite**
Academic Prestige: **Excellent**

Overall	**94**
Offense	**90**
Defense	**99**

TEAM INTRODUCTION

When you think about USC, you usually think about explosive offenses with players like Reggie Bush and Matt Leinart having passed through the program in recent years. While this team can still put points up on the board, the heart and soul is the defense.

This defense is stacked from top to bottom.

The linebacker corp is one of the best in *NCAA Football 09* and has the speed to get after the QB and cover receivers across the middle. Play aggressive bump-n-run coverage with your corners knowing that the safeties will be able to make plays to cover up mistakes.

When you are on offense look to get the ball into the hands of WR #1 as often as possible. He is your playmaker and should be the go-to guy.

IMPACT PLAYERS

MLB #58	OVR	SPD	AWR	TAK
Senior	96	87	85	92

DT #75	OVR	SPD	STR	TAK
Senior (RS)	95	69	89	89

WR #1	OVR	SPD	ACC	CTH
Senior	91	91	92	90

KEY PLAYS

Empty Trips Tight Screen

Spread the defense out and get the ball to your playmaker in open space. Take a quick peek at the corner route to see if it comes open.

Ace Big Twins Flood

This play is a zone buster. Three routes at three different levels on the left side will put even the best secondary to the test.

Ace Slot Flex Curl Flats

The Curl Flats is one of the staple route combinations in the game. We like to hot route one of the flats into a slant out to get deeper down the field.

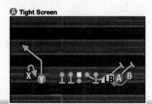

Strong Normal HB Dive

Pound the ball right up the gut with this run play. You can motion the FB over to the left if you want to attack that side of the line.

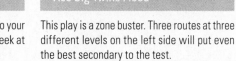
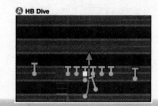

Weak Twins HB Gut

Here's another power run play to get your back up to full speed quickly. Get into the line as quickly as possible and use the juke move to beat the linebackers.

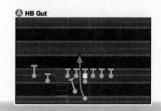

I-Form Twin TE X Slant

Break off a couple of nice runs from this formation. When the defense moves the linebackers in tight, hit the slant route behind them.

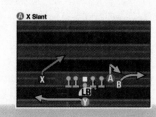
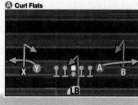

Top 20 Teams

TEAM REPORT CARD AND PRESTIGE

FLORIDA
Gators

Conference:	**SEC (East)**
Location:	**Gainesville, FL**
Overall Prestige:	★ ★ ★ ★ ★
Coach Prestige:	**Elite**
Academic Prestige:	**Excellent**

Overall	**94**
Offense	**96**
Defense	**94**

TEAM INTRODUCTION

The Florida Gators are back on the scene with more experience and a deadly combination of speed and misdirection. QB #15 is accurate and mobile with enough power to run over smaller corners and even linebackers.

WR #1 is the playmaker and should get as many touches as possible. Package him in all over the place. Put him in the slot for option plays, or use the Quick QB package with the Gator Heavy formation for a scary change of pace.

The defense is no slouch either. MLB #51 is a beast, and the secondary has greatly improved from last year's game. You'll have no problem scoring points with the Gators so you'll only need to make a stop or two to win the game.

IMPACT PLAYERS

QB #15 Junior	OVR 99	SPD 84	THP 97	THA 93

WR #1 Junior	OVR 96	SPD 98	ACC 99	CTH 93

MLB #51 Junior	OVR 94	SPD 85	AWR 85	TAK 96

KEY PLAYS

Shotgun Gator Heavy QB Blast

QB #15 is a load to bring down. This is a great short yardage play and is just about unstoppable in the red zone.

Shotgun Wing Trio TE PA QB Wrap

Lots of misdirection on this play. If the defense puts dime or quarters personnel on the field, hand it off. Otherwise, drop back and look for the corner route.

Shotgun Flip Trips FL Drive

The auto-motion receiver should be your first choice as he has a head of steam going over the middle. The deep in is choice number 2.

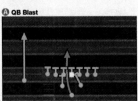

Shotgun Empty Trey Jet Sweep

Use the Z Left Slot package to get the ball to WR #1. His speed is hard to match as he comes around the corner on the sweep.

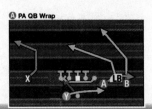

Shotgun Tight Circle

Option number one is the circle route run by the HB. This one is almost always open. The right side of the field has a nice flood as well to beat zone.

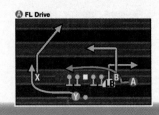

Shotgun Slot F Trips QB Slot Option

Use the Strong Slot or HB Slot package to get your best playmakers in as the pitch men. We like to sub in HB #8 to play the slot role here.

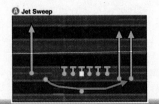

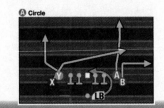

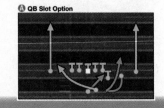

TEAM REPORT CARD AND PRESTIGE

LSU (LOUISIANA STATE)
Tigers

Conference:	**SEC (West)**
Location:	**Baton Rouge, LA**
Overall Prestige:	★ ★ ★ ★ ★ ★
Coach Prestige:	**Excellent**
Academic Prestige:	**Good**

Overall	**96**
Offense	**99**
Defense	**94**

TEAM INTRODUCTION

The defending BCS National Champion Tigers have some big shoes to fill this season. With 10 starters graduating and an untested QB, they may stumble a bit coming out of the blocks.

Fortunately, LSU still has plenty of talent to compete. HB #5 has excellent speed and will be the main threat on offense. Look to pound the ball behind the center and left side of the line. That is where their strength lies.

Defensively, RE #49 is your key to getting after the passer. The defensive line is strong and should get good pressure without having to send too many blitzers. FS #27 will anchor the secondary and is able to clean up any mistakes that are made by the cover corners.

IMPACT PLAYERS

FS #27 Senior (RS)	OVR	SPD	AWR	TAK
	94	**92**	**84**	**72**

RE #49 Senior (RS)	OVR	SPD	STR	TAK
	94	**84**	**80**	**82**

HB #5 Junior	OVR	SPD	AGI	BTK
	89	**93**	**92**	**86**

KEY PLAYS

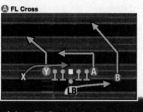

Pistol Ace FL Cross

The deep post route should clear out the safety so you can hit the underneath routes. If the safeties drop down to cover, hit the corner route.

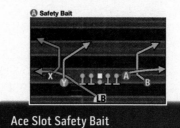

Ace Slot Safety Bait

This play is tough on zone coverage. The safety on the left side has to decide whether to pick up the post or the corner route.

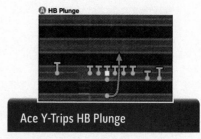

Ace Y-Trips HB Plunge

This is a quick hitting power run play. If the middle is clogged up, look to go outside, as you'll have two receivers to block for you.

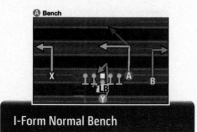

I-Form Normal Bench

Out routes are nasty against man coverage in *NCAA Football 09*. Look there first. You can check down to your HB if nothing is open.

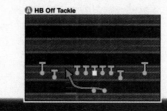

Shotgun Normal Wing TE HB Off Tackle

You'll need to establish the pass out of the Shotgun before running this play. Once you do, you should be able to get your HB going.

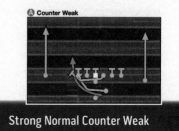

Strong Normal Counter Weak

HB #5 has good speed and should be able to make it to the corner on this play. Don't overrun your blockers and you should pick up yards.

Top 20 Teams

TEAM REPORT CARD AND PRESTIGE

MISSOURI
Tigers

Conference: **Big 12 (North)**
Location: **Columbia, MO**
Overall Prestige: ★★★★
Coach Prestige: **Very Good**
Academic Prestige: **Very Good**

Overall	**94**
Offense	**96**
Defense	**92**

TEAM INTRODUCTION

Missouri is a lot of fun to play with. QB #10 has a super accurate arm and can pretty much put the ball wherever he wants on the field. Line it up in Shotgun and play pitch and catch all over the field. WR #9 should be your main target, but you have plenty of other great options including your TE.

The trick to playing with Missouri is to get just enough of a run game going to take the pressure off your QB. Work quick runs and draws out of the Shotgun to make the defense play you honestly.

On defense you have a strong linebacking group. You can send these guys on the blitz behind RE #38 to get the maximum amount of pressure on the QB. FS #1 is the playmaker in your secondary. Let him help the corners in deep coverage.

IMPACT PLAYERS

QB #10 Senior
OVR	SPD	THP	THA
97	76	90	97

WR #9 Sophomore (RS)
OVR	SPD	ACC	CTH
94	97	98	93

MLB #34 Senior
OVR	SPD	AWR	TAK
89	82	86	88

KEY PLAYS

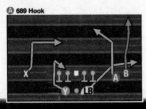

Shotgun Split Slot 689 Hook

Your primary read is going to be the outside receiver on the streak route. If the safety steps over to cover him, look for the post route.

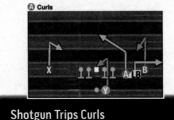

Shotgun Trips Curls

Curl routes are very effective against man coverage this year. If the defense plays zone, look for the out route or delay on the right side.

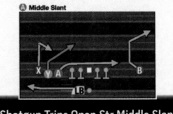

Shotgun Trips Open Str Middle Slant

This play attacks the middle of the field with a drag route and a slant. The slant is your #1 option, but keep an eye on the curl too.

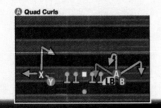

Shotgun 5WR Bunch Quad Curls

The right side of the field is flooded with short routes. These routes should break down both man and zone coverage. Somebody will be open.

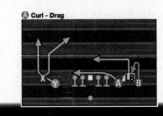

Shotgun 5WR Trio Curl-Drag

Spread 'em out and throw it around is the Missouri philosophy. This play attacks just about every area of the field: short, middle and deep.

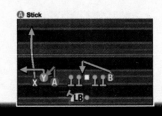

Shotgun Trio HB Wk Stick

The route combinations on the left side put a lot of pressure on zone defenses. The outside curl right is very effective against man coverage as well.

TEAM REPORT CARD AND PRESTIGE

WEST VIRGINIA
Mountaineers

Conference:	**Big East**
Location:	**Morgantown, WV**
Overall Prestige:	★ ★ ★ ★ ★
Coach Prestige:	**Good**
Academic Prestige:	**Good**

Overall	**84**
Offense	**90**
Defense	**80**

TEAM INTRODUCTION

West Virginia's offense is all about speed. QB #5 is one of the fastest signal callers in the game and is well able to beat the defense and go for six every time he takes a snap. HB #7, another speed demon with elusive skills, joins him in the backfield. Run the option, option & more option!

The offensive line is solid and will clear plenty of holes for you to run through. With all the speed in the backfield, the defense is going to have to creep up to stop them. Take advantage of this with play action passes deep over the middle.

The defense is going to be a bit of a trouble spot for you. You'll probably need to play a bend but don't break style. Or you can throw caution to the wind, blitz a ton and hope that you can get into a shoot out.

IMPACT PLAYERS

QB #5
Senior (RS)

OVR	SPD	THP	THA
97	92	94	88

HB #7
Sophomore (RS)

OVR	SPD	AGI	BTK
90	97	96	86

MLB #47
Junior (RS)

OVR	SPD	AWR	TAK
86	78	82	88

KEY PLAYS

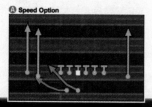

Shotgun Normal HB Wk Speed Option

This should be a bread and butter play for your offense. You have tons of speed in QB #5 and HB #7. Get to the corner and say goodbye to the D.

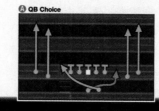

Shotgun Spread QB Choice

Your backfield has speed to burn on this play. Read the defense. If they overload left, keep it. If they overload right, hand it off.

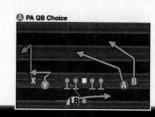

Shotgun Spread HB Wk PA QB Choice

If you've run the QB Choice before, the defense should buy your play fake. Look for one of the deep post routes on the right side of the field.

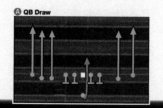

Shotgun 5WR Trips QB Draw

QB #5 gets to show off his skills on this play. The receivers all run deep routes to pull the coverage away so you can run in open space.

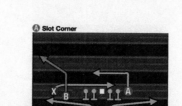

Shotgun Split Twins Slot Corner

This play puts pressure on both flats. If you can't find anything open down the field, check down to your speed back and get what you can.

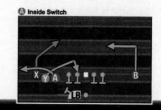

Shotgun Trips Open Str Inside Switch

The two inside receivers on the left side will cross over as they run their routes. Against man coverage one will get open quickly.

Top 20 Teams

TEAM REPORT CARD AND PRESTIGE

WISANSIN
WISCONSIN
Badgers

Conference: **Big Ten**
Location: **Madison, WI**
Overall Prestige: ★★★★
Coach Prestige: **Great**
Academic Prestige: **Excellent**

Overall **89**
Offense **92**
Defense **89**

TEAM INTRODUCTION

Wisconsin has a strong offensive line and a stable of quality running backs. Your gameplan should be to pound the ball down the throat of the defense. The QB situation is a bit up in the air with neither player being a real star so try to avoid third and long situations.

TE #9 is the go-to receiver in the passing game. If you can get your run game going, use play action and hit the TE on corner routes. He'll be your third and short possession guy. Burn up the clock with your running game and be opportunistic with the pass.

The defense has enough playmakers to keep you in the game. There are some weak spots on the team, but they are surrounded by strong enough players to cover things up.

IMPACT PLAYERS

RE #92 Senior	OVR	SPD	STR	TAK
	94	82	74	84

TE #9 Senior	OVR	SPD	ACC	CTH
	94	88	90	92

HB #39 Junior (RS)	OVR	SPD	AGI	BTK
	93	88	88	96

KEY PLAYS

Ace Wing Trips HB Wham

Slam and wham should be the motto for the Wisconsin offense this season. Pound the ball up the middle right into the heart of the defensive line.

Ace Big Twins HB Power

Your pulling LG will seal the outside so you can make this off tackle run. If the receivers pull their defenders deep, you can kick it outside.

I Form Twin TE Iso

This is another strong running play that attacks the middle of the defense. Follow your FB into the hole and drop your shoulder on the linebackers.

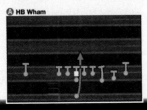

Strong Y-Trips Sail

This overload passing play is good for busting zone coverage. The inside release corner route and streak will force the safety into a decision.

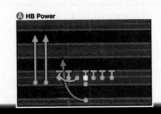

Weak Normal Outside Zone

Zone run plays don't have a designated hole. As soon as you see a hole develop in the line of scrimmage, dart in with your HB.

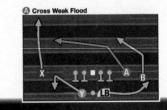

Shotgun Split Y-Flex Cross Weak Flood

The crossing route/post by the flexed TE is the money route on this play. If the safeties chase him down, look for the post or streak routes.

Top 20 Teams

TEAM REPORT CARD AND PRESTIGE

TEXAS
Longhorns

Conference: **Big 12 (South)**
Location: **Austin, TX**
Overall Prestige: ★ ★ ★ ★ ★ ★
Coach Prestige: **Elite**
Academic Prestige: **Excellent**

Overall	**89**
Offense	**88**
Defense	**92**

TEAM INTRODUCTION

Texas is reloading this year in the skill position department. Even with new starters in the fold, don't underestimate their scoring potential. You have a veteran QB to spread the ball around to your playmakers. You'll need to run a balanced offense with a good split between the run and the pass to be effective with Texas.

The strength of the Texas defense is the defensive line. The two bookends, RE #21 and LE #33, can defend the run or get after the passer. The linebackers are a solid if unspectacular unit. Against top-flight teams you must play conservatively on defense. The Texas defense is good enough to keep you in the game as long as you don't turn the ball over and give your opponent the short field.

IMPACT PLAYERS

DT #99 Senior	OVR	SPD	STR	TAK
	90	**62**	**90**	**88**

QB #12 Junior (RS)	OVR	SPD	THP	THA
	89	**76**	**90**	**88**

WR #6 Senior	OVR	SPD	ACC	CTH
	89	**91**	**94**	**89**

KEY PLAYS

Shotgun 5WR Flex Trey Whip Indys

This play is excellent against both man and zone coverages. The whip routes tear up man and you have a right side flood for zone.

Shotgun Ace Twins Wk Curl Flat Corner

The route combo on the left side always gets a player open. Be sure to keep an eye on the backside post route as well.

Strong Normal HB Blast

With Texas, you need to hit this play over and over again to control the clock. Follow your FB and try to make a linebacker miss you.

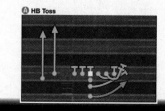

I Twins HB Toss

Against man coverage, the right side of the field should be open for you to turn the corner. Against zone, motion a receiver over to the right to block.

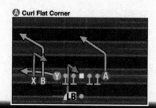

Shotgun Y-Trips Y Shallow Cross

The safety will be put to the test with the auto-motion post route and fade attacking the right side of the field. Watch the delay route as well against zone.

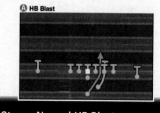

Shotgun Empty Trey Four Verticals

You are going for it all on this play. Four vertical routes can beat both cover 2 and cover 3 defenses. The slant curl is your hot read.

Top 20 Teams

TEAM REPORT CARD AND PRESTIGE

CLEMSON
Tigers

Conference: **ACC (Atlantic)**
Location: **Clemson, SC**
Overall Prestige: ★ ★ ★ ★
Coach Prestige: **Great**
Academic Prestige: **Great**

Overall	**89**
Offense	**90**
Defense	**92**

TEAM INTRODUCTION

Clemson is one of the few teams in the game that is blessed with two absolute studs at running back. HB #1 and HB #28 both are 90+ rated backs and can mow through defenses like a knife through warm butter.

Use plenty of two back sets: I-Form, Strong I and Shotgun Split formations. Get both players on the field as often as absolutely possible. WR #80 is no slouch either and if the defense crowds the run make them pay deep.

Defensively, you want to get SS #25 involved in the game as much as you can. He can drop the hammer in the secondary, which is the strongest part of the defense.

Send him after the quarterback, and punish receivers coming over the middle.

IMPACT PLAYERS

HB #1 Senior	OVR	SPD	AGI	BTK
	95	93	94	92

SS #25 Senior	OVR	SPD	TAK	AWR
	95	91	76	84

HB #28 Junior	OVR	SPD	AGI	BTK
	95	96	97	84

KEY PLAYS

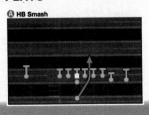

Ace Big HB Stretch

The offensive line is zone blocking and there isn't a designated hole. Find the first available running lane and attack the defense.

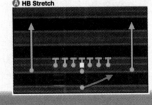

Ace Twin TE HB Smash

This play is a quick hitter between the RG and RT. Experiment with motioning the second TE across to act as a lead blocker.

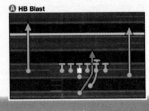

Strong H Pro HB Blast

Follow your FB and break into the secondary. With two solid running backs at your disposal, you can run this play again and again.

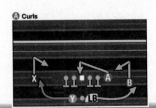

Shotgun Split Curls

Man coverage will really struggle against this play as both outside receivers button hook. If the heat comes, hit one of your backs in the flats.

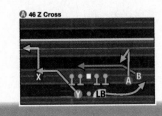

Shotgun Split Shot 46 Z Cross

The curl and flat routes on the right side attack zone coverage nicely. The out route on the left side will beat man coverage.

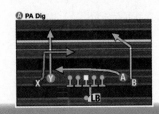

Shotgun Double Flex PA Dig

The strength of this play is that it attacks on many levels. Drag, dig and post will put a lot of pressure on the middle of the defensive secondary.

Top 20 Teams

TEAM REPORT CARD AND PRESTIGE

TEXAS TECH
Red Raiders

Conference: **Big 12 (South)**
Location: **Lubbock, TX**
Overall Prestige: ★★★★
Coach Prestige: **Very Good**
Academic Prestige: **Good**

Overall	**86**
Offense	**92**
Defense	**85**

TEAM INTRODUCTION

The Texas Tech Air Raid offense is one of the most fun to run in this game. If you like shootouts and want to bring a loaded gun to the fight, then TTU is a great squad to play with.

QB #6 has one of most accurate throwing arms in the game. You'll be able to spread it out all over the field and pretty much hit any target that you desire. You have a stable of highly rated receivers so you'll have little drop off if you run 4WR and 5WR sets.

The question mark for Texas Tech has been on defense. The squad is solid across the board, but a little thin at linebacker. That's okay. You'll be putting up so many points that you'll force teams to throw all game. You can sell out for pass defense pretty early.

IMPACT PLAYERS

QB #6 Senior (RS) — OVR 96 | SPD 65 | THP 90 | THA 97

WR #5 Sophomore (RS) — OVR 96 | SPD 94 | ACC 95 | CTH 96

CB #3 Junior — OVR 88 | SPD 91 | ACC 92 | AWR 82

KEY PLAYS

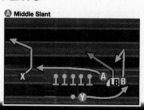
Shotgun 4WR Trey Str Middle Slant

The inside release corner route works well against Cover 2 defenses. The middle slant can get open behind the linebackers.

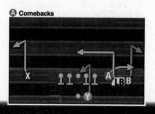
Shotgun 4WR Trey Str Comebacks

Deep comeback routes are effective against man coverage. You can use smart routes to extend them if necessary. Routes flood the zone on the right.

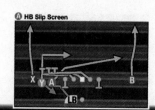
Shotgun Trips Open Str HB Slip Screen

Lots of blockers will get out to clear the way for your HB. Sprint out with your QB to the right to draw away defenders before throwing the ball.

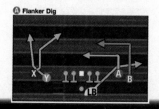
Shotgun Spread Flex Flanker Dig

Two levels of dig routes put pressure on the middle of the field. The fade/post combo on the left side strains the deep safety on that side.

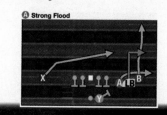
Shotgun Trips Strong Flood

The right side of the play floods the zone and forces the safeties into tough decisions. This can clear out the backside route for a big gain.

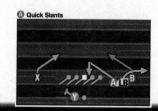
Shotgun Trips HB Wk Quick Slants

The slant routes are good for carving up man coverage. If the defense goes straight man without safety help you can often take the slant in for six.

Top 20 Teams

TEAM REPORT CARD AND PRESTIGE

PENN STATE
Nittany Lions

Conference: **Big Ten**
Location: **University Park, PA**
Overall Prestige: ★★★★★
Coach Prestige: **Elite**
Academic Prestige: **Elite**

Overall **91**
Offense **88**
Defense **94**

TEAM INTRODUCTION

With Penn State you truly have the option to run a balanced offensive attack. With two impact player receivers and quality backups, you can go spread and run 4 wide receivers out on the field.

The offensive line is seasoned and has the ability to split open defensive fronts for the running game. Penn State has two equally skilled quarterbacks with different styles of play. Rotate them in a 2 QB system and the defense will be in trouble.

Defensively you can rely on LOLB #45 to be your playmaker. The secondary is strong enough that you can pin your ears back and attack with your linebackers.

RE #47 is a tough match up for even the best offensive tackles.

IMPACT PLAYERS

LOLB #45 Senior	OVR 96	SPD 87	AWR 88	TAK 86

WR #2 Senior	OVR 92	SPD 97	ACC 98	CTH 88

WR #3 Senior (RS)	OVR 89	SPD 94	ACC 95	CTH 88

KEY PLAYS

Ace Twin TE Slot Inside Cross

The TE corner route on the right side should open things up for your HB sneaking out of the backfield on the out route.

I Form Twins China Special

You get a great zone flood on the left side of this play. The corner route will beat Cover 2 and the slant can break down man coverage.

Strong H Pro Counter Lead

Your LG pulls to seal the outside of the line. If you can't find anything between the tackle and RG, break it outside.

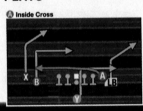

Shotgun Spread Slot Outs

This is a great play to attack man coverage. The out routes should get open, as well as the HB's angle route.

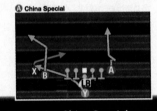

Ace Slot HB Dive

Spread out the defense and then hit them right up the middle. Be sure to work in passes from this same formation.

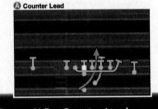

I Form Tight Iso

You can't go wrong with a good iso run play. The FB leads the way for your HB to get into the secondary.

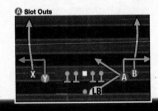

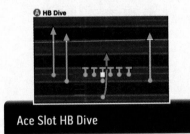

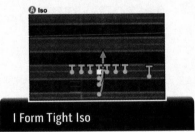

Top 20 Teams

TEAM REPORT CARD AND PRESTIGE

ARIZONA STATE
Sun Devils

Conference:	**PAC-10**
Location:	**Tempe, AZ**
Overall Prestige:	★ ★ ★ ★
Coach Prestige:	**Great**
Academic Prestige:	**Good**

Overall **86**
Offense **88**
Defense **87**

TEAM INTRODUCTION

Arizona State is making some changes this year by adding more 4WR and 5WR packages to their gameplan. They have the horses to make it work. QB #12 is accurate and has a strong arm. Spread the ball around to your wideouts, and don't forget to get HB #24 involved in the passing game as well.

The offensive line is young and unproven so you'll want to leave a back in to block, and be sure to get rid of the ball quickly. Focus your running attack behind your guards for best results.

The defense is full of solid performers. Be aggressive and bring the heat early and often. Use SS #14 to lay the wood on any receivers that try to come over the middle on you.

IMPACT PLAYERS

QB #12 Senior (RS)

OVR	SPD	THP	THA
92	72	93	92

HB #24 Senior

OVR	SPD	AGI	BTK
91	92	95	85

SS #14 Senior (RS)

OVR	SPD	AWR	TAK
88	89	82	76

KEY PLAYS

Shotgun 5WR Trey Strong Flood

The play name says it all. You have a flood to the strong side where you can go to work against zone coverage. The drag route beats man.

Shotgun Y Trips HB Wk Spacing

Spacing attacks the defense with four curl routes. This quick hitter will get you plenty of open receivers versus man coverage.

Ace Big Wing Y Option In

We like the post and corner routes on the left side of the play. Forcing the deep safety to choose a receiver always works to your advantage.

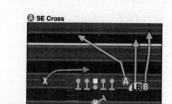

Ace Trey Open SE Cross

The cross/post route by the inside receiver can get open at several different points in the play. Two streaks on the right will beat Cover 2.

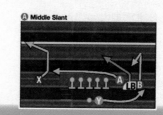

Shotgun 4WR Trey Str Middle Slant

Look for the trips receivers to draw the coverage so that you can hit the HB out in the flat. He should have room to operate.

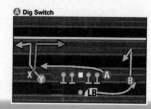

Shotgun Normal Dig Switch

The outside/in combination on the left side will often force the corners to switch assignments. While they hesitate in coverage, fire the pass in.

Top 20 Teams

TEAM REPORT CARD AND PRESTIGE

KANSAS
Jayhawks

Conference: **Big 12 (North)**
Location: **Lawrence, KS**
Overall Prestige: ★★★
Coach Prestige: **Good**
Academic Prestige: **Very Good**

Overall **77**
Offense **81**
Defense **78**

TEAM INTRODUCTION

QB #5 leads the Kansas offense and makes it tick. He has an accurate arm and decent mobility, which is good since he may have to run for his life at times.

On defense you are going to need to bring an extra safety down in the box to help stop the run as the interior of the defensive line is a bit shaky. Fortunately the outside of the line is in good shape with two solid defensive ends.

FS #25 is the ringleader in the secondary. He'll be needed to help the corners cover downfield if the defensive line is unable to get consistent pressure on the QB.

IMPACT PLAYERS

QB #5 Junior	OVR 92	SPD 76	THP 88	THA 94

RE #81 Senior	OVR 86	SPD 78	STR 72	TAK 80

FS #25 Junior (RS)	OVR 82	SPD 90	AWR 72	TAK 65

KEY PLAYS

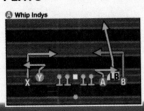

Shotgun 5WR Flex Trio Whip Indys

The "whip routes" on either side are tough for man coverage to handle. Take a peek at the deep route to keep the defense honest.

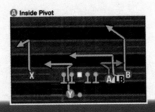

Shotgun Trips HB Wk Inside Pivot

We like to key in on the HB's route on this play. He will usually shake his coverage and get open. Eyeball the post against Cover 2.

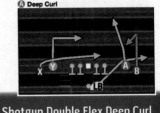

Shotgun Double Flex Deep Curl

The curl and streak routes on the right side should get plenty of attention deep. If they aren't open, the HB in the flat should be.

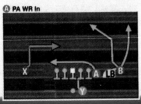

Shotgun Wing Trips PA WR In

You are hoping to see the safeties bite on your play action. If they do, you have two deep options to punish the defense's mistake.

Shotgun 4WR Trey Str HB Off Tackle

Being able to run from the Shotgun will keep the defense on its toes and force them to honor your play fakes when you go play action.

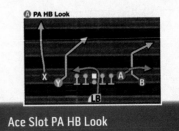

Ace Slot PA HB Look

This is another solid play action choice. If you can't hit the deep routes, look for the delay route out in the flat.

TEAM REPORT CARD AND PRESTIGE

AUBURN
Tigers

Conference: **SEC (West)**
Location: **Auburn, AL**
Overall Prestige: ★★★★★
Coach Prestige: **Excellent**
Academic Prestige: **Very Good**

Overall **84**
Offense **83**
Defense **87**

TEAM INTRODUCTION

Auburn made a big change right before their Bowl game last year. They added a new spread no-huddle package to their offensive plan of attack. Auburn has a good crop of receivers and a dynamite halfback. They are more than capable of running this style of offense.

The WRs are pretty much all rated the same with the exception of impact WR #80. You can be confident throwing to any of these targets. HB #44 is a solid performer and you should give him plenty of chances with the ball.

The defense is strong through the middle of the line and should be able to stuff the run inside the tackles. Get LOLB #59 involved in the blitz game as your playmaking linebacker.

IMPACT PLAYERS

DT #94 Junior (RS)	OVR	SPD	STR	TAK
	95	73	90	84

HB #44 Junior	OVR	SPD	AGI	BTK
	90	92	94	90

WR #80 Senior	OVR	SPD	ACC	CTH
	88	89	96	89

KEY PLAYS

Ace Trips HB Counter Strg

The LG pulls to seal the outside of the line at the point of attack. The HB's misdirection should free up some room on the right side.

Shotgun Y Flex-Z Slant Y Corner

The corner/slant combo on the right side will give defenses fits. The routes create picks and rubs to help break receivers open.

Shotgun Normal HB Off Tackle

You must establish the run from the Shotgun if you want to keep the defense from teeing off on your quarterback. This play will do just that.

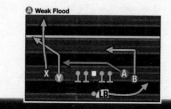

Shotgun Flanker Close Weak Flood

The play name says it all. You get a great flood on the weak side to destroy zone coverage. One of your deep routes should get open.

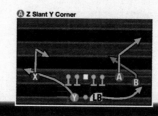

Shotgun Double Flex PA Dig

If you can get the safeties to buy the play action, then the post and streak routes have a good chance of getting open.

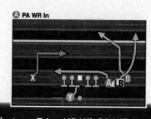

Shotgun Trips HB Wk PA WR In

The wheel/fade route on the right side of the play releases so that the post route gets downfield first and draws the safety.

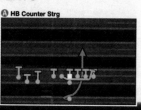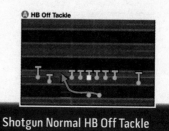

Top 20 Teams

TEAM REPORT CARD AND PRESTIGE

VIRGINIA TECH
Hokies

Conference: **ACC (Coastal)**
Location: **Blacksburg, VA**
Overall Prestige: ★ ★ ★ ★ ★
Coach Prestige: **Excellent**
Academic Prestige: **Great**

Overall	**84**
Offense	**79**
Defense	**89**

TEAM INTRODUCTION

Virginia Tech is in the enviable position of having two quality QBs. The main difficulty you will have with them is finding enough playmakers at WR to take advantage of your QB's skills.

Fortunately, the Virginia Tech defense is rock solid. You have a lock down corner in CB #1 and a pro class safety in FS #17. Run press coverage and send the heat on safety blitzes with your SS. The rest of your secondary will be able to handle its coverage assignments.

The defensive line is strong on the edges, and is backed up by a solid group of linebackers. You may struggle to put points on the board with Virginia Tech, but then again so will your opponent.

IMPACT PLAYERS

FS #17	OVR	SPD	AWR	TAK
Junior	95	92	85	76

CB #1	OVR	SPD	ACC	AWR
Senior	94	95	93	80

QB #5	OVR	SPD	THP	THA
Sophomore	84	86	91	87

KEY PLAYS

Ace Slot Flex HB Slant 18

This is a zone blocking run play. You can freelance a bit as you look for an open hole to break free.

I Form Normal Power O

Power O is a new play this year to Next Gen NCAA Football. It has a nasty blocking scheme with a pulling guard and lead fullback.

Weak Twins HB Slip Screen

Roll out to the left to draw the defense and then hit the HB. You will have plenty of blockers in front of you to clear the way.

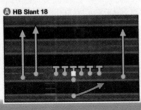

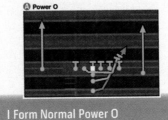

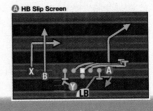

Pistol Slot Flex Curl Flats

Curl/Flats combos work well against man coverage. Against zone coverage you will often see the delay route come open.

Shotgun Y Trips HB Wk Levels Switch

Levels Switch is a great play if you want to attack the middle of the field. Three in routes, each at a different depth, create openings against all coverages.

Shotgun Normal Flex Wk FL Drive

The deep routes push the coverage back so that you can slip under for the dig or drag routes. Hit the HB if the defense brings the heat.

NCAA FOOTBALL 09

TEAM REPORT CARD AND PRESTIGE

ILLINOIS
Fighting Illini

Conference: **Big Ten**
Location: **Champaign, IL**
Overall Prestige: ★ ★ ★
Coach Prestige: **Good**
Academic Prestige: **Excellent**

Overall	**81**
Offense	**81**
Defense	**85**

TEAM INTRODUCTION

The Illinois offensive attack revolves around impact QB #7. He is fast, elusive and has a good enough arm to get the job done. Line him up in the Shotgun with 4 receivers and let him go to work.

The Spread Option is the key with Illinois. You'll want QB #7 to get out of the pocket and put the pressure on the defense. If they step up, hit impact WR #9. If they back off and play coverage, let him take off for the first down.

On defense, let CB #1 take his man one-on-one and give CB #28 help over the top. You should be able to lock down the passing game this way. The line is solid and should be able to handle pass rushing and run defense.

IMPACT PLAYERS

WR #9 Sophomore	OVR	SPD	ACC	CTH
	93	94	96	90

QB #7 Junior	OVR	SPD	THP	THA
	86	86	91	82

DT #68 Senior (RS)	OVR	SPD	STR	TAK
	85	72	85	80

KEY PLAYS

Shotgun Normal QB Choice

This play spreads out the defense so that QB #7 can get to work. If the defense stacks the left side of the field, make the handoff instead.

Shotgun Normal Y Slot Speed Option

Get to the corner with your QB. If the defense cuts him off, make the pitch. Otherwise, use your speed to get the ball downfield.

Shotgun 4WR Trio Smash

The combo of the post and corner route makes it difficult for the safety to handle his responsibilities. You also have a nice flat route by the HB if heat comes.

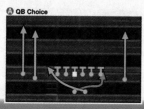

Shotgun 5WR Trips Pivot Z In

The post and whip routes on the left side cross over, often forcing the defenders to switch assignments. This usually gives you an opening for a pass.

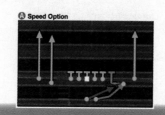

Shotgun Split Slot Backs Cross

The crossing routes by the backs are pretty much guaranteed to create an open man. You can also hit the outside curl against man coverage.

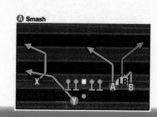

Shotgun Trips HB Mid Draw

Against man coverage, the corners and safeties will be pulled out of the middle of the field. This will give you room to operate with your HB.

Top 20 Teams

TEAM REPORT CARD AND PRESTIGE

TENNESSEE
Volunteers

Conference: **SEC (East)**
Location: **Knoxville, TN**
Overall Prestige: ★★★★★★
Coach Prestige: **Elite**
Academic Prestige: **Very Good**

Overall **84**
Offense **79**
Defense **89**

TEAM INTRODUCTION

Tennessee is set up perfectly to run a pro-style offense. You can go I-Form, Ace 3WR or pull out some Shotgun. The line has plenty of big bodies and should open holes for impact HB #27.

You won't have to score a ton on offense because Tennessee's defense is pretty stout. The defensive line should stuff the run at the line of scrimmage and has the horses to get after the passers.

ROLB #5 is your key linebacking playmaker. Get him after the QB or let him match up on receivers out of the backfield. SS #14 is a punishing tackler and should hold down his side of the field.

IMPACT PLAYERS

RE #91 Senior (RS) — OVR 94 | SPD 80 | STR 80 | TAK 82

ROLB #5 Junior (RS) — OVR 91 | SPD 85 | AWR 78 | TAK 84

HB #27 Senior (RS) — OVR 89 | SPD 90 | AGI 86 | BTK 90

KEY PLAYS

Ace Big HB Sprint

This is a quick hitting play that gets your back to the line as fast as possible. Don't be afraid to take it outside if the middle is clogged.

Ace Bunch Destroy

Double move routes typically break down man coverage. If the defense goes zone on you, you have a nice flood to the right side.

I Form Normal X Post

The post route is your primary pass route. You also have a quick flat route to your HB if you need to avoid pressure.

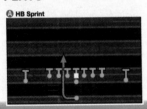

Weak H Twins Cross Under

The seam route (streak) can be hit at various points in the route depending on the coverage. The slant route works well against man coverage.

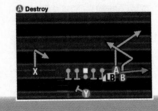

Shotgun Trips HB Wk Stick

A flood route to the right and a backside post route make this effective against both man and zone coverages. Look deep from time to time as well.

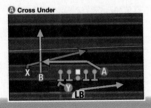

Shotgun Normal Dig Switch

The dig switch creates a nice pick for the two routes on the left side. Against man coverage you are bound to get an open receiver.

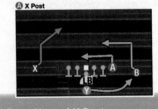
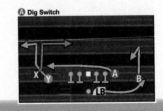
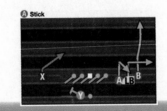

Top 20 Teams

TEAM REPORT CARD AND PRESTIGE

BYU
Cougars

Conference: **Mountain West**
Location: **Provo, UT**
Overall Prestige: ★ ★ ★
Coach Prestige: **Great**
Academic Prestige: **Great**

Overall	**79**
Offense	**88**
Defense	**73**

TEAM INTRODUCTION

BYU has been the elite program in the Mountain West Conference, but they will need to step up their game to go national. QB #15 has the skills to hang with anybody, and his backfield counterpart HB #45 is up to the task as well.

Against the Mountain West, you can go 4WR spread and be effective. If you are playing elite Top 10 competition, you'll want to focus in on your two starting WRs and move them around by packaging them into the slot.

Defensively, BYU is one of the few teams in *NCAA Football 09* that use a 3-4 defense. They have plenty of good linebackers and a star in RE #84. The corners will struggle against top-drawer receivers so you had better give them help deep.

IMPACT PLAYERS

RE #84 Junior (RS)	OVR	SPD	STR	TAK
	90	84	78	74

QB #15 Junior (RS)	OVR	SPD	THP	THA
	89	72	89	90

HB #45 Sophomore (RS)	OVR	SPD	AGI	BTK
	87	87	84	85

KEY PLAYS

Shotgun Split HB Off Tackle
This is a nice run play out of the Shotgun. It is rare that you get a lead blocker from the Shotgun, so take advantage of it.

Shotgun Normal Y Slot Slot Outside
This play is mainly geared towards defeating man coverage. The curl/flat combo on the right side gets you a pick. The HB runs a delay to beat zone.

Shotgun Spread Flex PA Jet Sweep
This is a great misdirection play. The Jet Sweep fake gets the defense moving to the right, while all the routes cut across the grain.

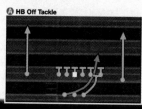
Shotgun Trips Open HB Burst
The flood on the left side is good against man coverage. The later releasing HB will often find room across the middle. Use the curl against man.

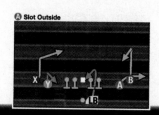
Shotgun 4WR Trey Str Curl Flat Corner
A great route combination on the right side will break down just about any kind of zone coverage that is thrown at you. The curl seems particularly effective.

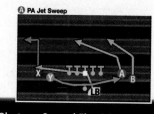
Ace Spread PA Slot Crosses
This play is about as money as it can be. The streak pushes the safeties deep, leaving room underneath for the crossing routes to do their magic.

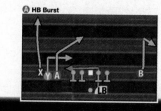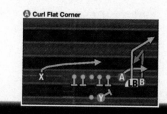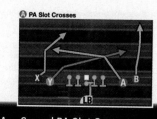

Running vs Base Defenses

▲ *Busting through the middle*

In this section of the book, we are going to talk about some simple solutions to counter your opponent when he tries to stop your game with base defensive formations.

3-4 DEFENSE VS RUN GAME

Solution: The best way to attack the 3-4 defense is to run quick inside run plays. With only three defensive linemen, it's almost always a guarantee that the running back will be able to pick up a few yards regardless of the defense. Any two or three tight end set will do nicely against the 3-4. Don't try to run the ball outside if the outside linebackers are fast; you will find it difficult to get running room on the perimeter.

PROBLEM 4-3 DEFENSE VS THE RUN GAME

▲ *Get to the corner quickly*

Solution: The 4-3 defense is easier to run outside on than the 3-4 because the line-backers are typically lined up closer inside. Sweeps, tosses, counters, and option plays are all good choices to run against the 4-3. Inside run plays can also be effective, but offensive linemen must get a push and hold their blocks. Dives, smashes, plunges, and slams are all good inside run plays to attack the 4-3 with. Watch for your opponent to bring the strong safety in the box to stop the inside run. If he does, audible to an outside run or deep pass play.

4-4 DEFENSE VS THE RUN GAME

Solution: With 8 defenders stacked in the box, forget about trying the run inside. There just isn't a lot of running room to be found. Instead call outside run plays such as sweeps, tosses, and option plays. Another option is to call pass plays that vertically stretch the field with three or four receivers running vertical routes. The free safety playing the deep middle will have a hard time trying to help the cornerbacks when that many receivers are going deep.

46 BEAR VS THE RUN GAME

Solution: The 46 Bear has eight defenders in the box, making it difficult to run inside. Just like the 4-4, it's best to call outside run plays. However if you call run plays from spread formations, it will force the linebackers and strong safety to play out wide. Ace Spread HB Dive is a good inside run play to attack the 46 Bear with providing that the linebackers and safety move out wide to cover the receivers in the slot. If they stay inside, then formation audible and call a pass play from the Ace Spread.

5-2 VS THE RUN GAME

Solution: Of all the defenses we have talked about so far, the 5-2 is the hardest to run on. With five defensive linemen and two linebackers, it's very hard to run inside or outside. The 5-2 is more of a hybrid Goal Line formation. If your opponent keeps calling this defense to stop the run, start calling pass plays with three, four, and five receivers. We guarantee your opponent won't stay in the 5-2 very long once his defense gets toasted with a few big pass plays deep down the field.

Passing vs Extra DB Sets

▲ Open on the Seam route

Knowing how to attack each pass defense set is essential to moving the ball through the air. The three pass defense sets in *NCAA Football 09* are Nickel (Normal, 3-3-5, and Strong) Dime (Normal, 3-2-6), and Quarter 3 Deep.

NICKEL NORMAL/STRONG

The Nickel Normal/Strong adds one extra defensive back in place of a linebacker. This means if you call four and five receiver sets, the defense won't have enough speed on the field to cover the inside receivers. To make it even more difficult, use packages to match up your fastest receivers on the linebackers. If you are able to get these match ups, call plays that have the receivers running crossing routes. The linebackers will have no chance to keep up with them.

NICKEL 3-3-5

The Nickel 3-3-5 has three linebackers in the line up and an extra defensive back. The same strategies apply to the 3-3-5 as the Nickel Normal. Be mindful that there are better blitz schemes from the 3-3-5 than there are from Nickel Normal/Strong. If you are playing against a veteran opponent, you can bet he has a few enhanced blitz set ups to get to your quarterback quickly. If you run into these set ups, make sure you have a few quick pass plays in your pocket. Running the ball inside is always an option as well.

DIME NORMAL

Having fast tight ends can really cause problems for players that call Dime Normal. This really holds true when the tight end runs a seam route against zone coverage. We can't tell you how many times we found the tight end wide open down the field for a quick bullet pass. If man coverage is called from the Dime Normal, have the tight end run crossing routes and drags. The inside defensive back covering him normally plays outside of where he lines up. Because of this the tight end will get inside position. If he has speed, he will be open for an 8 to 15 yard pick-up.

DIME 3-2-6

This pass defense can be tricky as well to attack. With an extra linebacker in the mix, there is good pressure that can be created. Since there are six defensive backs in pass coverage, going to four and five receiver sets is not always going to be to your advantage. If your team has a fast running back, look to match him up with one of the linebackers. Look for pass plays that have him running angle, circle, flat, and out routes. Once the running back breaks, he should get separation from the linebacker. Once he does, throw him a bullet pass. Again, the inside run game is always a good option.

QUARTER 3 DEEP

▲ Work the short passing game

With several of the Quarter 3 Deep defenses having at least three defenders playing deep coverage, it's best to attack it with underneath routes such as drags, slants, and crossing routes. Screens can also be called because there are seven defensive backs on the field. They will have a very hard time avoiding being knocked to the ground. Look to pound the ball inside, even if in third and long situations. You might be surprised at the amount of yardage that can be picked up.

PASS DEFENSE QUICK TIPS:

☐ Vary your pass coverages. Don't get in the habit of calling the same pass coverage over and over.

☐ Use defense individual hot routes to give your opponent different looks.

☐ Mix in all coverage from time to time. This means dropping 11 defenders in pass coverage. This tactic is very effective against the CPU controlled offense.

☐ Don't leave your cornerbacks on an island by themselves if they don't have the speed to cover the receiver they are matched up with. It's hard enough to defend a receiver in one-on-one coverage as is, so don't compound the problem.

☐ Develop blitz schemes that don't sacrifice too much pass coverage. The rule of thumb that most players use when blitzing is to try to achieve pressure with the least number of pass rushers possible.

☐ Use bump-n-run coverage to disrupt the timing of short to intermediate pass routes.

☐ Get your defensive user stick control up. Learn to take control of defenders while the ball is up in the air. You will find your pass defense is much better than if you let the CPU controlled defenders do all the work.

Inside Run Game

▲ *Preparing to pound the rock*

▲ *Nice hole in the middle*

Obviously having a big running back that can break tackles while pounding the ball inside is a huge asset. However, another key that is often overlooked by players is having a big offensive line up front. More specifically having big, strong interior offensive linemen: center, left guard, and right guard.

The offensive line play in our opinion is in many cases more important than the overall talents of the featured ball carrier. If the offensive line isn't able to create any sort of push for the ball carrier, he'll usually struggle just to pound out even the smallest of gains. Obviously every team doesn't have big physical All-American offensive linemen paving the way for their running game, but nonetheless you'll still want to identify who are the best run blockers along the offensive line on your team and focus the bulk of your interior running game behind them.

▲ *Who are your best run blockers?*

When looking over offensive linemen player ratings, look for ones with high run blocking ratings. The higher they are, the bet-

ter the chance that they will open holes for your running backs to follow through. Also look at the defensive linemen's ratings. If the defensive lineman is an elite player, chances are he is going to make short work of the offensive lineman in front of him.

SINGLEBACK TWIN TE HB PLUNGE

▲ *Misdirection run play*

There are several types of inside run plays in *NCAA Football 09*. Examples include the HB Dive, HB Slam, and HB Plunge. Each one of these plays gets the ball into the ball carrier's hands and gets him quickly through the line of scrimmage. The Singleback Twin TE HB Plunge is strong because with two tight ends lined up on the right our opponents tend to overload that side of the ball. This allows us to run to the weak side behind our left tackle and left guard, who are generally better run blockers than the right side of the offensive line.

The quarterback quickly hands the ball off to the running back.

The play is designed to have the running

back follow behind the left guard, but that doesn't mean we can't look for another area to run. Our center has opened up a pretty nice hole to run through, so that's where we go. The key here is not to press the Sprint button too early.

▲ *Follow your blockers to daylight*

Once through the hole, we press down on the sprint and shoot through for a 5 yard pick up.

QUICK INSIDE RUNNING TIPS

☐ Cover the ball up when you are just about to be tackled (+ on Xbox 360, R1 on PS3).

☐ Use the stiff arm, but be aware of fumbles. Try to use it on the sidelines.

☐ Use the Highlight Stick to run over defenders when using a big power back.

☐ Avoid dancing around with the running back. Most inside run plays are quick and precise.

☐ There are some inside run plays that can be bounced to the outside to pick up extra yardage.

☐ If the run play has a fullback, follow him through the hole. He often will break open big holes for you to pick up yardage.

Outside Running Game

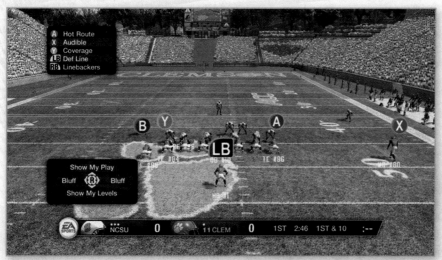

▲ Readying an outside run

▲ Set up your blockers

we then bounce back outside.

We now have plenty of room to pick up yardage down the sideline.

▲ Getting the ball outside

Running the ball outside successfully requires you to let the blocks set up. If you out-run your blockers, chances are the play is not going to work out. Having a fast running back also helps to increase the chances of a positive running play. If the running back doesn't have the speed to get to the corner, he more than likely will be tackled for a minimum gain or worse yet, a loss of yardage.

Another key to having a successful outside running game is having effective blockers along the offensive line with the speed to get outside to block. Effective outside running also depends on the blocks of the wide receivers. If a wide receiver is able to hold his block, it makes it that much easier to get outside and pick up yardage.

The tackles and tight ends play a crucial role in the outside running game as do the overall talents of the featured ball carrier. If the offensive tackles and tight ends aren't able to create any sort of push for the ball carrier, the outside running game can really struggle just to avoid a negative gain on the play.

ACE JUMBO HB TOSS STRONG

The Ace Jumbo HB Toss Strong is an excellent outside run play choice. With the extra tight end added to the play side, you'll get help sealing off the defenders.

Against man coverage, the cornerback covering the outside tight end will move

▲ The RG and RT will pull for you

inside to cover him. This leaves plenty of running room to the outside. The right guard and right tackle both pull to the running side. This gives the ball carrier two lead blockers once he gets out on the perimeter.

▲ Follow your blockers

Notice in the screen shot how the blockers are able to seal the defenders off.

Once to the outside, we don't want to overrun our blocking. We wait for the blocks to set up.

We actually cut back inside for a split second. We do this to give our blocker time to engage the defender in front of him.

Once the blocker engages the defender,

QUICK OUTSIDE RUNNING TIPS

☐ Don't outrun your blocking.

☐ Running backs with speed (93 or higher) have a better chance of success when running outside than slower running backs.

☐ If nothing develops outside, don't be afraid to cut back inside and pick up what you can. Don't try to make something happen and end up losing yardage.

☐ If your opponent likes to call man coverage, look for outside run plays that have twin receivers or compressed sets. This will bring the corners inside. This helps open up more running room to the outside.

Pass Protection Schemes

To have a successful passing attack, the offense must be able to protect its quarterback. Otherwise the passing attack may never get off the ground. Thankfully in *NCAA Football 09*, there are several options available to improve your pass protection. We are going to show you a few pass protection schemes you can use to keep your quarterback upright so he can deliver a strike to the open receiver.

▶ BACKS LEFT IN TO BLOCK

▲ *Use your blocking hot routes*

When your opponent is blitzing from the outside and from both sides of the field, it's best to leave both backs in to pass block where possible. One of the most popular Shotgun formations in the game is the Split. The reason is it has two backs lined up in the backfield. They can be hot routed to pass block to the right and left sides of the field.

If an outside blitz is called, they both will be in position to block the pass rush.

▲ *Plenty of time to throw*

With extra pass protection this gives us plenty of time in the pocket to find the open receiver down the field.

We make the catch for a 25 yard pick up.

▶ MOTION BLOCK

▲ *Sending the back in motion*

Another common pass protection technique is to hot route a running back or receiver to pass block and then put him in motion.

Once the running back or receiver gets to the area where the blitz looks like it's going to be most effective, snap the ball.

▲ *Snap it when he is in position*

This allows the blocker in motion to pick up the blitz and help provide extra pass protection so the quarterback can find the open receiver.

▲ *Our QB has time in the pocket*

▶ SLIDE PROTECTION

▲ *Setting slide protection inside*

▲ *The line picks up the inside blitz*

New to the Xbox 360/PS3 version of *NCAA Football 09* this year is the ability to slide protect. We have already shown the basics of slide protection in another section of the book. For this section, we want to show an example of how it can be implemented to improve your passing game.

If an inside blitz looks to be called, such as in the screen shot, we like to use slide protection pinch to counter the inside pass rush.

This prevents any A or B Gap heat from getting to our quarterback. We now can step up in the pocket with confidence and deliver a strike.

▶ SLIDE PROTECTION QUICK TIPS

☐ If slide protection to the left is used, consider rolling the quarterback out to the right. Hot route one of your backs to block to the right as well. This will buy you some extra time to find an open receiver and pick up the blitz to the roll side.

☐ When hot routing a receiver to pass block, make sure it's not an elite receiver. You want this type of receiver to go out on pass routes.

☐ When using the pinch slide protection, you may need to leave a running back in to pass block to the outside. The offensive tackles will block inside, leaving the outside pass rushers unblocked.

☐ Some players use slide protection to run the ball. You may consider looking into this and see if it's something you want implemented into your running game.

Pass Routes

We have already covered several of the pass routes in the game in the Hot Routes section of the book. Now we want to show six more common pass routes that you should implement in your passing attack. Master these and you will see big gains in your passing yardage, completion percentage, and touchdown totals.

CIRCLE ROUTE

▲ Two Circle Routes

The Circle Route run by a running back is best used against man coverage. The key is waiting for the receiver to break over the middle. Once he does, throw him a bullet pass. The Split Backs 3WR RB Circles is an example of a play that makes good use of the circle route. Notice the halfback and fullback are both running circle routes. At least one of them is almost always open.

▲ The back slides out of the backfield

The halfback starts off by going outside. He then will cut back over the middle. Once he does, he will get inside position on the defender covering them. As soon as we spot him open,

▲ The QB makes the throw

▲ Nice grab for 20 yards

we throw him a hard bullet pass.
We make the catch for a 20 yard pick up.

CROSSING ROUTE

▲ Crossing routes are deadly

If you have been playing on the Xbox 360 or PS3 over the last few years, then you know how effective the crossing routes are. This route is effective against man and zone coverage. One of the more popular sets to run the crossing route from is the Split Backs 3WR Slot Cross. This play has the split end running a deep post. His pass route forces the safeties to drop back, leaving the slot running a crossing route open over the middle.

Notice how the slot receiver gets inside position against the defender in coverage. This is what makes this route so effective against man.

▲ Waiting for the route to come open

Once he gets a few yards of separation, we throw him a bullet pass.
We make the catch about 17 yards down the field and have room to run to pick up some YAC (yards after catch).

▲ Easy game of pitch and catch

DELAY ROUTE

▲ Delay routes kill zone coverage

The delay route is one that many players overlook. This is a highly effective route, especially the delayed seam route version. This route is a zone coverage killer. Defenders playing zone coverage will continue to drop back provided that no other receiver comes in their area. By the time the receiver running the delay seam route goes out, the defenders have dropped too far back to make any type of play on the ball.

The Ace Slot Strong PA has the tight end running a delayed seam route.

Before he goes out on his pass route, he will chip the left end. This helps slow down the left end's pass rush.

▲ The QB fakes the handoff

While the tight end is chipping the left end, the defenders playing zone coverage are dropping back in coverage.

This allows the tight end to get open once he finally goes out on his delayed seam route. Notice how far the defenders are from him.

Pass Routes continued...

▲ *The route is opening up*

This makes for an easy pitch and catch.

▲ *The QB throws a strike*

We make the catch 10 yards down the field. The closest defender is still five yards away.

OPTION ROUTE

▲ *Slot receiver is assigned an option route*

Option routes are somewhat tricky to use because you have to rely on the CPU AI controlled receiver to make the correct decision on what pass route to run based on the coverage he sees. For that reason, some players tend to shy away from using them. Option routes give the receiver two or three routes he can run based on the type of pass coverage that is called. Notice in the screen shot, the slot has three routes he can run. His default route is a curl, his two options routes are a seam and a corner.

The defense coverage called is Cover 3. Against this type of coverage, the best route for the CPU AI controlled receiver is the corner route, which is what he chooses. We throw him a hard bullet pass once he makes his break.

▲ *The Slot runs the corner route*

We take control of the receiver and go up to make the catch for a big gain down the field.

POST ROUTE

▲ *Post routes hurt Cover 2*

The post route works best against Cover 2 type coverages because the safeties split out wide, leaving the deep middle open. The post route takes time for the receiver to run, so pass protection is a must to give the quarterback time to make the throw.

The Ace Slot Post has the receiver in the slot running a deep post route. The tight end running the drag route underneath will hold any linebackers playing hook zones. This will keep them out of the area where the slot receiver is running his post route.

Notice there is no defender playing the deep middle. The middle linebacker was held by the tight end long enough for the slot receiver to get behind him. This gives us enough space to throw to him on the deep post.

We make the catch 25 yards down field.

▲ *The middle is wide open*

SCREEN ROUTE

▲ *Use the screen to beat the blitz*

Screen plays to running backs and receivers should not be overlooked. They are some of the safest and best pass plays in the game. The biggest key to running them is giving the blockers enough time to set up their blocks. The Shotgun 5-Wide Tiger WR Screens has the split end and flanker both running screens. The split ends screen route is more of a decoy since no blockers pull to his side to set up blocking. The flanker, who is lined up on the right, is the go-to receiver.

We like to roll our quarterback away from where the screen is setting up. We are able to draw some of the defensive linemen away from the flanker and give us more room to run.

▲ *Roll away from the screen*

Once the blockers get out in front, we throw a bullet pass to the flanker.

We make the catch and follow our blockers.

▲ *WR#82 has plenty of room to run*

Reading Coverages

▲ Determining man or zone coverage

Being able to read whether the coverage is man or zone before and after the snap is very important to having a successful passing game. Reading the coverage before the play starts makes it much easier to know where to go with the ball. We are going to take a look at a few tried and true methods for reading man and zone coverage before and after the snap.

TWIN FORMATIONS

Calling plays from Twin formations is probably the simplest way to tell if your opponent is in man or zone coverage. This only works when the defense calls a base defense line 4-3, 3-4, 4-4, 46 Bear, or 5-2.

If both cornerbacks line up on the same side as the receivers, then it's some sort of man coverage.

If one cornerback lines up on the same side as the twin receivers, and the other cornerback lines up on the opposite side, then it's some type of zone coverage.

MOTION

▲ Using motion to read coverage

▲ Defense in Man Coverage

Putting players in motion can be used to tell if there is man or zone coverage. The only downside of this is if you are playing against a human opponent, he may audible to another coverage if he sees you getting a read on this play.

Notice we sent the flanker in motion in the screen shot. The right cornerback is following him all the way across to the other side of the field. This tells us man coverage has been called.

If zone coverage was called, the right cornerback will not follow the receiver across the field. This tells us the defensive coverage is some type of zone.

▲ Defense in Zone Coverage

Note: *Keep in mind if you play against a human opponent he can use defensive hot routes to change up the coverages and disguise his pass coverage scheme much better than what the CPU AI will do. So using motion may not always tell you what the pass coverage is, but it is a good foundation to use for reading the defense before the snap.*

QUESTIONS TO ASK BEFORE THE BALL IS SNAPPED

- ☐ What are the alignments of the safeties?
- ☐ Are the safeties up near the line of scrimmage?
- ☐ Are they in a one deep or two deep look?
- ☐ How is the defense adjusting to motion?
- ☐ What are the linebackers doing?
- ☐ Is the defense playing bump-and-run or loose coverage?

The answers to these questions will give you further clues as to what type of coverage has been called.

READING MAN ZONE

▲ We read Man Coverage

AFTER THE SNAP

If you can't tell or are unsure if the defense called is man or zone, don't panic. You can still tell after the ball is snapped.

If you see defenders following the receivers, then it's some type of man coverage.

If the defenders don't follow the receivers, then it's some type of zone coverage.

Red Zone Offense

A football team's red zone efficiency in many cases can be the determining factor in whether or not that team wins a close football game. The case can be made that the red zone (inside the opponent's 20 yard line) is probably one of the most difficult places on the field to consistently move the ball. Once an offense reaches their opponent's 20 yard line, it's a different game altogether.

▲ *The Red Zone*

Defenses will often blitz more, sending linebackers or defensive backs after the quarterback to disrupt the offense's rhythm. The cornerbacks and safeties can play tighter coverage because they don't have to worry about giving up the deep pass. In essence the back of the end zone becomes an extra defender. Playing inside the red zone alters the plays that can be called by the offensive team.

With this being the case, certain types of plays will always be more viable inside the red zone than others. For starters the running game will always be an option to a team once they reach their opponent's red zone. Running the football is relatively safe and in many instances is the best way to go. If your offense is able to continually pound the ball at the defense in this area of the field, it's a good idea to do so. However, sooner or later the need for passing the ball inside the red zone will arise. The types of plays that you'll want to consider are quick hitting pass plays and play action passes.

▲ *Run the ball in the red zone*

Quick passing routes such as slants, drags, screens and other short routes are good in this area of the field due to the condensed nature of the defense. A quick throw gets the ball out of the QB's hands before the defense has had a chance to really focus in on what the offense is doing. Slant routes are a favorite to use by offenses due to the quick timing of the throw.

▲ *Use quick routes in the red zone*

The most popular types of passing plays inside of the red zone are play action passes. Play action passes are effective in this area of the field because the defense has to honor the running game this close to their end zone. A well conceived play action pass play could mean all the difference in the world between scoring a touchdown or kicking a field goal.

▲ *Use play action in the red zone*

The following two plays are examples of two goal line plays we like to use when we get inside the 5 yard line. These two plays won't guarantee you success each and every time you use them, but will give you a solid foundation to build the rest of your goal line offensive package from.

GOAL LINE NORMAL POWER O

The Goal Line Normal Power O is a very effective run play to use when down near the goal line. With extra beef up front, the defense will have a very hard time defend-

▲ *Goal Line Normal Power O*

ing this run play.

We like to take control of the outside tight end on the right and motion him to the left. Once he gets behind the inside tight end or right tackle, we snap the ball.

This gives us another blocker to follow through the line of scrimmage.

We are able to move into the end zone untouched.

GOAL LINE NORMAL PA POWER O

▲ *Goal Line Normal PA Power O*

The Goal Line Normal PA Power O plays off of the Power O.

Instead of the quarterback handing the ball off to the halfback, he keeps it.

Once we gain control of the quarterback, we look for the tight end running the corner or the fullback in the flat.

The fullback is covered, but the tight end is open. We throw him a hard bullet pass as he breaks towards the corner of the end zone.

We make the easy catch for six points.

Note: *If you are still on first or second down, get outside and throw the ball away if nothing opens up. There is nothing worse than throwing an interception in the end zone when you are so close to pay dirt.*

Pass Coverages

In *NCAA Football 09* there are several types of pass coverage that can be called. Being able to recognize their strengths and weaknesses will help improve your defensive play calling tremendously. In this section of the guide, we are going to show you the different types of coverage and how they work.

COVER 0

Cover 0 coverage is a very aggressive man coverage scheme that is used primarily to bring pressure on the quarterback. There is no safety help deep and it leaves each pass defender on an island by themselves. A Cover 0 defense has six or more pass rushers that attack the quarterback. This type of pass coverage is high risk/high reward. One of three things usually happens: either the defense forces a bad throw or sacks the quarterback, or the offense is able to pick up the blitz and has a big play deep down the field.

4-4 FS BLITZ

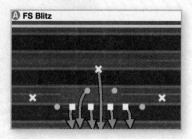

The 4-4 FS Blitz is perfect example of a Cover 0 defense. The free safety and right inside linebacker are both sent in on a blitz. Notice there are no safeties dropping back over the deep middle.

DIME 3-2-6 LIGHTING 0

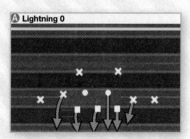

You can bet if you play online that you will see this Cover 0 blitz used to bring heat on the quarterback from all directions. A few lit-

tle shifts and this defense can bring serious A gap heat on the quarterback.

COVER 1

Much like Cover 0 coverage, Cover 1 (also known as Man Free) is also an aggressive man coverage scheme that is used to bring pressure on the quarterback. The main difference between Cover 0 and Cover 1 is instead of having no safety playing deep, one of the safeties drops back over the deep middle. This helps prevent the deep pass. The safety playing deep still has a lot of field to cover so he must have the speed for coverage to be effective. The other safety either plays man, zone coverage (robber coverage), or is sent in on a blitz. If the offense has more speed than the defenders do, Cover 1 can easily be exploited.

4-3 OVER COVER 1 PRESS

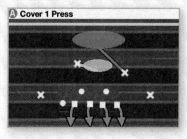

One of the new defensive playcall options added to *NCAA Football 09* is press coverage. The 4-3 Over Cover 1 Press has the strong safety rotating over the deep middle, while the free safety plays a hook zone underneath.

NICKEL NORMAL ROLB BLITZ

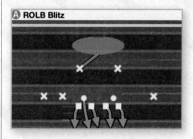

The Nickel Normal ROLB Blitz is a typical Cover 1 blitz scheme. The free safety rotates over the deep middle, while the right outside linebacker is sent on a blitz through the B Gap.

COVER 2 MAN

The coverage you will most often encounter while playing *NCAA Football 09* is Cover 2 Man (also known as 2 Man Under). The reason players like this coverage is it does a good job of covering all parts of the field with five defenders playing man coverage underneath and the safeties playing the deep halves. This pass coverage is not as aggressive as Cover 0 or Cover 1. However, that doesn't mean that it can't be used to apply pressure.

In most Cover 2 Man defenses, there is only a three or four man pass rush. There are some Cover 2 Man defenses that send up to five defenders. There also are a few where a linebacker plays QB Spy and the defensive ends are in QB Contain.

4-3 NORMAL 2 MAN UNDER

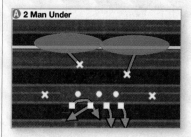

One of the most popular defenses in the game is the 4-3 Normal 2 Man Under. With the safeties playing 2 deep zones and five defenders playing man coverage underneath, this is one of the better overall defenses in the game.

4-3 UNDER SAM SHOOT FIRE 2

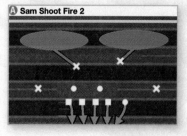

The 4-3 Under Sam Shoot Fire 2 adds an extra pass rusher by sending the left outside linebacker on a blitz. Although there is added pressure, the pass coverage is sacrificed somewhat since one receiver is left uncovered if all five go out on pass routes.

Pass Coverages continued...

COVER 2 ZONE

Cover 2 Zone coverage has both safeties playing the deep halves of the field, while five or six defenders play zone coverage underneath. The left and right cornerbacks play the flats taking away any type of pass in those areas of the field. Even though Cover 2 Zone is normally referred to as a bend-but-don't-break pass coverage, there are a few plays in the game that bring more than three or four pass rushers. If the opposing quarterback has time in the pocket, Cover 2 Zone coverage can be easily exploited deep, especially if a player has good stick skills while in control of a receiver. Because of this most players that run Cover 2 Zone normally use it inside the red zone, since the safeties don't have to cover as much ground.

COVER 2 BUC

Another form of Cover 2 is Cover 2 Buc (also known as Tampa 2). The same type of coverage is used as Cover 2 Zone, but with one added element. The middle linebacker drops back over the deep middle zone to take away the primary weakness of the Cover 2 zone. The middle linebacker needs to have speed to drop back in coverage. If he doesn't, the Cover 2 Buc can easily be exploited. Not only does the middle linebacker need to have speed, but so does the rest of the defense. If the defensive linemen can get to the quarterback quickly, it makes the pass coverage behind the pass rush that much stronger.

NICKEL 3-3-5 COVER 2 BUC

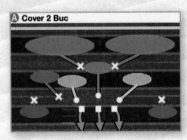

The Nickel 3-3-5 Cover 2 Buc is an excellent bend-but-don't-break defense. With five defenders playing underneath zone coverage, the middle linebacker playing the deep middle, and the safeties playing the deep halves, it is a hard defense to pass on. Just

don't expect to put a lot of pressure on the quarterback.

COVER 3

Cover 3 coverage has three defenders dropping back in deep coverage and four or five defenders playing zone coverage underneath. Typically, it's either the right and left cornerback plus the safety or one cornerback and both safeties playing three deep. The defender that is not playing deep will play a hook zone, flat, buzz zone, or blitz the quarterback. Cover 3 coverage does a much better job at taking away the deep pass than Cover 2 zone coverage, because of the extra defender playing the middle.

Cover 3 can also be used to help defend the run, because the strong safety can play closer to the line of scrimmage without sacrificing the pass coverage deep. A lot of zone blitz schemes in the game will have some type of Cover 3 coverage backing up the play.

NICKEL 3-3-5 COVER 3

A typical Cover 3 defense is the Nickel 3-3-5 Cover 3. The two cornerbacks and free safety drop back in 3 deep coverage. The strong safety and right outside linebacker play buzz zones. The nickelback and left outside linebacker play the flats. This Cover 3 defense has solid pass coverage all over the field, but not much of a pass rush with only the defensive linemen rushing the quarterback.

4-4 DOGS ZONE BLITZ

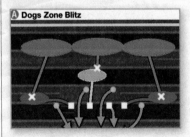

As mentioned already, several of the zone blitz concepts in the game have Cover 3 zone coverage behind them. The 4-4 Dogs Zone Blitz is a good example of what we are talking about. The DE drops in the flats, and the weak side defensive tackle drops in a hook zone. The four linebackers all blitz. The two CBs and FS drop back in 3 deep zone coverage.

COVER 4

Cover 4 is used mainly to defend intermediate and deep pass plays. With four defenders each playing a quarter of the field, it makes it very hard for the opposing offense to find any open receiver deep down the field. Typically the four defenders that drop deep are the two outside cornerbacks and two safeties. With this many defenders dropping deep, it leaves the underneath coverage vulnerable to be picked apart if the opposing quarterback has the patience to take what is given to him.

DIME 3-2-6 COVER 4

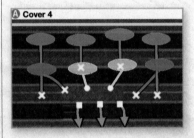

The Dime 3-2-6 Cover 4 drops four defenders underneath in zone coverage (two in hook zones, two in buzz zones, and four defenders in deep quarter zones). This defense does a good job at taking away intermediate and deep pass routes, but is vulnerable to short passes underneath.

PREVENT

The Prevent defense is not really a Cover 4 coverage, but it has some of the same elements. It's good for stopping the deep pass, but leaves short and intermediate pass routes open for the taking. Use this defense only at the end of a half when your opponent is throwing a Hail Mary pass or late in the fourth quarter when you have a big lead.

Blitzing 101

One of the first things top players look for when they get their hands on *NCAA Football* every year is ways to put pressure on the quarterback. They will spend several hours combing through defensive playbooks looking for plays that bring A, B, and C gap heat. They know that finding these defensive blitz schemes will disrupt their opponent's passing attack.

With the new Wide Open gameplay in this year's game, you had better be able to bring the heat inside, outside and with overloads.

INSIDE PRESSURE

▲ *46 Bear Plug Cover 1*

The quickest way to get to the quarterback is right up the middle. Having defenders coming up the gut will put the fear in most quarterbacks and make them get happy feet. When they see this type of pressure, they tend to throw off their back foot. When this happens, hurried and inaccurate passes are thrown. Often this leads to passes being intercepted.

The 46 Bear Plug Cover 1 is a good example of an inside blitz scheme that gets B Gap pressure from the strong safety. What makes this inside blitz scheme effective is it doesn't require any shifts or manual player movements.

The SS shoots through the B Gap and goes straight after the quarterback.

▲ *Here comes the heat*

Note: *Use this blitz scheme against base formations. Don't run it against 3, 4, and 5 WR formations. The pass coverage is not strong enough to handle that many receivers.*

OUTSIDE PRESSURE

▲ *Quarter 3 Deep Strike*

Outside pressure can come from one side or both sides of the field. Most players that bring outside pressure use it to keep the quarterback in the pocket. The outside heat makes it very difficult to roll out. The offensive pass protection usually can't handle outside pressure from both sides of the field. This means at least one of the outside pass rushers usually gets in.

A good example of an outside blitz scheme that brings pressure from both sides of the field is the Quarter 3 Deep Strike. The inside defensive backs are sent in on a blitz. The pass coverage is solid against the deep pass, but a quick pass can beat it.

The left and right tackles are put in a jam because they can't block two defenders at the same time. The left tackle is trying to block the right end and the blitzing defensive back on the left side of the field. He can't get both.

The result is a sack and a loss of yardage.

▲ *Good outside pressure*

OVERLOAD BLITZ

Overload blitz schemes are effective because they put more blitzing defenders in one area of the field than the offense can block. Using shifts and manually moving defenders are the standard methods for creating overloads. There are a few natural overload defensive blitz schemes in *NCAA Football 09*.

One such defense is the Nickel 3-3-5 Overload Fire. This overload blitz scheme has the NB, ROLB, and RE all pass rushing from the left side of the offensive line. The left tackle and left guard are outnumbered and won't be able to block all three. One of the three defenders will get a clean path to the quarterback.

▲ *Nickel 3-3-5 Overload Fire*

The RE is initially blocked by the LT, but he is able to free himself up. Notice the nickelback is not blocked.

▲ *The nickelback blitzes*

Since the RE frees himself from the tackle, the LT will now look to block the nickelback.

▲ *The RE gets the sack*

The RE is not picked up and is able to sack the quarterback.

Defending the Inside Run

▲ *The LOLB shoots the gap*

▲ *Stack the box to stop the run*

Once he sees that the weak side defensive tackle is blocked by the left tackle, he then looks to block the free safety.

This leaves the left inside linebacker a clear path to the ball carrier.

When a defensive coaching staff begins its weekly preparation for an upcoming opponent, stopping the running game will usually rank high on the list of things they feel they must accomplish. Few things can be more demoralizing to a defense than an offense that's able to consistently gain solid yardage on the ground.

A team that's not able to stop the run will usually lose the field position battle and eventually their defense will start to wear down. Needless to say it's important to have a good run stopping defense. Having a solid run defense starts with the front seven. If the front seven is not up to task, be prepared to be pounded on the inside all game long.

have a few tricks himself. The defense we use is the 4-4 LB Fire. By the design of the play, there are 8 defenders in the box. This gives you a solid inside defense, but we want to up the ante by bringing a ninth defender down in the box.

We take control of the free safety and move him down about 3 yards off the line of scrimmage and in front of the center.

From the top down zoom view, you can get a better idea of where the free safety is lined up before the ball is snapped.

▲ *Nowhere to go*

The ball carrier has no chance to even get back to the line of scrimmage before being tackled.

4-4 LB FIRE

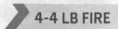

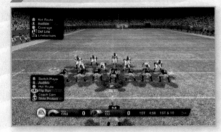
▲ *Loading up to stop the run*

Here is a simple run scheme that we have used to free up the inside linebackers, so at least one of them can have a shot at making a tackle on the ball carrier. Some may consider this run scheme shady, but when playing against a human opponent, you can bet he will

▲ *Positioning the Free Safety*

Once the ball is snapped, we move the free safety back. Notice the center goes to block the weak side defensive tackle initially.

▲ *Now drop the FS back*

▲ *The HB is stuffed*

DEFENDING THE INSIDE RUN QUICK TIPS

☐ This defensive scheme shuts down the inside run very well, but it can easily be exploited by a smart opponent on offense. Outside runs and pass plays will give this inside run scheme problems.

☐ Look for defensive play where linebackers are blitzing the A and B Gaps. The linebackers are more aggressive at attacking the gaps than if they were playing in man or zone coverage.

Defending the Outside Run

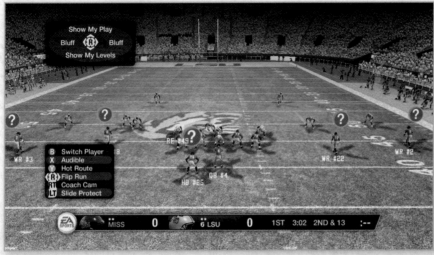

▲ Nickel 3-3-5 CB Dogs Blitz

If your defense is able to stop the inside run game, chances are likely that the offense will look to get outside on the perimeter with toss sweeps, counters, options, and in some cases the quarterback scrambling out of the pocket on passing plays. With that being the case, having good speed on your defense will help you negate those types of outside runs.

Teams such as Ohio State, Georgia, USC, and LSU all have tremendous defensive team speed, which makes it very tough to run outside on them. When evaluating your personnel to get a feel for how well they'll be able to handle the outside running game, we recommend starting with your defensive ends and the outside linebackers.

Defensive ends and outside linebackers are usually the players responsible for keeping plays from bouncing outside. Having a good defensive end is very important because more times than not he'll be aligned across the line of scrimmage from the tight end. If the defensive end is able to win his individual match up with the tight end or offensive tackle, this will go a long way towards helping the defense stop the play.

The outside linebackers are also important to an effective perimeter run defense. If the defensive line is able to use up blocks, the linebackers will be able to flow and pursue the ball carrier. Blitzing your outside linebackers off the edge of the formation is a good way of slowing down the outside running game.

DEFENSIVE SCHEME TO DEFEND THE OPTION

▲ Immediate pressure on the QB

One of the more frequent defenses used to defend the option is the Nickel 3-3-5 CB Dogs Blitz. The two blitzing corners make it tough to get the outside pitch going.

The corners are usually in position to make a tackle on the quarterback before he makes the pitch.

Even if the quarterback gets the pitch off, the cornerback is in position to quickly tackle the pitch man.

▲ No room for the pitch man

The left cornerback makes the tackle on the running back in the backfield for a small loss.

▲ The play results in a loss

DEFENDING THE OUTSIDE RUN QUICK TIPS

☐ Many players like to control one of the safeties to defend outside runs and the option. Human players with good stick control on defense normally do not fall for fakes like the CPU AI defenders do. Plus a human controlled defender can force the ball carrier back inside by keeping outside containment.

☐ The Nickel 3-3-5 CB Dogs Blitz and other blitz schemes with corners blitzing can be used to not only defend outside runs and options, but they also are used to prevent fast quarterbacks from taking off out of the pocket.

Defending the Mobile QB

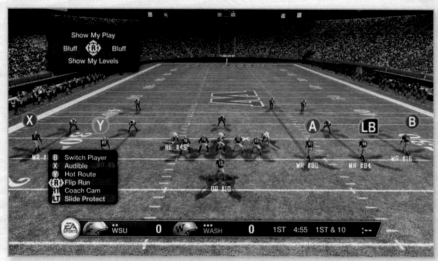

▲ *Quarter 3 Deep 2 Man Contain*

☐ Always contain the wide side of the field. If the ball is on the left hash mark, contain to the right. If the ball is on the right hash mark, contain to the left. Most players won't take off with the quarterback to the near side of the field because there is not much room to run.

☐ If the ball is in the middle of the field, contain to the side that the QB throws with. If he's right-handed, contain to the right. If he's left-handed, contain to the left. Doing this will force him to have to plant his feet in order to throw across his body as opposed to running to the side that he throws with.

☐ Don't put slow defenders in QB Spy such as defensive tackles. A fast quarterback will just outrun them. You are better off having them rush the passer or drop in zone coverage.

☐ One scheme to use to counter the mobile quarterback is to match speed with speed. If quarterback has an 87 speed rating, then hot route a defender with 87 speed or faster in QB Spy. That way the quarterback has no chance to get away from the defender. Keep in mind; you may need to make some coverage adjustments on the field. Some players will actually sub a non-starter cornerback that is fast in at free or strong safety. They will call some type of defense where the free or strong safety plays zone or is sent on a blitz. They then will hot route them into QB Spy. This scheme is very effective at countering the mobile quarterback.

☐ As a general rule, zone defenses are better at containing the mobile quarterback than man defenses since the defenders are not chasing receivers all over the field. Instead they keep themselves facing forward and are able to keep an eye on the quarterback. This doesn't apply if the man defense has defenders in QB Contain or QB Spy.

☐ Cornerback blitz schemes are effective to use against mobile quarterbacks. Often the quarterback will take off and run right into a blitzing cornerback.

With all the mobile quarterbacks in the college ranks, being able to negate their speed with creative defensive schemes is paramount if you plan on slowing down the opposing offense. Nothing is more frustrating than calling the right pass defense only to have a mobile quarterback take off and run for a first down.

Over the years, there have been several countermeasures implemented in NCAA Football to keep the mobile quarterback from dominating the games, such as QB Contain and QB Spy defensive individual hot routes. Thankfully all those countermeasures are still in the game.

QUARTER 3 DEEP 2 MAN CONTAIN

▲ *Good contain by the ends*

A common defensive scheme that is used to contain the mobile quarterback is having both defensive ends in QB Contain, and a linebacker in QB Spy. There are several of these schemes in each defensive playbook, or you can roll your own with hot routes. The Quarter 3 Deep 2 Man Contain is a good example of one of them. Notice the defensive ends are in QB Contain, while the lone linebacker on the field is in QB Spy.

If the quarterback tries to take off in any direction, he won't find much running room.

Once the ball is snapped, the defensive ends will hold their outside containment. They won't rush the quarterback.

▲ *The linebacker spies the QB*

If the quarterback does try to take off, the defensive ends and linebacker will be in position to make the tackle.

▲ *Tackled for a loss*

Pass Defense

▲ MLB#33 follows the QB's eyes

Being able to stop the run is only half the battle. Being is able to stop the pass is a real challenge this year. You have to call the right defenses, have good stick control, and even call down some luck if you plan on slowing down the high-powered college offenses in the game. With all the new formations and plays on offense, your defensive skills will be tested to the max. Hopefully after you read this section of the guide, you will be headed in the right direction.

SHORT AND MEDIUM PASS DEFENSE

▲ Closing on the receiver

Playing defense against the short and mid-ranged passing game can be more of a challenge in *NCAA Football 09* than it was in previous versions of the game. For the most part the cornerbacks do a very good job of playing their coverage responsibilities in the flats. This increases the difficulty for the offense when they try to attack a defense in this manner.

The coverage in the middle of the field isn't always as tight thanks to the game being more wide open than ever. The linebackers do a good job of breaking on the underneath throws into coverage if they have the awareness ratings to do so. There also are instances where they play very good man coverage against backs and receivers who are running routes over the middle of the field. With this said, if the defenders lack awareness or speed, they will have a hard time defending short to mid range passes, which is how the game should be.

For this reason some virtual defensive coordinators may choose to play a bend but don't break style of defense. With this philosophy your objective is not to give up the big play. The offense will in some instances be able to move the ball between the 20's. However, once the opposing offense gets inside the 20, it becomes tougher to score. Your ability to put the clamps on the opposing team's offense in this area of the field is based on the assumption that your run defense can hold up.

DEFENDING AGAINST THE VERTICAL PASS

Playing good solid pass defense against the vertical (deep) passing game can be a difficult task to accomplish in *NCAA Football 09*. This is especially true when playing a savvy human opponent who has good stick control. Gamers at varying skill levels are able to attack most defensive coverages with relative ease by throwing the long ball and manually getting their receiver in position to make the catch. Even if the defense chooses to sit back in coverages such as cover 2, 3, or 4, there will at times still be occasions where the offensive player is able to make the deep catch.

To compound matters, when playing against a team with a mobile quarterback, the quarterback will look to pull the ball down and run if no one is open. This even happens when playing against the CPU. The defense can send the all out blitz with straight man coverage to get heat on the quarterback, but this is risky because of the chance of being burnt deep.

Even if the quarterback isn't mobile, the human player may sprint back 15 to 20 yards and look to throw a deep bomb.

▲ Sprinting back in the pocket

So, what can the defense do? What we like to do when facing this type of offensive attack is to bring pressure while having the security of zone coverage over the top. We feel that a man or zone blitz is a good way of dealing with these types of offenses as long as one or more defenders are dropping back in deep coverage.

▲ Getting after the QB

In discussing this strategy with you we do realize that the quarterback will still be able to get his fair share of passes off regardless of how much pressure is put on him. The Swat button is a very useful tool to have at your disposal when trying to defend the deep areas of the field.

Favorite Plays

PISTOL BUNCH SPACING
(NEVADA PLAYBOOK)

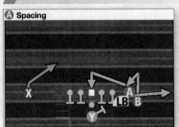

▲ Pistol Bunch Spacing

Learning to find bump-n-run man coverage beaters is very important if you plan on having any type of a successful passing attack. One play that we found that beats bump-n-run man coverage consistently is the Pistol Bunch Spacing.

This play has the tight end running a flat behind the slot receiver and flanker. This allows him to get off the line of scrimmage without being jammed.

▲ Coach Cam View

The only pre-snap adjustment we make is to hot route the flanker on a streak. We do this to clear out as much room for the tight end as we can.

▲ Hot route the flanker on a streak

Once the ball is snapped, we look immediately to the tight end.

If no defenders drop into the flat, we throw the ball to him.

The defender covering him almost always will be 3-5 yards away and won't have much

▲ An easy 6-yard gain

of a chance to make a play on the ball.

Once we make the catch, we turn up the field and pick up 6 yards.

KEY POINTS ABOUT THE PLAY

☐ If the tight end is not open for a quick pass, then look for the split end running the quick slant on the back side. He is our second option.

☐ Consider take controlling of the flanker and motioning him to the other side. This does two things. It tells you if man or zone coverage has been called, and it assures that the defender covering the flanker has no chance of being anywhere near the tight end once the ball is snapped.

SHOTGUN SPLIT SLOT CORNER STRIKE
(MISSOURI PLAYBOOK)

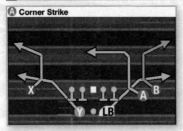

▲ Shotgun Split Slot Corner Strike

The Shotgun Split Slot Corner Strike is a good play to call against all the pass coverages in the game. As long as you are able to make the correct read after the snap, at least one receiver will be open.

The receiver we are going to key in on is the flanker lined up on the right. He is running a corner route with an inside release. His pass route is really effective against Cover 0, Cover 1, Cover 2 zone, and Cover 3.

▲ Hot route the SE on a streak

The only pre-snap adjustment we make is to hot route the split end on a streak. This gives us one deep threat.

Once the ball is snapped, notice where the free safety drops back. He is playing the deep middle of the field, but is cheating towards the split end running the streak.

▲ The receivers break to the corners

This tells us to look to the flanker running the corner route on the left side of the field.

Once he breaks to the corner, we throw him a hard bullet pass.

While the ball is up in the air, we take control of the flanker and move him towards the pass target icon.

We make the catch for an 18 yard pick up.

KEY POINTS ABOUT THE PLAY

☐ Look for the fullback in the flat on the right as a check down receiver if no receivers are open down the field.

☐ Consider leaving the halfback in to pass block. This will help with the pass protection, and give you more time to find the open receiver.

☐ The slot receiver running the dig route is another solid option to look for if man coverage is called.

SHOTGUN TRIPS CURL FLAT CORNER

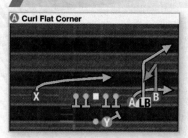

▲ *Shotgun Trips Curl Flat Corner*

Once you have found a few bump-n-run man beaters, it's time to switch to zone busters. The Shotgun Trips Curl Flat Corner is an excellent play to call to attack any type of zone coverage thrown at you.

By the play default there is a nice high/low combo on the right side of the field between the inside slot receiver running a flat route and the flanker running a curl. If the defense takes away the curl, then look for the flat. If the defense takes away the flat, then look for the curl. This pass combo is called a Curl/Flat combo. It's a pretty simple read that will net you 5-10 yards depending on which receiver you hit.

▲ *Coach Cam View*

If you would rather look to go deep to the slot receiver running the corner route, then all you need to do is hot route the flanker on the streak.

His pass route will help draw the deep defenders on his side away from the slot receiver running the corner route.

▲ *The corner is about to come open*

▲ *User catch!*

Once the slot receiver breaks to the corner, throw him a hard bullet pass.

We take control of the receiver and make the grab for a 25-yard pick up.

KEY POINTS ABOUT THE PLAY

☐ Look for the split end running a shallow crossing route on the backside. He is a good choice if nothing else opens up.

☐ If you have a fast quarterback, there is always the option of taking off and running the ball. That is why so many players choose teams with fast QBs.

SHOTGUN WING TRIO WK STRONG FLOOD
(FLORIDA PLAYBOOK)

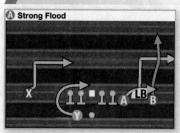

▲ *Shotgun Wing Trio Wk Strong Flood*

Calling pass plays that flood the zone are always good choices when the opposing defense likes to use this type of coverage. The Shotgun Wing Trio Wk Strong Flood is a great example of a passing concept that attacks all levels of zone coverage.

The play has three receivers flooding the right side of the field. Notice that each of the three routes attack a different level of the zone coverage. If Cover 4 is called, we look to throw to the tight end in the flat. If the flat is taken away, we then look for the slot receiver running the out. Our final option is the flanker

▲ *Coach Cam View*

running the go route. If Cover 2 or Cover 3 zone is called, we look to go deep to him.

The only pre-snap adjustment we make is to hot route the split end on a streak.

We look to the tight end first. He is covered like a blanket. The defender dropping in a buzz zone also covers the slot receiver running the out route.

This tells us to look up top to our impact receiver running the go route. Once we see him matched up with the strong safety, we let the ball fly.

While the ball is up in the air, we take control of the flanker.

▲ *Preparing for the user catch*

We use some stick control. Using the strafe button we turn our receiver back towards the ball while it's still up in the air.

We make the catch for a 30-yard gain deep down the field.

KEY POINTS ABOUT THE PLAY

☐ Don't forget about the split end running the streak (go) route down the left sideline. He is another deep option.

☐ Look for the running back underneath as a check down receiver. His circle route is a good option against most zone coverages.

Favorite Plays

Ⓐ Load Option

▲ *I-Form Y-Trips Load Option*

Over the last two pages we have shown a few of our favorite pass plays in *NCAA Football 09*. Now we want to show a run play we are sure you will want to check out.

I-FORM Y-TRIPS LOAD OPTION *(WEST VIRGINIA PLAYBOOK)*

▲ *Coach Cam View*

The I-Form Y-Trips Load Option has both receivers and the tight end all lined up on the same side of field. This alignment loads up the run blocking.

This makes this option run a very hard play to defend.

Notice the tight end has the left end

▲ *Sealing the left end*

▲ *In good pitch relationship*

blocked. The two receivers drive their men back. The fullback also lead blocks to the left.

At this point we could pitch the ball to the trailing halfback, but there is a defender closing in on him.

We decide to keep the ball and make a few shake and bake moves with the right stick.

▲ *Shake and bake time*

▲ *A good gain for our QB*

We avoid being tackled.
This allows us to pick up a few more yards before being tackled.

▶ KEY POINTS ABOUT THE PLAY

☐ Another way to run this play is to flip it to the opposite side of the tight end and receivers. The downside is that only the fullback will be out in front to block. If your opponent on defense overloads the side with the tight end and receivers, this option is one to consider.

☐ The Slip HB Screen is a nice passing complement to this play. Be sure to run it on occasion. You will find that it is one of the better running back screen plays in the game.

Campus Legend

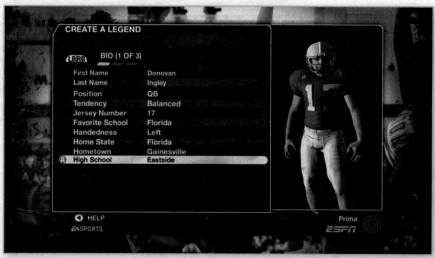
▲ *Our future Campus Legend*

▲ *Impressing the scouts*

CREATING YOUR PLAYER

Begin Campus Legend by either choosing an existing player or creating one from scratch. If you go with the existing player option, be sure to pick a younger player so that you will have time to turn him into a Legend. A Senior is not the best option here.

To get the most out of this mode, we suggest creating a High School player from scratch. You'll have three major choices to make when building your player: position, tendency and favorite school.

Position is certainly the most key of these choices, as you'll be playing at that position for the rest of your career. If you goal is to win the Heisman trophy, a running back or quarterback is your best bet. Going in as a quarterback is our recommendation if you really want to guarantee yourself a shot at the trophy.

As the quarterback, you can change the play at the line of scrimmage. So if you want to throw every down, you can override the coach's play call. The other positions don't afford you this luxury.

Tendency is important because it helps to define your base attributes. Try to pick a tendency that will match your style of play. Think about how you want to approach the game. If you desire to be a total gunslinger, a pocket passer is your best choice. If you want to be able to escape the pocket, a scrambling tendency is best. And finally, if you desire to play for a school like Georgia Tech, then an option

QB is your best choice.

Favorite school is the program that you most want to attend. You will automatically get an offer to this school.

HIGH SCHOOL

▲ *Playing in the State Playoffs*

If you're starting a player from scratch, you'll begin Campus Legend mode as a High School player in the state playoffs. College scouts will attend each game; so the deeper you go in the playoffs the better. Championships are great, but to attract the eye of the top programs, you have to load up on the stats.

Running backs, receivers and QBs need lots of yards and plenty of touchdowns to make the grade. Defensive players need tackles and forced turnovers to get the attention. If you play well enough, you'll reach your goal: becoming a 5-Star Prospect.

In Campus Legend, you will only play if you're a starter. As a second string QB, you'll hit the field to hold for kicks, but that's just about it. In addition to only playing games as a

starter, you'll only control your one player.

It is important that you study the play art before each snap. You will need to know your role and carry out your assignment even if you aren't the primary focus of the play. As a running back, you might be called on to block for passing plays, or have a route assignment to run. Running a poor route can result in an interception. On defense, you need to be active and try to get to every ball carrier that you can.

At the end of the game, you'll be able to view your caliber as a prospect, your game stats, and the scouts that were in attendance for your game. Get to that 5-star status so you can have your choice of college.

If you are blowing out the competition, don't be surprised if you end up on the bench during the fourth quarter of the game. Hopefully you've compiled enough stats in the first three quarters to impress the scouts.

SIGNING DAY

▲ *Scholarship offers come flooding in*

You've won the State Championship and hopefully have done enough to impress the college recruiters. Now it's decision time. Where are you going to go? The more prestigious the school you attend, the better the chance that you will be surrounded by big-time players, and the better the chance that you can win some serious team hardware.

The downside is you will probably be buried on the depth chart to start out your career. You will see a list of schools that have offered

Campus Legend continued...

you a scholarship, as well as the projected depth chart position you will have on that team once you finish High School.

There are a couple of different ways that you can approach your decision. You can go to a lower ranked school and step right into a starting role. You will most likely be able to dominate your conference, but whether you have enough exposure to win a Heisman trophy is uncertain. Or you can bide your time with a top tier program and wait for your chance.

It is entirely possible to move up from number two on the depth chart into the starting role by the fourth or fifth game of the season. So don't let early playing time influence your decision too much.

The final consideration is the playbook that your school will be running. For our Campus Legend, we wanted to be a prolific quarterback who would be called on to throw the ball just about every down. We accepted an offer to go to Texas Tech because we knew their playbook would give us plenty of opportunities to air it out.

CALENDAR

▲ The calendar keeps you on track

The calendar leads you through the season and includes classes, practices, games and evening events. You can always simulate through calendar, but if you want to really be a Campus Legend, then you need to take control and manage things day by day.

Class is really simple. It appears on your calendar, but you don't have to do anything with it. The CPU thankfully handles the rigors of that part of your life as a student athlete.

Practices have been reworked this year, so you can work on a week's worth of reps in just one practice session. Each practice is comprised of 10 reps of plays chosen by your coach. You get points for 1st downs, touchdowns, tackles, etc. The more points you are able to amass,

▲ That was a good workout!

the quicker you can become a starter. You will see a running total of how many practice points you need to achieve to move up to the next spot on the depth chart. If you have a really stellar practice session, you will see a jump in your attribute ratings as well.

The Evening Event is where you determine the things that are most important to your player besides practice. A typical event includes making a choice between going to the library, hitting the gym, studying your playbook or visiting the trainer. Each choice has a direct effect on your player in some way.

You can increase your awareness and other physical attributes by training and studying your playbook. You can increase your GPA by hitting the library. Remember, you have to

▲ Choose wisely

stay above a 2.0 GPA to be eligible to play. Don't forget to hit the books!

GAME TIME

▲ We get our first start

Practicing, studying, and working out are all import, but whether become a Campus

Legend or not comes down to what you do on the field come game day. Not only do you need to win games, but you also need to blow the crowd away with your gaudy statistics.

As a freshman, you will most likely be at the bottom of the depth chart so don't expect to see a lot of action right off the bat. As you move up the chart through practices or injury, you'll get your time to shine. The gameplay structure is similar to what you saw in the High School playoffs. You'll need to dominate the stat column to pick up awards and gain legendary status.

LEGEND SCORE

▲ Single game accomplishments

The Legend Meter is replaced by your Legend Score in *NCAA Football 09*. Achieving milestones for your position and team adds to your Legend Score. These accomplishments are broken down into several categories:

- ☐ Single Game Stats
- ☐ Season Stats
- ☐ Career Stats
- ☐ Big Games
- ☐ National Recognition
- ☐ Personal Goals

Dynasty Strategies

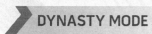

The ultimate Dynasty goal - BCS National Champions

▲ Recruiting Strategy

QB	Scrambler, Pocket Passer, Balanced
HB	Speed, Power, Balanced
FB/TE	Blocking, Receiving, Balanced
WR	Speed, Possession, Balanced
OL	Pass Block, Run Block, Balanced
DE	Pass Rusher, Run Stopper, Balanced
DT	Pass Rusher, Run Stopper, Balanced
LB	Coverage, Run Stopper, Balanced
CB	Coverage, Hard Hitter, Balanced
S	Coverage, Hard Hitter, Balanced

DYNASTY MODE

If you played Dynasty Mode in last year's game, then you should feel pretty comfortable with what you are going to see in *NCAA Football 09*. As you know, to have a successful long term Dynasty, you have to have top quality players. Thus, long-term Dynasty mode success boils down to being able to recruit well.

We had the opportunity to get unprecedented access to the EA SPORTS Dynasty mode design team and grill them on strategies for maximizing recruiting results. These tips and the changes to the recruiting module in *NCAA Football 09* will be the focus of this section of the guide.

RECRUITING STRATEGY

There is a lot to do when it comes to managing your recruiting program. You have to add players to your board, make calls, schedule visits, and offer scholarships. No head coach has the time to manage every aspect of the recruiting and neither do you (okay, you might if you are crazy serious about it). The Recruiting Strategy feature allows you to put your assistant coaches to work for you.

You can access the Recruiting Strategy menu from the Recruiting Carousel. You begin by determining how much power you will give the CPU to edit the recruiting board, offer scholarships and set up visits.

Next, you determine the style of offense you want to run and your base defensive set. Your choices will determine the positional needs for your team.

Offensive Types include:

- ☐ Spread
- ☐ Balanced
- ☐ Flexbone
- ☐ West Coast
- ☐ Option Run

Base Defenses include:

- ☐ 4-3
- ☐ 4-4
- ☐ 3-4
- ☐ 3-3-5 Stack
- ☐ 4-2-5

Now determine your preferred tendency within each position group. The CPU will use your choices to populate the Recruiting Board.

The final determination you will need to make is how much priority to place on each position. If you have specific needs, or you wish for your assistants to make sure to land a stud QB for example, you can set the priority to High. Setting all priorities to High, however, is a waste of time, as they will all get the same allotment of recruiting resources.

QUICK CALLS

▲ Making a quick call

Managing all the calls with your individual recruits can be very time consuming. You have to pull up the call interface, choose the different pitches that you want to try, get the results, and then pick a new recruit and start over.

Dynasty Strategies continued...

▲ Talking to a recruit

Quick calls enable you to get a ton of information about a prospect without having to spend the time doing it yourself. Simply decide how much time you want to devote to a player and whether you want to make a scholarship offer or not. Making an offer requires at least 15 extra minutes.

You will immediately get feedback as to how the call went. You'll learn which pitches were unlocked and what their priorities were. Once you have the basics nailed down for each of your prospects, you can go in and give them the extra special attention to hard sell these

pages and lock them up.

The downside of the quick call is you can't stop a pitch midstream if it is not working. The upside is that you can get a lot of recruiting business done in a short period of time. You'll also generally get more data about a player's interest than if you do a manual call.

INSIDER TIPS TO RECRUITING

In our sit-down with the EA SPORTS design team, we were able to pry out a couple of other hot tips about the recruiting process.

Instant Commits – there is a small chance that if you are #1 on a player's list and offer a scholarship right off the bat, you can get him to instantly commit.

Whenever you offer a scholarship to a player, you get an instant interest boost. So don't hold out too long when it comes to making a scholarship offer.

It is possible to land players that have no

interest in you to begin with, but it does take a lot of work.

Schedule player visits for the best games on your schedule for maximum interest boosts. Beating a rival at home provides a big jump in the prospect's feelings towards your school.

Repitch a player's most important interest from week to week. If he is high on an area that you are elite in, pound it over and over.

If you start a pitch and see the interest icon starting to frown, hit B (circle on PS3) to cancel the pitch and move on to another one.

Always try to leave your calls on a high note. Leave them smiling!

A good strategy for players that have zero interest in you is to start off with an immediate Hard Pitch on one of the pitches that your team is very strong in. If it matches one of his choices, you'll receive a huge boost to his interest level. It's risky so don't try this strategy on players that already show interest in your school.

Online Dynasty

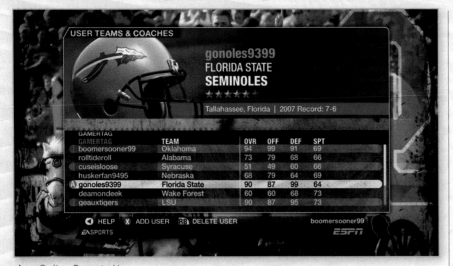

▲ Online Dynasty Users

At long last, Online Dynasty has made its way to Xbox 360 and PS3 consoles. You'll have every option available to you in Online Dynasty that you do in offline Dynasty. In this section of the guide we are going to walk you through setting up an Online Dynasty and working as Commissioner.

SETTING UP AN ONLINE DYNASTY

As the commissioner of the dynasty, the first thing you will want to do is select your team. Once you have set the commissioner's team, it is time to add additional users. You can

select someone from your friends list and assign him a team, or perform a search for a non-friend by entering their Gamertag/UserID.

After you have added all of the users and made the invites, it will be time to name your Online Dynasty. This is the name all the users will see when they log in to the dynasty.

Before you send out the invitations, you must determine the settings that will be used for the dynasty. The Commissioner can set the skill level, quarter length, penalty settings, Game AI, etc. You are not locked into these for the duration of your dynasty, but only the Commissioner can make changes to the settings.

Everyone in your Online Dynasty will use the same roster file. You can have the Dynasty auto-generate names for the players in the game or you can use a pre-edited roster file if you wish.

You do not have to have a hard drive to save the Dynasty file locally on your system. If you do have a drive and can save locally, you won't have to download the file again until it progresses to the next week. You can also

Online Dynasty continued...

convert your dynasty file to an offline dynasty whenever you want.

Once the file saves, invitations go out and the Dynasty is live and begins in the pre-season.

DYNASTY HEADQUARTERS

▲ Dynasty Headquarters

The Dynasty Headquarters screen is your one-stop shop for getting the latest information for your dynasty. Here you can see information about each user, how many users are currently online, and how close each user is to being ready to activate the next week/stage. You can refresh the page at any time to get more up-to-date info.

In the top bar of the screen you will see the current week/stage that the dynasty is in,

the total number of users participating in the dynasty, and the number of users currently logged into the dynasty.

Each user will have their very own pane that displays their information in the current week or stage. During the pre-season and off-season there will be a description of the tasks that need to be completed during that stage. During the regular season, game information and remaining recruiting time will be shown.

The game result window will also show you how many times a player restarted their game. If a user quit out of a game because they were losing and then restarted, everybody will be able to see their actions.

Each user will have the ability to add a message to their pane. Talk trash or simply let everybody know when you'll be done with your week.

PLAYING THE GAMES

If a user is scheduled to play a game against the CPU, the option will say "Play Game vs. CPU." If the user is scheduled to play another team owner, they will have the ability to send that user a game invite to play

▲ Weekly Schedule

their game online. Accepting the invitation will launch an online game between these two users.

If the two users want to play a head-to-head game (they are roommates or something of that nature), they can choose the "Play Game Offline vs. User" option.

▲ User Pane

FCS Team Rosters (PS2)

The depth charts featured earlier in the guide are based on the Xbox 360 and PS3 versions of *NCAA Football 09*. The Playstation 2 version of *NCAA Football 09* also features Division I FCS (Football Chapionship Subdivision) teams from nine conferences: Atlantic 10, Big Sky, Ivy League, Mid-Eastern

Athletic Conference (MEAC), Gateway Football, Ohio Valley, Southern, Southland and Southwestern Athletic Conference (SWC).

In this section of the guide, we have included the roster positions, numbers and overall ratings for all the players on these teams. You will notice the ratings are much

lower than their FBS counterparts. This doesn't mean that they play poorly, but it merely reflects the disparity between the two divisions.

It is possible to beat an FCS team with one of these squads, but you will have your work cut out for you.

Alabama A&M

POS	#	OVR
C	56	70
C	63	41
CB	36	73
CB	20	71
CB	23	69
CB	10	54
CB	21	47
DT	96	72
DT	54	71
DT	92	70
DT	93	48
FB	43	72
FS	28	71
FS	39	48
HB	17	79
HB	35	52
HB	41	43
HB	25	42
K	27	77
LE	91	77
LE	75	47
LG	71	72
LG	65	43
LOLB	32	71
LOLB	53	46
LT	76	69
LT	79	47
MLB	49	71
MLB	55	70
MLB	50	52
P	3	42
QB	9	67
QB	1	57
QB	15	47
RE	58	71
RE	90	60
RE	94	54
RG	66	70
ROLB	51	71
ROLB	45	45
ROLB	48	42
RT	68	70
RT	72	52
SS	4	70
SS	34	46
TE	88	66
TE	80	66
TE	7	40
WR	13	77
WR	81	73
WR	86	71
WR	24	70
WR	89	60
WR	84	55
WR	87	50
WR	85	43

Alabama State

POS	#	OVR
C	77	70
C	78	47
C	69	44
CB	22	75
CB	25	73
CB	30	71
CB	28	69
CB	16	51
CB	26	42
DT	94	72
DT	90	51
DT	97	42
DT	56	42
FB	42	42
FS	34	72
FS	38	52
HB	20	76
HB	6	73
HB	2	51
K	12	40
LE	95	71
LE	60	43
LG	75	73
LG	70	70
LG	64	47
LOLB	52	71
LOLB	55	49
LT	66	72
LT	67	40
MLB	48	69
MLB	40	47
MLB	54	42
P	49	47
QB	10	67
QB	5	59
QB	7	47
QB	3	42
RE	58	70
RE	98	45
RG	71	72
RG	73	47
ROLB	53	72
RT	68	70
RT	74	44
SS	4	75
SS	41	49
TE	88	71
TE	84	43
WR	9	78
WR	13	73
WR	83	71
WR	17	54
WR	11	51
WR	15	51
WR	80	42

Alcorn State

POS	#	OVR
C	63	70
C	79	59
CB	31	58
CB	11	55
CB	28	52
CB	32	49
CB	6	46
DT	45	73
DT	55	71
DT	98	70
DT	53	50
DT	57	50
DT	91	48
DT	95	40
FB	36	68
FB	35	43
FS	8	70
FS	4	53
HB	2	76
HB	23	70
HB	33	55
HB	25	51
HB	26	42
K	10	40
LE	76	70
LE	48	45
LG	68	71
LG	58	40
LOLB	46	71
LOLB	47	40
LT	74	71
LT	75	40
MLB	49	69
MLB	42	40
P	14	40
QB	1	70
QB	15	59
QB	12	46
RE	56	73
RE	92	45
RE	90	40
RG	60	71
RG	93	70
ROLB	44	75
RT	64	70
RT	72	57
SS	43	70
SS	20	50
TE	87	70
TE	86	50
TE	88	40
WR	82	80
WR	5	80
WR	7	72
WR	89	71
WR	85	70
WR	81	62
WR	17	48

Appalachian State

POS	#	OVR
C	57	70
C	63	57
CB	6	78
CB	18	75
CB	21	60
CB	36	45
DT	99	78
DT	98	76
DT	46	72
DT	95	50
DT	93	48
DT	71	46
DT	90	42
DT	95	40
FB	43	60
FB	33	51
FS	22	70
FS	13	45
HB	28	82
HB	30	59
K	91	51
LE	96	79
LE	68	62
LG	67	75
LG	79	46
LOLB	55	72
LOLB	48	43
LOLB	49	40
LT	72	70
LT	75	50
MLB	27	77
MLB	40	77
P	97	57
QB	14	86
QB	15	71
QB	10	59
RE	56	78
RE	58	76
RG	50	73
RG	61	67
ROLB	41	78
ROLB	31	74
ROLB	11	45
RT	76	74
RT	70	56
SS	47	80
SS	24	56
SS	25	46
TE	88	72
TE	35	65
TE	84	58
WR	3	82
WR	2	80
WR	16	79
WR	8	77
WR	82	75
WR	12	71
WR	81	58
WR	86	56

Ark-Pine Bluff

POS	#	OVR
C	70	72
C	79	49
CB	5	73
CB	7	71
CB	20	69
CB	3	52
CB	16	52
CB	33	40
CB	15	40
CB	24	40
DT	90	81
DT	99	70
DT	93	42
FB	40	68
FB	23	64
FS	4	71
FS	29	51
HB	8	77
HB	34	71
HB	45	55
HB	22	48
K	32	51
LE	98	72
LE	41	48
LG	92	69
LOLB	39	70
LOLB	53	54
LOLB	46	40
LT	75	72
LT	69	50
MLB	1	43
MLB	52	40
P	9	50
QB	17	70
QB	18	64
QB	12	53
RE	55	51
RE	91	40
RG	65	51
RG	50	40
ROLB	49	70
ROLB	58	45
RT	76	56
RT	74	44
SS	28	70
SS	30	40
TE	82	43
TE	10	40
WR	81	81
WR	87	72
WR	6	71
WR	19	51
WR	80	44

Bethune-Cookman

POS	#	OVR
C	75	71
C	65	69
C	55	40
CB	29	79
CB	4	76
CB	22	73
CB	16	72
CB	5	70
CB	25	61
CB	42	59
CB	35	54
DT	97	70
DT	98	51
DT	94	48
DT	45	45
FB	44	56
FS	20	71
FS	21	40
HB	37	77
HB	26	71
HB	33	58
K	47	40
LE	92	49
LE	93	46
LG	74	70
LG	78	46
LOLB	49	70
LOLB	40	40
LT	64	69
LT	61	66
MLB	57	70
MLB	48	40
P	39	40
QB	10	76
QB	12	61
QB	17	48
RE	52	70
RE	54	49
RG	73	70
RG	53	42
ROLB	3	72
ROLB	24	69
RT	56	69
RT	51	52
RT	71	45
SS	1	76
SS	6	55
SS	43	40
TE	82	66
TE	63	41
WR	80	72
WR	81	70
WR	85	68
WR	32	58
WR	13	56
WR	19	55
WR	88	50
WR	83	50

Brown

POS	#	OVR
C	64	69
C	70	40
CB	2	76
CB	18	72
CB	30	63
CB	7	50
DT	97	71
DT	94	69
DT	91	40
DT	57	40
DT	95	40
DT	96	40
FB	47	67
FB	36	53
FB	33	40
FS	21	50
FS	15	48
HB	22	84
HB	28	81
HB	35	73
HB	20	61
K	26	80
LE	93	70
LE	90	49
LE	79	41
LG	67	69
LG	62	45
LOLB	32	69
LOLB	52	41
LT	77	71
LT	60	70
MLB	54	78
MLB	31	74
MLB	42	71
MLB	48	40
MLB	50	40
P	51	40
QB	14	69
QB	12	58
QB	11	52
RE	99	71
RE	44	70
RE	92	46
RG	66	73
RG	68	51
ROLB	4	70
ROLB	45	64
RT	65	70
RT	76	45
SS	6	70
SS	39	65
TE	85	73
TE	82	68
TE	89	65
TE	87	43
WR	1	79
WR	19	77
WR	8	74
WR	5	72
WR	46	70
WR	81	68
WR	84	64

Chattanooga

POS	#	OVR
C	74	70
C	66	50
C	54	41
CB	21	80
CB	1	70
CB	23	70
CB	24	42
CB	4	42
DT	99	72
DT	69	71
DT	64	50
DT	92	40
FB	38	54
FS	41	70
FS	26	55
HB	28	70
HB	34	57
HB	22	51
HB	42	48
K	2	65
LE	97	70
LE	8	40
LG	60	71
LG	79	45
LOLB	27	70
LT	77	71
MLB	6	69
MLB	50	48
MLB	57	41
P	46	73
QB	12	71
QB	14	49
QB	10	41
RE	90	73
RE	93	56
RG	76	72
RG	67	52
ROLB	5	82
ROLB	58	44
RT	75	71
RT	72	41
SS	16	70
SS	17	53
TE	86	70
TE	83	68
TE	31	66
WR	80	74
WR	11	72
WR	18	64
WR	9	58
WR	19	45
WR	82	40

Columbia

POS	#	OVR
C	72	52
C	60	46
CB	20	76
CB	19	64
CB	35	51
CB	24	47
DT	99	46
DT	90	44
DT	63	43
DT	55	40
FB	43	41
FB	45	40
FS	1	63
FS	41	59
HB	36	75
HB	39	50
K	11	40
LE	95	43
LE	97	40
LG	66	49
LG	67	44
LOLB	57	44
LOLB	40	43
LT	64	54
LT	58	47
MLB	59	72
MLB	46	58
P	28	55
QB	16	75
QB	14	51
QB	17	44
RE	51	53
RE	96	41
RG	65	51
RG	76	48
ROLB	54	43
ROLB	56	40
RT	62	49
RT	61	44
SS	27	56
SS	38	48
TE	89	48
TE	81	41
WR	83	74
WR	2	54
WR	21	51
WR	9	51
WR	29	45

Cornell

POS	#	OVR
C	60	72
C	74	69
CB	22	71
CB	37	70
CB	24	51
CB	34	44
DT	67	70
DT	98	50
DT	56	41
DT	92	40
FB	36	52
FB	32	44
FS	7	70
FS	19	54
HB	25	75
HB	30	74
HB	26	44
K	39	40
LE	91	73
LG	75	50
LG	71	45
LOLB	55	70
LT	72	71
LT	76	45
MLB	52	41
MLB	54	40
MLB	50	40
P	10	40
QB	17	63
QB	12	59
RE	96	75
RE	94	49
RG	79	70
RG	53	42
ROLB	51	70
ROLB	58	47
RT	68	70
RT	73	45
SS	29	70
SS	35	49
SS	40	40
TE	80	66
TE	89	48
TE	83	43
WR	2	79
WR	18	74
WR	81	73
WR	5	70
WR	1	69
WR	82	57
WR	8	53

Dartmouth

POS	#	OVR
C	50	70
C	72	45
C	69	43
CB	4	74
CB	29	73
CB	22	71
CB	26	70
CB	5	57
CB	14	52
DT	90	72
DT	60	71
DT	85	70
DT	79	41
DT	62	41
DT	70	40
DT	97	40
FB	44	66
FB	36	50
FB	49	47
FS	17	71
FS	23	53
FS	28	40
HB	2	78
HB	1	74
HB	31	51
HB	45	49
HB	11	44
K	27	63
LE	94	70
LE	38	47
LG	54	61
LOLB	33	71
LOLB	57	44
LT	68	71
LT	78	70
MLB	56	73
MLB	46	43
P	93	40
QB	7	66
QB	10	62
QB	15	51
QB	19	44
RE	52	70
RE	99	42
RE	91	40
RG	61	70
RG	66	43
ROLB	59	77
ROLB	58	69
RT	74	70
RT	76	40
RT	73	40
SS	21	70
SS	39	46
SS	24	46
TE	82	68
TE	81	40
TE	86	40
WR	88	70
WR	9	69
WR	83	52
WR	47	50
WR	87	48

Delaware

POS	#	OVR
C	63	55
C	62	40
CB	20	77
CB	30	73
CB	24	72
CB	27	67
CB	23	56
DT	97	80
DT	11	70
DT	99	55
DT	52	53
DT	94	49
DT	90	40
FB	40	79
FS	9	70
FS	38	52
FS	22	47
HB	28	81
HB	29	76
HB	31	75
HB	35	71
K	16	44
LE	33	71
LE	98	48
LG	75	70
LOLB	56	70
LOLB	41	49
LT	69	70
LT	60	57
MLB	57	80
MLB	55	47
MLB	34	41
P	47	63
QB	15	73
QB	7	63
RE	92	75
RE	54	58
RG	70	72
RG	67	71
RG	74	58
ROLB	6	75
ROLB	44	57
RT	64	70
RT	73	42
SS	4	71
SS	37	58
TE	80	80
TE	89	66
TE	87	53
WR	85	75
WR	1	74
WR	21	72
WR	17	70
WR	82	64
WR	18	52
WR	86	47

Delaware State

POS	#	OVR
C	77	70
C	74	45
C	75	40
CB	27	72
CB	34	70
CB	37	47
CB	21	42
DT	94	72
DT	95	69
DT	65	60
DT	90	42
FB	24	66
FB	30	40
FS	20	70
FS	29	50
FS	41	49
HB	4	72
HB	23	51
HB	32	48
HB	22	46
K	51	40
LE	12	70
LE	98	43
LE	92	40
LG	70	47
LOLB	18	70
LOLB	43	48
LT	64	71
LT	70	70
MLB	45	68
MLB	55	43
P	42	40
QB	2	72
QB	10	60
RE	54	70
RE	93	66
RE	96	40
RG	57	70
RG	71	42
RG	63	41
ROLB	44	72
ROLB	53	43
ROLB	40	40
RT	68	71
RT	72	42
SS	35	80
SS	19	48
TE	80	66
TE	86	61
TE	81	46
WR	1	79
WR	7	74
WR	89	72
WR	3	69
WR	17	55
WR	84	55
WR	85	52

Eastern Illinois

POS	#	OVR
C	70	57
C	50	46
CB	23	73
CB	26	69
CB	31	66
CB	30	53
CB	15	53
CB	39	51
DT	97	74
DT	91	72
DT	92	55
DT	94	54
FB	44	73
FB	32	53
FS	28	71
FS	46	60
HB	37	74
HB	20	62
HB	22	55
K	41	60
LE	93	70
LE	55	48
LG	74	73
LG	57	44
LOLB	48	57
LOLB	49	47
LT	73	69
LT	68	59
MLB	54	79
MLB	53	41
P	33	46
QB	13	77
QB	10	72
QB	16	43
RE	90	71
RE	96	57
RG	63	73
RG	72	70
ROLB	47	70
ROLB	35	50
RT	66	65
RT	76	47
SS	42	65
SS	45	44
TE	88	68
TE	85	45
TE	87	42
WR	80	79
WR	18	73
WR	81	63
WR	19	59
WR	82	52
WR	89	47

Eastern Kentucky

POS	#	OVR
C	72	72
C	75	70
CB	26	75
CB	17	72
CB	6	72
CB	14	69
CB	36	54
DT	95	79
DT	33	72
DT	94	70
DT	60	56
DT	96	46
FB	39	67
FS	30	69
FS	38	52
HB	5	78
HB	28	72
HB	32	71
K	3	60
LE	93	70
LE	91	48
LG	57	66
LG	69	51
LOLB	48	72
LOLB	51	49
LT	77	72
MLB	50	71
MLB	46	69
MLB	52	40
P	49	73
QB	15	75
QB	2	67
QB	1	59
RE	40	81
RE	25	63
RE	97	48
RG	58	70
RG	71	62
RG	78	48
ROLB	24	72
ROLB	44	65
RT	56	70
RT	67	67
SS	10	70
SS	18	62
TE	7	65
TE	87	56
TE	88	46
WR	80	70
WR	11	70
WR	81	67
WR	8	63
WR	9	57
WR	22	43

Eastern Washington

POS	#	OVR
C	53	73
C	65	49
CB	37	74
CB	15	73
CB	6	72
CB	4	70
CB	29	58
CB	25	47
DT	97	71
DT	49	70
DT	90	58
DT	93	40
DT	98	40
FB	44	86
FS	2	70
FS	33	46
HB	20	74
HB	22	70
HB	30	56
HB	34	56
K	92	49
LE	94	72
LE	42	56
LG	64	70
LG	75	45
LOLB	52	57
LOLB	41	47
LT	71	70
LT	76	60
MLB	50	69
MLB	62	52
MLB	45	44
P	14	73
QB	16	77
QB	7	48
QB	12	43
RE	55	72
RE	99	64
RG	66	78
RG	73	47
RG	61	45
ROLB	27	70
ROLB	8	51
RT	77	62
RT	67	60
SS	3	70
SS	39	58
SS	21	50
TE	80	57
TE	91	47
TE	81	47
WR	26	78
WR	83	73
WR	9	71
WR	38	70
WR	31	50
WR	47	46

Elon

POS	#	OVR
C	71	70
C	61	46
C	72	40
CB	21	74
CB	5	72
CB	3	69
CB	28	60
CB	35	52
DT	86	76
DT	92	72
DT	94	71
DT	69	48
FB	42	57
FS	20	70
FS	2	51
HB	29	72
HB	32	58
HB	14	53
HB	34	47
K	50	54
LE	60	72
LE	90	70
LE	95	40
LG	51	70
LG	70	45
LOLB	39	61
LOLB	58	53
LT	66	73
MLB	10	76
MLB	9	50
P	97	40
QB	16	68
QB	6	61
QB	15	47
QB	17	40
RE	91	73
RE	98	70
RE	75	53
RG	62	72
RG	57	56
RG	76	41
ROLB	43	70
ROLB	46	61
ROLB	52	40
RT	67	70
RT	78	41
SS	48	70
SS	13	45
SS	4	42
TE	81	68
TE	85	66
TE	87	45
WR	82	78
WR	84	74
WR	1	73
WR	19	71
WR	8	70
WR	11	42

Florida A&M

POS	#	OVR
C	76	76
C	72	54
CB	28	73
CB	24	71
CB	21	69
CB	17	53
CB	12	50
CB	14	41
DT	71	73
DT	94	72
DT	93	70
DT	99	40
FB	32	41
FS	25	70
FS	9	47
HB	33	77
HB	38	72
HB	36	72
K	20	55
LE	98	41
LG	73	64
LOLB	44	71
LOLB	47	71
LT	60	75
MLB	27	69
MLB	57	40
P	49	59
QB	2	79
QB	16	66
QB	8	49
RE	90	70
RE	97	40
RE	62	40
RG	75	73
RG	64	70
RG	74	40
ROLB	4	76
ROLB	45	41
RT	70	69
RT	77	41
SS	31	48
SS	18	45
TE	82	67
TE	88	40
WR	85	75
WR	84	72
WR	3	71
WR	80	68
WR	89	62
WR	34	50

Furman

POS	#	OVR
C	60	71
C	52	50
CB	6	75
CB	1	73
CB	31	71
CB	28	69
CB	18	47
CB	24	40
DT	91	76
DT	97	74
DT	95	48
DT	99	40
DT	78	40
FB	45	85
FB	42	54
FS	8	73
FS	37	54
HB	22	79
HB	15	62
HB	21	58
K	29	76
LE	40	73
LE	70	72
LG	74	70
LG	64	51
LOLB	32	74
LOLB	49	54
LT	76	70
LT	59	45
MLB	20	73
MLB	33	40
P	87	40
QB	14	83
QB	9	63
QB	10	43
RE	55	78
RE	58	58
RG	62	72
RG	73	54
ROLB	41	77
ROLB	11	63
RT	65	70
RT	71	41
SS	3	70
SS	26	60
TE	84	72
TE	93	57
TE	85	48
WR	16	75
WR	13	72
WR	5	72
WR	4	69
WR	82	56
WR	23	49
WR	80	47

Georgia Southern

POS	#	OVR
C	70	72
C	68	62
CB	2	80
CB	28	73
CB	12	72
CB	29	60
CB	15	59
DT	90	81
DT	99	76
DT	92	65
DT	44	59
DT	73	50
FB	38	73
FB	34	61
FS	17	76
FS	20	61
HB	6	82
HB	5	82
HB	32	71
HB	24	60
K	42	63
LE	97	74
LE	95	63
LG	63	70
LG	65	66
LOLB	47	71
LOLB	50	51
LT	75	71
LT	69	58
MLB	1	79
MLB	52	69
MLB	57	40
P	33	49
QB	14	83
QB	13	64
RE	7	58
RE	55	80
RE	98	71
RE	96	61
RG	66	73
RG	64	69
RG	74	60
ROLB	53	73
ROLB	10	70
ROLB	54	50
RT	62	71
RT	79	55
SS	16	70
SS	35	49
TE	81	73
TE	87	67
WR	4	78
WR	84	76
WR	82	76
WR	86	74
WR	80	72
WR	25	69
WR	18	65
WR	83	60
WR	19	54

Grambling State

POS	#	OVR
C	67	72
C	69	42
C	63	41
CB	4	81
CB	8	72
CB	45	69
CB	19	64
CB	17	45
DT	91	82
DT	65	75
DT	94	70
DT	96	54
DT	46	41
DT	73	40
FB	81	52
FS	16	65
FS	20	57
HB	27	77
HB	23	76
HB	33	74
HB	24	71
HB	34	58
HB	43	43
K	30	71
LE	92	72
LE	77	63
LG	76	73
LG	61	72
LOLB	26	71
LOLB	44	40
LT	72	72
LT	68	69
MLB	59	70
MLB	42	60
MLB	36	57
MLB	50	40
P	32	40
QB	7	79
QB	14	61
QB	13	47
RE	95	72
RE	99	45
RE	90	40
RE	93	40
RG	78	74
RG	60	54
RG	74	44
RG	71	40
ROLB	47	72
ROLB	37	40
ROLB	56	40
ROLB	57	40
RT	75	71
RT	79	40
RT	70	40
SS	29	78
SS	10	51
TE	80	74
TE	86	70
TE	89	66
TE	87	42
WR	5	80
WR	11	77
WR	15	74
WR	85	72
WR	83	71
WR	9	69
WR	88	53
WR	18	52

Hampton

POS	#	OVR
C	70	44
C	55	40
CB	2	88
CB	30	81
CB	28	55
CB	10	49
CB	45	47
CB	47	45
DT	98	76
DT	97	73
DT	92	72
DT	94	69
DT	60	40
FB	33	52
FS	23	70
FS	42	40
HB	22	91
HB	21	74
HB	9	53
K	37	40
LE	99	70
LE	93	40
LG	69	72
LOLB	49	71
LOLB	58	70
LT	78	69
LT	63	44
MLB	43	75
MLB	41	40
P	3	41
QB	15	77
QB	4	67
QB	12	47
RE	71	71
RE	96	47
RE	95	40
RG	62	72
RG	65	70
ROLB	54	73
ROLB	46	71
RT	73	54
RT	72	42
SS	26	75
SS	48	45
SS	17	40
TE	89	67
TE	88	40
WR	19	80
WR	82	73
WR	80	71
WR	16	70
WR	85	50
WR	86	48

Harvard

POS	#	OVR
C	73	70
C	78	47
CB	4	81
CB	34	74
CB	24	73
CB	20	72
CB	17	69
CB	5	62
CB	25	60
CB	26	43
DT	62	50
DT	49	49
DT	56	44
DT	60	41
DT	61	40
FB	39	71
FB	32	65
FB	47	51
FS	2	71
FS	31	41
HB	22	85
HB	38	62
HB	21	54
HB	9	50
K	1	40
LE	97	72
LE	92	40
LG	68	70
LG	57	57
LOLB	30	69
LOLB	43	53
LT	64	71
LT	77	52
MLB	54	71
MLB	50	69
MLB	52	62
P	12	42
QB	7	71
QB	19	64
QB	8	43
RE	81	72
RE	91	48
RG	53	70
RG	74	51
RG	71	46
ROLB	29	73
ROLB	27	65
ROLB	41	40
RT	76	70
RT	72	47
RT	75	46
SS	37	76
SS	23	47
TE	95	68
TE	85	66
TE	93	43
TE	40	42
WR	83	76
WR	89	74
WR	82	73
WR	14	71
WR	86	70
WR	84	61
WR	18	55
WR	87	51

Hofstra

POS	#	OVR
C	58	74
C	72	45
C	62	42
CB	4	74
CB	9	71
CB	10	57
CB	27	55
DT	91	79
DT	92	70
DT	77	40
FB	26	69
FB	29	44
FS	5	70
FS	47	54
HB	2	81
HB	36	59
HB	24	53
K	18	84
K	40	53
LE	95	47
LE	63	41
LG	75	70
LG	60	42
LOLB	44	71
LOLB	28	50
LT	79	72
LT	57	70
MLB	55	77
MLB	56	69
MLB	45	62
MLB	43	58
P	49	42
QB	7	62
QB	14	52
QB	6	43
RE	94	73
RE	25	45
RG	70	70
RG	59	60
ROLB	42	73
ROLB	22	53
RT	71	71
RT	67	46
SS	8	70
SS	19	55
SS	23	51
TE	32	66
TE	90	40
WR	82	77
WR	88	73
WR	81	71
WR	80	69
WR	83	54
WR	86	45
WR	84	44

Howard

POS	#	OVR
C	66	73
C	91	70
CB	35	74
CB	43	71
CB	11	69
CB	17	52
CB	9	51
CB	26	51
DT	60	85
DT	56	71
DT	92	40
FB	32	42
FS	4	83
FS	47	70
HB	28	76
HB	25	75
HB	36	74
HB	29	67
HB	5	47
K	40	41
LE	99	73
LE	97	40
LG	71	69
LG	76	47
LOLB	45	68
LOLB	50	40
LT	77	70
LT	73	50
MLB	51	68
MLB	55	41
P	48	43
QB	13	67
QB	12	58
QB	7	40
RE	98	73
RE	54	40
RG	78	70
RG	64	50
RG	70	46
ROLB	42	70
ROLB	34	40
RT	79	70
RT	63	47
RT	68	42
SS	21	72
SS	37	48
SS	27	42
TE	3	66
TE	85	40
TE	89	40
WR	14	76
WR	1	73
WR	80	69
WR	84	50
WR	81	49
WR	82	47
WR	18	46

Idaho State

POS	#	OVR
C	71	70
C	74	41
CB	11	73
CB	3	71
CB	25	70
CB	7	60
CB	30	55
CB	27	45
DT	65	72
DT	92	70
DT	95	48
DT	96	42
FB	5	72
FS	2	70
FS	18	46
HB	8	77
HB	32	70
HB	33	54
K	13	54
LE	56	72
LE	90	53
LE	94	41
LG	66	70
LG	64	55
LOLB	12	70
LOLB	51	40
LT	58	72
LT	67	55
MLB	55	72
MLB	36	68
MLB	35	43
MLB	41	41
P	43	40
QB	17	65
QB	14	56
QB	15	51
RE	99	82
RE	54	70
RE	93	45
RG	72	71
RG	70	58
RG	75	44
ROLB	26	72
ROLB	50	53
RT	78	69
RT	73	55
SS	4	81
SS	28	43
TE	16	69
TE	44	65
TE	85	61
WR	21	73
WR	34	57
WR	84	57
WR	29	54
WR	81	54
WR	83	46

Illinois State

POS	#	OVR
C	77	48
C	71	46
CB	9	75
CB	39	71
CB	20	63
CB	31	47
CB	25	47
CB	93	49
DT	97	47
DT	98	40
DT	60	40
FB	34	65
FB	35	59
FS	38	49
FS	21	49
HB	23	75
HB	22	55
HB	33	53
K	26	48
LE	57	55
LE	91	46
LG	64	46
LG	69	40
LOLB	50	43
LOLB	56	43
LT	74	56
LT	67	48
MLB	45	80
MLB	48	40
QB	7	75
QB	16	57
QB	12	40
RE	94	77
RE	96	47
RE	92	44
RG	70	51
RG	68	45
ROLB	6	72
ROLB	54	43
ROLB	55	43
RT	61	52
RT	76	45
SS	37	45
SS	28	40
TE	11	51
TE	82	48
TE	84	47
WR	80	68
WR	10	59
WR	89	52
WR	85	50
WR	87	49
WR	18	49

Indiana State

POS	#	OVR
C	68	73
C	50	70
CB	8	73
CB	13	70
CB	33	50
CB	30	46
CB	15	42
CB	2	42
DT	99	74
DT	45	72
DT	69	71
DT	90	48
FB	47	51
FS	4	55
FS	21	55
HB	23	77
HB	32	74
HB	11	40
K	43	40
LE	93	71
LE	94	53
LG	66	52
LG	74	45
LOLB	52	51
LT	76	70
LT	79	41
MLB	17	75
MLB	91	41
MLB	26	40
P	46	83
QB	10	74
QB	16	53
QB	14	52
QB	18	41
RE	95	75
RE	71	59
RG	64	72
RG	55	47
ROLB	28	73
ROLB	51	45
RT	77	46
RT	72	41
SS	5	53
SS	34	42
TE	86	64
TE	84	45
WR	87	72
WR	81	72
WR	1	69
WR	83	62
WR	80	53
WR	19	52
WR	85	51

Jackson State

POS	#	OVR
C	76	72
C	54	70
C	70	43
CB	23	76
CB	26	73
CB	5	71
CB	21	70
CB	25	54
DT	50	71
DT	80	70
DT	94	50
DT	99	41
DT	52	40
DT	96	40
FB	47	40
FS	6	77
FS	15	51
HB	3	82
HB	29	74
HB	33	46
HB	11	45
K	39	40
LE	92	71
LE	69	40
LG	62	74
LG	71	72
LG	74	41
LOLB	56	72
LOLB	55	40
LT	78	72
LT	60	69
MLB	19	75
MLB	28	40
P	36	40
QB	9	78
QB	17	74
RE	97	78
RE	93	67
RG	57	74
RG	77	70
RG	66	52
ROLB	2	72
ROLB	42	70
ROLB	30	40
RT	79	71
RT	63	56
RT	75	50
SS	12	70
SS	16	50
TE	49	53
TE	14	40
WR	83	75
WR	18	74
WR	10	70
WR	4	69
WR	84	55
WR	88	52
WR	82	49

Jacksonville State

POS	#	OVR
C	55	70
C	76	63
C	71	52
CB	28	74
CB	32	72
CB	16	70
CB	29	66
CB	26	52
DT	91	74
DT	54	73
DT	57	70
DT	31	59
FB	46	71
FB	36	68
FB	30	55
FS	48	75
FS	13	55
HB	4	81
HB	19	79
HB	7	78
HB	22	76
K	41	54
LE	99	73
LE	92	48
LG	65	66
LG	68	48
LOLB	40	70
LOLB	34	51
LT	78	70
LT	51	65
LT	67	47
MLB	45	70
MLB	9	58
MLB	38	44
P	27	49
QB	11	73
QB	14	72
QB	15	60
QB	12	48
RE	63	73
RE	75	73
RG	73	71
RG	60	54
ROLB	39	79
ROLB	43	65
RT	79	69
RT	72	60
RT	61	58
SS	24	70
SS	17	45
TE	10	68
TE	84	66
TE	44	49
WR	1	77
WR	8	74
WR	5	72
WR	2	71
WR	3	69
WR	87	64
WR	89	57

James Madison

POS	#	OVR
C	53	79
C	76	70
CB	6	73
CB	20	72
CB	19	70
CB	24	61
CB	27	55
DT	90	73
DT	98	71
DT	96	70
DT	93	67
DT	58	55
FB	48	66
FB	35	49
FS	21	80
FS	37	68
HB	28	78
HB	14	77
HB	30	74
HB	17	67
K	40	75
LE	52	70
LE	77	56
LG	61	67
LG	75	54
LOLB	46	71
LOLB	51	57
LT	63	74
MLB	41	67
MLB	13	58
P	36	76
QB	7	76
QB	12	53
RE	99	78
RE	92	69
RE	69	55
RG	62	71
RG	71	61
ROLB	29	72
ROLB	9	60
RT	60	74
RT	78	70
SS	34	74
SS	18	70
TE	44	72
TE	85	68
TE	43	66
TE	81	57
WR	3	79
WR	15	75
WR	86	74
WR	5	71
WR	83	70
WR	84	66
WR	10	64

Maine

POS	#	OVR
C	50	65
C	72	46
CB	3	74
CB	23	69
CB	26	57
CB	28	46
CB	22	42
DT	96	74
DT	91	72
DT	95	59
DT	64	57
FB	80	69
FS	20	72
HB	32	81
HB	25	58
HB	21	56
K	13	54
LE	9	72
LE	43	44
LG	73	51
LOLB	10	71
LOLB	37	40
LT	55	72
LT	66	70
MLB	44	70
MLB	35	47
MLB	42	40
P	17	40
QB	15	68
QB	14	51
RE	98	84
RE	99	70
RG	75	72
RG	58	71
RG	63	48
ROLB	4	74
ROLB	30	49
RT	53	72
RT	74	41
SS	49	51
SS	24	47
TE	18	57
TE	11	40
WR	2	77
WR	8	71
WR	27	70
WR	88	52
WR	82	49
WR	6	48

McNeese State

POS	#	OVR
C	61	62
C	63	45
CB	35	79
CB	32	64
CB	9	55
CB	5	52
CB	1	52
DT	93	75
DT	96	61
DT	56	53
DT	42	40
DT	64	40
FB	24	65
FB	25	54
FS	39	69
FS	30	58
HB	27	65
HB	22	63
HB	4	56
K	15	70
LE	46	64
LE	97	46
LG	70	57
LG	65	44
LOLB	47	67
LOLB	51	47
LT	73	66
LT	79	53
MLB	58	57
MLB	40	44
P	11	54
QB	13	78
QB	10	60
QB	14	47
RE	99	82
RE	94	46
RG	66	64
RG	77	47
ROLB	52	74
ROLB	41	64
RT	75	61
RT	69	46
SS	34	60
SS	31	46
TE	85	48
TE	89	48
TE	84	47
WR	7	75
WR	88	64
WR	12	57
WR	6	54
WR	16	47
WR	87	43

Miss Valley State

POS	#	OVR
C	69	70
C	78	43
CB	37	75
CB	25	73
CB	28	72
CB	31	70
CB	23	50
CB	14	42
DT	96	75
DT	75	69
DT	90	49
FB	41	69
FB	26	47
FS	21	71
FS	27	62
FS	20	40
HB	9	75
HB	16	71
HB	15	70
K	11	40
LE	94	70
LE	95	46
LG	62	71
LG	67	46
LOLB	53	43
LOLB	50	40
LT	76	74
LT	61	69
MLB	54	69
MLB	59	44
P	36	40
QB	1	65
QB	3	55
QB	17	44
RE	55	70
RE	98	42
RG	74	72
RG	60	53
ROLB	58	78
ROLB	57	40
RT	71	70
RT	73	58
RT	64	44
SS	24	72
SS	29	40
TE	83	47
TE	89	40
WR	86	77
WR	82	71
WR	35	70
WR	8	58
WR	84	51

Missouri State

POS	#	OVR
C	73	50
C	77	41
CB	2	52
CB	27	50
CB	12	42
CB	29	42
DT	96	49
DT	98	41
DT	61	40
DT	92	40
FB	46	63
FS	31	83
HB	26	60
HB	24	51
HB	33	49
K	41	46
LE	90	56
LE	52	52
LG	71	51
LG	76	45
LOLB	50	51
LT	75	46
MLB	47	48
MLB	56	41
MLB	54	41
P	20	40
QB	15	77
QB	19	59
QB	11	55
RE	40	59
RE	39	53
RG	62	52
RG	72	47
ROLB	53	52
ROLB	42	45
RT	66	41
RT	74	41
SS	21	53
SS	44	42
TE	85	60
TE	86	45
WR	4	75
WR	80	65
WR	23	58
WR	84	54
WR	81	47

Montana

POS	#	OVR
C	75	74
C	73	71
CB	18	79
CB	34	75
CB	19	73
CB	21	72
CB	30	70
CB	9	69
DT	99	75
DT	59	73
DT	42	69
DT	67	57
DT	97	57
DT	95	54
FB	49	71
FB	40	67
FS	32	74
FS	27	64
FS	10	63
HB	38	83
HB	20	77
HB	33	67
K	29	69
LE	53	78
LE	91	71
LE	90	65
LG	74	72
LG	78	58
LOLB	37	75
LOLB	43	62
LT	71	77
LT	66	74
MLB	6	71
MLB	46	70
P	26	69
QB	14	77
QB	7	69
QB	16	54
RE	50	86
RE	96	72
RE	92	69
RG	69	82
RG	79	70
RG	72	51
ROLB	4	79
ROLB	35	65
ROLB	56	56
RT	55	75
RT	60	58
RT	64	57
SS	17	77
SS	31	62
SS	36	60
TE	88	72
TE	87	70
TE	89	67
WR	2	80
WR	82	77
WR	3	74
WR	5	74
WR	80	72
WR	8	70
WR	81	64
WR	11	59

Montana State

POS	#	OVR
C	61	73
C	70	70
CB	13	77
CB	8	73
CB	24	70
CB	2	69
CB	23	47
DT	92	75
DT	94	71
DT	60	69
DT	63	49
DT	91	40
FB	33	55
FS	31	75
FS	22	52
HB	1	77
HB	25	75
HB	35	47
K	39	52
LE	97	73
LE	90	43
LG	66	72
LG	89	70
LOLB	44	72
LOLB	56	42
LT	72	74
LT	73	51
MLB	41	71
MLB	50	69
MLB	49	40
P	82	40
QB	12	77
QB	15	60
RE	93	74
RE	99	73
RE	96	42
RG	76	72
RG	64	61
RG	69	43
ROLB	54	73
ROLB	47	69
ROLB	51	40
RT	53	70
RT	68	41
SS	27	72
SS	4	66
SS	26	42
TE	95	69
TE	84	66
TE	88	44
WR	10	76
WR	19	74
WR	80	74
WR	87	72
WR	16	52

Morgan State

POS	#	OVR
C	62	71
C	60	44
C	67	44
CB	4	77
CB	6	75
CB	8	51
CB	21	48
DT	53	77
DT	94	74
DT	58	72
FB	44	75
FB	37	51
FB	86	47
FS	25	70
FS	18	46
FS	24	44
HB	2	76
HB	3	60
HB	32	59
K	29	40
LE	9	70
LE	68	45
LG	71	71
LG	61	43
LOLB	41	70
LOLB	42	48
LT	72	72
LT	74	49
MLB	11	72
MLB	56	40
MLB	55	40
P	35	40
QB	1	71
QB	13	44
QB	16	40
RE	52	72
RE	98	49
RE	91	44
RE	97	40
RG	70	73
RG	69	46
ROLB	40	70
ROLB	54	40
ROLB	51	40
RT	77	69
RT	75	43
RT	64	40
SS	7	70
SS	19	48
TE	88	51
TE	89	40
WR	14	79
WR	20	74
WR	82	73
WR	84	71
WR	81	70
WR	85	46

Murray State

POS	#	OVR
C	68	72
C	64	70
CB	3	84
CB	20	71
CB	26	70
CB	36	66
CB	21	53
DT	59	71
DT	56	70
DT	78	60
DT	98	50
DT	91	49
DT	97	44
DT	95	40
FB	43	73
FB	41	53
FS	33	75
FS	24	72
HB	22	74
HB	5	64
HB	25	61
HB	32	53
K	1	63
LE	94	75
LE	90	48
LG	77	70
LG	72	49
LOLB	23	69
LOLB	53	50
LT	73	72
LT	79	55
MLB	44	69
MLB	37	51
P	16	46
QB	7	74
QB	18	70
RE	85	77
RE	65	72
RE	96	46
RG	66	70
RG	75	62
RG	76	44
ROLB	28	70
ROLB	14	62
ROLB	50	45
RT	71	67
RT	74	47
SS	2	60
SS	15	46
TE	8	79
TE	19	66
TE	83	40
WR	9	80
WR	4	73
WR	80	73
WR	27	52
WR	84	45

NC A&T State

POS	#	OVR
C	61	71
C	64	70
C	73	68
CB	26	77
CB	4	73
CB	27	71
CB	25	69
CB	20	62
DT	99	77
DT	90	72
DT	91	64
FB	44	77
FB	32	40
FS	7	70
FS	30	48
FS	48	48
HB	8	81
HB	39	78
HB	28	78
HB	22	53
K	49	40
LE	52	70
LE	97	40
LG	57	70
LG	68	53
LOLB	46	71
LOLB	50	40
LT	75	72
MLB	53	71
MLB	42	68
MLB	55	40
QB	19	63
QB	13	48
QB	12	45
QB	18	41
RE	98	72
RE	94	43
RE	93	40
RG	67	70
RG	70	57
ROLB	23	72
ROLB	96	70
ROLB	56	40
RT	76	69
RT	72	50
SS	9	81
SS	36	70
SS	40	47
TE	84	68
TE	24	43
WR	88	72
WR	1	71
WR	15	50
WR	3	55
WR	80	51
WR	82	48

New Hampshire

POS	#	OVR
C	58	70
C	60	67
C	77	67
CB	7	78
CB	10	73
CB	9	72
CB	15	69
CB	24	67
CB	40	58
DT	80	72
DT	93	69
DT	91	67
DT	72	66
DT	75	41
FB	38	65
FS	31	74
FS	43	66
HB	27	76
HB	32	74
HB	29	70
HB	1	70
K	99	68
LE	41	74
LE	50	71
LG	76	70
LG	73	60
LOLB	95	70
LOLB	30	66
LT	64	70
LT	79	60
MLB	34	72
MLB	56	65
MLB	48	50
P	18	52
QB	2	80
QB	14	69
QB	17	54
RE	90	77
RE	97	56
RG	74	75
RG	65	60
ROLB	53	71
ROLB	35	67
ROLB	54	65
RT	59	69
SS	33	72
SS	26	54
TE	85	66
TE	84	65
WR	19	80
WR	83	73
WR	82	71
WR	16	68
WR	6	59
WR	22	56

Nicholls State

POS	#	OVR
C	54	70
C	66	57
CB	7	75
CB	2	73
CB	20	70
CB	27	60
CB	37	41
DT	70	72
DT	90	71
DT	98	42
DT	85	40
FB	8	81
FB	1	72
FB	24	66
FS	5	82
FS	26	51
HB	46	78
HB	33	73
HB	40	70
HB	4	57
K	88	70
LE	11	69
LE	52	49
LG	64	70
LG	60	46
LOLB	45	70
LOLB	44	46
LT	76	70
LT	68	65
MLB	49	70
MLB	53	41
P	6	46
QB	9	72
QB	13	65
QB	14	58
QB	16	55
RE	91	75
RE	96	63
RE	92	48
RG	61	73
RG	71	62
RG	65	44
ROLB	43	71
ROLB	58	56
RT	95	69
RT	67	61
RT	62	47
SS	17	80
SS	34	57
SS	23	45
TE	86	65
TE	83	47
WR	3	79
WR	15	71
WR	87	70
WR	18	62
WR	36	51
WR	81	46

Norfolk State

POS	#	OVR
C	76	70
C	62	46
CB	27	82
CB	37	72
CB	18	69
CB	23	52
CB	33	52
CB	22	52
DT	98	74
DT	1	71
DT	97	70
DT	53	64
FB	5	81
FB	35	40
FB	32	40
FS	19	72
FS	46	50
HB	44	81
HB	25	70
HB	28	63
K	47	44
LE	54	69
LE	73	40
LG	63	69
LG	61	42
LOLB	48	72
LOLB	43	69
LT	77	72
LT	67	40
MLB	41	70
MLB	52	68
P	11	68
QB	3	65
QB	12	56
RE	92	71
RE	93	40
RG	64	73
RG	66	43
ROLB	56	72
ROLB	55	70
ROLB	51	65
RT	65	68
RT	74	45
SS	26	83
SS	13	40
TE	40	68
TE	85	65
TE	81	43
WR	84	72
WR	20	70
WR	83	53
WR	29	52
WR	17	48
WR	87	46
WR	86	40

Northeastern

POS	#	OVR
C	74	71
C	73	46
CB	20	72
CB	37	72
CB	21	70
CB	14	58
CB	2	44
DT	94	72
DT	55	69
DT	64	40
DT	96	40
DT	97	40
FB	26	56
FB	40	46
FS	7	71
FS	28	55
HB	11	79
HB	9	75
HB	27	59
HB	32	50
K	16	46
LE	43	70
LE	93	40
LG	54	70
LG	68	48
LOLB	34	71
LOLB	39	41
LT	70	71
LT	72	56
MLB	47	71
MLB	90	68
MLB	49	59
MLB	91	48
P	22	75
QB	4	73
QB	10	63
QB	12	62
RE	51	79
RE	57	52
RG	65	71
RG	71	45
RG	69	42
ROLB	52	72
ROLB	17	48
RT	62	70
RT	78	52
RT	63	41
SS	33	51
SS	24	45
TE	83	66
TE	89	41
WR	8	81
WR	5	72
WR	18	61
WR	81	54
WR	80	46
WR	23	45

Northern Arizona

POS	#	OVR
C	64	70
C	78	41
CB	4	76
CB	17	72
CB	43	70
CB	28	50
CB	34	48
DT	77	73
DT	90	73
DT	97	71
DT	95	44
DT	96	40
FB	30	71
FS	31	72
FS	6	62
HB	22	74
HB	13	71
HB	7	46
HB	20	46
K	38	48
LE	40	72
LE	94	40
LG	75	59
LG	61	46
LOLB	45	73
LOLB	37	70
LT	74	72
LT	62	56
MLB	33	71
MLB	44	69
P	36	47
QB	12	80
QB	15	64
QB	19	57
QB	5	52
RE	91	72
RE	89	43
RG	67	71
RG	73	58
ROLB	50	75
ROLB	53	71
ROLB	54	47
RT	68	70
RT	60	40
SS	27	70
SS	23	50
TE	11	66
TE	83	51
TE	86	44
WR	3	79
WR	82	75
WR	14	70
WR	87	59
WR	85	54
WR	8	46

Northwestern State

POS	#	OVR
C	63	60
C	62	48
CB	25	62
CB	31	58
CB	24	53
CB	7	52
CB	27	47
DT	94	82
DT	97	53
DT	96	44
DT	95	40
FB	29	62
FB	36	54
FS	39	69
FS	13	51
HB	22	79
HB	34	61
HB	20	54
K	32	68
LE	57	67
LE	45	48
LG	60	65
LG	71	45
LOLB	41	50
LOLB	55	45
LT	66	70
LT	77	50
MLB	56	57
MLB	37	43
P	1	51
QB	18	67
QB	10	58
QB	12	48
RE	52	85
RE	78	49
RG	61	74
RG	70	48
ROLB	43	60
ROLB	50	48
RT	65	68
RT	74	49
SS	2	61
SS	21	49
TE	86	60
TE	88	49
TE	5	42
WR	84	68
WR	85	62
WR	19	54
WR	83	51
WR	17	43

Penn

POS	#	OVR
C	62	70
C	70	59
CB	37	73
CB	6	71
CB	11	68
CB	30	60
CB	27	53
DT	94	82
DT	63	71
DT	69	70
DT	95	51
DT	92	43
DT	94	40
FB	43	82
FB	34	72
FB	38	48
FS	35	70
FS	14	53
FS	24	50
HB	28	73
HB	23	54
HB	22	51
K	89	57
LE	82	72
LE	56	40
LG	73	71
LG	64	40
LOLB	53	69
LOLB	52	42
LT	76	69
MLB	42	70
MLB	39	69
MLB	48	48
P	85	61
QB	17	72
QB	12	63
QB	9	52
QB	16	41
RE	47	76
RE	40	46
RG	65	72
RG	57	69
ROLB	58	71
ROLB	99	42
RT	72	57
RT	66	42
SS	3	49
SS	4	47
TE	80	68
TE	88	65
TE	87	44
WR	5	77
WR	32	70
WR	8	66
WR	19	50
WR	25	50
WR	31	50
WR	86	46

Portland State

POS	#	OVR
C	61	57
C	74	47
CB	21	67
CB	9	58
CB	18	46
CB	27	44
DT	58	59
DT	99	58
DT	96	45
DT	90	44
FB	78	50
FS	22	55
HB	37	63
HB	32	58
HB	46	45
K	29	40
LE	97	54
LE	93	45
LG	67	54
LG	62	43
LOLB	54	48
LOLB	26	43
LT	75	69
MLB	43	50
MLB	56	40
QB	12	69
QB	16	59
QB	10	52
RE	92	61
RE	45	49
RG	55	70
RG	63	49
RG	66	42
ROLB	49	76
ROLB	41	46
RT	77	60
RT	73	46
SS	24	50
SS	25	42
TE	19	58
TE	17	52
WR	5	78
WR	83	77
WR	82	62
WR	88	59
WR	85	51

Prairie View A&M

POS	#	OVR
C	68	49
C	64	43
CB	21	74
CB	3	70
CB	25	46
CB	5	44
DT	47	72
DT	92	48
DT	98	40
FB	40	40
FB	34	40
FS	33	53
FS	39	44
HB	24	73
HB	31	71
HB	30	47
K	27	40
LE	59	40
LG	67	51
LOLB	55	69
LT	51	72
LT	65	47
MLB	35	40
MLB	49	40
P	18	40
QB	8	71
QB	10	66
RE	93	70
RE	99	40
RG	71	70
RG	60	69
RG	72	47
ROLB	7	72
ROLB	52	42
RT	66	69
RT	76	45
SS	37	57
SS	22	49
TE	12	66
TE	87	40
TE	88	40
WR	81	71
WR	85	55
WR	89	50
WR	84	50
WR	83	49

Princeton

POS	#	OVR
C	76	70
C	60	40
CB	18	71
CB	26	69
CB	22	59
CB	32	48
CB	31	40
DT	96	73
DT	90	70
DT	98	48
DT	99	45
DT	61	40
FB	19	88
FB	49	46
FB	7	45
FS	25	70
FS	37	54
HB	15	72
HB	34	55
HB	36	46
K	38	40
LE	68	71
LE	94	40
LG	77	72
LG	78	49
LOLB	33	70
LOLB	52	41
LT	72	70
MLB	50	74
MLB	44	70
MLB	55	44
P	16	42
QB	11	71
QB	8	53
RE	97	77
RE	92	40
RG	75	72
RG	64	53
ROLB	51	71
ROLB	59	44
ROLB	39	40
RT	73	70
RT	69	40
SS	9	81
SS	43	44
TE	85	70
TE	88	67
TE	48	66
TE	83	46
WR	6	74
WR	84	73
WR	80	71
WR	89	55
WR	81	53
WR	82	49
WR	86	48

Rhode Island

POS	#	OVR
C	57	72
C	74	70
CB	23	74
CB	22	53
CB	29	50
CB	1	46
DT	92	80
DT	98	48
DT	58	41
DT	91	40
FB	37	83
FS	33	62
FS	49	43
HB	28	76
HB	3	72
HB	32	70
HB	4	62
HB	2	60
K	17	48
LE	65	50
LE	69	43
LG	78	70
LG	67	59
LOLB	41	73
LOLB	20	70
LT	60	70
LT	72	66
MLB	50	76
MLB	5	70
MLB	45	61
P	21	84
QB	10	65
QB	14	59
QB	8	55
RE	94	73
RE	95	47
RG	76	72
RG	62	55
RG	79	40
ROLB	51	74
ROLB	52	72
ROLB	25	69
RT	73	69
RT	64	47
SS	6	70
SS	24	43
TE	86	49
TE	36	48
WR	13	78
WR	85	71
WR	80	58
WR	81	56
WR	83	55

Richmond

POS	#	OVR
C	79	70
C	65	50
C	74	43
CB	5	76
CB	43	71
CB	24	69
CB	29	67
CB	21	53
DT	34	72
DT	8	70
DT	73	52
DT	93	46
DT	71	43
FB	41	54
FS	26	72
FS	27	50
HB	22	80
HB	3	79
HB	30	75
HB	32	67
HB	35	49
K	90	49
LE	62	72
LE	56	60
LG	60	58
LG	78	40
LOLB	23	71
LOLB	38	47
LT	66	75
MLB	49	49
MLB	42	40
P	25	56
QB	11	76
QB	12	70
QB	15	55
RE	55	72
RE	2	70
RE	92	47
RE	97	44
RG	76	70
RG	70	54
ROLB	33	73
ROLB	45	70
RT	52	74
RT	75	61
SS	39	71
SS	36	46
TE	87	69
TE	82	66
WR	14	76
WR	1	71
WR	7	70
WR	9	70
WR	80	66
WR	88	58
WR	83	57

Sacramento State

POS	#	OVR
C	61	48
C	70	45
CB	31	75
CB	10	63
CB	8	54
CB	28	52
DT	51	47
DT	91	46
DT	22	44
DT	95	41
FB	33	56
FS	25	50
HB	9	75
HB	30	49
HB	27	48
K	35	45
LE	93	49
LE	94	41
LG	62	47
LG	73	41
LOLB	32	49
LT	71	59
MLB	45	55
MLB	53	42
MLB	50	40
P	86	40
QB	5	72
QB	16	61
RE	55	52
RG	77	61
RG	68	45
ROLB	42	63
ROLB	47	46
RT	79	57
RT	78	40
SS	22	82
SS	20	47
TE	81	55
TE	89	48
WR	17	65
WR	2	57
WR	85	54
WR	14	48
WR	87	48
WR	84	45

Sam Houston State

POS	#	OVR
C	61	72
C	62	70
CB	21	79
CB	37	74
CB	11	74
CB	2	72
CB	13	70
CB	20	65
CB	14	53
CB	25	51
DT	95	72
DT	90	71
DT	91	54
DT	97	48
DT	92	44
DT	69	40
FB	40	60
FB	32	53
FS	31	72
FS	41	51
HB	33	77
HB	22	61
HB	28	55
K	17	60
LE	46	70
LE	98	57
LE	59	40
LG	58	56
LG	77	50
LOLB	42	71
LOLB	44	47
LT	68	72
LT	65	70
MLB	54	51
MLB	43	41
P	26	52
QB	7	83
QB	12	73
QB	16	65
QB	35	64
QB	10	49
RE	99	79
RE	96	61
RE	94	48
RG	78	70
RG	63	56
RG	64	49
ROLB	47	79
ROLB	45	45
RT	70	71
RT	71	50
SS	19	82
SS	36	51
SS	24	42
TE	84	74
TE	87	66
TE	86	45
WR	89	78
WR	4	74
WR	18	71
WR	3	70
WR	82	61
WR	88	51
WR	15	41

Samford

POS	#	OVR
C	72	70
C	63	57
CB	6	74
CB	42	73
CB	26	71
CB	16	70
CB	20	66
CB	89	52
DT	49	77
DT	97	71
DT	58	58
DT	95	50
DT	91	40
FB	46	62
FB	23	53
FS	28	71
FS	5	70
FS	34	57
HB	24	77
HB	33	71
HB	32	54
K	38	75
K	92	51
LE	98	74
LE	69	55
LG	50	70
LG	64	58
LOLB	51	71
LOLB	40	45
LT	60	71
LT	65	66
MLB	39	53
MLB	62	42
P	35	57
QB	3	76
QB	7	62
QB	2	46
RE	90	74
RE	93	70
RE	96	48
RG	78	73
RG	73	67
RG	56	52
RG	68	50
ROLB	22	72
ROLB	45	56
RT	61	71
RT	70	47
SS	21	73
SS	29	70
SS	10	44
TE	99	70
TE	15	55
WR	82	80
WR	8	74
WR	85	70
WR	12	69
WR	84	67
WR	30	52
WR	17	46

SE Missouri State

POS	#	OVR
C	71	61
C	74	48
CB	23	71
CB	29	62
CB	33	53
CB	4	51
DT	93	58
DT	99	52
DT	47	42
DT	90	40
FB	20	63
FB	25	53
FS	31	72
FS	12	55
HB	26	75
HB	28	60
HB	36	56
K	35	64
LE	92	64
LE	91	47
LG	60	65
LG	79	46
LOLB	45	58
LOLB	49	43
LT	73	69
LT	61	49
MLB	42	73
MLB	53	53
MLB	41	45
P	46	62
QB	14	78
QB	7	59
QB	1	47
RE	98	65
RE	57	53
RG	63	67
RG	78	51
ROLB	56	60
ROLB	17	51
RT	59	66
RT	76	48
SS	15	81
SS	8	46
TE	80	47
TE	85	45
WR	82	64
WR	87	63
WR	83	59
WR	22	57
WR	2	55
WR	86	46

South Carolina State

POS	#	OVR
C	55	70
C	73	57
CB	9	72
CB	11	71
CB	29	69
CB	8	67
CB	15	54
DT	95	73
DT	91	71
DT	45	70
DT	99	62
DT	97	57
FB	47	52
FS	26	70
FS	37	50
HB	28	80
HB	21	73
HB	32	57
K	43	40
LE	42	70
LE	92	47
LG	76	70
LG	64	47
LOLB	35	57
LT	71	74
LT	52	69
MLB	53	68
MLB	59	42
MLB	49	40
P	36	40
QB	19	78
QB	7	63
RE	94	70
RE	98	53
RE	96	40
RG	62	70
RG	79	52
ROLB	44	68
ROLB	39	40
RT	78	73
RT	72	41
SS	31	73
SS	5	70
SS	46	58
SS	27	57
TE	88	72
TE	81	66
TE	41	47
TE	86	40
WR	10	76
WR	3	75
WR	2	73
WR	12	71
WR	82	70
WR	80	70
WR	6	68
WR	83	60

Southeastern

POS	#	OVR
C	65	45
C	78	40
CB	32	58
CB	27	55
CB	24	52
CB	23	42
DT	93	56
DT	90	43
DT	96	41
FB	44	42
FS	18	57
FS	39	49
HB	20	51
HB	28	48
HB	31	46
K	16	47
LE	94	45
LE	97	40
LG	72	50
LG	70	41
LOLB	3	48
LOLB	5	40
LT	64	51
MLB	40	51
MLB	53	40
P	49	62
QB	14	76
QB	10	54
QB	13	51
RE	59	46
RE	91	43
RG	61	68
RG	68	47
ROLB	54	76
ROLB	45	40
RT	71	49
RT	74	42
SS	6	49
SS	8	47
TE	85	58
TE	86	56
WR	80	76
WR	84	70
WR	11	68
WR	87	67
WR	81	60

Southern

POS	#	OVR
C	76	71
C	54	69
CB	23	77
CB	17	75
CB	3	71
CB	21	63
CB	22	62
CB	20	60
DT	91	78
DT	71	72
DT	98	40
DT	70	40
FB	45	40
FS	2	78
HB	34	74
HB	42	68
HB	25	58
K	37	69
LE	93	49
LE	94	45
LG	65	44
LOLB	49	73
LT	77	71
LT	79	44
MLB	51	52
MLB	53	40
MLB	55	40
P	11	46
QB	16	75
QB	14	58
RE	96	83
RE	72	47
RG	75	74
RG	63	41
ROLB	33	73
ROLB	58	40
RT	74	71
RT	68	43
SS	32	54
SS	44	47
TE	81	72
TE	84	40
WR	80	80
WR	7	77
WR	86	76
WR	89	73
WR	83	66
WR	6	58
WR	88	54
WR	13	51
WR	39	48

Southern Illinois

POS	#	OVR
C	61	70
C	50	56
C	76	47
CB	36	73
CB	19	71
CB	8	69
CB	24	63
CB	9	62
CB	15	56
CB	30	48
DT	90	73
DT	99	71
DT	55	69
DT	92	63
DT	58	55
DT	66	43
FB	31	71
FB	46	66
FB	44	58
FS	6	87
FS	20	70
FS	42	58
HB	21	81
HB	32	58
HB	35	56
K	25	60
LE	56	73
LE	98	58
LG	75	70
LG	69	47
LOLB	10	70
LOLB	43	48
LT	68	71
LT	72	58
MLB	53	69
MLB	39	40
P	67	50
QB	17	76
QB	12	59
QB	14	47
RE	96	74
RE	33	71
RE	95	52
RG	77	73
RG	74	66
RG	64	45
ROLB	51	70
ROLB	3	52
ROLB	45	44
RT	79	69
RT	73	40
SS	2	70
SS	28	54
TE	86	73
TE	84	72
TE	87	46
WR	4	82
WR	89	74
WR	5	71
WR	18	67
WR	22	64
WR	26	57
WR	83	55
WR	88	47

Stephen F. Austin

POS	#	OVR
C	65	70
C	75	58
C	70	46
CB	83	75
CB	40	73
CB	28	71
CB	2	69
CB	23	67
CB	25	53
CB	37	53
CB	42	42
DT	92	71
DT	96	70
DT	60	54
DT	91	47
DT	97	40
DT	95	40
FB	39	72
FB	33	53
FS	41	72
FS	27	69
HB	31	81
HB	11	75
HB	34	74
HB	24	60
HB	32	54
K	29	64
LE	51	70
LE	94	48
LG	57	70
LG	78	59
LG	76	44
LOLB	17	74
LOLB	44	50
LT	59	75
LT	61	68
MLB	4	74
MLB	49	71
P	26	46
QB	7	75
QB	18	67
QB	3	58
QB	12	40
RE	99	73
RE	47	61
RE	62	44
RG	54	70
RG	77	62
RG	79	49
ROLB	55	81
ROLB	58	73
ROLB	53	45
RT	73	72
RT	74	49
SS	30	71
SS	21	49
TE	80	72
TE	98	66
TE	86	45
WR	1	77
WR	5	74
WR	8	72
WR	14	70
WR	9	56
WR	87	52
WR	84	48

Tennessee State

POS	#	OVR
C	64	70
C	63	47
CB	21	76
CB	45	75
CB	8	73
CB	32	71
CB	34	56
CB	9	50
DT	99	82
DT	13	70
DT	91	60
DT	95	53
DT	68	40
FB	30	72
FB	6	60
FS	42	75
FS	2	70
FS	44	57
HB	28	89
HB	25	75
HB	31	70
HB	26	61
HB	20	55
K	46	72
LE	59	80
LE	48	63
LG	60	64
LG	77	50
LOLB	80	64
LOLB	47	50
LT	67	74
LT	78	54
MLB	55	69
MLB	51	55
MLB	38	45
QB	7	78
QB	15	68
QB	14	58
QB	10	44
RE	93	80
RE	90	78
RE	92	47
RG	65	70
RG	74	61
RG	71	44
ROLB	4	71
ROLB	57	61
ROLB	41	46
RT	72	63
RT	70	49
SS	11	70
SS	29	62
SS	24	44
TE	43	71
TE	88	47
TE	85	45
WR	12	72
WR	82	72
WR	5	72
WR	89	64
WR	81	63
WR	18	56
WR	86	52

Tennessee Tech

POS	#	OVR
C	74	71
C	50	48
CB	21	76
CB	6	74
CB	25	70
CB	20	64
CB	1	49
DT	60	71
DT	56	71
DT	80	53
DT	98	41
DT	96	40
FB	35	69
FB	41	68
FS	3	75
FS	22	52
HB	33	69
HB	36	61
HB	23	53
K	15	63
LE	58	71
LE	95	65
LG	51	70
LG	78	44
LOLB	46	69
LOLB	91	56
LT	75	70
LT	71	65
MLB	48	70
MLB	52	40
P	43	49
QB	11	78
QB	12	61
QB	10	48
RE	57	87
RE	94	70
RE	93	52
RG	70	73
RG	76	62
ROLB	2	71
ROLB	55	57
ROLB	42	47
RT	77	68
RT	62	56
RT	79	47
SS	26	71
SS	16	70
TE	85	66
TE	88	59
TE	83	46
WR	5	80
WR	14	78
WR	82	74
WR	86	73
WR	17	71
WR	4	69
WR	84	54
WR	81	51
WR	89	43

Tennessee-Martin

POS	#	OVR
C	54	70
C	70	63
C	52	47
CB	26	72
CB	10	63
CB	13	53
CB	36	50
CB	14	46
DT	71	59
DT	99	51
DT	97	46
DT	91	40
FB	41	61
FB	35	53
FS	25	69
FS	31	51
HB	2	77
HB	29	63
HB	32	57
K	39	72
LE	95	68
LE	96	50
LG	79	66
LG	65	46
LOLB	11	61
LOLB	38	44
LT	72	70
LT	78	55
MLB	19	53
MLB	18	41
P	44	60
QB	12	76
QB	4	64
QB	7	44
RE	40	85
RE	94	51
RG	61	68
RG	60	52
ROLB	51	65
ROLB	17	54
RT	62	65
RT	68	50
SS	28	87
SS	24	52
TE	81	53
TE	82	46
WR	16	66
WR	8	66
WR	6	61
WR	88	56
WR	43	49

Texas Southern

POS	#	OVR
C	73	70
C	64	44
C	67	44
CB	25	78
CB	3	71
CB	42	69
CB	33	53
CB	16	47
CB	23	46
DT	78	76
DT	90	74
DT	17	70
DT	99	69
FB	30	72
FB	13	42
FB	44	40
FS	38	73
HB	24	75
HB	31	70
HB	21	45
HB	22	40
K	12	67
LE	98	71
LE	92	40
LG	62	48
LG	76	40
LOLB	51	45
LOLB	50	40
LT	68	75
LT	77	43
MLB	52	76
MLB	54	40
MLB	39	40
P	85	40
QB	14	88
QB	7	55
RE	95	76
RE	79	70
RE	91	40
RG	69	69
RG	74	47
ROLB	97	73
ROLB	11	40
RT	65	69
RT	63	40
SS	43	73
SS	5	70
TE	89	71
TE	48	53
TE	81	40
WR	19	77
WR	88	74
WR	87	73
WR	2	72
WR	8	69
WR	80	45

Texas State

POS	#	OVR
C	73	72
C	72	70
CB	3	81
CB	24	75
CB	4	73
CB	37	71
CB	30	70
CB	25	61
CB	38	51
CB	31	47
DT	60	78
DT	99	77
DT	97	73
DT	94	71
DT	98	48
DT	92	41
FB	18	84
FB	42	53
FS	29	72
FS	28	70
FS	47	52
HB	16	73
HB	22	72
HB	33	63
HB	32	61
HB	6	53
K	95	60
LE	78	74
LE	46	71
LE	91	48
LG	74	62
LG	64	49
LOLB	39	74
LOLB	51	70
LOLB	57	50
LT	70	76
LT	75	65
MLB	9	69
MLB	26	51
MLB	44	41
P	34	77
QB	14	80
QB	8	71
QB	10	55
QB	7	43
RE	50	83
RE	43	71
RE	71	70
RG	53	70
RG	65	56
RG	68	44
ROLB	54	75
ROLB	40	73
ROLB	52	57
ROLB	36	47
RT	66	72
RT	76	49
SS	27	73
SS	35	72
TE	88	71
TE	90	45
WR	5	79
WR	21	76
WR	81	74
WR	23	71
WR	17	69
WR	82	69
WR	20	53
WR	19	47

The Citadel

POS	#	OVR
C	71	70
C	73	52
C	78	50
CB	27	80
CB	2	74
CB	31	72
CB	3	69
CB	22	51
CB	13	46
DT	96	71
DT	91	70
DT	92	45
DT	94	44
DT	95	44
DT	93	41
FB	23	78
FB	26	55
FS	28	72
FS	29	57
HB	32	79
HB	20	70
HB	38	59
K	41	42
LE	99	71
LE	98	43
LG	79	71
LG	61	55
LOLB	34	49
LOLB	30	40
LT	74	71
LT	76	65
MLB	44	45
MLB	56	40
P	36	74
QB	7	71
QB	12	60
QB	16	47
RE	90	74
RE	55	52
RE	77	40
RG	77	72
RG	69	57
ROLB	54	77
ROLB	46	45
RT	70	68
RT	67	56
SS	1	70
SS	24	46
TE	83	73
TE	84	66
TE	86	47
WR	11	78
WR	17	76
WR	37	74
WR	5	71
WR	87	55
WR	81	53
WR	82	50
WR	39	50

Towson

POS	#	OVR
C	78	71
C	65	52
CB	22	75
CB	17	73
CB	33	71
CB	7	65
CB	26	58
DT	95	77
DT	91	75
DT	4	74
DT	92	56
DT	45	46
FB	18	75
FB	23	64
FS	25	73
FS	9	49
HB	32	74
HB	34	70
HB	44	55
K	35	83
LE	62	70
LE	51	44
LG	93	70
LG	71	51
LOLB	21	74
LOLB	57	50
LT	75	79
LT	69	70
MLB	36	80
MLB	8	43
P	12	61
QB	13	78
QB	3	62
QB	14	55
QB	19	50
RE	97	78
RE	59	66
RE	77	40
RG	63	73
RG	73	62
RG	53	44
ROLB	41	75
ROLB	60	51
RT	76	72
RT	72	69
SS	15	70
SS	24	61
TE	82	70
TE	42	66
TE	87	56
TE	99	42
WR	86	74
WR	2	74
WR	80	72
WR	16	70
WR	89	60
WR	83	54
WR	84	41

UMASS

POS	#	OVR
C	71	70
C	62	54
CB	21	76
CB	4	74
CB	16	72
CB	26	70
CB	39	61
DT	54	73
DT	56	70
DT	99	52
DT	79	47
FB	24	82
FB	33	70
FB	40	61
FS	6	88
FS	38	53
HB	32	77
HB	17	74
HB	25	69
K	29	52
LE	46	80
LE	94	43
LG	72	70
LG	67	40
LOLB	45	70
LOLB	37	57
LOLB	53	42
LT	63	71
LT	77	59
MLB	11	71
MLB	2	69
MLB	49	59
MLB	58	43
P	42	52
QB	12	70
QB	19	53
QB	14	44
RE	48	84
RE	98	76
RG	68	75
RG	73	54
ROLB	43	75
ROLB	36	58
ROLB	57	53
RT	60	68
RT	70	57
SS	5	80
SS	9	60
SS	27	46
TE	83	70
TE	84	68
TE	82	67
WR	8	80
WR	3	76
WR	15	74
WR	1	74
WR	80	72
WR	85	71
WR	88	70
WR	89	69
WR	22	54

UNI (Northern Iowa)

POS	#	OVR
C	77	74
C	74	48
C	64	41
CB	23	75
CB	24	73
CB	27	70
CB	29	70
CB	47	50
DT	98	74
DT	44	72
DT	95	70
DT	90	47
FB	34	74
FS	10	72
FS	8	58
HB	1	83
HB	32	74
HB	20	73
HB	30	60
HB	31	48
K	16	40
LE	99	74
LE	93	61
LE	85	43
LG	59	52
LG	65	46
LOLB	7	76
LOLB	52	41
LT	54	72
LT	79	59
MLB	94	72
MLB	46	56
MLB	43	41
P	41	40
QB	12	75
QB	13	58
QB	15	48
RE	96	76
RE	97	70
RE	91	57
RG	62	72
RG	73	53
RG	60	51
ROLB	39	78
ROLB	38	70
RT	71	71
RT	72	54
SS	18	71
SS	22	52
SS	37	47
TE	48	67
TE	80	66
TE	87	51
TE	82	45
WR	4	79
WR	2	76
WR	6	74
WR	88	69
WR	5	57
WR	9	52
WR	89	50
WR	11	46

Villanova

POS	#	OVR
C	60	70
C	70	48
C	58	42
CB	10	79
CB	7	75
CB	16	72
CB	20	71
CB	14	69
CB	23	55
CB	39	42
CB	35	40
DT	56	74
DT	94	70
DT	55	70
DT	93	48
DT	97	40
FB	30	54
FB	34	47
FS	28	76
FS	26	51
HB	24	75
HB	22	56
K	31	68
LE	52	70
LE	90	42
LG	61	70
LG	76	50
LOLB	91	71
LOLB	49	46
LT	71	72
MLB	2	69
MLB	53	43
MLB	42	41
P	36	40
QB	5	67
QB	12	58
QB	17	43
QB	18	40
RE	96	71
RE	44	51
RG	75	76
RG	72	64
RG	66	40
ROLB	54	74
ROLB	45	61
ROLB	41	40
RT	67	70
RT	74	52
SS	21	70
SS	27	41
TE	84	72
TE	89	48
WR	4	73
WR	3	73
WR	11	69
WR	81	49
WR	1	47
WR	88	45

Weber State

POS	#	OVR
C	62	76
C	53	72
CB	22	74
CB	23	72
CB	7	70
CB	9	69
CB	26	55
CB	19	44
CB	29	41
DT	94	76
DT	98	74
DT	96	71
DT	55	70
DT	93	40
FB	39	65
FB	38	55
FS	4	82
FS	24	48
HB	28	75
HB	33	70
HB	32	46
K	49	40
LE	91	74
LE	99	46
LG	63	61
LG	90	56
LOLB	30	69
LOLB	28	61
LT	74	74
MLB	44	77
MLB	54	70
P	16	40
QB	15	76
QB	12	66
QB	10	60
RE	86	75
RE	40	70
RE	58	41
RG	66	72
RG	77	40
ROLB	37	72
ROLB	34	68
ROLB	59	47
RT	68	72
RT	71	69
SS	17	69
SS	45	51
TE	85	51
TE	31	44
WR	81	75
WR	5	73
WR	88	71
WR	6	70
WR	80	67
WR	41	65
WR	84	53
WR	89	43

Western Carolina

POS	#	OVR
C	63	70
C	74	61
C	65	55
CB	2	79
CB	1	75
CB	16	73
CB	43	71
CB	15	70
DT	99	72
DT	53	70
DT	92	63
DT	96	56
DT	62	53
FB	33	57
FS	7	70
FS	20	51
HB	42	74
HB	30	64
HB	35	54
K	58	50
LE	82	73
LE	95	66
LG	73	74
LOLB	28	74
LOLB	57	59
LT	79	75
LT	78	53
MLB	44	72
MLB	50	69
P	39	59
QB	8	71
QB	10	65
QB	17	41
RE	97	84
RE	41	70
RE	90	46
RG	70	75
RG	68	73
ROLB	48	81
ROLB	46	71
RT	71	70
RT	77	45
RT	51	43
SS	34	70
SS	26	47
TE	32	77
TE	16	68
TE	52	68
WR	9	86
WR	19	80
WR	80	73
WR	11	69
WR	12	50

Western Illinois

POS	#	OVR
C	65	72
C	68	46
CB	10	71
CB	4	60
CB	8	58
CB	11	57
CB	27	45
DT	15	80
DT	71	72
DT	56	70
DT	39	68
DT	90	40
FB	18	53
FS	1	75
HB	3	78
HB	26	74
HB	20	54
HB	22	47
K	19	48
LE	94	70
LE	53	46
LG	69	75
LG	66	70
LOLB	35	73
LOLB	24	67
LOLB	30	42
LT	75	70
LT	58	53
MLB	47	70
MLB	40	69
MLB	55	44
MLB	52	40
P	16	40
QB	14	75
QB	12	70
QB	17	65
QB	13	40
RE	5	70
RE	92	51
RE	97	44
RG	72	72
RG	57	45
ROLB	6	73
ROLB	42	72
ROLB	31	58
RT	61	69
RT	73	51
RT	78	41
SS	38	72
SS	9	70
TE	87	55
TE	89	42
WR	2	79
WR	7	73
WR	81	72
WR	84	70
WR	85	55
WR	83	48

William & Mary

POS	#	OVR
C	59	74
C	51	54
CB	17	89
CB	22	80
CB	6	74
CB	24	69
CB	47	66
CB	31	61
CB	32	43
CB	30	42
DT	66	70
DT	83	68
DT	58	51
DT	92	48
DT	90	45
FB	46	78
FB	45	69
FS	9	76
FS	81	56
HB	25	75
HB	5	74
HB	8	73
HB	30	65
K	87	81
LE	95	77
LE	65	75
LG	72	72
LG	56	70
LOLB	54	71
LT	75	75
LT	79	71
MLB	56	71
MLB	39	71
MLB	35	60
P	80	77
QB	11	71
QB	16	62
QB	10	56
QB	15	53
RE	93	85
RE	96	76
RE	76	73
RG	63	72
RG	53	70
RG	70	59
ROLB	44	81
ROLB	97	71
ROLB	40	48
RT	67	71
RT	71	68
SS	37	71
SS	48	66
TE	86	71
TE	98	70
WR	82	65
WR	27	80
WR	2	79
WR	89	66
WR	41	65
WR	3	63

Wofford

POS	#	OVR
C	76	70
C	51	47
C	69	42
CB	5	79
CB	7	69
CB	24	57
CB	11	47
CB	32	43
CB	30	42
DT	91	71
DT	93	46
DT	94	42
DT	40	67
FS	10	70
FS	23	57
HB	20	75
HB	22	74
HB	18	71
HB	3	70
HB	34	52
K	25	40
LE	95	72
LE	98	53
LG	65	54
LOLB	43	69
LOLB	37	49
LT	73	72
LT	78	54
MLB	54	71
MLB	50	69
MLB	46	42
P	31	53
QB	12	75
QB	19	64
RE	96	73
RG	61	70
RG	62	60
RG	67	47
ROLB	15	78
ROLB	28	50
RT	54	70
RT	72	48
SS	26	70
SS	33	54
TE	88	66
TE	86	52
TE	87	47
WR	6	74
WR	84	73
WR	17	71
WR	89	58
WR	82	40

Yale

POS	#	OVR
C	62	51
C	67	40
CB	42	70
CB	10	69
CB	9	63
CB	24	57
CB	21	53
CB	29	46
DT	97	73
DT	93	71
DT	90	69
DT	31	54
DT	34	44
DT	45	40
DT	63	40
FB	5	76
FB	35	65
FB	38	63
FS	25	75
FS	3	45
HB	28	78
HB	14	74
HB	23	73
K	43	68
LE	33	72
LE	56	45
LE	79	40
LG	73	70
LG	82	45
LOLB	26	56
LOLB	47	40
LT	65	70
LT	64	58
MLB	44	74
MLB	51	64
P	41	40
QB	11	74
QB	7	65
QB	18	50
RE	60	72
RE	94	70
RE	95	41
RG	54	74
RG	58	48
RG	74	40
ROLB	39	74
ROLB	66	52
RT	61	70
RT	71	51
RT	69	41
SS	1	70
SS	20	40
TE	19	79
TE	83	69
TE	17	49
WR	88	72
WR	4	68
WR	87	60
WR	27	60
WR	85	56
WR	30	50
WR	13	46

Youngstown State

POS	#	OVR
C	50	70
C	61	64
C	74	46
CB	27	76
CB	21	74
CB	6	72
CB	16	72
CB	4	70
CB	32	50
DT	98	74
DT	94	73
DT	70	53
DT	92	40
FB	30	69
FB	34	66
FS	18	71
FS	10	43
HB	28	82
HB	48	65
HB	36	61
K	43	57
LE	55	70
LE	95	42
LG	51	70
LG	62	50
LOLB	59	70
LOLB	7	47
LT	64	71
LT	76	70
MLB	25	76
MLB	39	40
P	13	57
QB	24	76
QB	15	57
RE	96	79
RE	68	51
RG	67	70
RG	77	65
RG	69	42
ROLB	56	75
ROLB	53	60
ROLB	40	44
RT	78	71
RT	66	66
RT	75	46
SS	8	70
SS	3	49
TE	81	83
TE	87	67
WR	83	72
WR	11	69
WR	9	69
WR	82	60
WR	22	58
WR	84	54